Relative atomic masses (atomic weights) of the elements

1	Hydrogen	1.00794	54	Xenon	131.29
2	Helium	4.002602	55	Caesium	132.9054
3	Lithium	6.941	56	Barium	137.27
4	Beryllium	9.01218	57	Lanthanum	138.9055
5	Boron	10.81	58	Cerium	140.115
6	Carbon	12.011	59	Praseodymium	140.90765
7	Nitrogen	14.00674	60	Neodymium	144.24
8	Oxygen	15.9994	61	Promethium	(145)
9	Fluorine	18.9984032	62	Samarium	150.36
10	Neon	20.1797	63	Europium	151.965
11	Sodium	22.9897768	64	Gadolinium	157.25
12	Magnesium	24.3050	65	Terbium	158.92534
13	Aluminium	26.98154	66	Dysprosium	162.50
14	Silicon	28.0855	67	Holmium	164.93032
15	Phosphorus	30.97376	68	Erbium	167.26
16	Sulfur	32.066	69	Thulium	168.93421
17	Chlorine	35.4527	70	Ytterbium	173.04
18	Argon	39.948	71	Lutetium	174.967
19	Potassium	39.0983	72	Hafnium	178.49
20	Calcium	40.078	73	Tantalum	180.9479
21	Scandium	44.9559	74	Tungsten	183.85
22	Titanium	47.88	75	Rhenium	186.207
23	Vanadium	50.9415	76	Osmium	190.2
24	Chromium	51.9961	77	Iridium	192.22
25	Manganese	54.93805	78	Platinum	195.08
26	Iron	55.847	79	Gold	196.96654
27	Cobalt	58.93320	80	Mercury	200.59
28	Nickel	58.69	81	Thallium	204.3833
29	Copper	63.546	82	Lead	207.2
30	Zinc	65.39	83	Bismuth	208.9804
31	Gallium	69.723	84	Polonium	(209)
32	Germanium	72.61	85	Astatine	(210)
33	Arsenic	74.9216	86	Radon	(222)
34	Selenium	78.96	87	Francium	(223)
35	Bromine	79.904	88	Radium	226.0254
36	Krypton	83.80	89	Actinium	(227)
37	Rubidium	85.4678	90	Thorium	232.0381
38	Strontium	87.62	91	Protactinium	231.03588
39	Yttrium	88.90585	92	Uranium	238.0289
40	Zirconium	91.224	93	Neptunium	237.0482
41	Niobium	92.90638	94	Plutonium	(244)
42	Molybdenum	95.94	95	Americium	(243)
43	Technetium	98.9062	96	Curium	(247)
44	Ruthenium	101.07	97	Berkelium	(247)
45	Rhodium	102.90550	98	Californium	(251)
46	Palladium	106.42	99	Einsteinium	(254)
47	Silver	107.8682	100	Fermium	(257)
48	Cadmium	112.411	101	Mendelevium	(258)
49	Indium	114.82	102	Nobelium	(259)
50	Tin	118.710	103	Lawrencium	(260)
51	Antimony	121.75	104	Unnilquadium	(261)
52	Tellurium	127.60	105	Unnilpentium	(262)
53	Iodine	126.90447			

THE
ELEMENTS

SECOND EDITION

.

Written and compiled by

JOHN EMSLEY

Science Writer in Residence,
Imperial College, London

CLARENDON PRESS · OXFORD

Oxford University Press, Walton Street, Oxford OX2 6DP

Oxford New York Toronto
Delhi Bombay Calcutta Madras Karachi
Kuala Lumpur Singapore Hong Kong Tokyo
Nairobi Dar es Salaam Cape Town
Melbourne Auckland Madrid
and associated companies in
Berlin Ibadan

Oxford is a trade mark of Oxford University Press

Published in the United States
by Oxford University Press Inc., New York

First published 1989
Reprinted (with corrections) 1989, 1990 (twice)
Second edition 1991
Reprinted (with corrections) 1992 (twice), 1993

British Library Cataloguing in Publication Data
Emsley, John
The elements.
1. Chemical elements, chemical compounds—
Technical data—For schools
I. Title
540'.212
ISBN 0-19-855568-7 (pbk)

Library of Congress Cataloging in Publication Data
Emsley, J. (John)
The elements/written and compiled by John Emsley.
Includes index.
1. Chemical elements—Handbooks, manuals, etc. I. Title.
QD466.E48 1988   546—dc19   88-19011
ISBN 0-19-855568-7 (pbk)

Printed in Great Britain by
Bookcraft (Bath) Ltd
Midsomer Norton, Avon

Preface to the second edition

WHEN I compiled the first edition of *The Elements* I hoped that if the book were successful, and had to be reprinted, then all I would have to do was correct errors and insert new data. I little thought that I would be writing a second edition within two years. However, the response from readers and reviewers has made this necessary.

In the first edition I naturally took a chemist's view, and saw the information about each element in terms of atoms and their components. I began at the nucleus and worked outwards. In other words I had sections on Nuclear Properties, Electron Shell Properties, and bulk properties which I divided along the traditional lines of Chemical Properties and Physical Properties. I also gave a brief explanation of each element's name, who discovered it, where, and when.

But why stop there? The elements have a role to play in biology, health, geology, and even the world economy. The second edition takes these into account with an Environmental Properties section. This is divided into abundance, geological data, and biological role. Included in the first of these are the abundances in the Sun, the Earth's crust, and the oceans. The geological section gives the chief ores or sources, the annual production of each element and the extent of its known reserves. Under the biological heading is a brief outline of the element's role in living species, its level in human muscle, bone and blood, the average daily intake, and the level at which the element can produce a toxic, even lethal, response.

I have also added two new elements—104, unnilquadium, and 105, unnilpentium—although the information about them is sparse. I have reduced the number of tables of properties at the end of the book, keeping only those for which a complete listing can be justified on either educational or comparative grounds. Finally, I have added a questionnaire which you can complete and return to the publisher.

In preparing the second edition I want to thank all those people who responded to the first edition with criticisms, support, advice and help. These are, in alphabetical order: T. A. Bak; S. B. Baliga; R. E. Banks; M. Berry; V. Braütigam; P. G. Bruce; R. de Pasquale; J. Dillon; J. B. Farmer; F. Gallway; N. N. Greenwood; M. Griffin; E. Grimble; T. K. Halstead; W. F. Harrigan; D. A. Harris, A. F. Harrison; L. A. Hobbs; M. Kenward; J. King; A. Lekies; D. McCurrie; D. Margerison; R. Mason; P. G. Nelson; S. C. Nyburg; J. Thomas, D. R. Turner; J. Wachter; and M. Whitfield.

In particular I would like to thank the staff of Oxford University Press, Alfred and Isabel Bader of the Aldrich Chemical Company, and Marshall and Mary Smalley of Macfarland Smith, without whom the first edition would have not enjoyed the success it has. Finally my thanks to my daughter, Helen, for her practical help, and, most important of all, to my wife Joan for her encouragement and so much more.

London J.E.
September 1990

Preface to the first edition

MOST people are aware that everything we see around us is composed of a limited number of chemical elements. Most scientists occasionally need to find information about individual elements, and it comes as a surprise to them to discover that such information is not always easily obtained. Even chemists may have difficulty in tracking down certain pieces of data. Chemists have at their disposal several excellent collections of numerical facts, but we tend to view our world through the eyes of analytical, organic, inorganic, or physical chemists, and compile our data accordingly.

Curiously, a handbook about the elements themselves may be seen as the province of all, and yet be the responsibility of no one. This may explain why it has remained neglected for so long, but hopefully the book you now hold fills this gap. It should not be seen as just a chemistry book, but as a general book to which all scientists could refer. That there is a widespread interest in the chemical elements was made clear to me a few years ago when I produced the *New Scientist* Periodic Table to commemorate the 150th anniversary of the birth of Dimitri Mendeleyev, who first devised the Periodic Table of the Elements in 1869.

Many years ago I began my own collection of data about the elements. To start with I simply bought a large notebook with over 100 pages and wrote the name of a different element at the top of each page. Over the years my collection of numerical information about each element grew until the book finally burst its binding as I stuck in more and more leaves. It is an edited version of this book that you now have in your hands. Not all the information about every element is here, nor could it be, since I have deliberately kept within the format of a double page for each element, although I have tried to include as much data as possible within this framework.

For each element I have grouped together properties under the headings chemical, physical, nuclear, and electronic, as well as giving the history and derivation of the element's name. I have also included something on its environmental and biological importance. All the data are given in SI units in the main tables, but there are full details of how to convert this information into other, commonly used, units in the 'The key to *The Elements*' section.

The final part of the book consists of a series of double tables of properties, arranged first in order of the elements and then in order of the property itself. Again the choice is partly my own, but these tables were mainly determined by the need to include as many elements as possible for each property, and there are only a certain number of properties that are common to all, or most, of the elements.

Finally I make no apologies for including tables of such 'obvious' data as the elements in alphabetical order with their chemical symbols, and chemical symbols in alphabetical order with their full names (see back end papers). The need for these came home to me as I was preparing the *New Scientist* version of the periodic table. Opinion among other scientists is that chemists assume too much, and while we know without thinking that W is tungsten and Sn is tin, many of our fellow scientists need these symbols confirmed when they encounter them.

London   J.E.
December 1987

Contents

The key to *The Elements*

THE curious thing about numerical information is the way it varies slightly from book to book. Usually these variations are of the order of ± 2 per cent, small but irritating. The need to standardize data has been recognized by several organizations, such as the International Union of Pure and Applied Chemistry (IUPAC) and the National Bureau of Standards (NBS) in Washington DC. When such bodies set up committees to assess data and decide on the most reliable values, the job of an author like myself becomes much easier. For example, the table of thermodynamic data of the elements comes from an NBS book while the standard reduction potentials come from an IUPAC publication.

Rather than quote alternative values, or a range of values, for certain properties I have assumed that well established specialists in the collecting of data, such as those of the *CRC handbook of chemistry and physics* (reference 1) and *Lange's handbook of chemistry* (reference 2) provide reliable information, even though it may not be in SI units. Other compilations with extensive chemical data are references 3–6. In the sections which follow I give the sources of my information, explain the SI units used, and convert the data to other commonly used units.

Note: n.a. used in the tables means not available.

The elements: discovery, names, formulae, and relative atomic masses

IUPAC is the official body responsible for approving the names and formulae given to elements, and authenticating their relative atomic masses. The US names of aluminium (aluminum) and caesium (cesium) are so near to the recommended names that they present no problem, except that the latter name leads to a slightly different position in a list of elements arranged alphabetically. Changes are reported in *Pure and Applied Chemistry*, IUPAC's official journal. The relative atomic masses given here are taken from *Pure and Applied Chemistry*, 1986, **58**, 1677.

The most comprehensive volume on the discovery and history of the elements is M. E. Weeks and H. M. Leicester's, *Discovery of the elements*, published by the *Journal of Chemical Education*, Easton, Penn., 1968. An outline of the discovery of each element is also given in reference 1. Individual articles in the *Journal of Chemical Education* from time to time give excellent histories of individual elements.

D. W. Ball, in the *Journal of Chemical Education*, 1985, **62**, 787, and J. G. Stark and H. G. Wallace, in *Education in Chemistry*, 1970, 152, explain how the names of the elements were chosen.

Chemical properties

Descriptions

The brief descriptions of the elements and their reactivity towards air, water, acids, and alkalis have been taken from references 7–9. The *Encyclopedia of the chemical elements*, edited by C. A. Hampel (Reinhold Book Corporation, New York, 1968) gives a comprehensive, if somewhat dated account, of the uses of each element. The uses to which the lanthanide elements are put are taken from J. T.

Kilbourn *Metallurgical applications of the lanthanides and yttrium* (Molycorp Inc., White Plains, NY, 1987).

Radii

To convert radii, which are given in picometres (pm), to metres divide by 10^{12}. To convert to nanometres (nm) divide by 1000; and to convert to angstroms (Å) divide by 100.

The radius of an atom depends upon several factors: oxidation state, degree of ionization, and coordination number (for metals this is generally 12). When it is part of a molecule two radii are defined: the covalent radius, which refers to the role it plays in forming bonds, and the van der Waals radius, which refers to the radius it presents to the world beyond the molecule. Many textbooks quote some of these radii, but the best sources appear to be references 2 and 4.

Electronegativity

This quantity is well understood but ill-defined. It refers to the potential of an atom to attract electrons to itself. The higher the electronegativity the stronger is this ability. Fluorine is the most electronegative of all elements.

Electronegativity was first calculated by Pauling, whose method is based on bond energies, and these values have been up-dated from time to time, e.g. by A. L. Allred, in *Journal of Inorganic and Nuclear Chemistry*, 1961, **17**, 215. Pauling's values are given in most reference works, such as reference 4. Allred, in collaboration with E. G. Rochow, proposed an alternative method of calculating electronegativity based on the effective nuclear charge and the covalent radius of an atom: see A. L. Allred and E. G. Rochow (*Journal of Inorganic and Nuclear Chemistry*, 1958, **5**, 261). Again these values, labelled (Allred), have been amended by later workers. The units of electronegativity are rarely quoted for either Pauling's or Allred and Rochow's values.

R. G. Pearson (*Inorganic chemistry*, 1988, **27**, 734) has proposed a scale of absolute electronegativity, which is defined as the average of the first ionization energy and the electron affinity of the neutral atom. Pearson uses units of electron volts (eV) for these quantities, and consequently the absolute electronegativity is in eV, and is given here as such. To convert from eV to kJ mol^{-1} multiply by 96.486. Established electronegativity scales generally lie in the range 0 to 4, and this is extended from 0 to 10.41 for absolute electronegativities. There is little to be gained by converting absolute electronegativities to SI units.

Calculating the absolute electronegativities of the f block elements cannot be done with precision since individual electron affinities are known only to be ≤ 50 kJ mol^{-1}; the absolute negativities for these metals should therefore be quoted with caution. For the noble gases it is also possible to calculate absolute electronegativities with more precision, and for krypton (6.8 eV) and xenon (5.85 eV) the values have meaning in that compounds are known for these elements. For helium, neon, and argon it is also possible to give values, showing these to be the most electronegative of the elements, e.g. helium $= 12.3$ eV. Since these elements form no molecules the electronegativity values are enclosed in square brackets.

Effective nuclear charge, Z_e

Like electronegativity, this quantity is easier to understand than calculate. Although Z_e can be defined for any electron within an atom, only the Z_e for the valence shell electrons is of interest to the chemist. Z_e is the charge due to the protons of the nucleus less a screening factor due to the other electrons of the atom. There are several slightly different ways of calculating this screening, and consequently there are several values for Z_e. Those quoted were computed by J. C. Slater (*Physical Review*, 1930, **36**, 57), E. Clementi and D. L. Raimondi (*Journal of Chemical Physics*, 1963, **38**, 2686), E. Clementi, D. L. Raimondi, and W. P. Reinhardt (*Journal of Chemical Physics*, 1967, **47**, 1300), and C. Froese-Fischer (*Atomic Data*, 1972, **4**, 301, and *Atomic Data and Nuclear Data Tables*, 1973, **12**, 87).

Standard reduction potentials

In these diagrams the element is arranged with the highest oxidation state on the left. Potentials are given in volts. The higher the value of $E^{\ominus}$, the stronger is the oxidant as an oxidizing agent; the lower $E^{\ominus}$, the stronger is the reductant as a reducing agent. These diagrams are taken from *Standard potentials in aqueous solutions*, edited by A. J. Bard, R. Parsons, and J. Jordan. [Marcel Dekker (for IUPAC), New York, 1985.] Other compilations of $E^{\ominus}$ data are to be found in references 1–6.

Oxidation states

Although it is merely a formalism, the concept of oxidation number is much used in describing the changes that happen to an element in its chemical reactions. Consequently it is a useful way of classifying and explaining the compounds of that element. From the multitude of compounds known for elements in their various oxidation states I have chosen where possible to give the oxides, hydroxides or acids, hydrides, fluorides, and chlorides (after which 'etc.' means the corresponding bromides and iodides), and the species present in aqueous solutions of simple salts of the element (denoted 'aq'). Salts, complexes, and organometallic compounds are also given if these are special; otherwise I have merely indicated that such substances exist, and references 7–9 should be consulted for further details.

Covalent bonds

To convert bond lengths, r, given in picometres, to metres, divide by 10^{12}; to convert them to nanometres (nm) divide by 1000. To convert them to angstroms (Å) divide by 100. To convert bond energies, i.e. bond enthalpies, E, given in kJ mol^{-1} to kcal mol^{-1}, divide by 4.184.

The values are taken from various sources, notably bond lengths from references 1 and 4, and bond enthalpies from references 1, 3, and 4, and from *Bond energies, ionization potentials and electron affinities* by V. I. Vedeneyev, L. V. Gurvich, V. N. Kondrat'yev, V. A. Mededev, and Ye. L. Frankevich (Edward Arnold, London, 1966). *SI chemical data* by G. H. Aylward and T. J. V. Findley (Wiley, Sydney, 1971) also gives r and E for many bonds.

Physical properties

Melting points and boiling points

These are given in Kelvin (K). They can be converted to degrees Celsius (C) by subtracting 273.15. The values quoted are based on reference 1, but are also given with slight variations in all major data books (references 2–9). Critical temperatures, pressures, and volumes are also given for the gaseous elements. Pressure is reported in kilopascals (kPa); to convert to bars divide by 100, to convert to Torr (mmHg) multiply by 7.500; to convert to atmospheres divide by 101.325. Values are taken from R. C. Reid, J. M. Prausnitz, and T. K. Sherwood, *The properties of gases and liquids* (3rd edition) (McGraw-Hill, New York, 1977).

Enthalpy of fusion, ΔH_{fusion} and Enthalpy of vaporization, ΔH_{vap}

These, given in kJ mol^{-1}, can be converted to kcal mol^{-1} by dividing by 4.184.

The values are taken mainly from R. Loebel's compilation in reference 1 (where they are given in c.g.s. units), supplemented by references 4 and 6, where they are in SI units. The values for ΔH_{vap} are taken mainly from reference 6.

Thermodynamic properties

To convert kJ mol^{-1} to kcal mol^{-1} divide by 4.184. To convert entropies in J K^{-1} mol^{-1} to eu (entropy units, i.e. cal K^{-1} mol^{-1}) divide by 4.184. To convert specific heats, C_p, to cal g^{-1} K^{-1} divide first by 4.184 and then by the relative atomic mass of the element concerned.

The thermodynamic properties are taken from *The NBS tables of chemical thermodynamic properties* by D. D. Wagman, W. H. Evans, and V. B. Parker, which was published jointly by the American Chemical Society and the American Institute of Physics for the National Bureau of Standards, Washington DC, in 1982. Although thermodynamic data for the elements are to be found in references 1–5, the NBS compilation is preferred and is in SI units.

Density

Since the basic SI unit of weight is the kilogram (kg) and of length the metre (m), the preferred unit of density is kg m^{-3}. The more common unit, however, is g cm^{-3} and to convert from kg m^{-3} to g cm^{-3} divide by 1000.

Many sources list densities at only one temperature, such as reference 2 (293 K), others at various temperatures, e.g. reference 6, which reports them in SI units. The densities used here are based mainly on reference 1 for the solid elements. In the same work can be found the densities of the liquid elements at their melting points, compiled by G. Lang.

Thermal conductivity

The SI unit for this property is watts per metre per Kelvin (W m^{-1} K^{-1}). To convert to W cm^{-1} K^{-1} divide by 100.

The values are taken from C. Y. Ho, R. W. Powell, and P. E. Liley (*Journal of Physical Chemistry Reference Data*, 1974, **3**, suppl. 1), with the values for carbon being taken from reference 1 for the directions perpendicular and parallel to the graphite axis. Reference 2 also reports the thermal conductivity of the elements.

Electrical resistivity

The SI units are ohm metres (Ω m) and the electrical resistivity of metals are of the order of 10^{-8} Ω m. To convert to the more common units of $\mu\Omega$ cm multiply the Ω m values by 10^8.

The data are taken from reference 1. Reference 6, pp. 102–3, also gives the electrical resistivity in Ω m at temperatures of 78, 273, 373, 573, and 1473 K. Values in non-SI units are given in reference 3, pp. 580–684.

Mass magnetic susceptibility, χ

This is obtained from the volume magnetic susceptibility, κ, which is unitless, by dividing by the density (kg m^{-3} in SI units). To convert mass magnetic susceptibilities from the SI units of kg^{-1} m^3 to c.g.s. units of g^{-1} cm^3, multiply by $1000/4\pi$, i.e. 79.6. To convert to molar magnetic susceptibility multiply first by 79.6 then by the relative atomic mass of the element. The use of SI units for magnetic properties is discussed by T. I. Quickenden and R. C. Marshall, in the *Journal of Chemical Education*, 1972, **49**, 114.

The magnetic susceptibility data are taken from *Constantes sélectionnées. Diamagnétisme et paramagnétisme* by G. Foëx (Masson et Cie, Paris, 1957), and *Modern magnetism* (4th edition) by L. F. Bates (Cambridge University Press, Cambridge, 1963). Values for certain of the lanthanides were taken from J. M. Lock (*Proceedings of the Physical Society*, 1957, **B70**, 476 and 566). Reference 1 reports molar magnetic susceptibilities in c.g.s. units.

Coefficient of linear thermal expansion, α

This is the same in SI and c.g.s. units, i.e. K^{-1}. It is often reported as $10^6\alpha$. The data are taken from reference 3 (pp. 580–684).

Molar volume (or atomic volume)

This represents a slight problem for SI whose unit of volume is m^3. Traditionally atomic volume is obtained by dividing the relative atomic mass of an element in grams by the density in $g\ cm^{-3}$, and is consequently traditionally expressed in cm^3. To express the molar volume in m^3 divide the values given by 10^6. Expressing it in this way, however, implies a density measured in $g\ m^{-3}$, which is not a recognized way of expressing this quantity.

Since atomic volume for an element depends upon the density, it also depends upon the phase, the allotrope, and the temperature. The values reported here are based where possible on the solid state at room temperature (298 K or as indicated), and are taken mainly from C. N. Singman (*Journal of Chemical Education*, 1984, **61**, 137).

Crystal structure

To convert the cell parameters to angstroms (Å) divide by 100. To convert them to nm divide by 1000.

The abbreviation b.c.c. means body-centred cubic, f.c.c. means face-centred cubic, and h.c.p. means hexagonal close packed. The data are taken from *Landolt–Bornstein*, New Series, Group III, Vol. 6, edited by K. H. Hellwege and A. M. Hellwege. Crystal structure data are also to be found in references 3, 5, and 9; and *The structures of the elements* by J. Donohue (John Wiley & Sons, 1974).

X-ray diffraction mass absorption coefficients

These are taken from *International tables for X-ray crystallography*, Vol. III, Physical and Chemical Tables, section 3.2, published for the International Union of Crystallographers by the Kynock Press (Birmingham, UK, 1962).

Nuclear properties

Thermal neutron capture cross-section

The barn is defined as $10^{-24}\ cm^2$, which is $10^{-28}\ m^2$. The values are taken from reference 1.

Key isotopes

This lists all stable isotopes and the longest lived radioactive nuclides, plus those used in research. The per cent natural abundance is given as 'trace' for certain short-lived nuclides that are part of a natural decay series. The half-life, $T_{1/2}$, is expressed in seconds (s), minutes (m), hours (h), days (d), or years (y). The decay mode is shown as β^- for electron emission, β^+ for positron emission, α for alpha decay, EC for electron capture, IT for isomeric transition, and SF for spontaneous fission. Some nuclei decay by two routes. The energy (in mega electronvolts,

MeV) of the radiation is given in parentheses. γ indicates the emission of gamma radiation.

The nuclide data is taken from reference 1. Similar tables are given in references 2 and 3. The most comprehensive listing is to be found in the *Table of isotopes* (7th edition) by C. M. Lederer and V. S. Shirley (John Wiley & Sons, New York, 1978). This work lists the full data on 2600 known isotopes, and its compilation was supported by the US NBS Office of Standard Reference Data.

Nuclear spin (I) is reported in units of $h/2\pi$. The nuclear magnetic moment (μ) is reported in nuclear magnetons with diamagnetic correction. Both I and μ are taken from *Nuclear spins and moments* by G. H. Fuller (*Journal of Physical Chemistry Reference Data*, 1976, **5**, 835).

Use is made of isotopes in various areas of research, denoted by 'NMR', 'tracer', or 'med' short for medical. Nuclear magnetic resonance spectroscopy (NMR) details are given directly below the Key Isotopes table. The radioactive isotopes used as tracers and in medicine are taken from the *Merck index* (10th edition), edited by M. Windholz (Merck & Co., Inc., Rahway (NY), 1983); *Isotopes, products and services catalog* (Oak Ridge National Laboratory, P.O. Box X, Oak Ridge, Tennessee 37831, USA); and *Biochemicals* (The Radiochemical Centre, P.O. Box 16, Amersham, Bucks, HP7 9LL, UK). *Radionuclide tracers* by M. F. L'Annunziata (Academic Press, New York, London, 1987), also contains appendices of available isotopes and their radiation characteristics.

Nuclear magnetic resonance

Where data for two nuclei are given, the one enclosed in square brackets is less frequently used for NMR studies. Nuclear spins are given in the Key Isotopes table.

Relative sensitivity is at constant field for equal numbers of nuclei. Absolute sensitivity or receptivity is commonly quoted relative to $^{13}C = 1.00$.

The magnetogyric ratio is given in rad T^{-1} s^{-1}, but is often quoted as γ values which are in units of rad T^{-1} s^{-1} multiplied by 10^7. Thus for ^1H $\gamma = 26.75$, as opposed to 26.75×10^7 rad T^{-1} s^{-1}. γ is a constant of proportionality between frequency and field strength, and so the units are frequency (rad s^{-1})/field (T), i.e. rad T^{-1} s^{-1}.

Quadrupole moments are given in units of m^2. They can be converted to cm^2 by multiplying by 10^4, or to barns by multiplying by 10^{28}.

Frequency is quoted relative to the ^1H signal of $Si(CH_3)_4$, which is exactly 100 MHz in a magnetic field of 2.3488 T. For NMR spectrometers with ^1H at 60, 90, 200, 250, 360, or 400 MHz the frequency and field vary in direct proportion; in other words multiply the frequencies given in the tables by 0.6, 0.9, 2, 2.5, 3.6, or 4 respectively.

The data for the NMR tables were compiled from the *Handbook of high resolution multinuclear NMR* by C. Brevard and P. Granger (John Wiley & Sons, New York, 1981), *NMR and the periodic table* by R. K. Harris and B. E. Mann (Academic Press, London, 1978), *Multinuclear NMR* by J. Mason (Plenum Press, New York and London, 1987), and from Bruker Scientific Instruments publications.

Electron shell properties

Ground state electron configuration and term symbol

These are given in most inorganic textbooks, such as references 7 and 8. The data given here were taken from the *Handbook of atomic data* by S. Fraga, J. Karwowski, and K. M. S. Saxena (Elsevier, Amsterdam, 1976).

Electron affinity

To convert the values given in kJ mol^{-1} to electron volts (eV) divide by 96.486; to convert to MJ mol^{-1} divide by 1000.

Electron affinity is conventionally reported as positive if the addition of an electron to an atom releases energy, as it almost invariably does for the step $M \rightarrow M^{-}$, and negative if the process is energy absorbing, as it is for the addition of a second electron, i.e. $M^{-} \rightarrow M^{2-}$. This energy convention is the opposite of that used in reporting ionization energies and most other energy changes.

Although many chemistry textbooks report some electron affinities, and the major compilations, references 1 and 2, give extensive lists (in eV), the data reported here come from H. Hotop and W. C. Lineberger (*Journal of Physical Chemistry Reference Data*, 1985, **14**, 731), also reported in eV. An earlier compilation by R. J. Zollweg (*Journal of Chemical Physics*, 1969, **50**) also gives some values for the heavier elements. Their variation from element to element is discussed by E. C. M. Chen and W. E. Wentworth (*Journal of Chemical Education*, 1975, **52**, 486).

Ionization energies (ionization potentials)

To convert from kJ mol^{-1} to electron volts (eV) divide the values given by 96.486; to convert to MJ mol^{-1} divide by 1000.

Ionization energies are known to a high degree of accuracy for removal of the first, second, third, fourth, and fifth electrons for most elements, and for subsequent electron removal from the lighter elements. Values given in parentheses are less reliable. For some elements ionization energies beyond the tenth are available.

Many textbooks and compilations list ionization energies, some in SI units such as reference 4. The NBS has at different times published ionization data, beginning with E. C. Moore's *Atomic energy levels*, Volume III (NBS Circular 467, 1958). Reference 1 quotes *Analyses of optical spectra*, NSRDS-NBS 34 (Office of Standard Reference Data, NBS, Washington DC, 1970). The values for the lanthanides and actinides were taken from W. C. Martin, L. Hagan, J. Reader, and J. Sugar (*Journal of Physical Chemistry Reference Data*, 1974, **3**, 771).

Principal lines in atomic spectrum

The wavelengths are given in nanometres (nm); to convert to angstrom units (Å) multiply by 10. The stronger lines in the spectrum are listed with the strongest shown in bold. Lines arising from the neutral atom are indicated by Species I, and those arising from the singly charged ion M^{+} are Species II. Application in atom absorption spectrometry is indicated by (AA) and is taken from *Pye Unicam atomic absorption data book* (3rd edition) by P. J. Whiteside (Pye Unicam, Cambridge, UK, 1979). For some transuranium elements, with many intense lines, only the first seven lines identified as arising from the neutral atom are given.

Data are taken from *Line spectra of the elements* by J. Reader and C. H. Corliss in reference 1, and were prepared under the auspices of the Committee on Line Spectra of the Elements of the National Academy of Science – National Research Council, USA.

Environmental and biological properties

Abundances

For atmosphere, Earth's crust, and seawater the units are parts per million (p.p.m.), defined in the case of the atmosphere as cubic centimetres per cubic metre, in the case of the Earth's crust as grams per metric tonne (1000 kg), which is the same as milligrams per kilogram. The relative abundance of elements in the Sun are taken from J. E. Ross and L. H. Aller, *Science*, 1976, **191**, 1223, where they are reported relative to hydrogen (taken as 1×10^{12}) and given as log(relative abundances). These logarithmic values are also reproduced in Appendix A of reference 10. Solar abundances for arsenic, selenium, tellurium, iodine, tantalum, krypton, and xenon are not available because their spectra lines are masked by lines of more abundant elements. Some elements, notably the heavier radioactive elements, are not reported because they are too rare to be detected.

The atmospheric abundances are taken from reference 6. The abundance of elements in the Earth's crust are an average taken from Table 3.3 of reference 11.

The concentrations of the elements in the oceans, their residence times, and oxidation states are taken chiefly from M. Whitfield and D. R. Turner, *Aquatic surface chemistry*, Chapter 17, pp. 457–93, edited by W. Stumm (John Wiley & Sons Inc., New York, 1987). The values are expressed as parts per million (p.p.m.) by weight, i.e. milligram of the element per kilogram of seawater. To convert to molarities, multiply by the relative density of seawater (e.g. average at 277 K is 1.028 g cm^{-3}), divide by 1000 and by the relative atomic mass of the element. The more restricted data for the rarer elements are taken from Appendix A of reference 10, which is based on K. W. Bruland, *Trace elements in the ocean*, in *Chemical oceanography*, Volume 8, edited by J. Riley and R. Chester (Academic Press, New York, 1983), P. Henderson, *Inorganic geochemistry* (Pergamon Press, Oxford, 1982), and K. Schwochau, *Extraction of metals from seawater*, in *Topics in Current Chemistry*, 1984, **124**, 91.

Whitfield and Turner classify the elements as accumulating, recycled, and scavenged according to their oceanic profiles. 'Accumulating' means residence times in excess to 10^5 years with a concentration little changed with depth; 'recycled' refers to residence times of 10^3 to 10^5 years with a concentration that increases with depth; and scavenged elements have residence times of less than 1000 years and a concentration profile that decreases with depth. Readers requiring an approximate general value of ocean abundance should take an average of the Atlantic and Pacific deep values.

Geological data

Chief ores and sources can be found in reference 7. Reference 11 gives the important minerals and their annual production (y^{-1}). For certain key elements the data has been taken from W. Büchner, R. Schliebs, G. Winter, and K. H. Büchel, *Industrial inorganic chemistry*, translated by D. R. Terrell (CVH. Weinheim), 1989, which also gives the known reserves. The *Annual review of mining 1986*, published by Mining Journal Ltd, London, gives an account of 55 elements of commercial importance. Together these two publications give most of the data for the year 1985, which I have taken as representing a normal year, if there can be such a thing in the world economy. J. E. Ferguson, *Inorganic chemistry and the earth* (Pergamon Press, Oxford, 1982), also has some useful data, including Table 3.4 listing reserves for certain key metals.

The production figures refer to total world production of the element or its principal compound, although for some elements this should be treated with caution. The data for carbon were taken from *BP statistical review of world energy* (London, June, 1990). The data for the rare earth elements (f block) was provided by Molycorp Inc., White Plains, NY, and for the platinum group of metals by Johnson Matthey, London, UK

Biological role

Information about essential elements is from reference 11 and the *Handbook of vitamins, minerals and hormones* (2nd edition) by R. J. Kutsky (Van Nostrand

Reinhold, New York, 1981). The term stimulatory is used to describe the general effect on human metabolism; carcinogenic means that it can trigger cancer; teratogenic means that it can cause a deformed fetus.

Reference 11 has tables of the elemental composition of various human tissue of which muscles and bone are given here (p.p.m. refers to milligrams per kilogram of dry weight). Also given is the total mass of the element in an average human of 70 kg weight. The elemental composition of human blood (whole blood) is given as milligrams per $dm^3(=litre)$ also taken from reference 11. The daily dietary intake is taken from the same source, which also gives the toxic and lethal dosage for humans, although in some cases this refers to rats and is indicated as such.

Toxicological information about the elements depends on individual compounds, as well as the elements themselves. Useful sources of information are *Metal toxicology in mammals* (2 volumes) by T. D. Luckey and B. Venugopal (Plenum Press, New York, 1977), and the *Handbook of toxicity of inorganic compounds*, edited by H. G. Seiler and H. Sigel (Marcel Dekker, New York, 1988), which covers a majority of elements in alphabetical order.

General references

1. Weast, R. C. (ed.) *CRC handbook of chemistry and physics*, (70th edn), CRC Press, Boca Raton, Fl 1989.
2. Dean, J. A. (ed.) *Lange's handbook of chemistry* (13th edn). McGraw-Hill, New York, 1985.
3. Moses, A. J. *The practising scientist's handbook*. Van Nostrand Reinhold, New York, 1978.
4. Ball, M. C. and Norbury, A. H. *Physical data for inorganic chemists*. Longman, London, 1974.
5. Samsonov, G. V. (ed.) *Handbook of the physicochemical properties of the elements*. IFI-Plenum, New York, 1968.
6. Kaye, G. W. C. and Laby, T. H. *Tables of physical and chemical constants* (14th edn), Longman, London, 1973.
7. Greenwood, N. N. and Earnshaw, A. *Chemistry of the elements*. Pergamon Press, Oxford, 1984.
8. Cotton, F. A. and Wilkinson, G. *Advanced inorganic chemistry* (5th edn), John Wiley & Sons, New York, 1988
9. Bailar, J. C., Emeléus, H. J., Nyholm, R., and Trotman-Dickenson, A. F. (eds) *Comprehensive inorganic chemistry* (5 vols). Pergamon Press, Oxford, 1973.
10. Cox, P. A. *The elements: their origin, abundance and distribution*. Oxford University Press, Oxford, 1989
11. Bowen, H. J. M. *Environmental chemistry of the elements*. Academic Press, London, 1979.

THE
ELEMENTS

Ac

Atomic number: 89
Relative atomic mass ($^{12}C = 12.0000$): (227)

Chemical properties

Soft, silvery-white metal which glows in the dark. Reacts with water to evolve H_2.

Radii/pm: Ac^{3+} 118; atomic 187.8
Electronegativity: 1.1 (Pauling); 1.00 (Allred)
Effective nuclear charge: 1.80 (Slater)

Standard reduction potentials $E^{\ominus}/V$

	III		0
Acidic solution	Ac^{3+}	-2.13	Ac
Basic solution	$Ac(OH)_3$	-2.6	Ac

Oxidation states

Ac^0 ($d^1 s^2$)
Ac^{III} ([Rn]) Ac_2O_3, $Ac(OH)_3$ insoluble
[AcH_2 and AcH_3 are probably Ac^{III} compounds]

Physical properties

Melting point/K: 1320 ± 50
Boiling point/K: 3470 ± 300
ΔH_{fusion}/kJ mol^{-1}: 14.2
ΔH_{vap}/kJ mol^{-1}: 293

Thermodynamic properties (298.15 K, 0.1 MPa)

State	$\Delta_f H^{\ominus}$/kJ mol^{-1}	$\Delta_f G^{\ominus}$/kJ mol^{-1}	$S^{\ominus}$/J K^{-1} mol^{-1}	C_p/J K^{-1} mol^{-1}
Solid	0	0	56.5	27.2
Gas	406	366	188.1	20.84

Density/kg m^{-3}: 10060 [293 K]
Thermal conductivity/W m^{-1} K^{-1}: 12 [300 K]
Electrical resistivity/Ω m: n.a.
Mass magnetic susceptibility/kg^{-1} m^3: n.a.
Molar volume/cm^3: 22.6
Coefficient of linear thermal expansion/K^{-1}: 14.9×10^{-6}

Crystal structure (cell dimensions/pm), space group

f.c.c. ($a = 531.1$), Fm3m

X-ray diffraction: mass absorption coefficients (μ/ρ)/cm^2 g^{-1}:
CuK_α n.a. MoK_α n.a.

Actinium

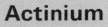

Thermal neutron capture cross-section/barns: 810 (^{227}Ac)
Number of isotopes (including nuclear isomers): 26
Isotope mass range: 210→232

Nuclear properties

Key isotopes

Nuclide	Atomic mass	Natural abund. (%)	Half-life $T_{1/2}$	Decay mode and energy (MeV)	Nuclear spin I	Nuclear magnetic moment μ	Uses
^{225}Ac	225.023 205	0	10.0d	α(5.935); γ	3/2+		tracer
^{227}Ac	227.027 750	trace	21.77y	β^-(0.0410) 98.6%; α(5.043); 1.4%; γ	3/2−	+1.1	NMR
^{228}Ac	228.031 015	trace	6.13h	β^-(2.142); γ	3+		

NMR

^{227}Ac

Relative sensitivity (^{1}H = 1.00) —
Receptivity (^{13}C = 1.00) —
Magnetogyric ratio/rad T^{-1} s^{-1} 3.5×10^7
Quadrupole moment/m^2 1.7×10^{-28}
Frequency (^{1}H = 100 MHz; 2.3488 T)/MHz 13.1

Ground state electron configuration: [Rn]6d^{1}7s^2
Term symbol: ^{2}D$_{3/2}$
Electron affinity (M→M$^-$)/kJ mol^{-1}: n.a.

Electron shell properties

Main lines in atomic spectrum

Wavelength/nm	Species
386.312	II
408.844	II
416.840	II
438.641	II
450.720	II
591.085	II

Ionization energies/kJ mol^{-1}

1. M → M$^+$ 499	6. M^{5+} → M^{6+}	(7 300)
2. M$^+$ → M^{2+} 1170	7. M^{6+} → M^{7+}	(9 200)
3. M^{2+} → M^{3+} 1900	8. M^{7+} → M^{8+}	(10 500)
4. M^{3+} → M^{4+} (4700)	9. M^{8+} → M^{9+}	(11 900)
5. M^{4+} → M^{5+} (6000)	10. M^{9+} → M^{10+}	(15 800)

Environmental properties

Biological role

None; never encountered, but would be toxic due to radioactivity
Levels in humans: nil

Abundances

Sun (relative to H = 1 × 10^{12}): n.a.
Earth's crust/p.p.m.: trace
Seawater/p.p.m.: nil

Geological data

Chief sources: decay product of ^{235}U with 0.2 p.p.m. in uranium ores. Obtained in milligram quantities by neutron bombardment of ^{226}Ra

Al

Atomic number: 13

Relative atomic mass ($^{12}C=12.0000$): **26.981 54**

Pure aluminium is soft and malleable, but can be toughened by the addition of small amounts of other metals such as copper and magnesium. Aluminium is protected by oxide film from reacting with air and water. Soluble in hot concentrated HCl and NaOH solution. Hundreds of uses as metal and alloys in aircraft, construction industry, containers, foil, etc.

Radii/pm: Al^{3+} 57; covalent 125; atomic 143.1: van der Waals 205

Electronegativity: 1.61 (Pauling); 1.47 (Allred); 3.23 eV (absolute)

Effective nuclear charge: 3.50 (Slater); 4.07 (Clementi); 3.64 (Froese-Fischer)

Standard reduction potentials $E^{\ominus}/V$

	III		0
Acid solution	Al^{3+}	$\xrightarrow{-1.676}$	Al
	AlF_6^{3-}	$\xrightarrow{-2.067}$	Al
Alkaline solution	$Al(OH)_3$	$\xrightarrow{-2.300}$	Al
	$Al(OH)_4^-$	$\xrightarrow{-2.310}$	Al

Covalent bonds r/pm E/kJ mol^{-1}

	r/pm	E/kJ mol^{-1}
Al–H	c. 170	285
Al–C	224	225
Al–O	162	585
Al–F	163	665
Al–Cl	206	498
Al–Al	286	c. 200

Oxidation states

Al^I AlCl in gas phase
Al^{III} Al_2O_3 (amphoteric)
AlO(OH), $Al(OH)_3$
$Al(H_2O)_6^{3+}$ (aq)
Al^{3+} salts, AlH_3
$LiAlH_4$, AlF_3,
Na_3AlF_6, Al_2Cl_6

Melting point/K: 933.52

Boiling point/K: 2740

ΔH_{fusion}/kJ mol^{-1}: 10.67

ΔH_{vap}/kJ mol^{-1}: 293.72

Thermodynamic properties   (298.15 K, 0.1 MPa)

State	$\Delta_f H^{\ominus}$/kJ mol^{-1}	$\Delta_f G^{\ominus}$/kJ mol^{-1}	$S^{\ominus}$/J K^{-1} mol^{-1}	C_p/J K^{-1} mol^{-1}
Solid	0	0	28.33	24.35
Gas	326.4	285.7	165.54	21.38

Density/kg m^{-3}: 2698 [293 K]; 2390 [liquid at m.p.]

Thermal conductivity/W m^{-1} K^{-1}: 237 [300 K]

Electrical resistivity/Ω m: 2.6548×10^{-8} [293 K]

Mass magnetic susceptibility/kg^{-1} m^3: $+7.7 \times 10^{-9}$ (s)

Molar volume/cm^3: 10.00

Coefficient of linear thermal expansion/K^{-1}: 23.03×10^{-6}

Crystal structure (cell dimensions/pm), space group

f.c.c. ($a = 404.959$), Fm3m

X-ray diffraction: mass absorption coefficients (μ/ρ)/cm^2 g^{-1}:
CuK$_\alpha$ 48.6   MoK$_\alpha$ 5.16

Discovered in 1825 by Hans Christian Oersted at Copenhagen, Denmark

[Latin, *alumen* = alum]

Aluminium (Aluminum)

Thermal neutron capture cross-section/barns: 0.233
Number of isotopes (including nuclear isomers): 11
Isotope mass range: 22→31

Key isotopes

Nuclide	Atomic mass	Natural abundance (%)	Half-life $T_{1/2}$	Decay mode and energy (MeV)	Nuclear spin I	Nuclear magnetic moment μ	Uses
^{26}Al	25.986 892	0	7.4×10^5y	β^+ (4.003) 82%; EC, 18%; γ	5+		tracer
^{27}Al	26.981 540	100	stable		5/2+	+3.6415	NMR

NMR

	^{27}Al
Relative sensitivity (^{1}H = 1.00)	0.21
Receptivity (^{13}C = 1.00)	1.17×10^3
Magnetogyric ratio/rad T^{-1} s^{-1}	6.9704×10^7
Quadrupole moment/m^2	0.4193×10^{-28}
Frequency (^{1}H = 100 MHz; 2.3488 T)/MHz	26.057

Reference: $Al(H_2O)_6^{3+}$

Ground state electron configuration: [Ne] $3s^2 3p^1$
Term symbol: $^2P_{1/2}$
Electron affinity (M→M$^-$)/kJ mol^{-1}: 44

Main lines in atomic spectrum

Wavelength/nm	Species
308.215	I
309.271 (AA)	I
309.281 (AA)	I
394.401	I
396.152	I

Ionization energies/kJ mol^{-1}

1. M → M$^+$	577.4	6. M^{5+} → M^{6+} 18 376
2. M$^+$ → M^{2+}	1816.6	7. M^{6+} → M^{7+} 23 293
3. M^{2+} → M^{3+}	2744.6	8. M^{7+} → M^{8+} 27 457
4. M^{3+} → M^{4+}	11 575	9. M^{8+} → M^{9+} 31 857
5. M^{4+} → M^{5+}	14 839	10. M^{9+} → M^{10+} 38 459

Environmental properties

Biological role

None; accumulates in the body from the daily intake; implicated in Alzheimer's disease (senile dementia)

Levels in humans:
Muscle/p.p.m.: 0.7–28
Bone/p.p.m.: 4–27
Blood/mg dm^{-3}: 0.39
Daily dietary intake: 2.45 mg
Toxic intake: 5 g
Lethal intake: n.a.
Total mass of element in average (70 kg) person: 61 mg

Abundances

Sun (relative to H = 1×10^{12}): 3.3×10^6

Earth's crust/p.p.m.: 82 000

Seawater/p.p.m.:
Atlantic surface: 9.7×10^{-4}
Atlantic deep: 5.2×10^{-4}
Pacific surface: 1.3×10^{-4}
Pacific deep: 0.13×10^{-4}
Residence time/years: 150
Classification: scavenged
Oxidation state: III

Geological data

Chief ores and sources:
bauxite, found as boehmite [AlO(OH)] and gibbsite [Al(OH)$_3$].

World production/tonnes y^{-1}: 15×10^6

Reserves/tonnes: 6×10^9

Am

Atomic number: 95
Relative atomic mass ($^{12}C = 12.0000$): **(243)**

Chemical properties

Radioactive, silvery metal which does not occur naturally. Attacked by air, steam, and acids, but not alkalis.

Radii/pm: Am^{6+} 80; Am^{5+} 86; Am^{4+} 92; Am^{3+} 107; atomic 184
Electronegativity: 1.3 (Pauling); n.a. (Allred)
Effective nuclear charge: 4.65 (Slater)

Standard reduction potentials $E^{\ominus}$/V

	VI		V		IV		III		0

Acid solution

$$AmO_2^{2+} \xrightarrow{1.59} AmO_2^{+} \xrightarrow{0.82} Am^{4+} \xrightarrow{2.62} Am^{3+} \xrightarrow{-2.07} Am$$

with $AmO_2^{+} \xrightarrow{1.72} Am^{4+}$ above, $AmO_2^{2+} \xrightarrow{1.20} Am^{4+}$ and $Am^{4+} \xrightarrow{-0.90} Am$ below.

Alkaline solution $AmO_2(OH)_2 \xrightarrow{0.9} AmO_2(OH) \xrightarrow{0.7} AmO_2 \xrightarrow{0.22} Am(OH)_3 \xrightarrow{-2.53} Am$

Oxidation states

Am^{II}	(f^7)	AmO, $AmCl_2$, etc.
Am^{III}	(f^6)	Am_2O_3, AmF_3, $AmCl_3$, etc. $[AmCl_6]^{3-}$, $Am^{3+}(aq)$
Am^{IV}	(f^5)	AmO_2, AmF_4
Am^{V}	(f^4)	AmO_2^{+} (aq) $\rbrace$ unstable due to reduction by radioactive
Am^{VI}	(f^3)	AmO_2^{2+} (aq) $\rbrace$ decay products

Physical properties

Melting point/K: 1267
Boiling point/K: 2880
ΔH_{fusion}/kJ mol^{-1}: 14.4
ΔH_{vap}/kJ mol^{-1}: 238.5

Thermodynamic properties (298.15 K, 0.1 MPa)

State	$\Delta_f H^{\ominus}$/kJ mol^{-1}	$\Delta_f G^{\ominus}$/kJ mol^{-1}	$S^{\ominus}$/J K^{-1} mol^{-1}	C_p/J K^{-1} mol^{-1}
Solid	0	0	n.a.	n.a.
Gas	n.a.	n.a.	n.a.	n.a.

Density/kg m^{-3}: 13 670 [293 K]
Thermal conductivity/W m^{-1} K^{-1}: 10 est. [300 K]
Electrical resistivity/Ω m: 68×10^{-8}
Mass magnetic susceptibility/kg^{-1} m^3: $+5 \times 10^{-8}$ (s)
Molar volume/cm^3: 17.78
Coefficient of linear thermal expansion/K^{-1}: n.a.

Crystal structure (cell dimensions/pm), space group

α-Am h.c.p. ($a = 346.80$; $c = 1124.0$), P6$_3$/mmc
β-Am f.c.c. ($a = 489.4$), Fm3m
$T(\alpha \rightarrow \beta) = 1347$ K

X-ray diffraction: mass absorption coefficients (μ/ρ)/cm^2 g^{-1}:
n.a.

Discovered in 1944 by G. T. Seaborg, R. A. James, L. O. Morgan, and A. Ghiorso at Chicago, Illinois, USA

[English, *America*]

Americium

Thermal neutron capture cross-section/barns: 74 (^{243}Am)
Number of isotopes (including nuclear isomers): 14
Isotope mass range: 237→247

Nuclear properties

Key isotopes

Nuclide	Atomic mass	Natural abund. (%)	Half-life $T_{1/2}$	Decay mode and energy (MeV)	Nuclear spin I	Nuclear magnetic moment μ	Uses
^{241}Am	241.056 823	0	432.2y	α(5.637); γ	5/2−	+1.61	tracer; medical
^{243}Am	243.061 375	0	7.37×10^3y	α(5.439); γ	5/2−	+1.61	NMR

NMR

	^{243}Am
Relative sensitivity (^{1}H = 1.00)	—
Receptivity (^{13}C = 1.00)	—
Magnetogyric ratio/rad T^{-1} s^{-1}	1.54×10^7
Quadrupole moment/m^2	4.9×10^{-28}
Frequency (^{1}H = 100 MHz; 2.3488 T)/MHz	5.76

Ground state electron configuration: [Rn]5f^{7}7s^2
Term symbol: ^{8}S$_{7/2}$
Electron affinity (M→M$^-$)/kJ mol^{-1}: n.a.

Electron shell properties

Main lines in atomic spectrum

Wavelength/nm	Species
283.226	II
348.331	II
351.013	I
356.916	II
367.312	I
377.750	II
392.625	II
408.929	II
428.926	I
450.945	II
457.559	II
466.279	II
605.464	I

Ionization energies/kJ mol^{-1}

1. M →M$^+$ 578.2
2. M$^+$→M^{2+}
3. M^{2+}→M^{3+}
4. M^{3+}→M^{4+}
5. M^{4+}→M^{5+}

Environmental properties

Biological role	Abundances	Geological data
None; never encountered, but would be toxic due to radioactivity **Levels in humans:** nil	**Sun** (relative to H = 1 × 10^{12}): n.a. **Earth's crust**/p.p.m.: nil **Seawater**/p.p.m.: nil	**Chief source:** produced in 100 g quantities as ^{243}Am by neutron bombardment of ^{239}Pu

Sb

Atomic number: 51
Relative atomic mass ($^{12}C = 12.0000$): 121.75

Chemical properties

Metalloid element with various allotropes, of which metal is bright, silvery, hard, and brittle. Stable in dry air and not attacked by dilute acids or alkalis. Used to harden other metals, in storage batteries, bearings, etc.

Radii/pm: Sb^{5+} 62; Sb^{3+} 89; covalent 141; atomic 182; van der Waals 220; Sb^{2-} 245

Electronegativity: 2.05 (Pauling); 1.82 (Allred); 4.85 eV (absolute)

Effective nuclear charge: 6.30 (Slater); 9.99 (Clementi); 12.37 (Froese-Fischer)

Standard reduction potentials $E^{\ominus}/V$

	V	IV	III	0	−III
Acid solution	Sb_2O_5	—0.605—	SbO^+ —0.204—	Sb	
Neutral solution	Sb_2O_5 —1.055—	Sb_2O_4 —0.342—	Sb_4O_6 —0.150—	Sb —−0.510—	SbH_3
		—0.699—			
Alkaline solution	$Sb(OH)_6^-$	—−0.465—	$Sb(OH)_4^-$ —−0.639—	Sb —−1.338—	SbH_3

Covalent bonds r/pm E/kJ mol^{-1}

	r/pm	E/kJ mol^{-1}
Sb–H	170.7	257
Sb–C	220	215
Sb–O	200	314
Sb–F	203	389
Sb–Cl	233	313
Sb–Sb	290	299

Oxidation states

Sb^{-III}	SbH_3
Sb^{III}	Sb_4O_6, SbO_3^{3-} (aq)
	SbF_3, $SbCl_3$, etc.
	$[SbF_5]^{2-}$, Sb_2S_3
Sb^V	Sb_4O_{10}, $[Sb(OH)_6]^-$ (aq)
	SbF_5, $SbCl_5$, $[SbCl_6]^-$
	$[SbBr_6]^-$

Physical properties

Melting point/K: 903.89
Boiling point/K: 1908
ΔH_{fusion}/kJ mol^{-1}: 20.9   **ΔH_{vap}/kJ mol^{-1}:** 67.91

Thermodynamic properties (298.15 K, 0.1 MPa)

State	$\Delta_f H^{\ominus}$/kJ mol^{-1}	$\Delta_f G^{\ominus}$/kJ mol^{-1}	$S^{\ominus}$/J K^{-1} mol^{-1}	C_p/J K^{-1} mol^{-1}
Solid	0	0	45.69	25.23
Gas	262.3	222.1	180.27	20.79

Density/kg m^{-3}: 6691 [293 K]; 6483 [liquid at m.p.]
Thermal conductivity/W m^{-1} K^{-1}: 24.3 [300 K]
Electrical resistivity/Ω m: 39.0×10^{-8} [273 K]
Mass magnetic susceptibility/kg^{-1} m^3: -1.0×10^{-8} (s)
Molar volume/cm^3: 18.20
Coefficient of linear thermal expansion/K^{-1}: 8.5×10^{-6}

Crystal structure (cell dimensions/pm), space group

Grey rhombohedral ($a = 430.84$; $c = 1124.7$), R3m
(Grey) cubic ($a = 298.6$), Pm3m
Metal h.c.p. ($a = 336.9$, $c = 533$), P6$_3$/mmc

X-ray diffraction: mass absorption coefficients (μ/ρ)/cm^2 g^{-1}:
CuK$_\alpha$ 270   MoK$_\alpha$ 33.1

Antimony

Thermal neutron capture cross-section/barns: 5.4
Number of isotopes (including nuclear isomers): 40
Isotope mass range: $109 \rightarrow 134$

Nuclear properties

Key isotopes

Nuclide	Atomic mass	Natural abundance (%)	Half-life $T_{1/2}$	Decay mode and energy (MeV)	Nuclear spin I	Nuclear magnetic moment μ	Uses
^{121}Sb	120.903 821	57.3	stable		$5/2+$	$+3.3592$	NMR
^{122}Sb	121.905 179	0	2.71d	β^- (1.982); β^+; EC; γ	$2-$	-1.90	tracer
^{123}Sb	122.904 216	42.7	stable		$7/2+$	$+2.5466$	NMR
^{124}Sb	123.905 038	0	60.4d	β^- (2.905); γ	3	± 1.3	tracer
^{125}Sb	124.905 252	0	2.76y	β^- (0.767); γ	$1/2+$	± 2.61	tracer

NMR

	^{121}Sb	$[^{123}$Sb$]$
Relative sensitivity (^{1}H = 1.00)	0.16	4.57×10^{-2}
Receptivity (^{13}C = 1.00)	520	111
Magnetogyric ratio/rad T^{-1} s^{-1}	6.4016×10^7	3.4668×10^7
Quadrupole moment/m^2	-0.53×10^{-28}	-0.68×10^{-28}
Frequency (^{1}H = 100 MHz; 2.3488 T)/MHz	23.930	12.959

Reference: $Et_4N^+SbCl_6^-$

Ground state electron configuration: $[Kr] 4d^{10}5s^25p^3$
Term symbol: $^4S_{3/2}$
Electron affinity $(M \rightarrow M^-)$/kJ mol^{-1}: 101

Electron shell properties

Main lines in atomic spectrum

Wavelength/nm	Species
206.833 (AA)	I
217.581	I
231.147	I
252.852	I
259.805	I

Ionization energies/kJ mol^{-1}

1. $M \rightarrow M^+$	833.7	6. $M^{5+} \rightarrow M^{6+}$	10 400
2. $M^+ \rightarrow M^{2+}$	1794	7. $M^{6+} \rightarrow M^{7+}$	(12 700)
3. $M^{2+} \rightarrow M^{3+}$	2443	8. $M^{7+} \rightarrow M^{8+}$	(15 200)
4. $M^{3+} \rightarrow M^{4+}$	4260	9. $M^{8+} \rightarrow M^{9+}$	(17 800)
5. $M^{4+} \rightarrow M^{5+}$	5400	10. $M^{9+} \rightarrow M^{10+}$	(20 400)

Environmental properties

Biological role

None; toxic; stimulatory

Levels in humans:
Muscle/p.p.m.: 0.042–0.191
Bone/p.p.m.: 0.01–0.6
Blood/mg dm^{-3}: 0.0033
Daily dietary intake:
  0.002–1.3 mg
Toxic intake: 100 mg
Lethal intake: n.a.
Total mass of element in
  average (70 kg) person: n.a.
  but low

Abundances

Sun (relative to H = 1×10^{12}):
  10
Earth's crust/p.p.m.: 0.2
Seawater/p.p.m.: c. 0.3×10^{-3}
Residence time/years:
  c.3.5×10^5
Classification: accumulating
Oxidation state: III

Geological data

Chief deposits and sources:
  stibnite $[Sb_2S_3]$, ullmanite
  [NiSbS]
World production/tonnes y^{-1}:
  53 000
Reserves/tonnes: 2.5×10^6

Ar

Chemical properties

Colourless, odourless gas comprising 1 per cent of the atmosphere. Used as inert atmosphere in lamps and high temperature metallurgy.

Radii/pm: atomic 174; van der Waals 191

Electronegativity: n.a. (Pauling); n.a. (Allred); [7.70 eV (absolute)]

Effective nuclear charge: 6.75 (Slater); 6.76 (Clementi); 7.52 (Froese-Fischer)

Oxidation states

Ar^0	$Ar_8(H_2O)_{46}$ and $Ar(quinol)_3$. These are not true compounds but clathrates in which argon atoms are trapped inside a lattice of other molecules

Physical properties

Melting point/K: 83.78
Boiling point/K: 87.29
ΔH_{fusion}/kJ mol^{-1}: 1.21
ΔH_{vap}/kJ mol^{-1}: 6.53

Critical temperature/K: 150.8
Critical pressure/kPa: 4870
Critical volume/cm^3 mol^{-1}: 74.9

Thermodynamic properties (298.15 K, 0.1 MPa)

State	$\Delta_f H^\circ$/kJ mol^{-1}	$\Delta_f G^\circ$/kJ mol^{-1}	S°/J K^{-1} mol^{-1}	C_p/J K^{-1} mol^{-1}
Gas	0	0	154.843	20.786

Density/kg m^{-3}: 1656 [40 K]; 1380 [liquid b.p.], 1.784 [273 K]
Thermal conductivity/W m^{-1} K^{-1}: 0.0177 [300 K]$_g$
Mass magnetic susceptibility/kg^{-1} m^3: -6.16×10^{-9} (g)
Molar volume/cm^3: 24.12 [40 K]

Crystal structure (cell dimensions/pm), space group

f.c.c. (40 K) ($a = 531.088$), Fm3m

X-ray diffraction: mass absorption coefficients (μ/ρ)/cm^2 g^{-1}: CuK$_\alpha$ 123 MoK$_\alpha$ 13.5

Argon

Thermal neutron capture cross-section/barns: 0.650–0.030
Number of isotopes (including nuclear isomers): 15
Isotope mass range: $32 \rightarrow 46$

**Nuclear
properties**

Key isotopes

Nuclide	Atomic mass	Natural abundance (%)	Half-life $T_{1/2}$	Decay mode and energy (MeV)	Nuclear spin I	Nuclear magnetic moment μ	Uses
^{36}Ar	35.967 545	0.337	stable		0+		
^{37}Ar	36.966 776	0	34.8d	EC (0.814); no γ	3/2+	+0.95	
^{38}Ar	37.962 732	0.063	stable		0+		
^{39}Ar	38.962 314	0	269y	β^- (3.44); no γ	7/2−	−1.3	
^{40}Ar	39.962 384	99.600	stable		0+		

Ground state electron configuration: [Ne] $3s^2 3p^6$
Term symbol: $^1S_0$
Electron affinity $(M \rightarrow M^-)$/kJ mol^{-1}: -35 (calc.)

**Electron
shell
properties**

Main lines in atomic spectrum

Wavelength/nm	Species
696.5431	I
706.7218	I
750.3869	I
801.4786	I
811.5311	I
912.2967	I
965.7786	I

Ionization energies/kJ mol^{-1}

1.	$M \rightarrow M^+$	1520.4	6.	$M^{5+} \rightarrow M^{6+}$	8811
2.	$M^+ \rightarrow M^{2+}$	2665.2	7.	$M^{6+} \rightarrow M^{7+}$	12021
3.	$M^{2+} \rightarrow M^{3+}$	3928	8.	$M^{7+} \rightarrow M^{8+}$	13844
4.	$M^{3+} \rightarrow M^{4+}$	5770	9.	$M^{8+} \rightarrow M^{9+}$	40759
5.	$M^{4+} \rightarrow M^{5+}$	7238	10.	$M^{9+} \rightarrow M^{10+}$	46186

Environmental properties

Biological role	Abundances	Geological data
None; non-toxic but could asphyxiate **Levels in humans:** very low	**Sun** (relative to $H = 1 \times 10^{12}$): 1×10^6 **Earth's crust**/p.p.m.: 1.2 **Seawater**/p.p.m.: Concentration/p.p.m.: 0.45 Residence time/years: 28000 Oxidation state: 0 **Atmosphere**/p.p.m. (by volume): 9300	**Chief resource**: Liquid air **World production**/tonnes y^{-1}: 700000 **Reserves**/tonnes: 6.6×10^{13} (atmosphere)

As

Atomic number: 33

Relative atomic mass ($^{12}C = 12.0000$): **74.9216**

Chemical properties

Metalloid with several allotropes. Grey α-arsenic is metallic—brittle, tarnishes, burns in O_2, resists attack by water, acids, and alkalis. Attacked by hot acids and molten NaOH. Uses: alloys; semiconductors; pesticides; wood preservatives; glass.

Radii/pm: As^{5+} 46; As^{3+} 69; covalent 121; atomic 125; van der Waals 200

Electronegativity: 2.18 (Pauling); 2.20 (Allred); 5.3 eV (absolute)

Effective nuclear charge: 6.30 (Slater); 7.45 (Clementi); 8.98 (Froese-Fischer)

Standard reduction potentials $E^{\ominus}/V$

	V		III		0		−III
Acid solution	H_3AsO_4	$\xrightarrow{0.560}$	$HAsO_2$	$\xrightarrow{0.240}$	As	$\xrightarrow{-0.225}$	AsH_3
Alkaline solution	AsO_4^{3-}	$\xrightarrow{-0.67}$	AsO_2^-	$\xrightarrow{-0.68}$	As	$\xrightarrow{1.37}$	AsH_3

Covalent bonds

	r/pm	E/kJ mol^{-1}
As–H	151.9	$c.$ 245
As–C	198	200
As–O	178	477
As–F	171	464
As–Cl	216	293
As–As	244	348

Oxidation states

As^{-III}	AsH_3
As^{III}	As_4O_6, H_3AsO_3, $H_2AsO_3^-$ (aq), AsF_3, $AsCl_3$, etc.
As^{V}	As_4O_{10}, H_3AsO_4, $H_2AsO_4^-$, etc. (aq), $NaAsO_3$, AsF_5

Physical properties

Melting point/K: 1090 (α) under pressure
Boiling point/K: 889 (sublimes)
ΔH_{fusion}/kJ mol^{-1}: 27.7
ΔH_{vap}/kJ mol^{-1}: 31.9

Thermodynamic properties (298.15 K, 0.1 MPa)

State	$\Delta_f H^{\ominus}$/kJ mol^{-1}	$\Delta_f G^{\ominus}$/kJ mol^{-1}	$S^{\ominus}$/J K^{-1} mol^{-1}	C_p/J K^{-1} mol^{-1}
Solid (α)	0	0	35.1	24.64
Gas	302.5	261.0	174.21	20.786

Density/kg m^{-3}: 5780 (α); 4700 (β) [293 K]
Thermal conductivity/W m^{-1} K^{-1}: 50.0 (α) [300 K]
Electrical resistivity/Ω m: 26×10^{-8} [273 K]
Mass magnetic susceptibility/kg^{-1} m^3: -9.17×10^{-10} (α); -3.97×10^{-9} (β)

Molar volume/cm^3: 12.95 (α); 15.9 (β)
Coefficient of linear thermal expansion/K^{-1}: 4.7×10^{-6}

Crystal structure (cell dimensions/pm), space group

α-As rhombohedral ($a = 413.18$; $\alpha = 54°10'$), $R\bar{3}m$, metallic form
β-As hexagonal ($a = 376.0$, $c = 10.548$), yellow
grey amorphous

$T(\alpha \rightarrow \beta) = 501$ K
$T(\beta \rightarrow \text{grey}) = \text{room temperature}$

X-ray diffraction: mass absorption coefficients (μ/ρ)/cm^2 g^{-1}:
CuK$_\alpha$ 83.4 MoK$_\alpha$ 69.7

Arsenic

Thermal neutron capture cross-section/barns: 4.30
Number of isotopes (including nuclear isomers): 21
Isotope mass range: $67 \rightarrow 86$

Key isotopes

Nuclide	Atomic mass	Natural abundance (%)	Half-life $T_{1/2}$	Decay mode and energy (MeV)	Nuclear spin I	Nuclear magnetic moment μ	Uses
^{73}As	72.923 827	0	80.3d	EC(0.35); γ	$3/2-$		tracer
^{74}As	73.923 827	0	17.78d	β^-(1.36); β^+; EC; γ	$2-$	-1.597	tracer
^{75}As	74.921 594	100	stable		$3/2-$	$+1.439\,47$	NMR
^{76}As	75.922 393	0	26.3h	β^-(2.97); γ	$2-$	-0.906	tracer

NMR

^{75}As

Relative sensitivity (^{1}H = 1.00) 2.51×10^{-2}
Receptivity (^{13}C = 1.00)   143
Magnetogyric ratio/rad T^{-1} s^{-1} 4.5804×10^7
Quadrupole moment/m^2 0.3×10^{-28}
Frequency (^{1}H = 100 MHz; 2.3488 T)/MHz 17.126
Reference: KAsF$_6$

Ground state electron configuration: [Ar] $3d^{10}4s^24p^3$
Term symbol: $^4S_{3/2}$
Electron affinity (M $\rightarrow$ M$^-$)/kJ mol^{-1}: 78

Main lines in atomic spectrum

Wavelength/nm	Species
193.759 (AA)	I
419.008	II
445.847	II
446.635	II
449.423	II
450.766	II
454.348	II

Ionization energies/kJ mol^{-1}

1. M $\rightarrow$ M$^+$	947.0	6. M$^{5+}\rightarrow$M^{6+} 12 305
2. M$^+\rightarrow$M^{2+}	1798	7. M$^{6+}\rightarrow$M^{7+} (15 400)
3. M$^{2+}\rightarrow$M^{3+}	2735	8. M$^{7+}\rightarrow$M^{8+} (18 900)
4. M$^{3+}\rightarrow$M^{4+}	4837	9. M$^{8+}\rightarrow$M^{9+} (22 600)
5. M$^{4+}\rightarrow$M^{5+}	6042	10. M$^{9+}\rightarrow$M^{10+} (26 400)

Environmental properties

Biological role

Essential to some species
  including humans; toxic;
  stimulatory; carcinogenic

Levels in humans:
Muscle/p.p.m.: 0.009–0.65
Bone/p.p.m.: 0.08–1.6
Blood/mg dm^{-3}: 0.0017–0.09
Daily dietary intake:
  0.04–1.4 mg
Toxic intake: 5–50 mg
Lethal intake: 50–340 mg
Total mass of element in
  average (70 kg) person:
  18 mg.

Abundances

Sun (relative to H = 1×10^{12}):
  n.a.
Earth's crust/p.p.m.: 1.5
Seawater/p.p.m.:
Atlantic surface: 1.45×10^{-3}
Atlantic deep: 1.53×10^{-3}
Pacific surface: 1.45×10^{-3}
Pacific deep: 1.75×10^{-3}
Residence time/years: 90 000
Classification: (As)III
  scavenged, As(V) recycled
Oxidation state: some III but
  mainly V
Atmosphere/p.p.m. (volume):
  trace

Geological data

Chief deposits and sources:
  realgar [As$_4$S$_4$], orpiment
  [As$_2$S$_3$], loellingite [FeAs$_2$]
World production of
  As$_2$O$_3$/tonnes y^{-1}: 47 000
Reserves/tonnes: n.a.

At

Atomic number: 85

Relative atomic mass ($^{12}C = 12.0000$): (210)

Radioactive non-metal element. Relatively unknown because of short half-life.

Radii/pm: At^{I} 57; At$^-$ 227

Electronegativity: 2.2 (Pauling); 1.96 (Allred); 6.2 eV (absolute)

Effective nuclear charge: 7.60 (Slater); 15.16 (Clementi); 19.61 (Froese-Fischer)

Standard reduction potentials $E^{\ominus}/V$

	V		I		0		−I
Acid solution	$HAtO_3$	—1.4—	$HAtO$	—0.7—	At_2	—0.2—	At^-
Alkaline solution	AtO_3^-	—0.5—	AtO^-	—0.0—	At_2	—0.2—	At^-

Covalent bonds

	r/pm	E/kJ mol^{-1}
At–At	c. 290 (estimated)	110

Oxidation states

At^{-1}	([Rn])	At$^-$ (aq)
At^{I}	(s^{2}p^4)	AtBr$_2^-$
At^{V}	(s^2)	AtO$_3^-$ (aq)

Melting point/K: 575 (est.)

Boiling point/K: 610 (est.)

ΔH_{fusion}/kJ mol^{-1}: 23.8

ΔH_{vap}/kJ mol^{-1}: n.a.

Thermodynamic properties (298.15 K, 0.1 MPa)

State	$\Delta_f H^{\ominus}$/kJ mol^{-1}	$\Delta_f G^{\ominus}$/kJ mol^{-1}	$S^{\ominus}$/J K^{-1} mol^{-1}	C_p/J K^{-1} mol^{-1}
Solid (α)	0	0	n.a.	n.a.
Gas	n.a.	n.a.	n.a.	n.a.

Density/kg m^{-3}: n.a.

Thermal conductivity/W m^{-1} K^{-1}: 1.7·[300 K]

Mass magnetic susceptibility/kg^{-1} m^3: n.a.

Molar volume/cm^3: n.a.

Crystal structure (cell dimensions/pm), space group

n.a.

X-ray diffraction: mass absorption coefficients (μ/ρ)/cm^2 g^{-1}:
n.a.

Produced by D. R. Corson, K. R. Mackenzie, and E. Segré in
1940 at the University of California, USA

[Greek, *astatos* = unstable]

Astatine

Thermal neutron capture cross-section/barns: n.a.

Number of isotopes (including nuclear isomers): 29

Isotope mass range: $196 \rightarrow 219$

**Nuclear
properties**

Key isotopes

Nuclide	Atomic mass	Natural abund. (%)	Half-life $T_{1/2}$	Decay mode and energy (MeV)	Nuclear spin I	Nuclear magnetic moment μ
^{210}At	209.987 126	0	8.1h	EC(3.98); α(5.63)<1%	5+	
^{211}At	210.987 469	0	7.2h	EC(0.784) 59%; α(5.981) 41%	9/2−	

Ground state electron configuration: [Xe] $4f^{14}5d^{10}6s^26p^5$

Term symbol: $^3P_{3/2}$

Electron affinity $(M \rightarrow M^-)$/kJ mol^{-1}: 270

**Electron
shell
properties**

Main lines in atomic spectrum

Wavelength/nm	Species
216.225	I
224.401	I

Ionization energies/kJ mol^{-1}

1. $M \rightarrow M^+$	930	6. $M^{5+} \rightarrow M^{6+}$ (7 500)
2. $M^+ \rightarrow M^{2+}$	1600	7. $M^{6+} \rightarrow M^{7+}$ (8 800)
3. $M^{2+} \rightarrow M^{3+}$	(2900)	8. $M^{7+} \rightarrow M^{8+}$ (13 300)
4. $M^{3+} \rightarrow M^{4+}$	(4000)	9. $M^{8+} \rightarrow M^{9+}$ (15 400)
5. $M^{4+} \rightarrow M^{5+}$	(4900)	10. $M^{9+} \rightarrow M^{10+}$ (17 700)

Environmental properties

Biological role	Abundances	Geological data
None; toxic due to radioactivity	**Sun** (relative to H $= 1 \times 10^{12}$): n.a.	**Chief sources:** obtainable in various ways, e.g. neutron bombardment of ^{209}Bi produces ^{211}At but not in weighable amounts
Levels in humans: nil	**Earth's crust**/p.p.m.: trace amount in some minerals	
	Seawater/p.p.m.: n.a.	

Ba

Atomic number: 56
Relative atomic mass (^{12}C = 12.0000): 137.327

Chemical properties

Relatively soft, silvery-white metal. Obtained from BaO on heating with aluminium. Attacked by air and water. Used mainly as Ba SO$_4$ in drilling fluids for oil and gas exploration; small amounts used in paints, glass, etc.

Radii/pm: Ba^{2+} 143; atomic 217.3; covalent 198
Electronegativity: 0.89 (Pauling); 0.97 (Allred); 2.4 eV (absolute)
Effective nuclear charge: 2.85 (Slater); 7.58 (Clementi); 10.27 (Froese-Fischer)

Standard reduction potentials $E^{\ominus}$/V

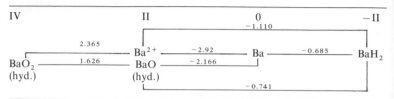

Oxidation states

Ba ^{II} ([Xe])   BaH$_2$, BaO, Ba(OH)$_2$ basic,
BaO$_2$ (peroxide), Ba^{2+}(aq),
BaF$_2$, BaCl$_2$, etc., BaCO$_3$,
BaSO$_4$ insoluble, many other salts

Physical properties

Melting point/K: 1002
Boiling point/K: 1910
ΔH_{fusion}/kJ mol^{-1}: 7.66
ΔH_{vap}/kJ mol^{-1}: 150.9

Thermodynamic properties (298.15 K, 0.1 MPa)

State	$\Delta_f H^{\ominus}$/kJ mol^{-1}	$\Delta_f G^{\ominus}$/kJ mol^{-1}	$S^{\ominus}$/J K^{-1} mol^{-1}	C_p/J K^{-1} mol^{-1}
Solid	0	0	62.8	28.07
Gas	180	146	170.243	20.786

Density/kg m^{-3}: 3594 [293 K]; 3325 [liquid at m.p.]
Thermal conductivity/W m^{-1} K^{-1}: 18.4 [300 K]
Electrical resistivity/Ω m: 50 × 10^{-8} [273 K]
Mass magnetic susceptibility/kg^{-1} m^3: +1.9 × 10^{-9} (s)
Molar volume/cm^3: 38.21
Coefficient of linear thermal expansion/K^{-1}: 18.1–21.0 × 10^{-6}

Crystal structure (cell dimensions/pm), space group

b.c.c. (a = 502.5), Im3m

High pressure form: (a = 390.1, c = 615.5), P6$_3$mmc

X-ray diffraction: mass absorption coefficients (μ/ρ)/cm^2 g^{-1}:
CuK$_\alpha$ 330 MoK$_\alpha$ 43.5

Barium

Thermal neutron capture cross-section/barns: 1.3
Number of isotopes (including nuclear isomers):   35
Isotope mass range: 120→148

Key isotopes

Nuclide	Atomic mass	Natural abundance (%)	Half-life $T_{1/2}$	Decay mode and energy (MeV)	Nuclear spin I	Nuclear magnetic moment μ	Uses
^{130}Ba	129.906 282	0.106	stable		0+		
^{132}Ba	131.905 042	0.101	stable		0+		
^{133}Ba	132.905 988	0	10.53y	EC(0.52); γ	1/2+		tracer
^{134}Ba	133.904 486	2.417	stable		0+		
^{135}Ba	134.905 665	6.592	stable		3/2+	+0.8365	NMR
^{135m}Ba		0	28.7h	IT(0.268); γ	11/2−		tracer
^{136}Ba	135.904 553	7.854	stable		0+		
^{137}Ba	136.905 812	11.23	stable		3/2+	+0.9357	NMR
^{138}Ba	137.905 232	71.70	stable		0+		
^{140}Ba	139.910 581	0	12.76d	β^-(1.03); γ	0+		tracer

NMR

	$[^{135}$Ba$]$	^{137}Ba
Relative sensitivity (^{1}H = 1.00)	4.90×10^{-4}	7.76×10^{-4}
Receptivity (^{13}C = 1.00)	1.83	4.41
Magnetogyric ratio/rad T^{-1} s^{-1}	2.6575×10^7	2.9728×10^7
Quadrupole moment/m^2	0.18×10^{-28}	0.28×10^{-28}
Frequency (^{1}H = 100 MHz; 2.3488 T)/MHz	9.934	11.113

Reference: $BaCl_2$ (aq)

Ground state electron configuration: $[Xe]6s^2$
Term symbol: $^1S_0$
Electron affinity (M→M$^-$)/kJ mol^{-1}: -46

Main lines in atomic spectrum

Wavelength/nm	Species
350.111	I
455.403	II
493.409	II
553.548 (AA)	II
614.172	II
649.690	II
705.994	I

Ionization energies/kJ mol^{-1}

1. M →M$^+$	502.8	6. M^{5+}→M^{6+} (7 700)
2. M$^+$→M^{2+}	965.1	7. M^{6+}→M^{7+} (9 000)
3. M^{2+}→M^{3+}	(3600)	8. M^{7+}→M^{8+} (10 200)
4. M^{3+}→M^{4+}	(4700)	9. M^{8+}→M^{9+} (13 500)
5. M^{4+}→M^{5+}	(6000)	10. M^{9+}→M^{10+} (15 100)

Environmental properties

Biological role	Abundances	Geological data
None; toxic; stimulatory	**Sun** (relative to H = 1×10^{12}): 123	**Chief ore:** baryte [$BaSO_4$]
Levels in humans:	**Earth's crust**/p.p.m.: 500	**World production of** $BaSO_4$/tonnes y^{-1}: 6×10^6
Muscle/p.p.m.: 0.09	**Seawater**/p.p.m.:	**Reserves**/tonnes: 450×10^6
Bone/p.p.m.: 3–70	Atlantic surface: 4.7×10^{-3}	
Blood/mg dm^{-3}: 0.068	Atlantic deep: 9.3×10^{-3}	
Daily dietary intake: 0.60–1.7 mg	Pacific surface: 4.7×10^{-3}	
Toxic intake: 200 mg	Pacific deep: 20.0×10^{-3}	
Lethal intake: 3.7 g	Residence time/years: 10 000	
Total mass of element in average (70 kg) person: 22 mg.	Classification: recycled	
	Oxidation state: II	

Bk

Atomic number: 97

Relative atomic mass ($^{12}C = 12.0000$): **(247)**

Radioactive silvery metal. Attacked by oxygen, steam, and acids, but not by alkalis.

Radii/pm: Bk^{2+} 118; Bk^{3+} 98; Bk^{4+} 87

Electronegativity: 1.3 (Pauling); n.a. (Allred)

Effective nuclear charge: 1.65 (Slater)

Standard reduction potentials $E^{\ominus}/V$

	III		IV		0
			-1.05		
Acid solution	Bk^{4+}	1.67	Bk^{3+}	-2.01	Bk

Oxidation states

Bk^{II}	(f^9)	BkO
Bk^{III}	(f^8)	Bk_2O_3, BkF_3, $BkCl_3$ etc.,
		$[BkCl_6]^{3-}$, Bk^{3+} (aq)
Bk^{IV}	(f^7)	BkO_2, BkF_4

Physical properties

Melting point/K: n.a.

Boiling point/K: n.a.

ΔH_{fusion}/kJ mol^{-1}: n.a.

ΔH_{vap}/kJ mol^{-1}: n.a.

Thermodynamic properties (298.15 K, 0.1 MPa)

State	$\Delta_f H^{\ominus}$/kJ mol^{-1}	$\Delta_f G^{\ominus}$/kJ mol^{-1}	$S^{\ominus}$/J K^{-1} mol^{-1}	C_p/J K^{-1} mol^{-1}
Solid	0	0	n.a.	n.a.
Gas	n.a.	n.a.	n.a.	n.a.

Density/kg m^{-3}: 14 790 [293 K]

Thermal conductivity/W m^{-1} K^{-1}: 10 (est.) [300 K]

Electrical resistivity/Ω m: n.a.

Mass magnetic susceptibility/kg^{-1} m^3: n.a.

Molar volume/cm^3: 16.70

Coefficient of linear thermal expansion/K^{-1}: n.a.

Crystal structure (cell dimensions/pm), space group

n.a.

X-ray diffraction: mass absorption coefficients (μ/ρ)/cm^2 g^{-1}: n.a.

Produced in December 1949 by S. G. Thompson, A. Ghiorso, and
G. T. Seaborg at Berkeley, California, USA
[English, *Berkeley*]

Berkelium

Thermal neutron capture cross-section/barns: 710 (^{249}Bk)
Number of isotopes (including nuclear isomers): 10
Isotope mass range: 243→250

Key isotopes

Nuclide	Atomic mass	Natural abundance (%)	Half-life $T_{1/2}$	Decay mode and energy (MeV)	Nuclear spin I	Nuclear magnetic moment μ	Uses
^{247}Bk	247.070 300	0	1.4×10^3y	α(5.889); γ	3/2−		
^{249}Bk	249.074 980	0	320d	β^-	7/2+	2.0	

Ground state electron configuration: [Rn]$5f^97s^2$
Term symbol: $^6H_{15/2}$
Electron affinity (M→M$^-$)/kJ mol^{-1}: n.a.

Main lines in atomic spectrum

Wavelength/nm	Species
329.972	I
325.219	I
328.875	I
329.935	I
333.526	I
340.828	I
342.093	I

Ionization energies/kJ mol^{-1}

1. M → M$^+$ 601
2. M$^+$ → M^{2+}
3. M^{2+} → M^{3+}
4. M^{3+} → M^{4+}
5. M^{4+} → M^{5+}

Environmental properties

Biological role	Abundances	Geological data
None; toxic due to radioactivity **Levels in humans:** nil	**Sun** (relative to H $= 1 \times 10^{12}$): n.a. **Earth's crust**/p.p.m.: nil **Seawater**/p.p.m.: nil	**Chief sources:** made in mg quantities as ^{249}Bk by neutron bombardment of ^{239}Pu

Be

Atomic number: 4
Relative atomic mass ($^{12}C = 12.0000$): 9.012 18

<table>
<tr><td>**Chemical properties**</td><td>Silvery-white, lustrous, relatively soft metal, obtained e.g. by the electrolysis of fused $BeCl_2$. Unaffected by air or water even at red heat. Used in alloys with copper and nickel, and imparts excellent electrical and thermal conductivities. Copper alloy used to make spark-proof tools.</td></tr>
</table>

Radii/pm: Be^{2+} 34; atomic 113.3; covalent 89
Electronegativity: 1.57 (Pauling); 1.47 (Allred); 4.9 eV (absolute)
Effective nuclear charge: 1.95 (Slater); 1.91 (Clementi); 2.27 (Froese-Fischer)

Standard reduction potentials $E^{\ominus}/V$

II		0
Be^{2+}	$\underline{\quad -1.97 \quad}$	Be

Covalent bonds r/pm E/kJ mol^{-1} **Oxidation states**

	r/pm	E/kJ mol^{-1}		
Be–H	163	226	Be^{II}	BeO, $Be(OH)_2$,
Be–O	133	523		BeH_2, $[Be(H_2O)_4]^{2+}$aq
Be–F	143	615		BeF_2, $BeCl_2$ etc.,
Be–Cl	177	293		$BeCO_3$, salts
Be–C	193			
Be–Be	222.6			

Physical properties

Melting point/K: 1551 ± 5
Boiling point/K: 3243 (under pressure)
ΔH_{fusion}/kJ mol^{-1}: 9.80
ΔH_{vap}/kJ mol^{-1}: 308.8

Thermodynamic properties (298.15 K, 0.1 MPa)

State	$\Delta_f H^{\ominus}$/kJ mol^{-1}	$\Delta_f G^{\ominus}$/kJ mol^{-1}	$S^{\ominus}$/J K^{-1} mol^{-1}	C_p/J K^{-1} mol^{-1}
Solid	0	0	9.50	16.44
Gas	324.6	286.6	136.269	20.786

Density/kg m^{-3}: 1847.7 [293 K]
Thermal conductivity/W m^{-1} K^{-1}: 200 [300 K]
Electrical resistivity/Ω m: 4.0×10^{-8} [293 K]
Mass magnetic susceptibility/kg^{-1} m^3: -1.3×10^{-8} (s)
Molar volume/cm^3: 4.88
Coefficient of linear thermal expansion/K^{-1}: 11.5×10^{-6}

Crystal structure (cell dimensions/pm), space group

α-Be   h.c.p. ($a = 228.55$, $c = 358.32$), P6$_3$/mmc
β-Be   b.c.c. ($a = 255.15$), Im3m

$T(\alpha \rightarrow \beta) = 1523$ K

X-ray diffraction: mass absorption coefficients (μ/ρ)/cm^2 g^{-1}:
CuK$_\alpha$ 1.50   MoK$_\alpha$ 0.298

Discovered in 1797 by N.-L. Vauquelin at Paris, France. Isolated in 1828 by F. Wöhler at Berlin, Germany, and independently by A. A. B. Bussy at Paris, France
[Greek, *beryllos* = beryl]

Beryllium

Thermal neutron capture cross-section/barns: 0.0092

Number of isotopes (including nuclear isomers): 6

Isotope mass range: $6 \rightarrow 11$

Nuclear properties

Key isotopes

Nuclide	Atomic mass	Natural abundance (%)	Half-life $T_{1/2}$	Decay mode and energy (MeV)	Nuclear spin I	Nuclear magnetic moment μ	Uses
^{7}Be	7.016 928	0	53.29d	EC(0.862); γ	3/2−		tracer
^{9}Be	9.012 182	100	stable		3/2−	−1.1776	NMR
^{10}Be	10.013 534	trace	1.6×10^6y	β^- (0.555); no γ	0+		

NMR

	^{9}Be
Relative sensitivity (^{1}H = 1.00)	1.39×10^{-2}
Receptivity (^{13}C = 1.00)	78.8
Magnetogyric ratio/rad T^{-1} s^{-1}	3.7589×10^7
Quadrupole moment/m^2	5.2×10^{-30}
Frequency (^{1}H = 100 MHz; 2.3488 T)/MHz	14.053

Reference: Be(NO$_3$)$_2$ (aq)

Ground state electron configuration: [He]2s^2

Term symbol: $^1S_0$

Electron affinity (M→M$^-$)/kJ mol^{-1}: −18

Electron shell properties

Main lines in atomic spectrum

Wavelength/nm	Species
234.861 (AA)	I
381.345	I
436.099	II
467.333	II
467.342	II
527.081	II

Ionization energies/kJ mol^{-1}

1. M → M$^+$	899.4
2. M$^+$ → M^{2+}	1 757.1
3. M^{2+} → M^{3+}	14 848
4. M^{3+} → M^{4+}	21 006

Environmental properties

Biological role	Abundances	Geological data
None; toxic (replaces Mg in enzymes), carcinogenic; fumes and dust cause berylliosis of the lungs	**Sun** (relative to H = 1×10^{12}): 14	**Chief ores**: beryl [Be$_3$Al$_2$Si$_6$O$_{18}$]; bertrandite [Be$_4$Si$_2$O$_7$(OH)$_2$]
Levels in humans:	**Earth's crust**/p.p.m.: 2.6	**World production**/tonnes y^{-1}: 364
Muscle/p.p.m.: 0.00075	**Seawater**/p.p.m.:	**Reserves**/tonnes: 400 000
Bone/p.p.m.: 0.003	Atlantic surface: 8.8×10^{-8}	
Blood/mg dm^{-3}: $<1 \times 10^{-5}$	Atlantic deep: 17.5×10^{-8}	
Daily dietary intake: 0.01 mg	Pacific surface: 3.5×10^{-8}	
Toxic intake: n.a.	Pacific deep: 22×10^{-8}	
Lethal intake: n.a.	Residence time/years: 4000	
Total mass of element in average (70 kg) person: 0.036 mg	Classification: recycled	
	Oxidation state: II	

Chemical properties

Brittle metal, silvery lustre with pink tinge. Stable to oxygen and water. Dissolves in concentrated nitric acid. Basic oxide. Used in alloys, pharmaceuticals, electronics, catalysts, cosmetics, and pigments.

Radii/pm: Bi^{5+} 74; Bi^{3+} 96; covalent 152; atomic 155; van der Waals 240

Electronegativity: 2.02 (Pauling); 1.67 (Allred); 4.69 eV (absolute)

Effective nuclear charge: 6.30 (Slater); 13.34 (Clementi); 16.90 (Froese-Fischer)

Standard reduction potentials $E^{\ominus}$/V

V		III		0		−III
Bi^{5+}	ca. 2	Bi^{3+}	0.317	Bi	−0.97	BiH_3

Covalent bonds

	r/pm	E/kJ mol^{-1}
Bi–H	n.a.	194
Bi–C	230	143
Bi–O	232	339
Bi–F	235	314
Bi–Cl	248	285
Bi–Bi	309	200

Oxidation states

Bi^{-III}	BiH_3
Bi^{I}	Bi^+
Bi^{III}	Bi_2O_3, $Bi(OH)_3$, Bi^{3+}(aq), BiOCl, BiF_3, $BiCl_3$ etc. $[BiBr_6]^{3-}$, salts
Bi^{V}	Bi_2O_5 unstable, $[Bi(OH)_6]^-$(aq), $NaBiO_3$, BiF_5, $KBiF_6$

Physical properties

Melting point/K: 544.5
Boiling point/K: 1833 ± 5
ΔH_{fusion}/kJ mol^{-1}: 10.48
ΔH_{vap}/kJ mol^{-1}: 179.1

Thermodynamic properties (298.15 K, 0.1 MPa)

State	$\Delta_f H^{\ominus}$/kJ mol^{-1}	$\Delta_f G^{\ominus}$/kJ mol^{-1}	$S^{\ominus}$/J K^{-1} mol^{-1}	C_p/J K^{-1} mol^{-1}
Solid	0	0	56.74	25.52
Gas	207.1	168.2	187.005	20.786

Density/kg m^{-3}: 9747 [293 K]; 10 050 [liquid at m.p.]
Thermal conductivity/W m^{-1} K^{-1}: 7.87 [300 K]
Electrical resistivity/Ω m: 106.8 × 10^{-8} [273 K]
Mass magnetic susceptibility/kg^{-1} m^3: −1.684 × 10^{-8} (s)
Molar volume/cm^3: 21.44
Coefficient of linear thermal expansion/K^{-1}: 13.4 × 10^{-6}

Crystal structure (cell dimensions/pm), space group

Rhombohedral (a = 454.950, c = 1186.225), R$\bar{3}$m

X-ray diffraction: mass absorption coefficients (μ/ρ)/cm^2 g^{-1}:
CuK$_\alpha$ 240   MoK$_\alpha$ 120

Bismuth

Thermal neutron capture cross-section/barns: 0.034
Number of isotopes (including nuclear isomers). 35
Isotope mass range: 190→215

Nuclear properties

Key isotopes

Nuclide	Atomic mass	Natural abund. (%)	Half-life $T_{1/2}$	Decay mode and energy (MeV)	Nuclear spin I	Nuclear magnetic moment μ	Uses
^{206}Bi	205.978 478	0	6.243d	EC(3.761); γ	6+	+4.56	tracer
^{207}Bi	206.987 446	0	32.2y	EC(2.40); γ	9/2−	4.10	
^{208}Bi	207.979 717	0	3.68×10^5y	EC(2.878); γ	5+		
^{209}Bi	208.980 347	100	stable		9/2−	+4.110	NMR
^{210m}Bi		0	3×10^6y	α(4.96); β^-; γ	9−		
^{210}Bi	209.984 095	trace	5.01d	β^-(1.16); α; no γ	1−	−0.044	tracer

NMR

^{209}Bi

Relative sensitivity (^{1}H = 1.00)   0.13
Receptivity (^{13}C = 1.00)   777
Magnetogyric ratio/rad T^{-1} s^{-1} 4.2986×10^7
Quadrupole moment/m^2 -0.4×10^{-28}
Frequency (^{1}H = 100 MHz; 2.3488 T)/MHz   16.069
Reference: KBiF$_6$

Ground state electron configuration: [Xc]4f^{14}5d^{10}6s^{2}6p^3
Term symbol: ^{4}S$_{3/2}$
Electron affinity (M→M$^-$)/kJ mol^{-1}: 91.3

Electron shell properties

Main lines in atomic spectrum

Wavelength/nm	Species
202.121	I
206.170	I
211.026	I
223.061 (AA)	I
289.798	I
306.772	I

Ionization energies/kJ mol^{-1}

1. M →M$^+$	703.2	6. M^{5+}→M^{6+} 8 520
2. M$^+$→M^{2+}	1610	7. M^{6+}→M^{7+} (10 300)
3. M^{2+}→M^{3+}	2466	8. M^{7+}→M^{8+} (12 300)
4. M^{3+}→M^{4+}	4372	9. M^{8+}→M^{9+} (14 300)
5. M^{4+}→M^{5+}	5400	10. M^{9+}→M^{10+} (16 300)

Environmental properties

Biological role

None; non-toxic
Levels in humans:
Muscle/p.p.m.: 0.032
Bone/p.p.m.: <0.2
Blood/mg dm^{-3}: c. 0.016
Daily dietary intake:
  0.005–0.02 mg
Toxic intake: n.a.
Lethal intake: n.a.
Total mass of element in
  average (70 kg) person: n.a.
  but low

Abundances

Sun (relative to H = 1×10^{12}):
  <80
Earth's crust/p.p.m.: 0.048
Seawater/p.p.m.:
Atlantic surface: 5.1×10^{-8}
Atlantic deep: n.a.
Pacific surface: 4×10^{-8}
Pacific deep: 0.4×10^{-8}
Residence time/years: n.a.
Classification: scavenged
Oxidation state: III

Geological data

Chief ores and sources:
bismite [α-Bi$_2$O$_3$];
bismuthinite [Ba$_2$S$_3$];
bismutite [(BiO)$_2$CO$_3$];
main source is by-product
from lead and copper
smelters

World production/tonnes y^{-1}:
3000

Reserves/tonnes: n.a.

B

Atomic number: 5

Relative atomic mass ($^{12}C = 12.0000$): **10.81**

Chemical properties

Non-metal with several allotropes. Amorphous boron is dark powder unreactive to oxygen, water, acids, and alkalis. Forms metal borides with most metals. Used in borosilicate glass, detergents, and fire retardants.

Radii/pm: B^{3+} 23; covalent 88; atomic 83; van der Waals 208

Electronegativity: 2.04 (Pauling); 2.01 (Allred); 4.29 eV (absolute)

Effective nuclear charge: 2.60 (Slater); 2.42 (Clementi); 2.27 (Froese-Fischer)

Standard reduction potentials $E^{\ominus}/V$

III		0
$B(OH)_3$	$\xrightarrow{-0.890}$	B
BF_4^-	$\xrightarrow{-1.284}$	B

Covalent bonds r/pm E/kJ mol^{-1} **Oxidation states**

	r/pm	E/kJ mol^{-1}
B–H	119	381
B–H–B	132	439
B–C	156	372
B–O	136	523
B–F	129	644
B–Cl	174	444
B–B	175	335

B^{III} B_2O_3, H_3BO_3 ($= B(OH)_3$), borates e.g. borax $Na_2[B_4O_5(OH)_4] \cdot 8H_2O$, B_2H_6, B_4H_{10} etc., $NaBH_4$, BF_3, BCl_3 etc.

Physical properties

Melting point/K: 2573
Boiling point/K: 3931
ΔH_{fusion}/kJ mol^{-1}: 22.2
ΔH_{vap}/kJ mol^{-1}: 538.9

Thermodynamic properties (298.15 K, 0.1 MPa)

State	$\Delta_f H^{\ominus}$/kJ mol^{-1}	$\Delta_f G^{\ominus}$/kJ mol^{-1}	$S^{\ominus}$/J K^{-1} mol^{-1}	C_p/J K^{-1} mol^{-1}
Solid (α)	0	0	5.86	11.09
Gas	562.7	518.8	153.45	20.799

Density/kg m^{-3}: 2340 (β-rhomb.) [293 K]
Thermal conductivity/W m^{-1} K^{-1}: 27.0 [300 K]
Electrical resistivity/Ω m: 18 000 [273 K]
Mass magnetic susceptibility/kg^{-1} m^3: -7.8×10^{-9} (s)
Molar volume/cm^3: 4.62
Coefficient of linear thermal expansion/K^{-1}: 5×10^{-6}

Crystal structure (cell dimensions/pm), space group

Tetragonal ($a = 874.0$; $c = 506$), P4$_2$/nnm
α-B rhombohedral ($a = 506.7$, $\alpha = 58°4'$), R$\bar{3}$m
β-B rhombohedral ($a = 1014.5$, $\alpha = 65°12'$), R$\bar{3}$m, R32, R3m
Orthorhombic ($a = 1015$, $b = 895$, $c = 1790$)
Monoclinic ($a = 1013$, $b = 893$, $c = 1786$, $\alpha \simeq 90°$, $\beta \simeq 90°$, $\gamma \simeq 90°$) or triclinic
Hexagonal ($a = 1198$, $c = 954$)

X-ray diffraction: mass absorption coefficients (μ/ρ)/cm^2 g^{-1}:
CuK$_\alpha$ 2.39   MoK$_\alpha$ 0.392

Discovered in 1808 by L. J. Lussac and L. J. Thenard in Paris,
France, and Sir Humphry Davy in London, UK

[Arabic, *buraq*]

Boron

Thermal neutron capture
cross-section/barns: 3837 ^{10}B, 0.005 ^{11}B

Number of isotopes (including nuclear isomers): 6

Isotope mass range: 8→13

Nuclear
properties

Key isotopes

Nuclide	Atomic mass	Natural abundance (%)	Half-life $T_{1/2}$	Decay mode and energy (MeV)	Nuclear spin I	Nuclear magnetic moment μ	Uses
^{10}B	10.012 937	19.9	stable		3+	+1.8007	NMR
^{11}B	11.009 305	80.1	stable		3/2−	+2.6886	NMR

NMR

	[^{10}B]	^{11}B
Relative sensitivity (^{1}H = 1.00)	1.99×10^{-2}	0.17
Receptivity (^{13}C = 1.00)	22.1	754
Magnetogyric ratio/rad T^{-1} s^{-1}	2.8740×10^7	8.5794×10^7
Quadrupole moment/m^2	7.4×10^{-30}	3.55×10^{-30}
Frequency (^{1}H = 100 MHz; 2.3488 T)/MHz	10.746	32.084

Reference: Et_2O/BF_3

Ground state electron configuration: [He]$2s^2 2p^1$

Term symbol: $^2P_{1/2}$

Electron affinity (M→M$^-$)/kJ mol^{-1}: 26.7

Electron
shell
properties

Main lines in atomic spectrum

Wavelength/nm	Species
208.891	I
208.957	I
249.667	I
249.773 (AA)	I
345.129	I
1166.004	I
1166.247	I

Ionization energies/kJ mol^{-1}

1. M →M$^+$ 800.6
2. M$^+$ →M^{2+} 2427
3. M^{2+} →M^{3+} 3 660
4. M^{3+} →M^{4+} 25 025
5. M^{4+} →M^{5+} 32 822

Environmental properties

Biological role

Essential to plants, toxic in
  excess

Levels in humans:
Muscle/p.p.m.: 0.33–1
Bone/p.p.m.: 1.1–3.3
Blood/mg dm^{-3}: 0.13
Daily dietary intake: 1–3 mg
Toxic intake: 4 g
Lethal intake: n.a.
Total mass of element in
  average (70 kg) person: n.a.

Abundances

Sun (relative to H = 1×10^{12}):
  <125

Earth's crust/p.p.m.: 10

Seawater/p.p.m.: 4.41
Residence time/years: 1×10^7
Classification: accumulating
Oxidation state: III

Geological data

Chief ores and sources: borax
{$Na_2[B_4O_5(OH)_4] . 8H_2O$};
colemanite
{$Ca_2[B_3O_4(OH)_3]_2 . 2H_2O$};
etc.

World production as
  B_2O_3/tonnes y^{-1}: 1×10^6

Reserves/tonnes: 270×10^6 (as
  B_2O_3)

Br

Atomic number: 35

Relative atomic mass ($^{12}C = 12.0000$): 79.904

Chemical properties

Deep red, dense, sharp smelling liquid, Br_2. Compounds used in fuel additives, pesticides, flame-retardants, and photography.

Radii/pm: covalent 114.2; Br^- 196; van der Waals 195

Electronegativity: 2.96 (Pauling); 2.74 (Allred); 7.59 eV (absolute)

Effective nuclear charge: 7.60 (Slater); 9.03 (Clementi); 10.89 (Froese-Fischer)

Standard reduction potentials $E^{\ominus}/V$

	VII		V		I		0		$-$I

Acid solution

BrO_4^- —1.853— BrO_3^- —1.447— HBrO —1.604— Br_2 —1.0652— Br^-

1.478 (BrO$_3^-$ to HBrO region)

Br_2 (aq) —1.0874—

1.341

Alkaline solution

BrO_4^- —1.025— BrO_3^- —0.492— BrO^- —0.455— Br_2 —1.0652— Br^-

0.766

0.584

Covalent bonds r/pm E/kJ mol^{-1}

Bond	r/pm	E/kJ mol^{-1}
Br–H	140.8	366
Br–C	194	285
Br–O	160	234
Br–F	176	285
Br–Br	229	193
Br–B	187	410
Br–Si	215	310
Br–P	218	264

Oxidation states

Br^{-I}	([Kr])	Br^-(aq), HBr, KBr etc.
Br^{I}	(s^2p^4)	Br_2O, $BrCl_2^-$
Br^{III}	(s^2p^2)	BrF_3, BrF_4^-
Br^{IV}	(s^2p^1)	BrO_2
Br^{V}	(s^2)	BrO_3^-(aq), BrF_5, BrF_6^-
Br^{VII}	(d^{10})	$KBrO_4$, BrF_6^+

Physical properties

Melting point/K: 265.9

Boiling point/K: 331.93

ΔH_{fusion}/kJ mol^{-1}: 10.8

ΔH_{vap}/kJ mol^{-1}: 30.0

Thermodynamic properties (298.15 K, 0.1 MPa)

State	$\Delta_f H^{\ominus}$/kJ mol^{-1}	$\Delta_f G^{\ominus}$/kJ mol^{-1}	$S^{\ominus}$/J K^{-1} mol^{-1}	C_p/J K^{-1} mol^{-1}
Liquid	0	0	152.231	75.689
Gas (atom)	111.884	82.396	175.022	20.786

Density/kg m^{-3}: 4050 [123 K]; 3122.6 [293 K]; 7.59 [gas]

Thermal conductivity/W m^{-1} K^{-1}: 0.122 [300 K]$_l$

Mass magnetic susceptibility/kg^{-1} m^3: -4.44×10^{-9} (l)

Molar volume/cm^3: 19.73 [123 K]

Crystal structure (cell dimensions/pm), space group

Orthorhombic (120 K) ($a = 673.7$; $b = 454.8$; $c = 876.1$), Cmca

X-ray diffraction: mass absorption coefficients (μ/ρ)/cm^2 g^{-1}: CuK_{α} 99.6 MoK_{α} 79.8

Bromine

Thermal neutron capture cross-section/barns: 6.8
Number of isotopes (including nuclear isomers): 28
Isotope mass range: 72→92

Nuclear properties

Key isotopes

Nuclide	Atomic mass	Natural abundance (%)	Half-life $T_{1/2}$	Decay mode and energy (MeV)	Nuclear spin I	Nuclear magnetic moment μ	Uses
^{77}Br	76.921 378	0	57.0h	EC(1.365); β^+; γ	$1+$		tracer
^{79}Br	78.918 336	50.69	stable		$3/2-$	$+2.1064$	NMR
^{81}Br	80.916 289	49.31	stable		$3/2-$	$+2.2706$	NMR
^{82}Br	81.914 802	0	35.30h	β^-(3.093); γ	$5-$	±1.6270	tracer

NMR

	$[^{79}$Br$]$	^{81}Br
Relative sensitivity (^{1}H $= 1.00$)	7.86×10^{-2}	9.85×10^{-2}
Receptivity (^{13}C $= 1.00$)	226	277
Magnetogyric ratio/rad T^{-1} s^{-1}	6.7023×10^7	7.2246×10^7
Quadrupole moment/m^2	0.33×10^{-28}	0.28×10^{-28}
Frequency (^{1}H $= 100$ MHz; 2.3488 T)/MHz	25.053	27.006

Reference: NaBr(aq)

Ground state electron configuration: $[Ar]3d^{10}4s^24p^5$
Term symbol: $^2P_{3/2}$
Electron affinity ($M \rightarrow M^-$)/kJ mol^{-1}: 324.7

Electron shell properties

Main lines in atomic spectrum

Wavelength/nm	Species
614.860	I
635.073	I
655.980	I
663.162	I
751.296	I
827.244	I
844.655	I
926.542	I

Ionization energies/kJ mol^{-1}

1. $M \rightarrow M^+$ 1139.9	6. $M^{5+} \rightarrow M^{6+}$ 8 550
2. $M^+ \rightarrow M^{2+}$ 2104	7. $M^{6+} \rightarrow M^{7+}$ 9 940
3. $M^{2+} \rightarrow M^{3+}$ 3500	8. $M^{7+} \rightarrow M^{8+}$ 18 600
4. $M^{3+} \rightarrow M^{4+}$ 4560	9. $M^{8+} \rightarrow M^{9+}$ (23 900)
5. $M^{4+} \rightarrow M^{5+}$ 5760	10. $M^{9+} \rightarrow M^{10+}$ (28 100)

Environmental properties

Biological role

None proved; Br$^-$ slightly
toxic; Br$_2$ very toxic

Levels in humans:
Muscle/p.p.m.: 7.7
Bone/p.p.m.: 6.7
Blood/mg dm^{-3}: 4.7
Daily dietary intake:
  0.8–24 mg
Toxic intake: 3 g
Lethal intake: >35 g
Total mass of element in
  average (70 kg) person:
  260 mg

Abundances

Sun (relative to H $= 1 \times 10^{12}$):
  n.a.
Earth's crust/p.p.m.: 0.37
Seawater/p.p.m.: 65
Residence time/years: 1×10^8
Classification: accumulating
Oxidation state: $-$I

Geological data

Chief deposits and sources:
  salt-lake evaporates,
  natural brines, Dead Sea,
  seawater
World production of
  Br$_2$/tonnes y^{-1}: 330 000
Reserves/tonnes: almost
  unlimited

Cd

Atomic number: 48

Relative atomic mass ($^{12}C = 12.0000$): 112.411

Chemical properties

Silvery metal. Tarnishes in air, soluble in acids but not alkalis. Used in rechargeable batteries, alloys, pigments.

Radii/pm: Cd^{2+} 103; Cd^+ 114; covalent 141; atomic 148.9

Electronegativity: 1.69 (Pauling); 1.46 (Allred); 4.33 eV (absolute)

Effective nuclear charge: 4.35 (Slater); 8.19 (Clementi); 11.58 (Froese-Fischer)

Standard reduction potentials $E^{\ominus}/V$

	II		0
Acid solution	Cd^{2+}	$\underline{-0.4025}$	Cd
Alkaline solution	$Cd(OH)_2$	$\underline{-0.824}$	Cd
	$[Cd(NH_3)_4]^{2+}$	$\underline{-0.622}$	Cd
	$[Cd(CN)_4]^{2-}$	$\underline{-1.09}$	Cd

Oxidation states

Cd^I	$(d^{10} s^1)$	rare, e.g. $Cd_2[AlCl_4]_2$
Cd^{II}	(d^{10})	CdO (basic), CdS, $Cd(OH)_2$, CdF_2, $CdCl_2$ etc., many salts, $[Cd(H_2O)_6]^{2+}$ (aq), many complexes, e.g. $[Cd(SCN)_4]^{2-}$

Physical properties

Melting point/K: 594.1

Boiling point/K: 1038

ΔH_{fusion}/kJ mol^{-1}: 6.11

ΔH_{vap}/kJ mol^{-1}: 99.87

Thermodynamic properties (298.15 K, 0.1 MPa)

State	$\Delta_f H^{\ominus}$/kJ mol^{-1}	$\Delta_f G^{\ominus}$/kJ mol^{-1}	$S^{\ominus}$/J K^{-1} mol^{-1}	C_p/J K^{-1} mol^{-1}
Solid	0	0	51.76	25.98
Gas	112.01	77.41	167.746	20.786

Density/kg m^{-3}: 8650 [293 K]; 7996 [liquid at m.p.]

Thermal conductivity/W m^{-1} K^{-1}: 96.8 [300 K]

Electrical resistivity/Ω m: 6.83×10^{-8} [273 K]

Mass magnetic susceptibility/kg^{-1} m^3: -2.21×10^{-9} (s)

Molar volume/cm^3: 13.00

Coefficient of linear thermal expansion/K^{-1}: 29.8×10^{-6}

Crystal structure (cell dimensions/pm), space group

h.c.p. ($a = 297.94$; $c = 561.86$), P6$_3$/mmc

X-ray diffraction: mass absorption coefficients (μ/ρ)/cm^2 g^{-1}:
CuK$_\alpha$ 231   MoK$_\alpha$ 27.5

Cadmium

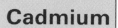

Thermal neutron capture cross-section/barns: 2450
Number of isotopes (including nuclear isomers): 31
Isotope mass range: 99→124

Nuclear properties

Key isotopes

Nuclide	Atomic mass	Natural abundance (%)	Half-life $T_{1/2}$	Decay mode and energy (MeV)	Nuclear spin I	Nuclear magnetic moment μ	Uses
^{106}Cd	105.906 461	1.25	stable		0+		
^{108}Cd	107.904 176	0.89	stable		0+		
^{109}Cd	108.904 953	0	462d	EC(0.16); γ	5/2+	−0.8270	tracer
^{110}Cd	109.903 005	12.51	stable		0+		
^{111}Cd	110.904 182	12.81	stable		1/2+	−0.5943	NMR
^{112}Cd	111.902 758	24.13	stable		0+		
^{113}Cd	112.904 400	12.22	stable		1/2+	−0.6217	NMR
^{114}Cd	113.903 357	28.72	stable		0+		
^{115m}Cd		0	44.6d	β^-(1.62); γ	11/2−	−1.042	tracer
^{115}Cd	114.905 430	0	53.5h	β^-(1.45); γ	1/2+	−0.648	tracer
^{116}Cd	115.904 754	7.47	stable		0+		

NMR

	$[^{111}$Cd]	^{113}Cd
Relative sensitivity (^{1}H = 1.00)	9.54×10^{-3}	1.09×10^{-2}
Receptivity (^{13}C = 1.00)	6.93	7.6
Magnetogyric ratio/rad T^{-1} s^{-1}	-5.6714×10^7	-5.9328×10^7
Frequency (^{1}H = 100 MHz; 2.3488 T)/MHz	21.205	22.182

References: Cd(ClO$_4$)$_2$ (aq) and Cd(CH$_3$)$_2$

Ground state electron configuration: [Kr]4d^{10}5s^2
Term symbol: ^{1}S$_0$
Electron affinity (M→M$^-$)/kJ mol^{-1}: −26

Electron shell properties

Main lines in atomic spectrum

Wavelength/nm	Species
214.441	II
226.502	II
228.802 (AA)	I
326.106	I
643.847	I

Ionization energies/kJ mol^{-1}

1. M → M$^+$	867.6	6. M^{5+} → M^{6+} (9 100)
2. M$^+$ → M^{2+}	1631	7. M^{6+} → M^{7+} (11 100)
3. M^{2+} → M^{3+}	3616	8. M^{7+} → M^{8+} (14 100)
4. M^{3+} → M^{4+}	(5300)	9. M^{8+} → M^{9+} (16 400)
5. M^{4+} → M^{5+}	(7000)	10. M^{9+} → M^{10+} (18 800)

Environmental properties

Biological role

None proved; toxic;
   stimulatory; carcinogenic;
   teratogenic
Levels in humans:
Muscle/p.p.m.: 0.14–3.2
Bone/p.p.m.: 1.8
Blood/mg dm^{-3}: 0.0052
Daily dietary intake:
   0.007–3 mg
Toxic intake: 3–330 mg
Lethal intake: 1.5–9 g
Total mass of element in
   average (70 kg) person:
   50 mg

Abundances

Sun (relative to H = 1×10^{12}):
   71
Earth's crust/p.p.m.: 0.11
Seawater/p.p.m.:
Atlantic surface: 1.1×10^{-6}
Atlantic deep: 38×10^{-6}
Pacific surface: 1.1×10^{-6}
Pacific deep: 100×10^{-6}
Residence time/years: 30 000
Classification: recycled
Oxidation state: II

Geological data

Chief deposits and sources:
   greenockite [CdS] but
   commercial source is by-
   product of zinc production
   from ZnS
World production/tonnes y^{-1}:
   14 000
Reserves/tonnes: see zinc

Cs

Atomic number: 55

Relative atomic mass ($^{12}C = 12.0000$): **132.9054**

Chemical properties

Soft, shiny, gold-coloured metal; reacts rapidly with oxygen and explosively with water. Used as catalyst promoter, in special glasses, and in radiation monitoring equipment.

Radii/pm: Cs^+ 165; atomic 265.4; covalent 235; van der Waals 262

Electronegativity: 0.79 (Pauling); 0.86 (Allred); 2.18 eV (absolute)

Effective nuclear charge 2.20 (Slater); 6.36 (Clementi); 8.56 (Froese-Fischer)

Standard reduction potentials $E^\ominus$/V

I		0
Cs^+	$\xrightarrow{-2.923}$	Cs

Oxidation states

Cs^{-1}	(s^2)	caesium metal in liquid ammonia
Cs^I	([Xe])	Cs_2O, Cs_2O_2, CsO_2, CsOH, CsH, CsF, CsCl etc., $[Cs(H_2O)_x]^+$(aq), Cs_2CO_3, many salts and salt hydrates, some complexes with crown ethers etc.

Physical properties

Melting point/K: 301.55

Boiling point/K: 951.6

ΔH_{fusion}/kJ mol^{-1}: 2.09

ΔH_{vap}/kJ mol^{-1}: 65.90

Thermodynamic properties (298.15 K, 0.1 MPa)

State	$\Delta_f H^\ominus$/kJ mol^{-1}	$\Delta_f G^\ominus$/kJ mol^{-1}	$S^\ominus$/J K^{-1} mol^{-1}	C_p/J K^{-1} mol^{-1}
Solid	0	0	85.23	32.17
Gas	76.065	49.121	175.595	20.786

Density/kg m^{-3}: 1873 [293 K]; 1843 [liquid at m.p.]

Thermal conductivity/W m^{-1} K^{-1}: 35.9 [300 K]

Electrical resistivity/Ω m: 20.0×10^{-8} [293 K]

Mass magnetic susceptibility/kg^{-1} m^3: $+2.8 \times 10^{-9}$ (s)

Molar volume/cm^3: 70.96

Coefficient of linear thermal expansion/K^{-1}: 97×10^{-6}

Crystal structure (cell dimensions/pm), space group

b.c.c. (78 K) ($a = 614$), Im3m

High pressure forms: ($a = 598.4$), Fm3m
($a = 580.0$), Fm3m

X-ray diffraction: mass absorption coefficients (μ/ρ)/cm^2 g^{-1}:
CuK$_\alpha$ 318 MoK$_\alpha$ 41.3

Discovered by R. Bunsen and G. R. Kirchhoff in 1860 at Heidelberg, Germany

[Latin, *caesius* = sky blue]

Caesium (Cesium)

Thermal neutron capture cross-section/barns: 29

Number of isotopes (including nuclear isomers): 40

Isotope mass range: $114 \rightarrow 145$

Key isotopes

Nuclide	Atomic mass	Natural abundance (%)	Half-life $T_{1/2}$	Decay mode and energy (MeV)	Nuclear spin I	Nuclear magnetic moment μ	Uses
^{133}Cs	132.905 429	100	stable		$7/2+$	$+2.579$	NMR
^{134}Cs	133.906 696	0	2.065y	β^- (2.06); γ	4	$+2.990$	tracer
^{135}Cs	134.905 885	0	3×10^6y	β^- (0.205); no γ	$7/2+$	$+2.729$	
^{137}Cs	136.907 073	0	30.17y	β^- (1.17); γ	$7/2+$	$+2.838$	tracer, medical

NMR

^{133}Cs

Relative sensitivity (^{1}H = 1.00)	4.74×10^{-2}
Receptivity (^{13}C = 1.00)	269
Magnetogyric ratio/rad T^{-1} s^{-1}	3.5087×10^7
Quadrupole moment/m^2	-3×10^{-31}
Frequency (^{1}H = 100 MHz; 2.3488 T)/MHz	13.117

Reference: 0.5M CsBr(aq)

Ground state electron configuration: [Xe]$6s^1$

Term symbol: $^2S_{1/2}$

Electron affinity (M$\rightarrow$M$^-$)/kJ mol^{-1}: 45.5

Main lines in atomic spectrum

Wavelength/nm	Species
455.528	I
460.376	II
522.704	II
592.563	II
852.113 (AA)	I
895.347	I

Ionization energies/kJ mol^{-1}

1. M $\rightarrow$M$^+$ 375.7	6. M$^{5+}\rightarrow$M^{6+} (7 100)
2. M$^+\rightarrow$M^{2+} 2420	7. M$^{6+}\rightarrow$M^{7+} (8 300)
3. M$^{2+}\rightarrow$M^{3+} (3400)	8. M$^{7+}\rightarrow$M^{8+} (11 300)
4. M$^{3+}\rightarrow$M^{4+} (4400)	9. M$^{8+}\rightarrow$M^{9+} (12 700)
5. M$^{4+}\rightarrow$M^{5+} (6000)	10. M$^{9+}\rightarrow$M^{10+} (23 700)

Environmental properties

Biological role	Abundances	Geological data
None	Sun (relative to H = 1×10^{12}): <80	Chief deposits and sources: pollucite [(Cs, Na)$_4$Al$_4$Si$_9$O$_{26}$.H$_2$O]
Levels in humans: Muscle/p.p.m.: 0.07–1.6 Bone/p.p.m.: 0.013–0.052 Blood/mg dm^{-3}: 0.0038 Daily dietary intake: 0.004–0.03 mg Toxic intake: non-toxic Total mass of element in average (70 kg) person: n.a.	Earth's crust/p.p.m.: 3 Seawater/p.p.m.: 3.0×10^{-4} Residence time/years: 600 000 Classification: accumulating Oxidation state: I	World production of caesium compounds/tonnes y^{-1}: *c*. 20 Reserves/tonnes: n.a.

Ca

Atomic number: **20**

Relative atomic mass ($^{12}C = 12.0000$): **40.078**

Chemical properties

Silvery white, relatively soft metal obtained formerly from fused calcium chloride by electrolysis but now got by heating CaO with aluminium metal in a vacuum. Protected by oxide/nitride film and can be worked as a metal. Attacked by oxygen and water. Used in alloys and in manufacture of Zr, Th, U, and rare earth metals. Lime (CaO) used in metallurgy, water treatment, chemicals industry, buildings, etc.

Radii/pm: Ca^{2+} 106; covalent 174; atom (α form) 197.3

Electronegativity: 1.00 (Pauling); 1.04. (Allred); 2.2 eV (absolute)

Effective nuclear charge: 2.85 (Slater); 4.40 (Clementi); 5.69 (Froese-Fischer)

Standard reduction potentials $E^{\ominus}/V$

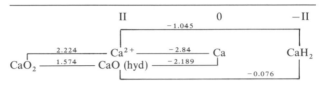

Oxidation states

Ca^{II}	([Ar])	CaO, CaO_2 (peroxide), $Ca(OH)_2$, CaH_2, CaF_2, $CaCl_2$ etc., Ca^{2+}(aq), $CaCO_3$, $CaSO_4 \cdot 2H_2O$ (gypsum) $CaSO_4 \cdot \frac{1}{2}H_2O$ (plaster of Paris) CaC_2 (calcium carbide), many salts, few complexes

Physical properties

Melting point/K: 1112

Boiling point/K: 1757

ΔH_{fusion}/kJ mol^{-1}: 9.33

ΔH_{vap}/kJ mol^{-1}: 149.95

Thermodynamic properties (298.15 K, 0.1 MPa)

State	$\Delta_f H^{\ominus}$/kJ mol^{-1}	$\Delta_f G^{\ominus}$/kJ mol^{-1}	$S^{\ominus}$/J K^{-1} mol^{-1}	C_p/J K^{-1} mol^{-1}
Solid (α)	0	0	41.42	25.31
Gas	178.2	144.3	154.884	20.786

Density/kg m^{-3}: 1550 [293 K]; 1365 [liquid at m.p.]

Thermal conductivity/W m^{-1} K^{-1}: 200 [300 K]

Electrical resistivity/Ω m: 3.43×10^{-8} [293 K]

Mass magnetic susceptibility/kg^{-1} m^3: $+1.4 \times 10^{-8}$ (s)

Molar volume/cm^3: 25.86

Coefficient of linear thermal expansion/K^{-1}: 22×10^{-6}

Crystal structure (cell dimensions/pm), space group

α-Ca f.c.c. ($a = 558.84$), Fm3m
β-Ca b.c.c. ($a = 448.0$), Im3m
γ-Ca h.c.p. ($a = 397$, $c = 649$), P6$_3$/mmc, [may contain H]

$T(\alpha \rightarrow \beta) = 573$ K
$T(\beta \rightarrow \gamma) = 723$ K

X-ray diffraction: mass absorption coefficients (μ/ρ)/cm^2 g^{-1}:
CuK$_\alpha$ 162   MoK$_\alpha$ 18.3

Isolated in 1808 by Sir Humphry Davy in London, UK

[Latin, *calx* = lime]

Calcium

Thermal neutron capture cross-section/barns: 0.43

Number of isotopes (including nuclear isomers): 16

Isotope mass range: $36 \rightarrow 51$

Key isotopes

Nuclide	Atomic mass	Natural abundance (%)	Half-life $T_{1/2}$	Decay mode and energy (MeV)	Nuclear spin I	Nuclear magnetic moment μ	Uses
^{40}Ca	39.962 591	96.941	stable		0+		
^{42}Ca	41.958 618	0.647	stable		0+		
^{43}Ca	42.958 766	0.135	stable		7/2−	1.3173	NMR
^{44}Ca	43.955 480	2.086	stable		0+		
^{45}Ca	44.956 185	0	163.8d	β^-(0.257); no γ	7/2−		tracer
^{46}Ca	45.953 689	0.004	stable		0+		
^{47}Ca	46.954 543	0	4.536h	β^-(1.988); γ	7/2−		tracer
^{48}Ca	47.952 5334	0.187	stable		0+		

NMR

^{43}Ca

Relative sensitivity (^{1}H = 1.00)	6.40×10^{-3}
Receptivity (^{13}C = 1.00)	0.0527
Magnetogyric ratio/rad T^{-1} s^{-1}	-1.8001×10^7
Quadrupole moment/m^2	-0.05×10^{-28}
Frequency (^{1}H = 100 MHz; 2.3488 T)/MHz	6.728

Reference: CaCl$_2$(aq)

Ground state electron configuration: [Ar]4s^2

Term symbol: ^{1}S$_0$

Electron affinity (M$\rightarrow$M$^-$)/kJ mol^{-1}: -186

Main lines in atomic spectrum

Wavelength/nm	Species
239.856	I
317.933	II
373.690	II
393.366	II
393.847	II
422.673 (AA)	I

Ionization energies/kJ mol^{-1}

1.	M $\rightarrow$ M$^+$	589.7	6. M$^{5+} \rightarrow$ M^{6+}	10 496
2.	M$^+ \rightarrow$ M^{2+}	1145	7. M$^{6+} \rightarrow$ M^{7+}	12 320
3.	M$^{2+} \rightarrow$ M^{3+}	4910	8. M$^{7+} \rightarrow$ M^{8+}	14 207
4.	M$^{3+} \rightarrow$ M^{4+}	6474	9. M$^{8+} \rightarrow$ M^{9+}	18 191
5.	M$^{4+} \rightarrow$ M^{5+}	8144	10. M$^{9+} \rightarrow$ M^{10+}	20 385

Environmental properties

Biological role

Essential to all species

Levels in humans:

Muscle/p.p.m.: 140–700

Bone/p.p.m.: 170 000

Blood/mg dm^{-3}: 60.5

Daily dietary intake:
600–1400 mg

Toxic intake: non-toxic

Total mass of element in
average (70 kg) person:
1.00 kg

Abundances

Sun (relative to H = 1×10^{12}):
2.24×10^6

Earth's crust/p.p.m.: 41 000

Seawater/p.p.m.:
Atlantic surface: 390
Atlantic deep: 430
Pacific surface: 390
Pacific deep: 440
Residence time/years: 1×10^6
Classification: recycled
Oxidation state: II

Geological data

Chief deposits and sources:
limestone [CaCO$_3$],
dolomite
[CaCO$_3$.MgCO$_3$],
gypsum [CaSO$_4$.2H$_2$O]

**World production of calcium
metal**/tonnes y^{-1}: 2000

**World production of lime
[CaO]**/tonnes y^{-1}:
112×10^6

Reserves/tonnes: almost
unlimited

Cf	**Atomic number: 98**
	Relative atomic mass ($^{12}C = 12.0000$): (251)

Chemical properties

Radioactive, silvery metal which does not occur naturally. Attacked by oxygen, steam, and acids, but not alkalis. ^{252}Cf used in cancer therapy.

Radii/pm: Cf^{4+} 86; Cf^{3+} 98; Cf^{2+} 117

Electronegativity: 1.3 (Pauling); n.a. (Allred)

Effective nuclear charge: 1.65 (Slater)

Standard reduction potentials $E^{\ominus}/V$

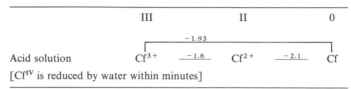

	III	II	0
		−1.93	
Acid solution	Cf^{3+} $\quad$ −1.6	Cf^{2+} $\quad$ −2.1	Cf

[Cf^{IV} is reduced by water within minutes]

Oxidation states

Cf^{II}	(f^{10})	CfO ?, $CfBr_2$, CfI_2
Cf^{III}	(f^9)	Cf_2O_3, CfF_3, $CfCl_3$ etc.
		Cf^{3+}(aq), $[Cf(C_5H_5)_3]$
Cf^{IV}	(f^8)	CfO_2, CfF_4

Physical properties

Melting point/K: n.a.

Boiling point/K: n.a.

ΔH_{fusion}/kJ mol^{-1}: n.a.

ΔH_{vap}/kJ mol^{-1}: n.a.

Thermodynamic properties (298.15 K, 0.1 MPa)

State	$\Delta_f H^{\ominus}$/kJ mol^{-1}	$\Delta_f G^{\ominus}$/kJ mol^{-1}	$S^{\ominus}$/J K^{-1} mol^{-1}	C_p/J K^{-1} mol^{-1}
Solid	0	0	n.a.	25.98
Gas	n.a.	n.a.	n.a.	n.a.

Density/kg m^{-3}: n.a.

Thermal conductivity/W m^{-1} K^{-1}: 10 (est.) [300 K]

Electrical resistivity/Ω m: n.a.

Mass magnetic susceptibility/kg^{-1} m^3: n.a.

Molar volume/cm^3: n.a.

Coefficient of linear thermal expansion/K^{-1}: n.a.

Crystal (cell dimensions/pm), space group

Cubic

X-ray diffraction: mass absorption coefficients (μ/ρ)/cm^2 g^{-1}: n.a.

Produced in 1950 by S. G. Thompson, K. Street Jr, A. Ghiorso, and G. T. Seaborg at Berkeley, California, USA
[English, *California*]

Californium

Nuclear properties

Thermal neutron capture cross-section/barns: 2900 (^{251}Cf)

Number of isotopes (including nuclear isomers): 16

Isotope mass range: 240→255

Key isotopes

Nuclide	Atomic mass	Natural abundance (%)	Half-life $T_{1/2}$	Decay mode and energy (MeV)	Nuclear spin I	Nuclear magnetic moment μ	Uses
^{249}Cf	249.074 844	0	351y	α(6.295)	9/2−		
^{251}Cf	251.079 580	0	890y	α(6.172)	1/2+		
^{252}Cf	252.081 621	0	2.64y	α(6.217); SF	0+		tracer, medical

Electron shell properties

Ground state electron configuration: [Rn]5f^{10}7s^2

Term symbol: $^5I_8$

Electron affinity (M→M$^-$)/kJ mol^{-1}: n.a.

Main lines in atomic spectrum

Wavelength/nm	Species
339.222	I
353.149	I
354.098	I
359.877	I
360.532	I
361.211	II
362.676	II

Ionization energies/kJ mol^{-1}

1. M →M$^+$	608
2. M$^+$→M^{2+}	
3. M^{2+}→M^{3+}	
4. M^{3+}→M^{4+}	
5. M^{4+}→M^{5+}	

Environmental properties

Biological role	Abundances	Geological data
None; never encountered, but would be toxic due to radioactivity **Levels in humans:** nil	**Sun** (relative to H = 1 × 10^{12}): n.a. **Earth's crust**/p.p.m.: nil **Seawater**/p.p.m.: nil	**Chief source:** none. Obtained in milligram quantities as ^{249}Cf and ^{252}Cf from neutron bombardment of ^{239}Pu

C

Atomic number: 6

Relative atomic mass ($^{12}C = 12.0000$): 12.011

Chemical properties

Used as coke (steel making), carbon black (printing), and activated charcoal (sugar refining, etc.).

Radii/pm: covalent bond 77; double 67; triple 60; C^{4-} 260;
van der Waals 185

Electronegativity: 2.55 (Pauling); 2.50 (Allred); 6.27 eV (absolute)

Effective nuclear charge: 3.25 (Slater); 3.14 (Clementi);
2.87 (Froese-Fischer)

Standard reduction potentials $E^\ominus/V$

	IV		II		0		$-$II		$-$IV
Acid solution	CO_2	$\xrightarrow{-0.106}$	CO	$\xrightarrow{0.517}$	C	$\xrightarrow{0.132}$	CH_4		
	CO_2	$\xrightarrow{-0.20}$	HCO_2H	$\xrightarrow{0.034}$	HCHO	$\xrightarrow{0.232}$	CH_3OH	$\xrightarrow{0.59}$	CH_4
Alkaline solution	CO_2	$\xrightarrow{-1.01}$	HCO_2^-	$\xrightarrow{-1.07}$	HCHO	$\xrightarrow{0.59}$	CH_3OH	$\xrightarrow{-0.2}$	CH_4

Covalent bonds*

	r/pm	E/kJ mol^{-1}
C—H	109.3	411
C—C	154	348
C=C	134	614
C≡C	120	839
C—N	147	305
C=N	130	615
C≡N	116	891
C—O	143	358
C=O	123	745
C≡O	112.8	1074

*See also other elements for bonds to carbon

Oxidation states

This concept is rarely used in discussing carbon and its compounds because of their subtleties of bonding. However, for simple compounds with a single carbon we can use it:

C^{-IV} CH_4
C^{II} CO
C^{IV} CO_2, CO_3^{2-}, CF_4, etc.

Physical properties

Melting point/K: *c.* 3820 (diamond)
Boiling point/K: 5100 (sublimes)
ΔH_{fusion}/kJ mol^{-1}: 105.0
ΔH_{vap}/kJ mol^{-1}: 710.9

Thermodynamic properties (298.15 K, 0.1 MPa)

State	$\Delta_f H^\ominus$/kJ mol^{-1}	$\Delta_f G^\ominus$/kJ mol^{-1}	$S^\ominus$/J K^{-1} mol^{-1}	C_p/J K^{-1} mol^{-1}
Solid (graphite)	0	0	5.740	8.527
Solid (diamond)	1.895	2.900	2.377	6.113
Gas	716.682	671.257	158.096	20.838

Density/kg m^{-3}: 3513 (diam.); 2260 (graph.) [293 K]
Thermal conductivity/W m^{-1} K^{-1}: 990–2320 (diam.);
5.7$^\perp$, 1960$^\parallel$ (graph.) [298 K]
Electrical resistivity/Ω m: 10^{11} (diam.); 1.375×10^{-5} (graph.) [293 K]
Mass magnetic susceptibility/kg^{-1} m^3: -6.3×10^{-9} (graph.);
-6.2×10^{-9} (diam.)
Molar volume/cm^3: 3.42 (diam.)
Coefficient of linear thermal expansion/K^{-1}: 1.19×10^{-6} (diam.)

Crystal structure (cell dimensions/pm), space group

Cubic diamond ($a = 356.703$), Fd3m
Hexagonal graphite ($a = 246.12$, $c = 670.78$), P6$_3$mc
Rhombohedral graphite ($a = 364.2$, $\alpha = 39°30'$), R3m
Hexagonal diamond ($a = 252$, $c = 412$), P6$_3$/mmc
Hexagonal carbon [chaoite] ($a = 894.8$, $c = 1408$)

X-ray diffraction: mass absorption coefficients (μ/ρ)/cm^2 g^{-1}:
CuK$_\alpha$ 4.60   MoK$_\alpha$ 0.625

Occurs naturally as graphite (and diamond); known to prehistoric humans

[Latin, *carbo* = charcoal]

Carbon

Thermal neutron capture cross-section/barns: 0.0035
Number of isotopes (including nuclear isomers): 8
Isotope mass range: 9→16

Key isotopes

Nuclide	Atomic mass	Natural abundance (%)	Half-life $T_{1/2}$	Decay mode and energy (MeV)	Nuclear spin I	Nuclear magnetic moment μ	Uses
^{11}C	11.011 430	0	20.3 m	β^+ (1.982); γ	$3/2-$	-0.964	tracer
^{12}C	12.000 000*	98.90	stable		$0+$		
^{13}C	13.003 355	1.10	stable		$1/2-$	$+0.702 41$	NMR
^{14}C	14.003 241	trace	5730y	β^- (0.15648); no γ	$0+$		tracer

*By definition.

NMR

^{13}C

Relative sensitivity ($^1H = 1.00$)	1.59×10^{-2}
Receptivity ($^{13}C = 1.00$)	1.00 (by definition)
Magnetogyric ratio/rad T^{-1} s^{-1}	6.7263×10^7
Frequency ($^1H = 100$ MHz; 2.3488 T)/MHz	25.144
Reference: $Si(CH_3)_4$	

Ground state electron configuration: $[He]2s^2 2p^2$
Term symbol: $^3P_0$
Electron affinity $(M \rightarrow M^-)$/kJ mol^{-1}: 121.9

Main lines in atomic spectrum

Wavelength/nm	Species
247.856	I
283.671	II
426.726	II
723.642	II

Ionization energies/kJ mol^{-1}

1. $M \rightarrow M^+$ 1086.2
2. $M^+ \rightarrow M^{2+}$ 2352
3. $M^{2+} \rightarrow M^{3+}$ 4620
4. $M^{3+} \rightarrow M^{4+}$ 6222
5. $M^{4+} \rightarrow M^{5+}$ 37 827
6. $M^{5+} \rightarrow M^{6+}$ 47 270

Environmental properties

Biological role

Constituent element of DNA

Levels in humans:
Muscle/p.p.m.: 670 000
Bone/p.p.m.: 360 000
Daily dietary intake: 300 g
Toxic intake: generally non-toxic, but can be very toxic as CO or cyanide [CN^-]
Total mass of element in average (70 kg) person: 16 kg.

Abundances

Sun (relative to $H = 1 \times 10^{12}$):
  4.17×10^8

Earth's crust/p.p.m.: 480

Seawater/p.p.m.:
Atlantic surface: 23
Atlantic deep: 26
Pacific surface: 23
Pacific deep: 28
Residence time/years: 800 000
Classification: recycled
Oxidation state: IV

Atmosphere/ppm
(by volume): CO_2, 335; CO, 0.02; CH_4, 1.7

Geological data

Chief deposits and sources: limestone [$CaCO_3$], etc.; coal; oil; natural gas. Some natural forms of the element as graphite and diamond

World production*/tonnes y^{-1}: 8×10^9 (1990)

Reserves (1990): natural gas, 110×10^{12} m^3 ($= 3 \times 10^6$ tonnes); coal, 1.1×10^{12} tonnes; oil 1.4×10^{11} tonnes

*Gas and coal expressed as equivalent amount of oil.

Ce

Atomic number: 58

Relative atomic mass ($^{12}C = 12.0000$): 140.115

Chemical properties

Reactive, grey metal; most abundant of the lanthanide metals. Tarnishes in air, burns when heated, reacts rapidly with water, dissolves in acids. Used in glass, flints, ceramics, and alloys.

Radii/pm: Ce^{3+} 107; Ce^{4+} 94; atomic 182.5; covalent 165

Electronegativity: 1.12 (Pauling); 1.06 (Allred); ≤ 3.0 eV (absolute)

Effective nuclear charge: 2.85 (Slater); 10.80 (Clementi); 10.57 (Froese-Fischer)

Standard reduction potentials $E^{\ominus}/V$

	IV		III		0
Acid solution	Ce^{4+}	—1.72—	Ce^{3+}	—-2.34—	Ce
Alkaline solution	CeO_2	—-0.7—	$Ce(OH)_3$	—-2.78—	Ce

Oxidation states

Ce^{III} ($4f^1$)	Ce_2O_3, $Ce(OH)_3$, CeF_3, $CeCl_3$ etc., Ce^{3+} salts, $[Ce(H_2O)_6]^{3+}$ (aq), complexes
Ce^{IV} ([Xe])	CeO_2, CeF_4, $CaCl_6^{2-}$, $[Ce(NO_3)_6]^{2-}$ (aq)

Physical properties

Melting point/K: 1072

Boiling point/K: 3699

ΔH_{fusion}/kJ mol^{-1}: 8.87

ΔH_{vap}/kJ mol^{-1}: 313.8

Thermodynamic properties (298.15 K, 0.1 MPa)

State	$\Delta_f H^{\ominus}$/kJ mol^{-1}	$\Delta_f G^{\ominus}$/kJ mol^{-1}	$S^{\ominus}$/J K^{-1} mol^{-1}	C_p/J K^{-1} mol^{-1}
Solid	0	0	72.0	26.94
Gas	423	385	191.776	23.075

Density/kg m^{-3}: 8240 (α); 6749 (β); 6773 (γ); 6700 (δ) [298 K]

Thermal conductivity/W m^{-1} K^{-1}: 11.4 [300 K]

Electrical resistivity/Ω m: 73×10^{-8} [273 K]

Mass magnetic susceptibility/kg^{-1} m^3: $+2.17 \times 10^{-7}$ (s)

Molar volume/cm^3: 17.00

Coefficient of linear thermal expansion/K^{-1}: 8.5×10^{-6}

Crystal structure (cell dimensions/pm), space group

α-Ce f.c.c. ($a = 485$), Fm3m
β-Ce hexagonal ($a = 367.3$, $c = 1180.2$), P6$_3$/mmc
γ-Ce f.c.c. ($a = 516.01$), Fm3m
δ-Ce f.c.c. ($a = 412$), Im3m
$T(\beta \rightarrow \gamma) = 441$ K

X-ray diffraction: mass absorption coefficients (μ/ρ)/cm^2 g^{-1}:
CuK$_\alpha$ 352   MoK$_\alpha$ 48.2

Discovered in 1803 by J. J. Berzelius and W. Hisinger at Vestmanland,
Sweden. First isolated by W. F. Hillebrand and T. H. Norton
in 1875 at Washington, DC, USA
[Named after asteroid Ceres, discovered in 1801]

Cerium

Thermal neutron capture cross-section/barns: 0.6
Number of isotopes (including nuclear isomers):   28
Isotope mass range: $129 \rightarrow 151$

Key isotopes

Nuclide	Atomic mass	Natural abundance (%)	Half-life $T_{1/2}$	Decay mode and energy (MeV)	Nuclear spin I	Nuclear magnetic moment μ	Uses
^{136}Ce	135.907 140	0.19	stable		0+		
^{138}Ce	137.905 985	0.25	stable		0+		
^{139}Ce	138.906 631	0	140d	EC(0.27); γ	3/2+	± 0.9	tracer
^{140}Ce	139.905 433	88.48	stable		0+		
^{141}Ce	140.908 271	0	32.5d	β^- (0.581); γ	7/2−	± 0.97	tracer
^{142}Ce	141.909 241	11.08	stable		0+		
^{143}Ce	142.912 383	0	33.0h	β^-(1.462); γ	3/2+	$c. \pm 1$	tracer
^{144}Ce	143.913 643	0	284.4h	β^- (0.318); γ	0+		

Ground state electron configuration: $[Xe]4f^2 6s^2$
Term symbol: $^3H_4$
Electron affinity $(M \rightarrow M^-)$/kJ mol^{-1}: ≤ 50

Main lines in atomic spectrum

Wavelength/nm	Species
349.275	II
395.254	II
399.924	II
401.239	II
413.380	II
418.660	II

Ionization energies/kJ mol^{-1}

1. $M \rightarrow M^+$	527.4	6. $M^{5+} \rightarrow M^{6+}$ (8 200)
2. $M^+ \rightarrow M^{2+}$	1047	7. $M^{6+} \rightarrow M^{7+}$ (9 700)
3. $M^{2+} \rightarrow M^{3+}$	1949	8. $M^{7+} \rightarrow M^{8+}$ (11 800)
4. $M^{3+} \rightarrow M^{4+}$	3547	9. $M^{8+} \rightarrow M^{9+}$ (13 200)
5. $M^{4+} \rightarrow M^{5+}$ (6800)		10. $M^{9+} \rightarrow M^{10+}$ (14 700)

Environmental properties

Biological role

None; stimulatory

Levels in humans:
Muscle/p.p.m.: n.a.
Bone/p.p.m.: 2.7
Blood/mg dm^{-3}: <0.002
Daily dietary intake: n.a. but
  very low
Toxic intake: non-toxic?
Total mass of element in
  average (70 kg) person: n.a.

Abundances

Sun (relative to $H = 1 \times 10^{12}$):
35.5
Earth's crust/p.p.m.: 68
Seawater/p.p.m.:
Atlantic surface: 9.0×10^{-6}
Atlantic deep: 2.6×10^{-6}
Pacific surface: 1.5×10^{-6}
Pacific deep: 0.5×10^{-6}
Residence time/years: 100
Classification: scavenged
Oxidation state: III

Geological data

Chief deposits and sources:
monazite
  [(Ce, La, etc.)PO$_4$];
bastnaesite
  [(Ce, La, etc.)(CO$_3$)F]
World production/tonnes y^{-1}:
9400
Reserves/tonnes: 40×10^6

Cl

Atomic number: 17
Relative atomic mass ($^{12}C = 12.0000$): 35.4527

Chemical properties

Yellow-green, dense, sharp smelling gas, Cl_2; produced on large scale by electrolysis of sodium chloride. Used as bleaching agent and to make organochlorine solvents and polymers (PVC)

Radii/pm: Cl^- 181; covalent 99; van der Waals 181
Electronegativity: 3.16 (Pauling); 2.83 (Allred); 8.30 eV (absolute)
Effective nuclear charge: 6.10 (Slater); 6.12 (Clementi); 6.79 (Froese-Fischer)

Standard reduction potentials $E^{\ominus}/V$

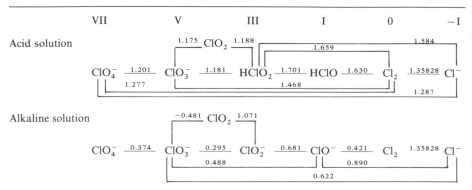

| | VII | V | III | I | 0 | −I |

Acid solution

Alkaline solution

Covalent bonds r/pm E/kJ mol^{-1}

	r/pm	E/kJ mol^{-1}
Cl–O	170	206
Cl–Cl	198.8	242
Cl–F	163	257

For other bonds see other elements

Oxidation states

Cl^{-I}	Cl^-(aq), HCl, NaCl etc
Cl^{I}	Cl_2O, HOCl, salts, ClO^-(aq), ClF
Cl^{III}	$NaClO_2$, ClF_3
Cl^{IV}	ClO_2
Cl^{V}	$HClO_3$, salts, ClO_3^- (aq), ClF_5, F_3ClO
Cl^{VI}	Cl_2O_6
Cl^{VII}	Cl_2O_7, $HClO_4$, salts, ClO_4^- (aq), $FClO_3$

Physical properties

Melting point/K: 172.17
Boiling point/K: 239.18   **Triple point/K:** 172.17
ΔH_{fusion}/kJ mol^{-1}: 6.41 ΔH_{vap}/kJ mol^{-1}: 20.4033

Thermodynamic properties (298.15 K, 0.1 MPa)

State	$\Delta_f H^{\ominus}$/kJ mol^{-1}	$\Delta_f G^{\ominus}$/kJ mol^{-1}	$S^{\ominus}$/J K^{-1} mol^{-1}	C_p/J K^{-1} mol^{-1}
Gas (Cl_2)	0	0	223.066	33.907
Gas (atoms)	121.679	105.680	165.198	21.840

Density/kg m^{-3}: 2030 [113 K]; 1507 [239 K]; 3.214 [273 K]
Thermal conductivity/W m^{-1} K^{-1}: 0.0089 [300 K]$_g$
Critical temperature/K: 417   **Critical pressure/kPa:** 7700
Critical volume/cm^3 mol^{-1}: 124
Mass magnetic susceptibility/kg^{-1} m^3: -7.2×10^{-9} (g)
Molar volume/cm^3: 17.46 [113 K]

Crystal structure (cell dimensions/pm), space group

Tetragonal ($a = 856$; $c = 612$), P4/ncm
Orthorhombic ($a = 624$, $b = 448$, $c = 826$), Cmca

T (tetragonal $\rightarrow$orthorhombic) = 100 K

X-ray diffraction: mass absorption coefficients (μ/ρ)/cm^2 g^{-1}:
CuK$_\alpha$ 106   MoK$_\alpha$ 11.4

Discovered in 1774 by C. W. Scheele at Uppsala, Sweden

[Greek, *chloros* = pale green]

Chlorine

Thermal neutron capture cross-section/barns: 35.5
Number of isotopes (including nuclear isomers): 13
Isotope mass range: 31→41

Key isotopes

Nuclide	Atomic mass	Natural abundance (%)	Half-life $T_{1/2}$	Decay mode and energy (MeV)	Nuclear spin I	Nuclear magnetic moment μ	Uses
^{35}Cl	34.968 852	75.77	stable		3/2+	+0.821 87	NMR
^{36}Cl	35.968 306	0	3.1×10^5y	β^- (0.709); β^+, EC; (2%); no γ	2+	+1.285 47	tracer
^{37}Cl	36.965 903	24.23	stable		3/2+	+0.684 12	NMR

NMR

	^{35}Cl	^{37}Cl
Relative sensitivity (^{1}H = 1.00)	4.70×10^{-3}	2.71×10^{-3}
Receptivity (^{13}C = 1.00)	20.2	3.8
Magnetogyric ratio/rad T^{-1} s^{-1}	2.6210×10^7	2.1718×10^7
Quadrupole moment/m^2	-8.0×10^{-30}	-6.32×10^{-30}
Frequency (^{1}H = 100 MHz; 2.3488 T)/MHz	9.798	8.156

Reference: NaCl (aq)

Ground state electron configuration: [Ne] $3s^2 3p^5$
Term symbol: $^2P_{3/2}$
Electron affinity $(M \rightarrow M^-)$/kJ mol^{-1}: 349.0

Main lines in atomic spectrum

Wavelength/nm	Species
479.455	II
489.677	II
542.323	II
837.574	I
858.597	I

Ionization energies/kJ mol^{-1}

1. $M \rightarrow M^+$	1251.1	6. $M^{5+} \rightarrow M^{6+}$ 9 362
2. $M^+ \rightarrow M^{2+}$	2297	7. $M^{6+} \rightarrow M^{7+}$ 11 020
3. $M^{2+} \rightarrow M^{3+}$	3826	8. $M^{7+} \rightarrow M^{8+}$ 33 610
4. $M^{3+} \rightarrow M^{4+}$	5158	9. $M^{8+} \rightarrow M^{9+}$ 38 600
5. $M^{4+} \rightarrow M^{5+}$	6540	10. $M^{9+} \rightarrow M^{10+}$ 43 960

Environmental properties

Biological role

Essential to many species including humans; very toxic as Cl_2 gas

Levels in humans:
Muscle/p.p.m.: 2000–5200
Bone/p.p.m.: 900
Blood/mg dm^{-3}: 2890
Daily dietary intake:
  3.00–6.60 g
Toxic intake: non-toxic
Total mass of element in average (70 kg) person: 95 g

Abundances

Sun (relative to H = 1×10^{12}):
  3.2×10^5
Earth's crust/p.p.m.: 130
Seawater/p.p.m.: 18 000
Residence time/years: 4×10^8
Classification: accumulating
Oxidation state: $-I$
Atmosphere: traces as organo-chlorine compounds

Geological data

Chief deposits and sources:
rock salt [NaCl]
World production of NaCl/
tonnes y^{-1}: 168×10^6
Reserves/tonnes: $> 10^{13}$

Cr

Atomic number: 24

Relative atomic mass ($^{12}C = 12.0000$): 51.9961

Chemical properties

Hard blue-white metal. Soluble in HCl and H_2SO_4 but not HNO_3, H_3PO_4 or $HClO_4$ due to formation of protective layer. Resists oxidation in air. Main use in alloys, chrome plating, and metal ceramics.

Radii/pm: Cr^{2+} 84; Cr^{3+} 64; Cr^{4+} 56; atomic 124.9

Electronegativity: 1.66 (Pauling); 1.56 (Allred); 3.72 eV (absolute)

Effective nuclear charge: 3.45 (Slater); 5.13 (Clementi); 6.92 (Froese-Fischer)

Standard reduction potentials $E^{\ominus}/V$

	VI	V	IV	III	II	0

Acid solution

$$Cr_2O_7^{2-} \xrightarrow{0.55} CrO_4^{3-} \xrightarrow{1.34} Cr(IV) \xrightarrow{2.10} Cr^{3+} \xrightarrow{-0.424} Cr^{2+} \xrightarrow{-0.90} Cr$$

(0.95 over VI–V; 1.38 below; 1.72 below; −0.74 over III–II)

Alkaline solution

$$CrO_4^{2-} \xrightarrow{-0.11} Cr(OH)_3 \xrightarrow{-1.33} Cr$$
$$\xrightarrow{-0.72} Cr(OH)_4^- \xrightarrow{-1.33}$$

Oxidation states

Cr^{-II}	(d^8)	$Na_2[Cr(CO)_5]$
Cr^{-I}	(d^7)	$Na_2[Cr_2(CO)_{10}]$
Cr^0	(d^6)	$Cr(CO)_6$
Cr^{I}	(d^5)	$[Cr(bipyridyl)_3]^+$
Cr^{II}	(d^4)	CrO, CrF_2, $CrCl_2$ etc., CrS
Cr^{III}	(d^3)	Cr_2O_3, CrF_3, $CrCl_3$ etc. $[Cr(H_2O)_6]^{3+}$ (aq), $Cr(OH)_3$, salts, complexes
Cr^{IV}	(d^2)	CrO_2, CrF_4
Cr^{V}	(d^1)	CrF_5
Cr^{VI}	(d^0)	CrO_3, $Na_2Cr_2O_7$, CrO_4^{2-}, $CrOF_4$

Physical properties

Melting point/K: 2130 ± 20

Boiling point/K: 2945

ΔH_{fusion}/kJ mol^{-1}: 15.3

ΔH_{vap}/kJ mol^{-1}: 348.78

Thermodynamic properties (298.15 K, 0.1 MPa)

State	$\Delta_f H^{\ominus}$/kJ mol^{-1}	$\Delta_f G^{\ominus}$/kJ mol^{-1}	$S^{\ominus}$/J K^{-1} mol^{-1}	C_p/J K^{-1} mol^{-1}
Solid	0	0	23.47	23.35
Gas	396.6	351.8	174.50	20.79

Density/kg m^{-3}: 7190 [293 K]; 6460 [liquid at m.p.]

Thermal conductivity/W m^{-1} K^{-1}: 93.7 [300 K]

Electrical resistivity/Ω m: 12.7×10^{-8} [273 K]

Mass magnetic susceptibility/kg^{-1} m^3: $+4.45 \times 10^{-8}$ (s)

Molar volume/cm^3: 7.23

Coefficient of linear thermal expansion/K^{-1}: 6.2×10^{-6}

Crystal structure (cell dimensions/pm), space group

---

b.c.c. ($a = 288.46$), Im3m

X-ray diffraction: mass absorption coefficients (μ/ρ)/cm^2 g^{-1}:
CuK_α 260 MoK_α 31.1

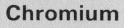

Nuclear properties

Thermal neutron capture cross-section/barns: 3.1
Number of isotopes (including nuclear isomers): 13
Isotope mass range: 45→57

Key isotopes

Nuclide	Atomic mass	Natural abundance (%)	Half-life $T_{1/2}$	Decay mode and energy (MeV)	Nuclear spin I	Nuclear magnetic moment μ	Uses
^{50}Cr	49.946 046	4.35	stable		0+		
^{51}Cr	50.944 768	0	27.70d	EC (0.751); γ	7/2−	±0.934	tracer, medical
^{52}Cr	51.940 509	83.79	stable		0+		
^{53}Cr	52.940 651	9.50	stable		3/2+	−0.47454	NMR
^{54}Cr	53.938 882	2.36	stable		0+		

NMR

^{53}Cr

Relative sensitivity (^{1}H = 1.00)	9.03×10^{-4}
Receptivity (^{13}C = 1.00)	0.49
Magnetogyric ratio/rad T^{-1} s^{-1}	-1.5120×10^7
Quadrupole moment/m^2	$\pm 0.3 \times 10^{-28}$
Frequency (^{1}H = 100 MHz; 2.3488 T)/MHz	5.652

Reference: CrO_4^{2-} (aq)

Electron shell properties

Ground state electron configuration: [Ar]3d^{5}4s^1
Term symbol: $^7S_3$
Electron affinity (M→M$^-$)/kJ mol^{-1}: 64.3

Main lines in atomic spectrum

Wavelength/nm	Species
357.869 (AA)	I
359.349	I
360.533	I
425.435	I
427.480	I
428.972	I
520.844	I

Ionization energies/kJ mol^{-1}

1. M → M$^+$	652.7	6. M^{5+} → M^{6+}	8 739
2. M$^+$ → M^{2+}	1592	7. M^{6+} → M^{7+}	15 550
3. M^{2+} → M^{3+}	2987	8. M^{7+} → M^{8+}	17 830
4. M^{3+} → M^{4+}	4740	9. M^{8+} → M^{9+}	20 220
5. M^{4+} → M^{5+}	6690	10. M^{9+} → M^{10+}	23 580

Environmental properties

Biological role

Essential to some species, including humans; stimulatory; carcinogenic

Levels in humans:
Muscle/p.p.m.: 0.024–0.84
Bone/p.p.m.: 0.1–33
Blood/mg dm^{-3}: 0.006–0.11
Daily dietary intake:
0.01–1.2 mg
Toxic intake: 200 mg
Lethal intake: > 3.0 g
Total mass of element in average (70 kg) person: n.a.

Abundances

Sun (relative to H = 1 × 10^{12}):
5.13 × 10^5
Earth's crust/p.p.m.: c. 100
Seawater/p.p.m.:
Atlantic surface: 1.8 × 10^{-4}
Atlantic deep: 2.3 × 10^{-4}
Pacific surface: 1.5 × 10^{-4}
Pacific deep: 2.5 × 10^{-4}
Residence time/years: 10 000
Classification: recycled
Oxidation state: VI

Geological data

Chief ore: chromite [FeCr$_2$O$_4$]
World production of Cr metal/tonnes y^{-1}: c. 20 000
World production of chromite/tonnes y^{-1}: 9.6 × 10^6
Reserves/tonnes: 1 × 10^9

Chemical properties

Lustrous, silvery-blue, hard metal; ferromagnetic. Stable in air, slowly attacked by dilute acids. ^{60}Co useful radio-isotope. Used in alloys for magnets, ceramics, catalysts, and paints

Radii/pm: Co^{2+} 82; Co^{3+} 64; atomic 125.3; covalent 116

Electronegativity: 1.88 (Pauling); 1.70 (Allred); 4.3 eV (absolute)

Effective nuclear charge: 3.90 (Slater); 5.58 (Clementi); 7.63 (Froese-Fischer)

Standard reduction potentials $E^{\ominus}$/V

	IV		III		II		0
Acid solution	CoO_2	$\underline{1.416}$	Co^{3+}	$\underline{1.92}$	Co^{2+}	$\underline{-0.277}$	Co
Alkaline solution	CoO_2	$\underline{0.7}$	$Co(OH)_3$	$\underline{0.17}$	$Co(OH)_2$	$\underline{-0.733}$	Co

Oxidation states

Co^{-I}	(d^{10})	rare $[Co(CO)_4]^-$
Co^0	(d^9)	rare $[Co_2(CO)_8]$
Co^I	(d^8)	rare $[Co(NCCH_2)_5]^+$
Co^{II}	(d^7)	CoO, Co_3O_4 ($= Co^{II}Co_2^{III}O_4$), $Co(OH)_2$, CoF_2, $CoCl_2$ etc., $[Co(H_2O)_6]^{2+}$ (aq), many salts and complexes
Co^{III}	(d^6)	$Co(OH)_3$, CoF_3, $[Co(H_2O)_6]^{3+}$ (aq), $[Co(NH_3)_6]^{3+}$, many complexes
Co^{IV}	(d^5)	CoO_2?, CoS_2, $[CoF_6]^{2-}$
Co^V	(d^4)	K_3CoO_4

Physical properties

Melting point/K: 1768

Boiling point/K: 3143

ΔH_{fusion}/kJ mol^{-1}: 15.2

ΔH_{vap}/kJ mol^{-1}: 382.4

Thermodynamic properties (298.15 K, 0.1 MPa)

State	$\Delta_f H^{\ominus}$/kJ mol^{-1}	$\Delta_f G^{\ominus}$/kJ mol^{-1}	$S^{\ominus}$/J K^{-1} mol^{-1}	C_p/J K^{-1} mol^{-1}
Solid	0	0	30.04	24.81
Gas	424.7	380.3	179.515	23.020

Density/kg m^{-3}: 8900 [293 K]; 7670 [liquid at m.p.]

Thermal conductivity/W m^{-1} K^{-1}: 100 [300 K]

Electrical resistivity/Ω m: 6.24×10^{-8} [293 K]

Mass magnetic susceptibility/kg^{-1} m^3: Ferromagnetic

Molar volume/cm^3: 6.62

Coefficient of linear thermal expansion/K^{-1}: 13.36×10^{-6}

Crystal structure (cell dimensions/pm), space group

α-Co f.c.c. ($a = 354.41$), Fm3m

ε-Co h.c.p. ($a = 250.7$; $c = 406.9$), P6$_3$/mmc

$T (\alpha \rightarrow \varepsilon) = 690$ K

X-ray diffraction: mass absorption coefficients (μ/ρ)/cm^2 g^{-1}: CuK$_\alpha$ 313 MoK$_\alpha$ 42.5

Thermal neutron capture cross-section/barns: 37.2
Number of isotopes (including nuclear isomers): 17
Isotope mass range: 35m→64

Key isotopes

Nuclide	Atomic mass	Natural abundance (%)	Half-life $T_{1/2}$	Decay mode and energy (MeV)	Nuclear spin I	Nuclear magnetic moment μ	Uses
^{56}Co	55.939 841	0	77.7d	β^+ (4.566); EC; γ	0+	±3.830	tracer
^{57}Co	56.936 294	0	271d	EC (0.836); γ	7/2−	+4.733	tracer, medical
^{58}Co	57.935 755	0	70.91d	β^+ (2.30); EC; γ	2+	+4.044	tracer, medical
^{59}Co	58.933 198	100	stable		7/2−	+4.627	NMR
^{60}Co	59.933 819	0	5.272y	β^- (2.824); γ	5+	+3.799	tracer, medical

NMR

	^{59}Co
Relative sensitivity (^{1}H = 1.00)	0.28
Receptivity (^{13}C = 1.00)	1570
Magnetogyric ratio/rad T^{-1} s^{-1}	6.3472×10^7
Quadrupole moment/m^2	0.40×10^{-28}
Frequency (^{1}H = 100 MHz; 2.3488 T)/MHz	23.614

Reference: K$_3$Co(CN)$_6$

Ground state electron configuration: [Ar] 3d^{7}4s^2
Term symbol: ^{4}F$_{9/2}$
Electron affinity (M→M$^-$)/kJ mol^{-1}: 63.8

Main lines in atomic spectrum

Wavelength/nm	Species
240.725 (AA)	I
242.493	I
340.512	I
344.364	I
345.350	I
350.228	I
356.938	I

Ionization energies/kJ mol^{-1}

1. M → M$^+$ 760.0	6. M^{5+}→M^{6+} 9 840
2. M$^+$→M^{2+} 1646	7. M^{6+}→M^{7+} 12 400
3. M^{2+}→M^{3+} 3232	8. M^{7+}→M^{8+} 15 100
4. M^{3+}→M^{4+} 4950	9. M^{8+}→M^{9+} 17 900
5. M^{4+}→M^{5+} 7670	10. M^{9+}→M^{10+} 26 600

Environmental properties

Biological role

Essential to most species, including humans; carcinogenic

Levels in humans:
Muscle/p.p.m.: 0.028–0.65
Bone/p.p.m.: 0.01–0.04
Blood/mg dm^{-3}: 0.0002–0.04
Daily dietary intake: 0.005–1.8 mg
Toxic intake: 500 mg
Lethal intake: n.a.
Total mass of element in average (70 kg) person: 1.5 mg

Abundances

Sun (relative to H = 1 × 10^{12}): 7.94 × 10^4
Earth's crust/p.p.m.: 20
Seawater/p.p.m.:
Atlantic surface: n.a.
Atlantic deep: n.a.
Pacific surface: 6.9 × 10^{-6}
Pacific deep: 1.1 × 10^{-6}
Residence time/years: 40
Classification: scavenged
Oxidation state: II

Geological data

Chief ores: smaltite [CoAs$_2$]; cobaltite [CoAsS]; linnaeite [Co$_3$S$_4$]
World production/tonnes y^{-1}: 19 000
Reserves/tonnes: n.a.

Cu

Atomic number: **29**

Relative atomic mass ($^{12}C = 12.0000$): **63.546**

Chemical properties

Reddish metal, malleable and ductile, with high electrical and thermal conductivities. Resistant to air and water but slowly weathers to green patina of carbonate. (Historically important alloy, bronze.) Used as wire for conducting electricity; coins; alloys, etc.

Radii/pm: Cu^+ 96; Cu^{2+} 72; atomic 127.8; covalent 117

Electronegativity: 1.90 (Pauling); 1.75 (Allred); 4.48 eV (absolute)

Effective nuclear charge: 4.20 (Slater); 5.84 (Clementi); 8.07 (Froese–Fischer)

Standard reduction potentials $E^{\ominus}$/V

II	I	0

$$Cu^{2+} \xrightarrow{\quad 0.159 \quad} Cu^+ \xrightarrow{\quad 0.520 \quad} Cu$$ (overall 0.340)

$$Cu(NH_3)_4^{2+} \xrightarrow{\quad 0.10 \quad} Cu(NH_3)_4^+ \xrightarrow{\quad -0.100 \quad} Cu$$

$$Cu(CN)_2 \xrightarrow{\quad 1.12 \quad} Cu(CN)_2^- \xrightarrow{\quad -0.44 \quad} Cu$$

Oxidation states

Cu^0	$(d^{10} s^1)$	rare, $[Cu(CO)_3]$ at 10 K
Cu^I	(d^{10})	Cu_2O, CuCl, $K[Cu(CN)_2]$
Cu^{II}	**(d^9)**	CuO, $CuCl_2$, Cu^{2+}(aq), Cu^{2+} salts
Cu^{III}	(d^8)	$K_3[CuF_6]$
Cu^{IV}	(d^7)	rare $Cs_2[CuF_6]$

Physical properties

Melting point/K: 1356.6

Boiling point/K: 2840

ΔH_{fusion}/kJ mol^{-1}: 13.0

ΔH_{vap}/kJ mol^{-1}: 304.6

Thermodynamic properties (298.15 K, 0.1 MPa)

State	$\Delta_f H^{\ominus}$/kJ mol^{-1}	$\Delta_f G^{\ominus}$/kJ mol^{-1}	$S^{\ominus}$/J K^{-1} mol^{-1}	C_p/J K^{-1} mol^{-1}
Solid	0	0	33.150	24.435
Gas	338.32	298.58	166.38	20.786

Density/kg m^{-3}: 8960 [293 K]; 7940 [liquid at m.p.]

Thermal conductivity/W m^{-1} K^{-1}: 401 [300 K]

Electrical resistivity/Ω m: 1.6730×10^{-8} [293 K]

Mass magnetic susceptibility/kg^{-1} m^3: -1.081×10^{-9} (s)

Molar volume/cm^3: 7.09

Coefficient of linear thermal expansion/K^{-1}: 16.5×10^{-6}

Crystal structure (cell dimensions/pm), space group

f.c.c. ($a = 361.47$), Fm3m

X-ray diffraction: mass absorption coefficients (μ/ρ)/cm^2 g^{-1}: CuK_α 52.9 MoK_α 50.9

Copper

Thermal neutron capture cross-section/barns: 3.78
Number of isotopes (including nuclear isomers): 18
Isotope mass range: $58 \rightarrow 73$

Key isotopes

Nuclide	Atomic mass	Natural abundance (%)	Half-life $T_{1/2}$	Decay mode and energy (MeV)	Nuclear spin I	Nuclear magnetic moment μ	Uses
^{63}Cu	62.939 598	69.17	stable		$3/2-$	$+2.2233$	NMR
^{64}Cu	63.929 765	0	12.701h	β^- (0.578) 39%;1+ β^+(1.675) 19%; EC 41%; γ		-0.217	tracer, medical
^{65}Cu	64.927 793	30.83	stable		$3/2-$	$+2.3817$	NMR
^{67}Cu	66.927 747	0	61.9h	β^- (0.58); γ	$3/2-$		tracer

NMR

	^{63}Cu	^{65}Cu
Relative sensitivity (^{1}H = 1.00)	9.31×10^{-2}	0.11
Receptivity (^{13}C = 1.00)	365	201
Magnetogyric ratio/rad T^{-1} s^{-1}	7.0965×10^7	7.6018×10^7
Quadrupole moment/m^2	-0.211×10^{-28}	0.195×10^{-28}
Frequency (^{1}H = 100 MHz; 2.3488 T)/MHz	26.505	28.394

Reference: Cu(MeCN)$_4^+$BF$_4^-$ in MeCN

Ground state electron configuration: $[Ar]3d^{10}4s^1$
Term symbol: $^2S_{1/2}$
Electron affinity (M$\rightarrow$M$^-$)/kJ mol^{-1}: 118.5

Main lines in atomic spectrum

Wavelength/nm	Species
216.509	I
217.894	I
324.754 (AA)	I
327.396	I
521.820	I

Ionization energies/kJ mol^{-1}

1. M $\rightarrow$ M$^+$	745.4	6. M$^{5+}\rightarrow$M^{6+} (9 940)
2. M$^+\rightarrow$M^{2+}	1958	7. M$^{6+}\rightarrow$M^{7+} (13 400)
3. M$^{2+}\rightarrow$M^{3+}	3554	8. M$^{7+}\rightarrow$M^{8+} (16 000)
4. M$^{3+}\rightarrow$M^{4+}	5326	9. M$^{8+}\rightarrow$M^{9+} (19 200)
5. M$^{4+}\rightarrow$M^{5+}	7709	10. M$^{9+}\rightarrow$M^{10+} (22 400)

Environmental properties

Biological role	Abundances	Geological data
Essential to all species	Sun (relative to H = 1×10^{12}): 1.15×10^4	Chief ores: chalcopyrite [CuFeS$_2$]; chalcocite [Cu$_2$S]; cuprite [Cu$_2$O]; malachite [Cu$_2$(CO$_3$)(OH)$_2$]
Levels in humans: Muscle/p.p.m.: 10 Bone/p.p.m.: 1–26 Blood/mg dm^{-3}: 1.01 Daily dietary intake: 0.50–6 mg Toxic intake: >250 mg Lethal intake: n.a. Total mass of element in average (70 kg) person: 72 mg	**Earth's crust**/p.p.m.: 50 **Seawater**/p.p.m.: Atlantic surface: 8.0×10^{-5} Atlantic deep: 12×10^{-5} Pacific surface: 8.0×10^{-5} Pacific deep: 28×10^{-5} Residence time/years: 3 000 Classification: recycled Oxidation state: II	**World production**/tonnes y^{-1}: $>7 \times 10^6$ **Reserves**/tonnes: 310×10^6

Chemical properties

Radioactive, silvery metal. Attacked by oxygen, steam, and acids but not alkalis.

Radii/pm: Cm^{2+} 119; Cm^{3+} 99; Cm^{4+} 88

Electronegativity: 1.3 (Pauling); n.a. (Allred)

Effective nuclear charge: 1.80 (Slater)

Standard reduction potentials $E^{\ominus}/V$

	IV		III		0
Acid solution	Cm^{4+}	$\underline{\quad 3.2 \quad}$	Cm^{3+}	$\underline{\quad -2.06 \quad}$	Cm
Alkaline solution	CmO_2	$\underline{\quad 0.7 \quad}$	$Cm(OH)_3$	$\underline{\quad -2.5 \quad}$	Cm

Oxidation states

Cm^{II}	$(f^7 d^1)$	CmO
Cm^{III}	(f^7)	Cm_2O_3, $Cm(OH)_3$, CmF_3, $CmCl_3$ etc., Cm^{3+} (aq)
Cm^{IV}	(f^6)	CmO_2, CmF_4, Cm^{4+} (aq) very unstable

Physical properties

Melting point/K: 1610 ± 40

Boiling point/K: n.a.

ΔH_{fusion}/kJ mol^{-1}: n.a.

ΔH_{vap}/kJ mol^{-1}: n.a.

Thermodynamic properties (298.15 K, 0.1 MPa)

State	$\Delta_f H^{\ominus}$/kJ mol^{-1}	$\Delta_f G^{\ominus}$/kJ mol^{-1}	$S^{\ominus}$/J K^{-1} mol^{-1}	C_p/J K^{-1} mol^{-1}
Solid	0	0	n.a.	n.a.
Gas	n.a.	n.a.	n.a.	n.a.

Density/kg m^{-3}: 13 300 [293 K]

Thermal conductivity/W m^{-1} K^{-1}: 10 (est.) [300 K]

Electrical resistivity/Ω m: n.a.

Mass magnetic susceptibility/kg^{-1} m^3: n.a.

Molar volume/cm^3: 18.6

Coefficient of linear thermal expansion/K^{-1}: n.a.

Crystal structure (cell dimensions/pm), space group

n.a.

X-ray diffraction: mass absorption coefficients (μ/ρ)/cm^2 g^{-1}:
n.a.

Prepared by G. T. Seaborg, R. A. James, and A. Ghiorso in 1944
at Berkeley, California, USA
[Named after Pierre and Marie Curie]

Curium

Thermal neutron capture cross-section/barns: 60 (^{247}Cm)
Number of isotopes (including nuclear isomers): 14
Isotope mass range: 238→251

**Nuclear
properties**

Key isotopes

Nuclide	Atomic mass	Natural abundance (%)	Half-life $T_{1/2}$	Decay mode and energy (MeV)	Nuclear spin I	Nuclear magnetic moment μ	Uses
^{242}Cm	242.058 830	0	162.9d	α (6.126); γ	0+		available
^{244}Cm	244.062 747	0	18.11y	α (5.902); γ	0+		in mg quantities
^{245}Cm	245.065 483	0	8.5×10^3y	α (5.623)	7/2+	0.5	
^{246}Cm	246.067 218	0	4.78×10^3y	α (5.476)	0+		
^{247}Cm	247.070 347	0	1.56×10^7y	α (5.352); γ	9/2−	+0.37	
^{248}Cm	248.072 343	0	3.4×10^5y	α (5.162); SF	0+		

Ground state electron configuration: [Rn]$5f^76d^17s^2$
Term symbol: $^9D_2$
Electron affinity (M→M$^-$)/kJ mol^{-1}: n.a.

**Electron
shell
properties**

Main lines in atomic spectrum*

Wavelength/nm	Species
299.939	I
310.969	I
311.641	I
313.716	I
314.733	I
315.510	I
315.860	I

* First seven lines associated with neutral atom.

Ionization energies/kJ mol^{-1}

1. M →M$^+$ 581
2. M$^+$→M^{2+}
3. M^{2+}→M^{3+}
4. M^{3+}→M^{4+}
5. M^{4+}→M^{5+}

Environmental properties

Biological role	Abundances	Geological data
None; never encountered, but would be toxic due to radioactivity	**Sun** (relative to H $= 1 \times 10^{12}$): n.a.	**Chief source:** None. Obtained in gram quantities as ^{242}Cm and ^{244}Cm from neutron bombardment of ^{239}Pu
Levels in humans: nil	**Earth's crust**/p.p.m.: nil	
	Seawater/p.p.m.: nil	

Dy

Atomic number: 66

Relative atomic mass (^{12}C = 12.0000): 162.50

Chemical properties

Reactive, hard, silvery metal of the rare earth group. Oxidized by oxygen, reacts rapidly with water, dissolves in acids. Used in alloys for making magnets.

Radii/pm: Dy^{3+} 91; atomic 177.3; covalent 159

Electronegativity: 1.22 (Pauling); 1.10 (Allred)

Effective nuclear charge: 2.85 (Slater); 8.34 (Clementi); 11.49 (Froese-Fischer)

Standard reduction potentials $E^{\ominus}$/V

	IV		III		II		0
					-2.29		
Acid solution	Dy^{4+}	$\underline{5.7}$	Dy^{3+}	$\underline{-2.5}$	Dy^{2+}	$\underline{-2.2}$	Dy
Alkaline solution	DyO_2	$\underline{3.5}$	$Dy(OH)_3$		-2.80		Dy

Oxidation states

Dy^{II}	(f^{10})	$DyCl_2$, DyI_2
Dy^{III}	(f^9)	Dy_2O_3, $Dy(OH)_3$, DyF_3, $DyCl_3$ etc., $[Dy(H_2O)_x]^{3+}$ (aq), Dy^{3+} salts, $DyCl_6^{3-}$
Dy^{IV}	(f^8)	Cs_3DyF_7

Physical properties

Melting point/K: 1685

Boiling point/K: 2835

ΔH_{fusion}/kJ mol^{-1}: 17.2

ΔH_{vap}/kJ mol^{-1}: 293

Thermodynamic properties (298.15 K, 0.1 MPa)

State	$\Delta_f H^{\ominus}$/kJ mol^{-1}	$\Delta_f G^{\ominus}$/kJ mol^{-1}	$S^{\ominus}$/J K^{-1} mol^{-1}	C_p/J K^{-1} mol^{-1}
Solid	0	0	74.77	28.16
Gas	290.4	254.4	196.63	20.79

Density/kg m^{-3}: 8550 [293 K]

Thermal conductivity/W m^{-1} K^{-1}: 10.7 [300 K]

Electrical resistivity/Ω m: 57.0×10^{-8} [273 K]

Mass magnetic susceptibility/kg^{-1} m^3: $+8.00 \times 10^{-6}$ (s)

Molar volume/cm^3: 19.00

Coefficient of linear thermal expansion/K^{-1}: 10.0×10^{-6}

Crystal structure (cell dimensions/pm), space group

Orthorhombic ($a = 359.5$; $b = 618.3$; $c = 567.7$), Cmcm
h.c.p. ($a = 359.03$; $c = 564.75$), P6$_3$/mmc
b.c.c. ($a = 398$), Im3m

T (orthorhombic→h.c.p.) = 86 K
High pressure form: ($a = 334$, $c = 245$), R$\bar{3}$m

X-ray diffraction: mass absorption coefficients (μ/ρ)/cm^2 g^{-1}:
CuK$_\alpha$ 286   MoK$_\alpha$ 70.6

Dysprosium

Thermal neutron capture cross-section/barns: 920
Number of isotopes (including nuclear isomers). 24
Isotope mass range: 147m→168

Key isotopes

Nuclide	Atomic mass	Natural abundance (%)	Half-life $T_{1/2}$	Decay mode and energy (MeV)	Nuclear spin I	Nuclear magnetic moment μ	Uses
^{154}Dy	153.924 429	0	3×10^6y	α	0+		
^{156}Dy	155.925 277	0.06	stable		0+		
^{158}Dy	157.924 403	0.10	stable		0+		
^{160}Dy	159.925 193	2.34	stable		0+		
^{161}Dy	160.926 930	18.9	stable		5/2+	−0.48	NMR
^{162}Dy	161.926 795	25.5	stable		0+		
^{163}Dy	162.928 728	24.9	stable		5/2−	+0.673	NMR
^{164}Dy	163.929 171	28.2	stable		0+		

NMR

	^{161}Dy	^{163}Dy
Relative sensitivity (^{1}H = 1.00)	4.17×10^{-4}	1.12×10^{-3}
Receptivity (^{13}C = 1.00)	0.509	1.79
Magnetogyric ratio/rad T^{-1} s^{-1}	-0.9206×10^7	1.2750×10^7
Quadrupole moment/m^2	1.4×10^{-28}	1.6×10^{-28}
Frequency (^{1}H − 100 MHz; 2.3488 T)/MHz	3.294	4.583

Ground state electron configuration: $[Xe]4f^{10}6s^2$
Term symbol: $^5I_8$
Electron affinity (M→M$^-$)/kJ mol^{-1}: n.a.

Main lines in atomic spectrum

Wavelength/nm	Species
353.170	II
364.540	II
394.468	II
396.839	II
404.597	I
418.682	I
421.172 (AA)	I

Ionization energies/kJ mol^{-1}

1. M →M$^+$	571.9	6. M^{5+}→M^{6+}
2. M$^+$→M^{2+}	1126	7. M^{6+}→M^{7+}
3. M^{2+}→M^{3+}	2200	8. M^{7+}→M^{8+}
4. M^{3+}→M^{4+}	4001	9. M^{8+}→M^{9+}
5. M^{4+}→M^{5+}		10. M^{9+}→M^{10+}

Environmental properties

Biological role

None; low toxicity; stimulatory

Levels in humans:
Muscle/p.p.m.: n.a., but low

Abundances

Sun (relative to H = 1×10^{12}): 11.5

Earth's crust/p.p.m.: 6

Seawater/p.p.m.:
Atlantic surface: 8×10^{-7}
Atlantic deep: 9.6×10^{-7}
Residence time/years: 300
Classification: recycled
Oxidation state: III

Geological data

Chief deposits and sources:
monazite
$[(Ce, La, etc.)PO_4]$;
bastnaesite
$[(Ce, La, etc.)(CO_3)F]$

World production/tonnes y^{-1}:
c. 100

Reserves/tonnes: *c.* 10^5

Es	Atomic number: **99**
	Relative atomic mass ($^{12}C = 12.0000$): **(254)**

Chemical properties

Radioactive, silvery metal which does not occur naturally. Attacked by oxygen, steam, and acids, but not alkalis.

Radii/pm: Es^{2+} 116; Es^{3+} 98; Es^{4+} 85

Electronegativity: 1.3 (Pauling); n.a. (Allred); ≤ 3.5 eV (absolute)

Effective nuclear charge: 1.65 (Slater)

Standard reduction potentials $E^{\ominus}/V$

	III		II		0
Acid solution	Es^{3+}	$\xrightarrow{-1.5}$	Es^{2+}	$\xrightarrow{-2.2}$	Es
			$\xrightarrow{-2.0}$		

Oxidation states

Es^{II}	(f^{11})	transient state
$\mathbf{Es^{III}}$	(f^{10})	Es_2O_3, $EsCl_3$, $EsBr_3$, Es^{3+} (aq), EsOCl

Physical properties

Melting point/K: 860 ± 30

Boiling point/K: n.a.

ΔH_{fusion}/kJ mol^{-1}: n.a.

ΔH_{vap}/kJ mol^{-1}: n.a.

Thermodynamic properties (298.15 K, 0.1 MPa)

State	$\Delta_f H^{\ominus}$/kJ mol^{-1}	$\Delta_f G^{\ominus}$/kJ mol^{-1}	$S^{\ominus}$/J K^{-1} mol^{-1}	C_p/J K^{-1} mol^{-1}
Solid	0	0	n.a.	n.a.
Gas	n.a.	n.a.	n.a.	n.a.

Density/kg m^{-3}: n.a.

Thermal conductivity/W m^{-1} K^{-1}: 10 (est.) [300 K]

Electrical resistivity/Ω m: n.a.

Mass magnetic susceptibility/kg^{-1} m^3: n.a.

Molar volume/cm^3: n.a.

Coefficient of linear thermal expansion/K^{-1}: n.a.

Crystal (cell dimensions/pm), space group

cubic

X-ray diffraction: mass absorption coefficients (μ/ρ)/cm^2 g^{-1}: n.a.

Discovered in the debris of the 1952 thermonuclear explosion in
the Pacific by G. R. Choppin, S. G. Thompson, A. Ghiorso, and
B. G. Harvey
[Named after Albert Einstein]

Einsteinium

Thermal neutron capture cross-section/barns: 160 (^{253}Es)
Number of isotopes (including nuclear isomers): 17
Isotope mass range: 243→256

Nuclear properties

Key isotopes

Nuclide	Atomic mass	Natural abundance (%)	Half-life $T_{1/2}$	Decay mode and energy (MeV)	Nuclear spin I	Nuclear magnetic moment μ	Uses
^{252}Es	252.082 944	0	1.29y	α (6.739); EC; γ	5−		
^{253}Es	253.084 818	0	20.47d	α (6.739); γ	7/2+	4.10	Available
^{254}Es	254.088 019	0	275d	α (6.617); γ	7+		
^{255}Es	255.090 270	0	39.8d	β^- (0.300)	7/2+		

Ground state electron configuration: $[Rn]4f^{11}7s^2$
Term symbol: $^5I_{15/2}$
Electron affinity $(M \to M^-)$/kJ mol^{-1}: ≤ 50

Electron shell properties

Main lines in atomic spectrum

Wavelength/nm	Species
270.866	II
342.848	I
349.811	I
351.433	I
352.138	I
352.049	I
354.775	II

Ionization energies/kJ mol^{-1}

1. $M \to M^+$ 619
2. $M^+ \to M^{2+}$
3. $M^{2+} \to M^{3+}$
4. $M^{3+} \to M^{4+}$
5. $M^{4+} \to M^{5+}$

Environmental properties

Biological role
None; never encountered, but
would be toxic due to
radioactivity
Levels in humans: nil

Abundances
Sun (relative to H = 1 × 10^{12}):
n.a.
Earth's crust/p.p.m.: nil
Seawater/p.p.m.: nil

Geological data
Chief source: None; obtained
in milligram quantities as
^{253}Es from neutron
bombardment of ^{239}Pu

Er

Atomic number: 68

Relative atomic mass ($^{12}C=12.0000$): 167.26

Chemical properties

Silver-grey metal of the rare earth group. Slowly tarnishes in air, slowly reacts with water, dissolves in acids. Used in infrared absorbing glass; alloys with titanium.

Radii/pm: Er^{3+} 89; atomic 175.7; covalent 157

Electronegativity: 1.24 (Pauling); 1.11 (Allred);
≤ 3.3 eV (absolute)

Effective nuclear charge: 2.85 (Slater); 8.48 (Clementi);
11.70 (Froese-Fischer)

Standard reduction potentials $E^{\ominus}/V$

	III		0
Acid solution	Er^{3+}	$\underline{-2.32}$	Er
Alkaline solution	$Er(OH)_3$	$\underline{-2.84}$	Er

Oxidation states

Er^{III}	(f^{11})	Er_2O_3, $Er(OH)_3$, ErF_3, $ErCl_3$ etc., $[Er(H_2O)_x]^{3+}$ (aq), Er^{3+} salts, $ErCl_6^{3-}$, complexes, etc.

Physical properties

Melting point/K: 1802
Boiling point/K: 3136
ΔH_{fusion}/kJ mol^{-1}: 17.2
ΔH_{vap}/kJ mol^{-1}: 292.9

Thermodynamic properties (298.15 K, 0.1 MPa)

State	$\Delta_f H^{\ominus}$/kJ mol^{-1}	$\Delta_f G^{\ominus}$/kJ mol^{-1}	$S^{\ominus}$/J K^{-1} mol^{-1}	C_p/J K^{-1} mol^{-1}
Solid	0	0	73.18	28.12
Gas	317.1	280.7	195.59	20.79

Density/kg m^{-3}: 9066 [298 K]
Thermal conductivity/W m^{-1} K^{-1}: 14.3 [300 K]
Electrical resistivity/Ω m: 87×10^{-8} [298 K]
Mass magnetic susceptibility/kg^{-1} m^3: $+3.33 \times 10^{-6}$ (s)
Molar volume/cm^3: 18.44
Coefficient of linear thermal expansion/K^{-1}: 9.2×10^{-6}

Crystal structure (cell dimensions/pm), space group

α-Er h.c.p. ($a=355.88$; $c=558.74$), P6$_3$/mmc
β-Er b.c.c. ($a=394$), Im3m

$T(\alpha \rightarrow \beta)=1640$ K

X-ray diffraction: mass absorption coefficients (μ/ρ)/cm^2 g^{-1}:
CuK$_\alpha$ 134   MoK$_\alpha$ 77.3

Erbium

Thermal neutron capture cross-section/barns: 160
Number of isotopes (including nuclear isomers). 25
Isotope mass range: $150 \to 173$

Key isotopes

Nuclide	Atomic mass	Natural abundance (%)	Half-life $T_{1/2}$	Decay mode and energy (MeV)	Nuclear spin I	Nuclear magnetic moment μ	Uses
^{162}Er	161.928 775	0.14	stable		0+		
^{164}Er	163.929 198	1.61	stable		0+		
^{166}Er	165.930 290	33.6	stable		0+		
^{167}Er	166.932 046	22.95	stable		7/2+	−0.5665	NMR
^{168}Er	167.932 368	26.8	stable		0+		
^{169}Er	168.934 588	0	9.4d	β (0.351); γ	1/2−	+0.515	tracer
^{170}Er	169.935 461	14.9	stable		0+		
^{171}Er	170.938 027	0	7.52h	β^- (1.490); γ	5/2−	0.70	tracer

NMR

^{167}Er

Relative sensitivity (^{1}H = 1.00) 5.07×10^{-4}
Receptivity (^{13}C = 1.00) 0.665
Magnetogyric ratio/rad T^{-1} s^{-1} -0.7752×10^7
Quadrupole moment/m^2 2.83×10^{-28}
Frequency (^{1}H = 100 MHz; 2.3488 T)/MHz 2.890

Ground state electron configuration: [Xe]4f^{12}6s^2
Term symbol: ^{3}H$_6$
Electron affinity (M$\to$M$^-$)/kJ mol^{-1}: ≤ 50

Main lines in atomic spectrum

Wavelength/nm	Species
369.265	II
386.285	I
389.268	I
390.631	II
400.796 (AA)	I
415.111	I

Ionization energies/kJ mol^{-1}

1. M $\to$ M$^+$ 588.7
2. M$^+$ $\to$ M^{2+} 1151
3. M^{2+} $\to$ M^{3+} 2194
4. M^{3+} $\to$ M^{4+} 4115
5. M^{4+} $\to$ M^{5+}

Environmental properties

Biological role	Abundances	Geological data
None; low toxicity; stimulatory	**Sun** (relative to H = 1×10^{12}): 5.8	**Chief ores**: monazite [(Ce, La, etc.)PO$_4$]; bastnaesite [(Ce, La, etc.)(CO$_3$)F]
Levels in humans: n.a., but low	**Earth's crust**/p.p.m.: 3.8	**World production**/tonnes y^{-1}: c. 100
	Seawater/p.p.m.: Atlantic surface: 5.9×10^{-7} Atlantic deep: 8.6×10^{-7} Residence time/years: 400 Classification: recycled Oxidation state: III	**Reserves**/tonnes: c. 10^5

Eu

Atomic number: 63

Relative atomic mass (^{12}C = 12.0000): 151.965

 Chemical properties

Rare, and most reactive of the rare earth metals. Soft, silvery metal which reacts quickly with oxygen and water. Little used. Some used in thin-film superconductor alloy.

Radii/pm: Eu^{2+} 112; Eu^{3+} 98; atomic 204.2; covalent 185

Electronegativity: n.a. (Pauling); 1.01 (Allred);
$\leq$ 3.1 eV (absolute)

Effective nuclear charge: 2.85 (Slater); 8.11 (Clementi);
11.17 (Froese-Fischer)

Standard reduction potentials $E^{\ominus}$/V

	III		II		0
		-1.99			
Acid solution	Eu^{3+}	$\underline{\quad -0.35 \quad}$	Eu^{2+}	$\underline{\quad -2.80 \quad}$	Eu
Alkaline solution	$Eu(OH)_3$		$\underline{\quad -2.51 \quad}$		Eu

Oxidation states

Eu^{II}	(f^7)	EuO, EuS, EuF_2, $EuCl_2$ etc.
Eu^{III}	(f^6)	Eu_2O_3, $Eu(OH)_3$, EuF_3, $EuCl_3$ etc.,
		$[Eu(H_2O)_x]^{3+}$ (aq), Eu^{3+} salts, complexes

 Physical properties

Melting point/K: 1095
Boiling point/K: 1870
ΔH_{fusion}/kJ mol^{-1}:   10.5
ΔH_{vap}/kJ mol^{-1}:   175.7

Thermodynamic properties   (298.15 K, 0.1 MPa)

State	$\Delta_f H^{\ominus}$/kJ mol^{-1}	$\Delta_f G^{\ominus}$/kJ mol^{-1}	$S^{\ominus}$/J K^{-1} mol^{-1}	C_p/J K^{-1} mol^{-1}
Solid	0	0	77.78	27.66
Gas	175.3	142.2	188.795	20.786

Density/kg m^{-3}:   5243 [293 K]
Thermal conductivity/W m^{-1} K^{-1}:   13.9 [300 K]
Electrical resistivity/Ω m: 90.0×10^{-8} [298 K]
Mass magnetic susceptibility/kg^{-1} m^3: $+2.81 \times 10^{-6}$ (s)
Molar volume/cm^3:   28.98
Coefficient of linear thermal expansion/K^{-1}: 32×10^{-6}

Crystal structure (cell dimensions/pm), space group

b.c.c. (a = 458.20), Im3m

X-ray diffraction: mass absorption coefficients (μ/ρ)/cm^2 g^{-1}:
CuK$_\alpha$ 425   MoK$_\alpha$ 61.5

Discovered in 1901 by E.-A. Demarçay at Paris, France

[Named after Europe]

Europium

Thermal neutron capture cross-section/barns: 4600
Number of Isotopes (Including nuclear isomers). 26
Isotope mass range: 141m→160

Key isotopes

Nuclide	Atomic mass	Natural abundance (%)	Half-life $T_{1/2}$	Decay mode and energy (MeV)	Nuclear spin I	Nuclear magnetic moment μ	Uses
^{151}Eu	150.919 847	47.8	stable		5/2+	+3.464	NMR
^{152}Eu	151.921 742	0	13.4y	EC (1.876) 72%; β^- (1.822) 28%; γ	3−	−1.924	tracer
^{152m}Eu		0	9.3h	β^-; γ	0−		tracer
^{153}Eu	152.921 225	52.2	stable		5/2+	+1.530	NMR

NMR

	^{151}Eu	^{153}Eu
Relative sensitivity (^{1}H = 1.00)	0.18	1.52×10^{-2}
Receptivity (^{13}C = 1.00)	4.64×10^2	45.7
Magnetogyric ratio/rad T^{-1} s^{-1}	6.5477×10^7	2.9371×10^7
Quadrupole moment/m^2	1.16×10^{-28}	2.9×10^{-28}
Frequency (^{1}H = 100 MHz; 2.3488 T)/MHz	24.801	10.951

Ground state electron configuration: $[Xe]4f^76s^2$
Term symbol: $^8S_{7/2}$
Electron affinity (M→M$^-$)/kJ mol^{-1}: ≤ 50

Main lines in atomic spectrum

Wavelength/nm	Species
318.967	II
412.974	II
420.505	II
459.402 (AA)	I
462.722	I
466.187	I

Ionization energies/kJ mol^{-1}

1. M →M$^+$ 546.7
2. M$^+$→M^{2+} 1085
3. M^{2+}→M^{3+} 2404
4. M^{3+}→M^{4+} 4110
5. M^{4+}→M^{5+}

Environmental properties

Biological role	Abundances	Geological data
None; low toxicity **Levels in humans:** n.a. but low	**Sun** (relative to H = 1×10^{12}): 5 **Earth's crust**/p.p.m.: 2.1 **Seawater**/p.p.m.: Atlantic surface: 0.9×10^{-7} Atlantic deep: 1.5×10^{-7} Pacific surface: 1.0×10^{-7} Pacific deep: 2.7×10^{-7} Residence time/years: 500 Classification: recycled Oxidation state: III	**Chief deposits and sources:** monazite [(Ce, La, etc.) PO$_4$]; bastnaesite [(Ce, La, etc.)(CO$_3$)F] **World production**/tonnes y^{-1}: c. 100 **Reserves**/tonnes: c. 10^5

Fm

Atomic number: **100**

Relative atomic mass ($^{12}C = 12.0000$): **(257)**

Chemical properties

Radioactive metal which does not occur naturally, and is of research interest only.

Radii/pm: Fm^{2+} 115; Fm^{3+} 97; Fm^{4+} 84

Electronegativity: 1.3 (Pauling); n.a. (Allred)

Effective nuclear charge: 1.65 (Slater)

Standard reduction potentials $E^\ominus$/V

	III		II		0
			−1.96		
Acid solution	Fm^{3+}	−1.15	Fm^{2+}	−2.37	Fm

Oxidation states

Fm^{II}	(f^{12})	?
Fm^{III}	(f^{11})	$[Fm(H_2O)_x]^{3+}$ (aq)

Physical properties

Melting point/K: n.a.

Boiling point/K: n.a.

ΔH_{fusion}/kJ mol^{-1}: n.a.

ΔH_{vap}/kJ mol^{-1}: n.a.

Thermodynamic properties (298.15 K, 0.1 MPa)

State	$\Delta_f H^\ominus$/kJ mol^{-1}	$\Delta_f G^\ominus$/kJ mol^{-1}	$S^\ominus$/J K^{-1} mol^{-1}	C_p/J K^{-1} mol^{-1}
Solid	0	0	n.a.	n.a.
Gas	n.a.	n.a.	n.a.	n.a.

Density/kg m^{-3}: n.a.

Thermal conductivity/W m^{-1} K^{-1}: 10 (est.) [300 K]

Electrical resistivity/Ω m: n.a.

Mass magnetic susceptibility/kg^{-1} m^3: n.a.

Molar volume/cm^3: n.a.

Coefficient of linear thermal expansion/K^{-1}: n.a.

Crystal structure (cell dimensions/pm), space group

n.a.

X-ray diffraction: mass absorption coefficients (μ/ρ)/cm^2 g^{-1}:
n.a.

Fermium

Thermal neutron capture cross-section/barns: 5800 (^{257}Fm)

Number of isotopes (including nuclear isomers). 18

Isotope mass range: 243→258

Nuclear properties

Key isotopes

Nuclide	Atomic mass	Natural abundance (%)	Half-life $T_{1/2}$	Decay mode and energy (MeV)	Nuclear spin I	Nuclear magnetic moment μ
^{253}Fm	253.085 173	0	3d	EC (0.334) 88%; α (7.200) 12%; γ	1/2+	
^{254}Fm	254.086 846	0	3.24h	α (7.303)	0+	
^{255}Fm	255.089 948	0	20.1h	α (7.240)	7/2+	
^{257}Fm	257.075 099	0	100.5d	α (6.871); γ	9/2+	

Ground state electron configuration: [Rn]$5f^{12}7s^2$

Term symbol: $^3H_6$

Electron affinity (M→M$^-$)/kJ mol^{-1}: n.a.

Electron shell properties

Main lines in atomic spectrum		Ionization energies/kJ mol^{-1}
Wavelength/nm	Species	1. M $\rightarrow$ M$^+$ 627
		2. M$^+ \rightarrow$ M^{2+}
n.a.		3. M$^{2+} \rightarrow$ M^{3+}
		4. M$^{3+} \rightarrow$ M^{4+}
		5. M$^{4+} \rightarrow$ M^{5+}

Environmental properties

Biological role	Abundances	Geological data
None; never encountered, but would be toxic due to radioactivity **Levels in humans:** nil	**Sun** (relative to H − 1 × 10^{12}): n.a. **Earth's crust**/p.p.m.: nil **Seawater**/p.p.m.: nil	**Chief source:** Obtained in microgram quantities as ^{253}Fm from neutron bombardment of ^{239}Pu

F

Atomic number: 9

Relative atomic mass ($^{12}C = 12.0000$): **18.998 4032**

Chemical properties

Pale yellow gas, F_2, most reactive of all elements and the strongest commercially available oxidant. Produced by electrolysis of molten KF.2HF. Used to make UF_6, SF_6, and fluorinating agents such as ClF_3. Organic compounds, polymers, and salts all used, notably CaF_2 as flux in metallurgy, and AlF_3 in aluminium production.

Radii/pm: F^- 133; covalent 58; atomic 70.9; van der Waals 135

Electronegativity: 3.98 (Pauling); 4.10 (Allred);
10.41 eV (absolute)

Effective nuclear charge: 5.20 (Slater); 5.10 (Clementi);
4.61 (Froese-Fischer)

Standard reduction potentials $E^\ominus$/V

$$
\begin{array}{ll}
0 & -I \\
F_2 \xrightarrow{\ 2.866\ } F^- \text{ (aq)} \\
F_2 \xrightarrow{\ 2.979\ } HF_2^- \\
F_2 \xrightarrow{\ 3.053\ } HF \text{ (aq)}
\end{array}
$$

Oxidation states

F^{-I}	([Ne])	F^- (aq), HF, KHF_2, CaF_2
		many salts and derivatives
		of other elements

Covalent bonds r/pm E/kJ mol^{-1}

	r/pm	E/kJ mol^{-1}
F–F	141.7	159
F–O	147	190
F–N	137	272

For other bonds see other elements

Physical properties

Melting point/K: 53.53	**Critical temperature**/K: 144.3
Boiling point/K: 85.01	**Critical pressure**/kPa: 5220
ΔH_{fusion}/kJ mol^{-1}: 5.10	**Critical volume**/cm^3 mol^{-1}: 66.2
ΔH_{vap}/kJ mol^{-1}: 6.548	

Thermodynamic properties   (298.15 K, 0.1 MPa)

State	$\Delta_f H^\ominus$/kJ mol^{-1}	$\Delta_f G^\ominus$/kJ mol^{-1}	$S^\ominus$/J K^{-1} mol^{-1}	C_p/J K^{-1} mol^{-1}
Gas (F_2)	0	0	202.78	31.30
Gas atoms	78.99	61.91	158.754	22.744

Density/kg m^{-3}: n.a. [solid]; 1516 [liquid, 85 K]; 1.696 [gas, 273 K]

Thermal conductivity/W m^{-1} K^{-1}:   0.0279 [300 K];
0.0248 [273 K]

Mass magnetic susceptibility/kg^{-1} m^3:   n.a.

Molar volume/cm^3:   18.05 [85 K]

Crystal structure (cell dimensions/pm), space group

α-F_2 monoclinic ($a = 550$, $b = 328$, $c = 728$, $\beta = 102.17°$, C2/C
β-F_2 cubic ($a = 667$), Pm3n

$T(\alpha \rightarrow \beta) = 45.6$ K

X-ray diffraction: mass absorption coefficients (μ/ρ)/cm^2 g^{-1}:
CuK$_\alpha$ 16.4   MoK$_\alpha$ 1.80

First isolated in 1886 by H. Moissan at Paris, France

[Latin, *fluere* = to flow]

Fluorine

Thermal neutron capture cross-section/barns: 0.0096
Number of isotopes (including nuclear isomers). 7
Isotope mass range: 17→23

Key isotopes

Nuclide	Atomic mass	Natural abundance (%)	Half-life $T_{1/2}$	Decay mode and energy (MeV)	Nuclear spin I	Nuclear magnetic moment μ	Uses
^{18}F	18.000 937	0	109.8m	β^+ (1.655), EC (3%), no γ			tracer, medical
^{19}F	18.998 403	100	stable		1/2+	+2.6887	NMR

NMR

	^{19}F
Relative sensitivity (^{1}H = 1.00)	0.83
Receptivity (^{13}C = 1.00)	4730
Magnetogyric ratio/rad T^{-1} s^{-1}	25.1665×10^7
Frequency (^{1}H = 100 MHz; 2.3488 T)/MHz	94.077

Reference: $CFCl_3$

Ground state electron configuration: [He]$2s^2 2p^5$
Term symbol: $^2P_{3/2}$
Electron affinity (M→M$^-$)/kJ mol^{-1}: 328

Electron
shell
properties

Main lines in atomic spectrum

Wavelength/nm	Species
685.603	I
690.248	I
703.747	I
712.787	I
775.470	I

Ionization energies/kJ mol^{-1}

1. M →M$^+$	1 681	6. M^{5+}→M^{6+} 15 164
2. M$^+$→M^{2+}	3 374	7. M^{6+}→M^{7+} 17 867
3. M^{2+}→M^{3+}	6 050	8. M^{7+}→M^{8+} 92 036
4. M^{3+}→M^{4+}	8 408	9. M^{8+}→M^{9+} 106 432
5. M^{4+}→M^{5+}	11 023	

Environmental properties

Biological role

Essential to mammals including humans; some compunds very toxic, e.g. HF and F_2 gas

Levels in humans:
Muscle/p.p.m.: 0.05
Bone/p.p.m.: 2000–12 000
Blood/mg dm^{-3}: 0.5
Daily dietary intake: 0.3–0.5 mg
Toxic intake: 20 mg (F$^-$)
Lethal intake: 2 g (F$^-$)
Total mass of element in average (70 kg) person: 2.6 g

Abundances

Sun (relative to H = 1×10^{12}): 3.63×10^{-4}
Earth's crust/p.p.m.: 950
Seawater/p.p.m.: 1.3
Residence time/years: 400 000
Classification: accumulating
Oxidation state: I

Geological data

Chief deposits and sources:
fluorspar [CaF_2];
fluorapatite [$Ca_5(PO_4)_3F$];
cryolite [Na_3AlF_6]
World production of fluorspar/tonnes y^{-1}: 4.7×10^6
Reserves of fluorspar/tonnes: 123×10^6
World production of fluorine gas/tonnes y^{-1}: 2400

Fr

Atomic number: 87

Relative atomic mass ($^{12}C = 12.0000$): **(223)**

Chemical properties

Intensely radioactive, short-lived metal element.

Radii/pm: Fr^+ 180; atomic $c.$ 270
Electronegativity: 0.7 (Pauling); 0.86 (Allred)
Effective nuclear charge: 2.20 (Slater)

Standard reduction potentials $E^{\ominus}/V$

I		0
Fr^+	$\xrightarrow{-3.09}$	Fr

Oxidation states

Fr^I	([Rn])	little studied, Fr^+ (aq), $FrClO_4$ insoluble

Physical properties

Melting point/K: 300
Boiling point/K: 950
ΔH_{fusion}/kJ mol^{-1}: n.a.
ΔH_{vap}/kJ mol^{-1}: n.a.

Thermodynamic properties (298.15 K, 0.1 MPa)

State	$\Delta_f H^{\ominus}$/kJ mol^{-1}	$\Delta_f G^{\ominus}$/kJ mol^{-1}	$S^{\ominus}$/J K^{-1} mol^{-1}	C_p/J K^{-1} mol^{-1}
Solid	0	0	95.4	n.a.
Gas	72.8	n.a.	n.a.	n.a.

Density/kg m^{-3}: n.a.
Thermal conductivity/W m^{-1} K^{-1}: 15 (est.) [300 K]
Electrical resistivity/Ω m: n.a.
Mass magnetic susceptibility/kg^{-1} m^3: n.a.
Molar volume/cm^3: n.a.
Coefficient of linear thermal expansion/K^{-1}: n.a.

Crystal structure (cell dimensions/pm), space group

n.a.

X-ray diffraction: mass absorption coefficients (μ/ρ)/cm^2 g^{-1}:
n.a.

Francium

Thermal neutron capture cross-section/barns: n.a.
Number of isotopes (including nuclear isomers): 30
Isotope mass range: $201 \rightarrow 229$

Nuclear properties

Key isotopes

Nuclide	Atomic mass	Natural abundance (%)	Half-life $T_{1/2}$	Decay mode and energy (MeV)	Nuclear spin I	Nuclear magnetic moment μ
^{212}Fr	211.996 130	0	20.0m	EC (5.070), 57%; α (6.529), 43%; γ	5+	
^{223}Fr	223.019 733	some	21.8m*	β^- (1.147); γ	3/2+	

* Longest lived isotope

Ground state electron configuration: $[Rn]7s^1$
Term symbol: $^2S_{1/2}$
Electron affinity $(M \rightarrow M^-)$/kJ mol^{-1}: 44 (calc.)

Electron shell properties

Main lines in atomic spectrum

Wavelength/nm	Species
717.7	I

Ionization energies/kJ mol^{-1}

1. $M \rightarrow M^+$ 400	6. $M^{5+} \rightarrow M^{6+}$ (6 900)
2. $M^+ \rightarrow M^{2+}$ (2100)	7. $M^{6+} \rightarrow M^{7+}$ (8 100)
3. $M^{2+} \rightarrow M^{3+}$ (3100)	8. $M^{7+} \rightarrow M^{8+}$ (12 300)
4. $M^{3+} \rightarrow M^{4+}$ (4100)	9. $M^{8+} \rightarrow M^{9+}$ (12 800)
5. $M^{4+} \rightarrow M^{5+}$ (5700)	10. $M^{9+} \rightarrow M^{10+}$ (29 300)

Environmental properties

Biological role

None; never encountered, but
  would be toxic due to
  radioactivity
Levels in humans: nil

Abundances

Sun (relative to $H = 1 \times 10^{12}$):
  n.a.
Earth's crust/p.p.m.: nil
Seawater/p.p.m.: nil

Geological data

Chief source: minute traces in
uranium ores. Obtained in
minute quantities from
actinium produced by the
neutron bombardment of
radium

Gd

Chemical properties

Silvery-white metal of rare earth group. Reacts slowly with oxygen and water, dissolves in acids. Used in magnets, electronics, refractories, neutron radiography, neutron radiography, and alloys, with iron for magneto-optic recording devices.

Radii/pm: Gd^{3+} 97; atomic 180.2; covalent 161

Electronegativity: 1.20 (Pauling); 1.11 (Allred); ≤ 3.3 eV (absolute)

Effective nuclear charge: 2.85 (Slater); 8.22 (Clementi); 11.28 (Froese-Fischer)

Standard reduction potentials $E^{\ominus}/V$

		III		0
Acid solution		Gd^{3+}	—2.28	Gd
Alkaline solution		$Gd(OH)_3$	—2.82	Gd

Oxidation states

Gd^{II}	(f^8)	GdI_2
Gd^{III}	(f^7)	Gd_2O_3, $Gd(OH)_3$, GdF_3, $GdCl_3$ etc., $[Gd(H_2O)_x]^{3+}$ (aq), Gd^{3+} salts and complexes

Physical properties

Melting point/K: 1586

Boiling point/K: 3539

ΔH_{fusion}/kJ mol^{-1}: 15.5

ΔH_{vap}/kJ mol^{-1}: 311.7

Thermodynamic properties (298.15 K, 0.1 MPa)

State	$\Delta_f H^{\ominus}$/kJ mol^{-1}	$\Delta_f G^{\ominus}$/kJ mol^{-1}	$S^{\ominus}$/J K^{-1} mol^{-1}	C_p/J K^{-1} mol^{-1}
Solid	0	0	68.07	37.03
Gas	397.5	359.8	193.314	27.547

Density/kg m^{-3}: 7900.4 [298 K]

Thermal conductivity/W m^{-1} K^{-1}: 10.6 [300 K]

Electrical resistivity/Ω m: 134.0×10^{-8} [298 K]

Mass magnetic susceptibility/kg^{-1} m^3: $+6.030 \times 10^{-5}$ (s)

Molar volume/cm^3: 19.90

Coefficient of linear thermal expansion/K^{-1}: 8.6×10^{-6}

Crystal structure (cell dimensions/pm), space group

α-Gd h.c.p. ($a = 363.60$, $c = 578.26$), P6$_3$/mmc

β-Gd b.c.c. ($a = 405$), Im3m

$T(\alpha \rightarrow \beta) = 1535$ K

high pressure form: ($a = 361$, $c = 2603$), R$\bar{3}$m

X-ray diffraction: mass absorption coefficients (μ/ρ)/cm^2 g^{-1}:
CuK$_\alpha$ 439   MoK$_\alpha$ 64.4

Discovered in 1880 by J.-C. Galissard de Marignac at Geneva, Switzerland. Isolated in 1886 by P.-E. Lecoq de Boisbaudran at Paris, France
[Named after J. Gadolin, a Finnish chemist]

Gadolinium

Thermal neutron capture cross-section/barns: 49 000
Number of isotopes (including nuclear isomers). 23
Isotope mass range: $143m \rightarrow 163$

Key isotopes

Nuclide	Atomic mass	Natural abundance (%)	Half-life $T_{1/2}$	Decay mode and energy (MeV)	Nuclear spin I	Nuclear magnetic moment μ	Uses
^{152}Gd	151.919 786	0.20	1.1×10^{14}y	α (2.24)	0+		
^{153}Gd	152.921 745	0	241.6d	EC (0.243); γ	3/2−		tracer
^{154}Gd	153.920 861	2.18	stable		0+		
^{155}Gd	154.922 618	14.80	stable		3/2−	−0.27	NMR
^{156}Gd	155.922 118	20.47	stable		0+		
^{157}Gd	156.923 956	15.65	stable		3/2−	−0.36	NMR
^{158}Gd	157.924 099	24.84	stable		0+		
^{160}Gd	159.927 049	21.86	stable		0+		

NMR

	^{155}Gd	^{157}Gd
Relative sensitivity (^{1}H = 1.00)	2.79×10^{-4}	5.44×10^{-4}
Receptivity (^{13}C = 1.00)	0.124	0.292
Magnetogyric ratio/rad T^{-1} s^{-1}	-0.8273×10^7	-1.0792×10^7
Quadrupole moment/m^2	1.6×10^{-28}	2×10^{-28}
Frequency (^{1}H = 100 MHz; 2.3488 T)/MHz	3.819	4.774

Ground state electron configuration: $[Xe]4f^75d^16s^2$
Term symbol: $^9D_2$
Electron affinity ($M \rightarrow M^-$)/kJ mol^{-1}: ≤ 50

Main lines in atomic spectrum

Wavelength/nm	Species
342.247	II
364.619	II
368.413	I
376.839	II
368.305	I
407.870 (AA)	I

Ionization energies/kJ mol^{-1}

1. $M \rightarrow M^+$	592.5	6. $M^{5+} \rightarrow M^{6+}$	
2. $M^+ \rightarrow M^{2+}$	1167	7. $M^{6+} \rightarrow M^{7+}$	
3. $M^{2+} \rightarrow M^{3+}$	1990	8. $M^{7+} \rightarrow M^{8+}$	
4. $M^{3+} \rightarrow M^{4+}$	4250	9. $M^{8+} \rightarrow M^{9+}$	
5. $M^{4+} \rightarrow M^{5+}$		10. $M^{9+} \rightarrow M^{10+}$	

Environmental properties

Biological role

None; low toxicity; stimulatory
Levels in humans: n.a. but low

Abundances

Sun (relative to H = 1×10^{12}): 13.2
Earth's crust/p.p.m.: 7.7
Seawater/p.p.m.:
Atlantic surface: 5.2×10^{-7}
Atlantic deep: 9.3×10^{-7}
Pacific surface: 6.0×10^{-7}
Pacific deep: 15×10^{-7}
Residence time/years: 300
Classification: recycled
Oxidation state: III

Geological data

Chief deposits and sources:
monazite
$[(Ce, La, etc.)PO_4]$;
bastnmaesite $[(Ce, La, etc.) (CO_3)F]$
World production/tonnes y^{-1}: c. 100
Reserves/tonnes: c. 10^5

Ga

Atomic number: **31**

Relative atomic mass ($^{12}C = 12.0000$): **69.723**

Soft, silvery-white metal, stable in air and with water. Soluble in acids and alkalis. Longest liquid range of all elements. Semiconductor properties with phosphorus, arsenic, and antimony. Used in light-emitting diodes; microwave equipment.

Radii/pm: Ga^{3+} 62; Ga^{+} 113; atomic 122.1; covalent 125

Electronegativity: 1.81 (Pauling); 1.82 (Allred); 3.2 eV (absolute)

Effective nuclear charge: 5.00 (Slater); 6.22 (Clementi); 6.72 (Froese-Fischer)

Standard reduction potentials $E^{\ominus}/V$

	III		II		0
			-0.53		
Acid solution	Ga^{3+}	$\underline{c. -0.65}$	Ga^{2+}	$\underline{c. -0.45}$	Ga

Oxidation states

Ga^{I}	(s^2)	Ga_2O, $GaCl_2$ etc., Ga_2Cl_4 is $Ga^{I}[Ga^{III}Cl_4]$
Ga^{II}	(s^1)	$[Ga_2Cl_6]^{2-}$
Ga^{III}	$([d^{10}])$	Ga_2O_3, $Ga(OH)_3$, $[Ga(H_2O)_6]^{3+}$ (aq) GaF_3, Ga_2Cl_6, $GaCl_6^{3-}$

Melting point/K: 302.93
Boiling point/K: 2676
$\Delta H_{fusion}/kJ\ mol^{-1}$: 5.59
$\Delta H_{vap}/kJ\ mol^{-1}$: 256.1

Thermodynamic properties (298.15 K, 0.1 MPa)

State	$\Delta_f H^{\ominus}/kJ\ mol^{-1}$	$\Delta_f G^{\ominus}/kJ\ mol^{-1}$	$S^{\ominus}/J\ K^{-1}\ mol^{-1}$	$C_p/J\ K^{-1}\ mol^{-1}$
Solid	0	0	40.88	25.86
Gas	277.0	238.9	169.06	25.36

Density/kg m^{-3}: 5907 [293 K]; 6113.6 [liquid at m.p.]

Thermal conductivity/W m^{-1} K^{-1}: 40.6 [300 K]

Electrical resistivity/Ω m: 27×10^{-8} [273 K] varies with axis

Mass magnetic susceptibility/kg^{-1} m^3: -3.9×10^{-9} (s)

Molar volume/cm^3: 11.81

Coefficient of linear thermal expansion/K^{-1}:
11.5×10^{-6} (a axis); 31.5×10^{-6} (b axis); 16.5×10^{-6} (c axis)

Crystal structure (cell dimensions/pm), space group

α-Ga orthorhombic ($a = 451.86$, $b = 765.70$, $c = 452.58$), Cmca
β-Ga orthorhombic ($a = 290$, $b = 813$, $c = 317$), Cmcm (metastable form)
γ-Ga orthorhombic ($a = 1060$, $b = 1356$, $c = 519$), Cmc2$_1$

$T(\gamma \rightarrow \alpha) = 238$ K
High pressure form: ($a = 279$, $c = 438$), I4/mmm

X-ray diffraction: mass absorption coefficients (μ/ρ)/cm^2 g^{-1}:
CuK$_\alpha$ 67.9   MoK$_\alpha$ 60.1

Discovered in 1875 by Paul-Émile Lecoq de Boisbaudran at Paris, France

[Latin, *Gallia* = France]

Gallium

Thermal neutron capture cross-section/barns: 2.9
Number of isotopes (including nuclear isomers): 23
Isotope mass range: $62 \rightarrow 83$

**Nuclear
properties**

Key isotopes

Nuclide	Atomic mass	Natural abundance (%)	Half-life $T_{1/2}$	Decay mode and energy (MeV)	Nuclear spin I	Nuclear magnetic moment μ	Uses
^{67}Ga	66.928 420	0	78.25h	EC(1.001); γ	$3/2-$	$+1.8507$	medical tracer
^{69}Ga	68.925 580	60.11	stable		$3/2-$	$+2.01659$	NMR
^{71}Ga	70.924 700	39.89	stable		$3/2-$	$+2.56227$	NMR
^{72}Ga	71.926 365	0	13.95h	β^-(3.99); γ	$3-$	-0.13224	tracer

NMR

	$[^{69}\text{Ga}]$	^{71}Ga
Relative sensitivity (^{1}H = 1.00)	6.91×10^{-2}	0.14
Receptivity (^{13}C = 1.00)	237	319
Magnetogyric ratio/rad T^{-1} s^{-1}	6.420×10^7	8.158×10^7
Quadrupole moment/m^2	0.178×10^{-28}	0.112×10^{-28}
Frequency (^{1}H = 100 MHz; 2.3488 T)/MHz	24.003	30.495

Reference: $\text{Ga(H}_2\text{O)}_6^{3+}$

Ground state electron configuration: $[\text{Ar}]3\text{d}^{10}4\text{s}^2 4\text{p}^1$
Term symbol: $^2\text{P}_{1/2}$
Electron affinity (M$\rightarrow$M$^-$)/kJ mol^{-1}: *c.* 30

**Electron
shell
properties**

Main lines in atomic spectrum

Wavelength/nm	Species
287.424 (AA)	I
294.364	I
403.299	I
417.204	I
639.656	I
641.344	I

Ionization energies/kJ mol^{-1}

1. $\text{M} \rightarrow \text{M}^+$ 578.8	6. $\text{M}^{5+} \rightarrow \text{M}^{6+}$ (11 400)
2. $\text{M}^+ \rightarrow \text{M}^{2+}$ 1979	7. $\text{M}^{6+} \rightarrow \text{M}^{7+}$ (14 400)
3. $\text{M}^{2+} \rightarrow \text{M}^{3+}$ 2963	8. $\text{M}^{7+} \rightarrow \text{M}^{8+}$ (17 700)
4. $\text{M}^{3+} \rightarrow \text{M}^{4+}$ 6200	9. $\text{M}^{8+} \rightarrow \text{M}^{9+}$ (22 300)
5. $\text{M}^{4+} \rightarrow \text{M}^{5+}$ (8700)	10. $\text{M}^{9+} \rightarrow \text{M}^{10+}$ (26 100)

Environmental properties

Biological role	Abundances	Geological data
None; stimulatory	**Sun** (relative to H = 1×10^{12}): 631	**Chief ores and sources**: occurs up to 1 per cent in other minerals. Gallium is recovered as a by-product of zinc and copper refining
Levels in humans:	**Earth's crust**/p.p.m.: 18	
Muscle/p.p.m.: 0.0014	**Seawater**/p.p.m.: 3×10^{-5}	
Bone/p.p.m.: n.a.	Residence time/years: 10 000	**World production**/tonnes y^{-1}: 30
Blood/mg dm^{-3}: <0.08	Classification: n.a.	
Daily dietary intake: n.a. but low	Oxidation state: III	**Reserves**/tonnes: n.a.
Toxic intake: low toxicity		
Total mass of element in average (70 kg) person: n.a.		

Ge

Atomic number: **32**

Relative atomic mass ($^{12}C = 12.0000$): **72.61**

Ultrapure it is a silvery-white brittle metalloid element. Stable in air and water, unaffected by acids, except nitric, and alkalis. Used in semiconductors, alloys, and special glasses for infrared devices.

Radii/pm: Ge^{2+} 90; atomic 122.5; covalent 122; Ge^{4-} 272

Electronegativity: 2.01 (Pauling); 2.02 (Allred); 4.6 eV (absolute)

Effective nuclear charge: 5.65 (Slater); 6.78 (Clementi); 7.92 (Froese-Fischer)

Standard reduction potentials $E^{\ominus}$/V

	IV		II		0		−IV
Acid solution	GeO_2	$\xrightarrow{-0.370}$	GeO	$\xrightarrow{0.255}$	Ge	$\xrightarrow{-0.29}$	GeH_4
	Ge^{4+}	$\xrightarrow{0.00}$	Ge^{2+}	$\xrightarrow{-0.247}$			

[Alkaline solutions contain many different forms]

Covalent bonds r/pm E/kJ mol^{-1}

	r/pm	E/kJ mol^{-1}
Ge–H	152.9	288
Ge–C	194	237
Ge–O	165	363
Ge–F	170	464
Ge–Cl	210	340
Ge–Ge	241	163

Oxidation states

Ge^{II} (s^2)   GeO, GeS, GeF_2, $GeCl_2$ etc.

Ge^{IV} (d^{10}) GeO_2, GeH_4 etc., GeF_4, $GeCl_4$ etc., GeF_6^{2-}, $GeCl_6^{2-}$, GeS_2, $[GeO(OH)_3]^-$ (aq)

Melting point/K: 1210.6

Boiling point/K: 3103

ΔH_{fusion}/kJ mol^{-1}:   34.7

ΔH_{vap}/kJ mol^{-1}:   334.3

Thermodynamic properties   (298.15 K, 0.1 MPa)

State	$\Delta_f H^{\ominus}$/kJ mol^{-1}	$\Delta_f G^{\ominus}$/kJ mol^{-1}	$S^{\ominus}$/J K^{-1} mol^{-1}	C_p/J K^{-1} mol^{-1}
Solid	0	0	31.09	23.347
Gas	376.6	335.9	167.900	30.731

Density/kg m^{-3}:   5323 [293 K]; 5490 [liquid at m.p.]

Thermal conductivity/W m^{-1} K^{-1}:   59.9 [300 K]

Electrical resistivity/Ω m: 0.46 [295 K]

Mass magnetic susceptibility/kg^{-1} m^3: -1.328×10^{-9} (s)

Molar volume/cm^3:   13.64

Coefficient of linear thermal expansion/K^{-1}: 5.57×10^{-6}

Crystal structure (cell dimensions/pm), space group

Cubic ($a = 565.754$), Fd3m, diamond structure

High pressure forms: ($a = 488.4$; $c = 269.2$), I4$_1$/amd
($a = 593$; $c = 698$), P4$_3$2$_1$2
($a = 692$), b.c.c.

X-ray diffraction: mass absorption coefficients (μ/ρ)/cm^2 g^{-1}:
CuK$_\alpha$ 75.6   MoK$_\alpha$ 64.8

Discovered in 1886 by C. A. Winkler at Freiberg, Germany

[Latin, *Germania* = Germany]

Germanium

Thermal neutron capture cross-section/barns: 2.2
Number of isotopes (including nuclear isomers): 24
Isotope mass range: $64 \rightarrow 83$

Key isotopes

Nuclide	Atomic mass	Natural abundance (%)	Half-life $T_{1/2}$	Decay mode and energy (MeV)	Nuclear spin I	Nuclear magnetic moment μ	Uses
^{68}Ge	67.928 096	0	288d	EC(0.11); γ	0+		tracer
^{70}Ge	69.924 250	20.5	stable		0+		
^{71}Ge	70.924 953	0	11.2d	EC(0.236); γ	1/2−	+0.547	tracer
^{72}Ge	71.922 079	27.4	stable		0+		
^{73}Ge	72.923 463	7.8	stable		9/2+	−0.879 46	NMR
^{74}Ge	73.921 177	36.5	stable		0+		
^{76}Ge	75.921 401	7.8	stable		0+		
^{77}Ge	76.923 548	0	11.30h	β^- (2.70); γ	7/2+		tracer

NMR
^{73}Ge

Relative sensitivity (^{1}H = 1.00) 1.4×10^{-3}
Receptivity (^{13}C = 1.00) 0.617
Magnetogyric ratio/rad T^{-1} s^{-1} -0.9331×10^7
Quadrupole moment/m^2 -0.2×10^{-28}
Frequency (^{1}H = 100 MHz; 2.3488 T)/MHz 3.488
Reference: $Ge(CH_3)_4$

Ground state electron configuration: [Ar] $3d^{10}4s^24p^2$
Term symbol: $^3P_0$
Electron affinity (M→M$^-$)/kJ mol^{-1}: 116

Main lines in atomic spectrum

Wavelength/nm	Species
204.171	I
206.866	I
209.426	I
259.253	I
265.117	I
265.157 (AA)	I

Ionization energies/kJ mol^{-1}

1. M → M$^+$ 762.1
2. M$^+$ → M^{2+} 1537
3. M^{2+} → M^{3+} 3302
4. M^{3+} → M^{4+} 4410
5. M^{4+} → M^{5+} 9020
6. M^{5+} → M^{6+} (11 900)
7. M^{6+} → M^{7+} (15 000)
8. M^{7+} → M^{8+} (18 200)
9. M^{8+} → M^{9+} (21 800)
10. M^{9+} → M^{10+} (27 000)

Environmental properties

Biological role

None; stimulatory
Levels in humans:
Muscle/p.p.m.: 0.14
Bone/p.p.m.: n.a.
Blood/mg dm^{-3}: *c.* 0.44
Daily dietary intake:
  0.4–1.5 mg
Toxic intake: non-toxic
Total mass of element in
  average (70 kg) person: n.a.

Abundances

Sun (relative to H = 1×10^{12}):
  3160
Earth's crust/p.p.m.: 1.8
Seawater/p.p.m.:
Atlantic surface: 0.07×10^{-6}
Atlantic deep: 0.14×10^{-6}
Pacific surface: 0.35×10^{-6}
Pacific deep: 7.00×10^{-6}
Residence time/years: 20 000
Classification: recycled
Oxidation state: IV

Geological data

Chief deposits and sources:
  germanite
  $[Cu_3(Ge, Fe)(S, As)_4]$ very
  rare;
  widely distributed in other
  minerals; Ge is recovered
  as a by-product of zinc and
  copper refining
World production/tonnes y^{-1}:
  80
Reserves/tonnes: n.a.

Au

Atomic number: 79

Relative atomic mass ($^{12}C = 12.0000$): 196.96654

Soft metal with characteristic yellow colour. Highest malleability and ductility of any element. Unaffected by air, water, acids (except HNO_3–HCl), and alkalis. Used as bullion, in jewellery, electronics, and glass (colouring and heat reflecting).

Radii/pm: Au^+ 137; Au^{3+} 91; atomic 144.2; covalent 134

Electronegativity: 2.54 (Pauling); 1.42 (Allred); 5.77 eV (absolute)

Effective nuclear charge: 4.20 (Slater); 10.94 (Clementi); 15.94 (Froese-Fischer)

Standard reduction potentials $E^{\ominus}/V$

	III		I		0
Acid solution	Au^{3+}	$\dfrac{1.36}{1.52}$	Au^+	1.83	Au
	$AuCl_4^-$	$\dfrac{0.926}{1.002}$	$AuCl_2^-$	1.154	Au
	$Au(SCN)_4^-$	$\dfrac{0.623}{0.636}$	$Au(SCN)_2^-$	0.662	Au

Oxidation states

Au^{-I}	$(d^{10} s^2)$	$[Au(NH_3)_n]^-$ in liquid NH_3
Au^0	$(d^{10} s^1)$	Gold clusters eg. $[Au_8(PPh_3)_8]^{2+}$
Au^I	(d^{10})	Au_2S, $[Au(CN)_2]^-$ and other complexes
Au^{II}	(d^9)	Rare but some complexes known
Au^{III}	(d^8)	Au_2O_3, $Au(OH)_4^-$ (aq), $AuCl_4^-$ (aq),
		$AuCl_3(OH)^-$ (aq), Au_2S_3, AuF_3,
		Au_2Cl_6, $AuBr_3$, complexes
Au^V	(d^6)	AuF_5
Au^{VII}	(d^4)	AuF_7

Melting point/K: 1337.58

Boiling point/K: 3080

ΔH_{fusion}/kJ mol^{-1}: 12.7

ΔH_{vap}/kJ mol^{-1}: 324.4

Thermodynamic properties (298.15 K, 0.1 MPa)

State	$\Delta_f H^{\ominus}$/kJ mol^{-1}	$\Delta_f G^{\ominus}$/kJ mol^{-1}	$S^{\ominus}$/J K^{-1} mol^{-1}	C_p/J K^{-1} mol^{-1}
Solid	0	0	47.40	25.418
Gas	336.1	326.3	180.503	20.786

Density/kg m^{-3}: 19 320 [293 K]; 17 280 [liquid at m.p.]

Thermal conductivity/W m^{-1} K^{-1}: 317 [300 K]

Electrical resistivity/Ω m: 2.35×10^{-8} [293 K]

Mass magnetic susceptibility/kg^{-1} m^3: -1.78×10^{-9} (s)

Molar volume/cm^3: 10.19

Coefficient of linear thermal expansion/K^{-1}: 14.16×10^{-6}

Crystal structure (cell dimensions/pm), space group

f.c.c. ($a = 407.833$), Fm3m

X-ray diffraction: mass absorption coefficients (μ/ρ)/cm^2 g^{-1}: CuK$_\alpha$ 208 MoK$_\alpha$ 115

Gold

Thermal neutron capture cross-section/barns: 98.7
Number of isotopes (including nuclear isomers): 39
Isotope mass range: $176 \rightarrow 204$

Key isotopes

Nuclide	Atomic mass	Natural abundance (%)	Half-life $T_{1/2}$	Decay mode and energy (MeV)	Nuclear spin I	Nuclear magnetic moment μ	Uses
^{195}Au	194.965 013	0	186.1d	EC(0.230); γ	3/2+	± 0.148	tracer
^{197}Au	196.966 543	100	stable		3/2+	+0.1457	NMR
^{198}Au	197.968 217	0	2.693d	β^-(1.372); γ	2−	+0.5934	tracer, medical
^{199}Au	198.968 740	0	3.14d	β^-(0.453); γ	3/2+	+0.2715	tracer

NMR (difficult to detect) ^{197}Au
Relative sensitivity (^{1}H = 1.00) 2.51×10^{-5}
Receptivity (^{13}C = 1.00)   0.06
Magnetogyric ratio/rad T^{-1} s^{-1} 0.357×10^7
Quadrupole moment/m^2 0.58×10^{-28}
Frequency (^{1}H = 100 MHz; 2.3488 T)/MHz   1.712

Ground state electron configuration: [Xe]$4f^{14}5d^{10}6s^1$
Term symbol: $^2S_{1/2}$
Electron affinity $(M \rightarrow M^-)$/kJ mol^{-1}: 222.8

Main lines in atomic spectrum

Wavelength/nm,	Species
201.200	I
202.138	I
242.795 (AA)	I
267.595	I
274.825	I
312.278	I

Ionization energies/kJ mol^{-1}

1. $M \rightarrow M^+$	890.1	6. $M^{5+} \rightarrow M^{6+}$ (7 000)
2. $M^+ \rightarrow M^{2+}$	1980	7. $M^{6+} \rightarrow M^{7+}$ (9 300)
3. $M^{2+} \rightarrow M^{3+}$	(2900)	8. $M^{7+} \rightarrow M^{8+}$ (11 000)
4. $M^{3+} \rightarrow M^{4+}$	(4200)	9. $M^{8+} \rightarrow M^{9+}$ (12 800)
5. $M^{4+} \rightarrow M^{5+}$	(5600)	10. $M^{9+} \rightarrow M^{10+}$ (14 800)

Environmental properties

Biological role

None; stimulatory
Levels in humans:
Muscle/p.p.m.: n.a.
Bone/p.p.m.: 0.016
Blood/mg dm^{-3}: (0.1–4.2) $\times$ 10^{-4}
Daily dietary intake: n.a. but very low
Toxic intake: non-toxic
Total mass of element in average (70 kg) person: n.a.

Abundances

Sun (relative to H = 1 $\times$ 10^{12}): 5.6
Earth's crust/p.p.m.: 0.0011
Seawater/p.p.m.: c. 1 $\times$ 10^{-5}
Residence time/years: n.a.
Classification: n.a.
Oxidation state: +I

Geological data

Chief deposits and sources: occurs as metal
World production/tonnes y^{-1}: 1423
Reserves/tonnes: 15 000

| **Hf** | Atomic number: **72** |
| | Relative atomic mass ($^{12}C = 12.0000$): **178.49** |

Chemical properties

Lustrous, silvery, ductile metal. Resists corrosion due to oxide film, but powdered Hf will burn in air. Unaffected by acids (except HF) and alkalis. Used in control rods for nuclear reactors; high temperature alloys and ceramics.

Radii/pm: Hf^{4+} 84; atomic 156.4; covalent 144

Electronegativity: 1.3 (Pauling); 1.23 (Allred); 3.8 eV (absolute)

Effective nuclear charge: 3.15 (Slater); 9.16 (Clementi); 13.27 (Froese-Fischer)

Standard reduction potentials $E^{\ominus}/V$

IV		0
Hf^{4+}	$\underline{\quad -1.70 \quad}$	Hf
HfO_2	$\underline{\quad -1.57 \quad}$	Hf

Oxidation states

Hf^I	(d^3)	HfCl?
Hf^{II}	(d^2)	$HfCl_2$?
Hf^{III}	(d^1)	$HfCl_3$, $HfBr_3$, HfI_3, Hf^{3+} reduces water
$\mathbf{Hf^{IV}}$	(d^0, f^{14})	HfO_2, $Hf(OH)^{3+}$ (aq), HfF_4, $HfCl_4$ etc., HfF_6^{2-}, HfF_7^{3-}, HfF_8^{4-}

Physical properties

Melting point/K: 2503
Boiling point/K: 5470
ΔH_{fusion}/kJ mol^{-1}: 25.5
ΔH_{vap}/kJ mol^{-1}: 661.1

Thermodynamic properties (298.15 K, 0.1 MPa)

State	$\Delta_f H^{\ominus}$/kJ mol^{-1}	$\Delta_f G^{\ominus}$/kJ mol^{-1}	$S^{\ominus}$/J K^{-1} mol^{-1}	C_p/J K^{-1} mol^{-1}
Solid	0	0	43.56	25.73
Gas	619.2	576.5	186.892	20.803

Density/kg m^{-3}: 13 310 [293 K]; 12 000 [liquid at m.p.]
Thermal conductivity/W m^{-1} K^{-1}: 23.0 [300 K]
Electrical resistivity/Ω m: 35.1×10^{-8} [293 K]
Mass magnetic susceptibility/kg^{-1} m^3: $+5.3 \times 10^{-9}$ (s)
Molar volume/cm^3: 13.41
Coefficient of linear thermal expansion/K^{-1}: 5.9×10^{-6}

Crystal structure (cell dimensions/pm), space group

α-Hf h.c.p. ($a = 319.46$; $c = 505.10$), P6$_3$/mmc
β-Hf cubic ($a = 362$)
$T(\alpha \rightarrow \beta) = 2033$ K

X-ray diffraction: mass absorption coefficients (μ/ρ)/cm^2 g^{-1}:
CuK$_\alpha$ 159   MoK$_\alpha$ 91.7

Discovered in 1923 by D. Coster and G. C. von Hevesey at Copenhagen, Denmark

[Latin, *Hafnia* = Copenhagen]

Hafnium

Thermal neutron capture cross-section/barns: 104
Number of isotopes (including nuclear isomers): 33
Isotope mass range: $158 \rightarrow 184$

Nuclear properties

Key isotopes

Nuclide	Atomic mass	Natural abundance (%)	Half-life $T_{1/2}$	Decay mode and energy (MeV)	Nuclear spin I	Nuclear magnetic moment μ	Uses
^{172}Hf	171.939 460	0	1.87y	EC(0.35); γ	0+		tracer
^{174}Hf	173.940 044	0.16	stable	α(2.55)	0+		
^{175}Hf	174.941 507	0	70d	EC(0.686)	5/2−	0.70	tracer
^{176}Hf	175.941 406	5.21	stable		0+		
^{177}Hf	176.943 217	18.6	stable		7/2+	+0.7935	
^{178}Hf	177.943 696	27.30	stable		0+		
^{179}Hf	178.945 812	13.63	stable		9/2+	−0.6409	NMR
^{180}Hf	179.946 545	35.10	stable		0		
^{181}Hf	180.949 096	0	42.4d	β^-(1.027); γ	1/2−		tracer
^{182}Hf	181.950 550	0	9×10^6y	β^-(0.431)	0+		tracer

NMR (difficult to observe)	^{177}Hf	^{179}Hf
Relative sensitivity (^{1}H = 1.00)	6.38×10^{-4}	2.16×10^{-4}
Receptivity (^{13}C = 1.00)	0.88	0.27
Magnetogyric ratio/rad T^{-1} s^{-1}	$+0.945 \times 10^7$	-0.609×10^7
Quadrupole moment/m^2	4.5×10^{-28}	5.1×10^{-28}
Frequency (^{1}H = 100 MHz; 2.3488 T)/MHz	3.120	1.869

Ground state electron configuration: [Xe]$4f^{14}5d^26s^2$
Term symbol: $^3F_2$
Electron affinity ($M \rightarrow M^-$)/kJ mol^{-1}: *c.* 0

Electron shell properties

Main lines in atomic spectrum

Wavelength/nm	Species
201.278	II
202.818	II
286.637	I
289.826	I
307.288 (AA)	I
329.980	II
368.224	I

Ionization energies/kJ mol^{-1}

1. $M \rightarrow M^+$ 642
2. $M^+ \rightarrow M^{2+}$ 1440
3. $M^{2+} \rightarrow M^{3+}$ 2250
4. $M^{3+} \rightarrow M^{4+}$ 3216
5. $M^{4+} \rightarrow M^{5+}$
6. $M^{5+} \rightarrow M^{6+}$
7. $M^{6+} \rightarrow M^{7+}$
8. $M^{7+} \rightarrow M^{8+}$
9. $M^{8+} \rightarrow M^{9+}$
10. $M^{9+} \rightarrow M^{10+}$

Environmental properties

Biological role	Abundances	Geological data
None; non-toxic **Levels in humans:** n.a.	**Sun** (relative to H = 1×10^{12}): 6 **Earth's crust**/p.p.m.: 5.3 **Seawater**/p.p.m.: 7×10^{-6} Residence time/years: n.a. Classification: n.a. Oxidation state: IV	**Chief ore and sources:** alvite [(Hf, Th, Zr)SiO$_4$. xH$_2$O]; but Hf is obtained as a by-product of zirconium refining **World production**/tonnes y^{-1}: *c.* 50 **Reserves**/tonnes: n.a.

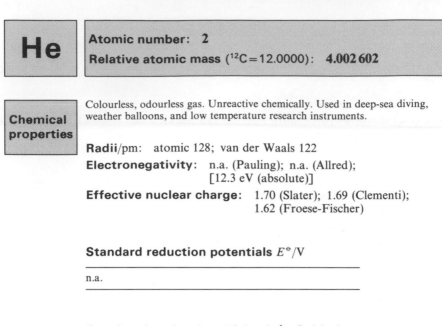

He	Atomic number: 2
	Relative atomic mass ($^{12}C = 12.0000$): **4.002 602**

Chemical properties

Colourless, odourless gas. Unreactive chemically. Used in deep-sea diving, weather balloons, and low temperature research instruments.

Radii/pm: atomic 128; van der Waals 122

Electronegativity: n.a. (Pauling); n.a. (Allred);
[12.3 eV (absolute)]

Effective nuclear charge: 1.70 (Slater); 1.69 (Clementi);
1.62 (Froese-Fischer)

Standard reduction potentials $E^{\ominus}$/V

n.a.

Covalent bonds r/pm E/kJ mol^{-1} | **Oxidation states**

none | only He^0 as a gas

Physical properties

Melting point/K: 0.95   **Critical temperature**/K: 5.19
(under pressure)   **Critical pressure**/kPa: 227
Boiling point/K: 4.216   **Critical volume**/cm^3 mol^{-1}: 57.3
ΔH_{fusion}/kJ mol^{-1}: 0.021
ΔH_{vap}/kJ mol^{-1}: 0.082

Thermodynamic properties (298.15 K, 0.1 MPa)

State	$\Delta_f H^{\ominus}$/kJ mol^{-1}	$\Delta_f G^{\ominus}$/kJ mol^{-1}	$S^{\ominus}$/J K^{-1} mol^{-1}	C_p/J K^{-1} mol^{-1}
Gas	0	0	126.150	20.786

Density/kg m^{-3}: n.a. [solid]; 124.8 [liquid at b.p.];
0.1785 [gas, 273 K]
Thermal conductivity/W m^{-1} K^{-1}: 0.152 [300 K]$_g$
Mass magnetic susceptibility/kg^{-1} m^3: -5.9×10^{-9} (g)
Molar volume/cm^3: 32.07 [4 K]

Crystal structure (cell dimensions/pm), space group [T, p]

α-He h.c.p. ($a = 353.1$; $c = 569.3$), P6$_3$/mmc. [$T = 1.15$ K, $p = 6.69$ MPa]
β-He f.c.c. ($a = 424.0$), Fm3m. [$T = 16$ K, $p = 127$ MPa]
γ-He b.c.c. ($a = 411$), Im3m. [$T = 1.73$ K, $p = 2.94$ MPa]

X-ray diffraction: mass absorption coefficients (μ/ρ)/cm^2 g^{-1}:
CuK$_\alpha$ 0.383   MoK$_\alpha$ 0.207

Isolated in 1895 by Sir William Ramsay at London, UK, and independently by P. T. Cleve and N. A. Langlet at Uppsala, Sweden
[Greek, *helios* = sun]

Helium

Thermal neutron capture cross-section/barns: *c.* 0.007
Number of isotopes (including nuclear isomers). *5*
Isotope mass range: $3 \rightarrow 8$ except 7

Key isotopes

Nuclide	Atomic mass	Natural abundance (%)	Half-life $T_{1/2}$	Decay mode and energy (MeV)	Nuclear spin I	Nuclear magnetic moment μ	Uses
^{3}He	3.016 03	0.000 138	stable		1/2	-2.12762	NMR, tracer
^{4}He	4.002 60	99.999 862	stable		$3/2-$		

NMR (no compounds known) ^{3}He
Relative sensitivity (^{1}H $= 1.00$)   0.44
Receptivity (^{13}C $= 1.00$)   0.003 26
Magnetogyric ratio/rad T^{-1} s^{-1} -20.378×10^7
Frequency (^{1}H $= 100$ MHz; 2.3488 T)/MHz   76.178

Ground state electron configuration: $1s^2$
Term symbol: $^1S_0$
Electron affinity $(M \rightarrow M^-)$/kJ mol^{-1}:   0.0

Main lines in atomic spectrum

Wavelength/nm	Species
388.865	I
587.562	I
1083.025	I
1083.034	I
1868.534	I
2058.130	I

Ionization energies/kJ mol^{-1}

1. $M \rightarrow M^+$ 2372.3
2. $M^+ \rightarrow M^{2+}$ 5250.4

Environmental properties

Biological role	Abundances	Geological data
None; non-toxic but can asphyxiate	**Sun** (relative to H $= 1 \times 10^{12}$): 6.31×10^{10}	**Chief sources:** natural gas may contain up to 7% helium
Levels in humans: n.a. but low	**Earth's crust**/p.p.m.: 0.008	**World production**/tonnes y^{-1}: *c.* 4500
	Seawater/p.p.m.: 4×10^{-6}	
	Residence time: n.a.	**Reserves**/tonnes: n.a.; atmosphere contains 3.7×10^9
	Oxidation state: 0	
	Atmosphere/p.p.m. by volume: 5.2	

Ho	Atomic number: 67
	Relative atomic mass ($^{12}C = 12.0000$): **164.93032**

Chemical properties

Silvery metal of the rare earth group. Slowly attacked by oxygen and water, dissolves in acid. Used as flux concentrator for high magnetic fields.

Radii/pm: Ho^{3+} 89; atomic 176.6; covalent 158

Electronegativity: 1.23 (Pauling); 1.10 (Allred); ≤ 3.3 eV (absolute)

Effective nuclear charge: 2.85 (Slater); 8.44 (Clementi); 11.60 (Froese-Fischer)

Standard reduction potentials $E^{\ominus}/V$

	III		0
Acid solution	Ho^{3+}	$\underline{-2.33}$	Ho
Alkaline solution	$Ho(OH)_3$	$\underline{-2.85}$	Ho

Oxidation states

Ho^{III}	(f^{10})	Ho_2O_3, $Ho(OH)_3$, $[Ho(H_2O)_x]^{3+}$ (aq), Ho^{3+} salts, HoF_3, $HoCl_3$ etc., $HoCl_6^{3-}$, complexes

Physical properties

Melting point/K: 1747
Boiling point/K: 2968
ΔH_{fusion}/kJ mol^{-1}: 17.2
ΔH_{vap}/kJ mol^{-1}: 251.0

Thermodynamic properties (298.15 K, 0.1 MPa)

State	$\Delta_f H^{\circ}$/kJ mol^{-1}	$\Delta_f G^{\circ}$/kJ mol^{-1}	S°/J K^{-1} mol^{-1}	C_p/J K^{-1} mol^{-1}
Solid	0	0	75.3	27.15
Gas	300.8	264.8	195.59	20.79

Density/kg m^{-3}: 8795 [298 K]
Thermal conductivity/W m^{-1} K^{-1}: 16.2 [300 K]
Electrical resistivity/Ω m: 87.0×10^{-8} [298 K]
Mass magnetic susceptibility/kg^{-1} m^3: $+5.49 \times 10^{-6}$ (s)
Molar volume/cm^3: 18.75
Coefficient of linear thermal expansion/K^{-1}: 9.5×10^{-6}

Crystal structure (cell dimensions/pm), space group

α-Ho h.c.p. ($a = 357.73$; $c = 561.58$), P6$_3$/mmc
β-Ho b.c.c. ($a = 396$), Im3m
$T(\alpha \rightarrow \beta)$ just below melting point
High pressure form: ($a = 334$; $c = 2410$), R$\bar{3}$m

X-ray diffraction: mass absorption coefficients (μ/ρ)/cm^2 g^{-1}:
CuK$_\alpha$ 128   MoK$_\alpha$ 73.9

Holmium

Thermal neutron capture cross-section/barns: 65
Number of isotopes (including nuclear isomers): 39
Isotope mass range: $148 \rightarrow 170$

Nuclear properties

Key isotopes

Nuclide	Atomic mass	Natural abundance (%)	Half-life $T_{1/2}$	Decay mode and energy (MeV)	Nuclear spin I	Nuclear magnetic moment μ	Uses
^{165}Ho	164.930 319	100	stable		$7/2-$	$+4.173$	NMR
^{166}Ho	165.932 281	0	1.117d	β^- (1.854)	$0-$		tracer

NMR

^{165}Ho

Relative sensitivity (^{1}H = 1.00)   0.18
Receptivity (^{13}C = 1.00) 1.16×10^3
Magnetogyric ratio/rad T^{-1} s^{-1} 5.710×10^7
Quadrupole moment/m^2 2.82×10^{-28}
Frequency (^{1}H = 100 MHz; 2.3488 T)/MHz   20.513

Ground state electron configuration: [Xe]$4f^{11}6s^2$
Term symbol: $^4I_{15/2}$
Electron affinity ($M \rightarrow M^-$)/kJ mol^{-1}: ≤ 50

Electron shell properties

Main lines in atomic spectrum

Wavelength/nm	Species
345.600	II
379.675	II
381.073	II
389.102	II
405.393	I
410.384 (AA)	I
416.303	I

Ionization energies/kJ mol^{-1}

1. $M \rightarrow M^+$ 580.7
2. $M^+ \rightarrow M^{2+}$ 1139
3. $M^{2+} \rightarrow M^{3+}$ 2204
4. $M^{3+} \rightarrow M^{4+}$ 4100
5. $M^{4+} \rightarrow M^{5+}$

Environmental properties

Biological role	Abundances	Geological data
None; low toxicity; stimulatory	**Sun** (relative to H = 1×10^{12}): n.a.	**Chief deposits and sources:** monazite [(Ce, La, etc.)PO$_4$]; bastnaesite [(Ce, La, etc.) (CO$_3$)F]
Levels in humans: n.a. but low	**Earth's crust**/p.p.m.: 1.4	**World production**/tonnes y^{-1}: *c.* 100
	Seawater/p.p.m.:	**Reserves**/tonnes: *c.* 10^5
	Atlantic surface: 2.4×10^{-7}	
	Atlantic deep: 2.9×10^{-7}	
	Pacific surface: 1.6×10^{-7}	
	Pacific deep: 5.8×10^{-7}	
	Residence time/years: n.a.	
	Classification: recycled	
	Oxidation state: III	

H	Atomic number: 1
	Relative atomic mass ($^{12}C = 12.0000$): **1.00794**

Chemical properties

Colourless, odourless gas, insoluble in water. Burns in air, forms explosive mixtures with air. Used for making ammonia, cyclohexane, methanol, etc.

Radii/pm: H^- 154; atomic 78; covalent 30;
van der Waals 120; H^+ 10^{-5}

Electronegativity: 2.20 (Pauling); n.a. (Allred); 7.18 eV (absolute)

Effective nuclear charge: 1.00 (Slater); 1.00 (Clementi);
1.00 (Froese-Fischer)

Standard reduction potentials $E^{\ominus}$/V

	I		0		$-$I
Acid solution	H_3O^+	$\underline{0.00}$	H_2	$\underline{-2.25}$	H^-
Alkaline solution	H_2O	$\underline{0.828}$	H_2	$\underline{-2.25}$	H^-

Covalent bonds r/pm E/kJ mol^{-1}

	r/pm	E/kJ mol^{-1}
H—H	74.14	453.6
H—F	91.7	566
H—Cl	127.4	431
H—Br	140.8	366
H—I	160.9	299

For covalent bonds to hydrogen
see other elements

^{2}H—^{2}H	74.14	447.3

Oxidation states

H^{-1}	NaH, CaH_2, etc.
H^0	H_2
H^I	H_2O, H_3O^+, etc.. OH^-, HF, HCl, etc., other acids, NH_3 etc., CH_4 etc.

Hydrogen is the most versatile of elements in its range of chemical bonds

Physical properties

Melting point/K: 14.01
Boiling point/K: 20.28
ΔH_{fusion}/kJ mol^{-1}: 0.12
ΔH_{vap}/kJ mol^{-1}: 0.46
Triple point/K: 13.96

Critical temperature/K: 33.2
Critical pressure/kPa: 1297
Critical volume/cm^3: 65.0

Thermodynamic properties (298.15 K, 0.1 MPa)

State	$\Delta_f H^{\ominus}$/kJ mol^{-1}	$\Delta_f G^{\ominus}$/kJ mol^{-1}	$S^{\ominus}$/J K^{-1} mol^{-1}	C_p/J K^{-1} mol^{-1}
Gas (H$_2$)	0	0	130.684	28.824
Gas (atoms)	217.965	203.247	114.713	20.784

Density/kg m^{-3}: 76.0 [solid, 11 K]; 70.8 [liquid, b.p.];
0.08988 [gas, 273 K]

Thermal conductivity/W m^{-1} K^{-1}: 0.1815 [300 K] g

Mass magnetic susceptibility/kg^{-1} m^3: -2.50×10^{-8} (g)

Molar volume/cm^3: 13.26 [11 K]

Crystal structure (cell dimensions/pm), space group

H_2 h.c.p. ($a = 377.6$, $c = 616.2$), P6$_3$/mmc
^{2}H$_2$ h.c.p. ($a = 360.0$, $c = 585.8$), P6$_3$/mmc
H_2 cubic ($a = 533.8$), Fm3m
^{2}H$_2$ cubic ($a = 509.2$), Fm3m
H_2 tetragonal ($a = 450$, $c = 368$), I4
^{2}H$_2$ tetragonal ($a = 338$, $c = 560$)
T (h.c.p.→cubic) = 4.5 K

X-ray diffraction: mass absorption coefficients (μ/ρ)/cm^2 g^{-1}:
CuK$_\alpha$ 0.435   MoK$_\alpha$ 0.380

Recognized as an element in 1766 by H. Cavendish at London, UK

[Greek, *hydro genes* = water forming]

Hydrogen

Thermal neutron capture cross-section/barns: 0.332
Number of isotopes (including nuclear isomers): 3
Isotope mass range: $1 \rightarrow 3$

Key isotopes

Nuclide	Atomic mass	Natural abundance (%)	Half-life $T_{1/2}$	Decay mode and energy (MeV)	Nuclear spin I	Nuclear magnetic moment μ	Uses
^{1}H	1.007825	99.985	stable		1/2	+2.79284	NMR
^{2}H	2.01400	0.015	stable		1	+0.85743	NMR
^{3}H	3.01605	0	12.26y	β^-(0.01861); no γ	1/2	+2.97896	tracer, medical

NMR

	^{1}H	^{2}H	^{3}H
Relative sensitivity (^{1}H = 1.00)	1.00 (by defn)	9.65×10^{-3}	1.21
Receptivity (^{13}C = 1.00)	5680	8.2×10^{-6}	—
Magnetogyric ratio/rad T^{-1} s^{-1}	26.7510×10^7	4.1064×10^7	28.5335×10^7
Quadrupole moment/m^2	—	2.73×10^{-31}	—
Frequency (^{1}H = 100 MHz; 2.3488 T)/MHz	100.000	15.351	106.663

Reference: $Si(CH_3)_4$

Ground state electron configuration: $1s^1$
Term symbol: $^2S_{1/2}$
Electron affinity $(M \rightarrow M^-)$/kJ mol^{-1}: 72.8

Main lines in atomic spectrum

Wavelength/nm	Species
434.047	I
486.133	I
656.272	I
656.285	I
1875.10	I

Ionization energies/kJ mol^{-1}

1. $M \rightarrow M^+$ 1312.0

Environmental properties

Biological role	Abundances	Geological data
Constituent element of DNA	**Sun** (relative to $H = 1 \times 10^{12}$): taken as standard	**Chief sources:** Methane $(CH_4 + 2H_2O = 3H_2 + CO)$; by-product of oil refineries and chemical industry, water electrolysis
Levels in humans: Muscle/p.p.m.: 93000 Bone/p.p.m.: 52000 Blood/mg dm^{-3}: constituent of water	**Earth's crust**/p.p.m.: 1520 **Seawater**/p.p.m.: constituent element of water	**World production**/m^3: 350×10^9
Daily dietary intake: mainly as water	**Atmosphere**/p.p.m. by volume: 0.53	**Reserves:** almost limitless
Toxic intake: non-toxic Total mass of element in average (70 kg) person: 7 kg		

In

Atomic number: **49**

Relative atomic mass ($^{12}C = 12.0000$): **114.82**

Chemical properties

Soft, silvery-white metal. Stable in air and with water, dissolves in acids. Used in low melting alloys in safety devices. Semiconductor uses as InAs and InSb in transistors, thermistors, etc.

Radii/pm: In^{3+} 92; In^+ 132; atomic 162.6; covalent 150

Electronegativity: 1.78 (Pauling); 1.49 (Allred); 3.1 eV (absolute)

Effective nuclear charge: 5.00 (Slater); 8.47 (Clementi); 9.66 (Froese-Fischer)

Standard reduction potentials $E^{\ominus}$/V

	III		I		0
Acid solution	In^{3+}	$\underset{}{\overset{-0.444}{\rule{1cm}{0.4pt}}}$	In^+	$\overset{-0.126}{\rule{1cm}{0.4pt}}$	In
			$\overset{-0.3382}{\rule{3cm}{0.4pt}}$		

Covalent bonds r/pm E/kJ mol^{-1}

	r/pm	E/kJ mol^{-1}
In–H	185	243
In–C	216	165
In–O	213	109
In–F	199	c.525
In–Cl	240	439
In–In	325.1	c. 85

Oxidation states

In^I	(s^2)	InCl, InBr, InI
In^{II}	(s^1)	$[In_2Cl_6]^{2-}$
		$[In_2Br_2]^{2-}$, $[In_2I_6]^{2-}$
$\mathbf{In^{III}}$	(d^{10})	In_2O_3, $In(OH)_3$,
		$[In(H_2O)_6]^{3+}$ (aq)
		InF_3, $InCl_3$ etc.,
		$InCl_5^{2-}$, $InCl_6^{3-}$,
		complexes

Physical properties

Melting point/K: 429.32

Boiling point/K: 2353

ΔH_{fusion}/kJ mol^{-1}: 3.27

ΔH_{vap}/kJ mol^{-1}: 226.4

Thermodynamic properties (298.15 K, 0.1 MPa)

State	$\Delta_f H^{\ominus}$/kJ mol^{-1}	$\Delta_f G^{\ominus}$/kJ mol^{-1}	$S^{\ominus}$/J K^{-1} mol^{-1}	C_p/J K^{-1} mol^{-1}
Solid	0	0	57.82	26.74
Gas	243.30	208.71	173.79	20.84

Density/kg m^{-3}: 7310 [298 K]; 7032 [liquid at m.p.]

Thermal conductivity/W m^{-1} K^{-1}: 81.6 [300 K]

Electrical resistivity/Ω m: 8.37×10^{-8} [293 K]

Mass magnetic susceptibility/kg^{-1} m^3: -7.0×10^{-9} (s)

Molar volume/cm^3: 15.71

Coefficient of linear thermal expansion/K^{-1}: 33×10^{-6}

Crystal structure (cell dimensions/pm), space group

Face centred tetragonal ($a = 325.30$, $c = 494.55$), I4/mmm

X-ray diffraction: mass absorption coefficients (μ/ρ)/cm^2 g^{-1}: CuK$_{\alpha}$ 243 MoK$_{\alpha}$ 29.3

Thermal neutron capture cross-section/barns: 194
Number of isotopes (including nuclear isomers): 59
Isotope mass range: $102 \rightarrow 132$

Key isotopes

Nuclide	Atomic mass	Natural abundance (%)	Half-life $T_{1/2}$	Decay mode and energy (MeV)	Nuclear spin I	Nuclear magnetic moment μ	Uses
^{111}In	110.905 109	0	2.81d	EC; γ			medical tracer
^{113}In	112.904 061	4.3	stable		9/2+	+5.5229	NMR
^{113m}In		0	1.657h	IT(0.3917)	1/2−	−0.210	medical tracer
^{114m}In	113.904 916	0	49.51	IT(0.190) 97%; EC(1.6) 3%; γ	5+	+4.7	tracer
^{115}In	114.903 880	95.7	6×10^{14}y	β^-(0.496); no γ	9/2+	+5.534	NMR

NMR

	$[^{113}\text{In}]$	^{115}In
Relative sensitivity (^{1}H = 1.00)	0.34	0.34
Receptivity (^{13}C = 1.00)	83.8	1890
Magnetogyric ratio/rad T^{-1} s^{-1}	5.8493×10^7	5.8618×10^7
Quadrupole moment/m^2	1.14×10^{-28}	1.16×10^{-28}
Frequency (^{1}H = 100 MHz; 2.3488 T)/MHz	21.866	21.914

Reference: $\text{In}(\text{H}_2\text{O})_6^{3+}$

Ground state electron configuration: $[\text{Kr}]4d^{10}5s^25p^1$
Term symbol: $^2P_{1/2}$
Electron affinity (M→M$^-$)/kJ mol^{-1}: $c.$ 30

Main lines in atomic spectrum

Wavelength/nm	Species
303.936 (AA)	I
325.609	I
325.856	I
410.176	I
451.131	I

Ionization energies/kJ mol^{-1}

1. M →M$^+$	558.3	6. M^{5+}→M^{6+} (9 500)
2. M$^+$→M^{2+}	1820.6	7. M^{6+}→M^{7+} (11 700)
3. M^{2+}→M^{3+}	2704	8. M^{7+}→M^{8+} (13 900)
4. M^{3+}→M^{4+}	5200	9. M^{8+}→M^{9+} (17 200)
5. M^{4+}→M^{5+}	(7400)	10. M^{9+}→M^{10+} (19 700)

Environmental properties

Biological role	Abundances	Geological data
None; stimulatory; teratogenic	**Sun** (relative to H = 1×10^{12}): 44.7	**Chief deposits and sources:** occurs up to 1% of zinc sulfide and galena (lead sulfide) ores; obtained as a by-product of zinc and lead smelting
Levels in humans:	**Earth's crust**/p.p.m.: 0.049	
Muscle/p.p.m.: $c.$ 0.015	**Seawater**/p.p.m.: 1×10^{-7}	
Bone/p.p.m.: n.a.	Residence time/years: n.a.	
Blood/mg dm^{-3}: n.a. but low	Oxidation state: III	**World production**/tonnes y^{-1}: 75
Daily dietary intake: n.a. but low		
Toxic intake: 30 mg		**Reserves**/tonnes: > 1500
Lethal intake: > 200 mg		
Total mass of element in average (70 kg) person: n.a.		

Atomic number: 53

Relative atomic mass (^{12}C $=12.0000$): **126.90447**

Chemical properties

Black, shiny non-metal solid, I_2. Sublimes easily. Used in disinfection, pharmaceuticals, food supplements, dyes, catalysts and photography.

Radii/pm: I^- 220; Covalent 133.3; van der Waals 215

Electronegativity: 2.66 (Pauling); 2.21 (Allred); 6.76 eV (absolute)

Effective nuclear charge: 7.60 (Slater); 11.61 (Clementi); 14.59 (Froese-Fischer)

Standard reduction potentials $E^{\ominus}/V$

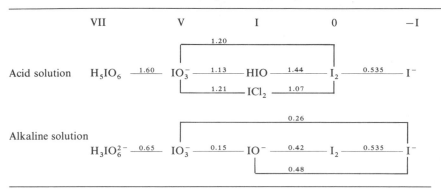

	VII	V	I	0	$-$I

Acid solution: $H_5IO_6 \xrightarrow{1.60} IO_3^- \xrightarrow{1.13} HIO \xrightarrow{1.44} I_2 \xrightarrow{0.535} I^-$; with $IO_3^- \xrightarrow{1.21} ICl_2 \xrightarrow{1.07}$; upper 1.20

Alkaline solution: $H_3IO_6^{2-} \xrightarrow{0.65} IO_3^- \xrightarrow{0.15} IO^- \xrightarrow{0.42} I_2 \xrightarrow{0.535} I^-$; 0.26; 0.48

Covalent bonds

	r/pm	E/kJ mol^{-1}	Oxidation states	
I–H	160.9	299	I^{-I}	I^-(aq), HI, KI, etc.
I–C	213	218	I^0	I_2, I_3^-, I_5^-, etc.
I–O	195	234	I^I	I_n^+, ICl_2^-, etc.
I–F	191	280	I^{III}	I_4O_9 ($=I^{3+}(IO_3^-)_3$)
I–Cl	232	208		ICl_3
I–I	266.6	151	I^V	I_2O_5, HIO_3, IO_3^-(aq)
I–Si	243	234		IF_5, IF_6^-
I–P	252	184	I^{VII}	H_5IO_6, $H_4IO_6^-$(aq) etc.,
				HIO_4, IO_4^-(aq), IF_7

Physical properties

Melting point/K: 386.7

Boiling point/K: 457.50

ΔH_{fusion}/kJ mol^{-1}: 15.27 $\qquad$ ΔH_{vap}/kJ mol^{-1}: 41.67

Thermodynamic properties (298.15 K, 0.1 MPa)

State	$\Delta_f H^{\ominus}$/kJ mol^{-1}	$\Delta_f G^{\ominus}$/kJ mol^{-1}	$S^{\ominus}$/J K^{-1} mol^{-1}	C_p/J K^{-1} mol^{-1}
Solid	0	0	116.135	54.438
Gas (I_2)	62.438	19.327	260.69	36.90
Gas (atoms)	106.838	70.250	180.791	20.786

Density/kg m^{-3}: 4930 [293 K]

Thermal conductivity/W m^{-1} K^{-1}: 0.449 [300 K]

Electrical resistivity/Ω m: 1.37×10^7 [293 K]

Mass magnetic susceptibility/kg^{-1} m^3: -4.40×10^{-9} (s)

Molar volume/cm^3: 25.74

Coefficient of linear thermal expansion/K^{-1}: n.a.

Crystal structure (cell dimensions/pm), space group

Orthorhombic ($a=726.47$, $b=478.57$, $c=979.08$), Cmca

X-ray diffraction: mass absorption coefficients (μ/ρ)/cm^2 g^{-1}: CuK$_\alpha$ 294 MoK$_\alpha$ 37.1

Iodine

Thermal neutron capture cross-section/barns: 6.2

Number of isotopes (including nuclear isomers). 37

Isotope mass range: $110 \rightarrow 140$

Nuclear properties

Key isotopes

Nuclide	Atomic mass	Natural abundance (%)	Half-life $T_{1/2}$	Decay mode and energy (MeV)	Nuclear spin I	Nuclear magnetic moment μ	Uses
^{123}I	122.905 594	0	13.1h	EC(1.23); γ	5/2+		tracer
^{125}I	124.904 620	0	59.9d	EC(0.178); γ	5/2+	+3.0	tracer medical
^{127}I	126.904 473	100	stable		5/2+	+2.808	NMR
^{129}I	128.904 986	0	1.67×10^7 y	β^-(0.193); γ	7/2+	+2.617	
^{131}I	130.906 114	0	8.040d	β^-(0.971); γ	7/2+	+2.74	tracer, medical

NMR

^{127}I

Relative sensitivity ($^1H = 1.00$)	9.34×10^{-2}
Receptivity ($^{13}C = 1.00$)	530
Magnetogyric ratio/rad T^{-1} s^{-1}	5.3525×10^7
Quadrupole moment/m^2	-0.79×10^{-28}
Frequency ($^1H = 100$ MHz; 2.3488 T)/MHz	20.007

Reference: NaI (aq)

Ground state electron configuration: $[Kr]4d^{10}5s^25p^5$

Term symbol: $^2P_{3/2}$

Electron affinity $(M \rightarrow M^-)$/kJ mol^{-1}: 295.2

Electron shell properties

Main lines in atomic spectrum

Wavelength/nm	Species
511.929	I
533.822	II
562.569	II
804.374	I
905.833	I
911.391	I

Ionization energies/kJ mol^{-1}

1. $M \rightarrow M^+$ 1008.4	6. $M^{5+} \rightarrow M^{6+}$ (7 400)
2. $M^+ \rightarrow M^{2+}$ 1845.9	7. $M^{6+} \rightarrow M^{7+}$ (8 700)
3. $M^{2+} \rightarrow M^{3+}$ 3200	8. $M^{7+} \rightarrow M^{8+}$ (16 400)
4. $M^{3+} \rightarrow M^{4+}$ (4100)	9. $M^{8+} \rightarrow M^{9+}$ (19 300)
5. $M^{4+} \rightarrow M^{5+}$ (5000)	10. $M^{9+} \rightarrow M^{10+}$ (22 100)

Environmental properties

Biological role

Essential to many species, including humans; toxic as I_2

Levels in humans:
Muscle/p.p.m.: 0.05–0.5
Bone/p.p.m.: 0.27
Blood/mg dm^{-3}: 0.057
Daily dietary intake:
  0.1–0.2 mg
Toxic iodide intake: 2 mg
Lethal iodide intake: 35–350 g
Total mass of element in
  average (70 kg) person:
  12–20 mg

Abundances

Sun (relative to $H = 1 \times 10^{12}$):
n.a.
Earth's crust/p.p.m.: 0.14
Seawater/p.p.m.:
Atlantic surface: 0.049
Atlantic deep: 0.056
Pacific surface: 0.043
Pacific deep: 0.058
Residence time/years: 300 000
Classification: scavenged as
  I($-$I); recycled as I(V)
Oxidation states: $-$I and V,
  mainly V

Geological data

Chief sources: brines; Chilean
  nitrates contain up to 0.3%
  calcium iodate; seaweed
World production/tonnes y^{-1}:
12 000
Reserves/tonnes: 2.6×10^6

Ir

Atomic number: 77
Relative atomic mass ($^{12}C=12.0000$): 192.22

Chemical properties

Hard, lustrous, silvery metal of the platinum group. Stable to air and water, inert to all acids but fused NaOH will attack it. Used in special alloys and spark plugs.

Radii/pm: Ir^{2+} 89; Ir^{3+} 75; Ir^{4+} 66; atomic 135.7; covalent 126

Electronegativity: 2.20 (Pauling); 1.55 (Allred); 5.4 eV (absolute)

Effective nuclear charge: 3.90 (Slater); 10.57 (Clementi);
15.33 (Froese-Fischer)

Standard reduction potentials $E^{\ominus}$/V

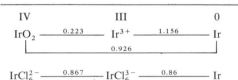

$$IrCl_6^{2-} \xrightarrow{\;0.867\;} IrCl_6^{3-} \xrightarrow{\;0.86\;} Ir$$

Oxidation states

Ir^{-I}	(d^{10})	rare $[Ir(CO)_3(PPh_3)]^-$
Ir^{0}	(d^{9})	rare $[Ir_4(CO)_{12}]$
Ir^{I}	(d^{8})	$[Ir(CO)Cl(PPh_3)_2]$
Ir^{II}	(d^{7})	$IrCl_2$
Ir^{III}	(d^{6})	IrF_3, $IrCl_3$ etc., $[IrCl_6]^{3-}$(aq)
Ir^{IV}	(d^{5})	IrO_2, IrF_4, IrS_2, $[IrCl_6]^{2-}$(aq)
Ir^{V}	(d^{4})	IrF_5, $[IrF_6]^-$
Ir^{VI}	(d^{3})	IrF_6

Physical properties

Melting point/K: 2683
Boiling point/K: 4403
ΔH_{fusion}/kJ mol^{-1}:   26.4
ΔH_{vap}/kJ mol^{-1}:   563.6

Thermodynamic properties   (298.15 K, 0.1 MPa)

State	$\Delta_f H^{\ominus}$/kJ mol^{-1}	$\Delta_f G^{\ominus}$/kJ mol^{-1}	$S^{\ominus}$/J K^{-1} mol^{-1}	C_p/J K^{-1} mol^{-1}
Solid	0	0	35.48	25.10
Gas	665.3	617.9	193.578	20.786

Density/kg m^{-3}:   22 560 [290 K]; 20 000 [liquid at m.p.]
Thermal conductivity/W m^{-1} K^{-1}:   147 [300 K]
Electrical resistivity/Ω m: 5.3×10^{-8} [293 K]
Mass magnetic susceptibility/kg^{-1} m^3: $+1.67 \times 10^{-9}$ (s)
Molar volume/cm^3:   8.57
Coefficient of linear thermal expansion/K^{-1}: 6.4×10^{-6}

Crystal structure (cell dimensions/pm), space group

f.c.c. ($a=383.92$), Fm3m

X-ray diffraction: mass absorption coefficients (μ/ρ)/cm^2 g^{-1}:
CuK$_\alpha$ 193   MoK$_\alpha$ 110

Discovered in 1803 by S. Tennant at London, UK

[Latin, *iris* = rainbow]

Iridium

Thermal neutron capture cross-section/barns: 425
Number of isotopes (including nuclear isomers): 40
Isotope mass range: 170→198

Nuclear properties

Key isotopes

Nuclide	Atomic mass	Natural abundance (%)	Half-life $T_{1/2}$	Decay mode and energy (MeV)	Nuclear spin I	Nuclear magnetic moment μ	Uses
^{191}Ir	190.960 584	37.3	stable		3/2+	+0.1461	NMR
^{192}Ir	191.962 580	0	73.83d	β^- (1.454); γ	4−	+1.880	tracer medical
^{193}Ir	192.962 917	62.7	stable		3/2+	+0.1591	NMR

	^{191}Ir	^{193}Ir
NMR (never used)		
Relative sensitivity (^{1}H = 1.00)	2.53×10^{-5}	3.27×10^{-5}
Receptivity (^{13}C = 1.00)	0.023	0.050
Magnetogyric ratio/rad T^{-1} s^{-1}	0.539×10^7	0.391×10^7
Quadrupole moment/m^2	1.5×10^{-28}	1.4×10^{-28}
Frequency (^{1}H = 100 MHz; 2.3488 T)/MHz	1.718	1.871

Ground state electron configuration: [Xe]$4f^{14}5d^76s^2$
Term symbol: $^4F_{9/2}$
Electron affinity (M→M$^-$)/kJ mol^{-1}: 151

Electron shell properties

Main lines in atomic spectrum

Wavelength/nm	Species
203.357	I
208.882 (AA)	I
209.263	I
215.805	I
254.397	I
263.971	I
322.078	I

Ionization energies/kJ mol^{-1}

1. M → M$^+$ 880	6. M^{5+} → M^{6+} (6 900)
2. M$^+$ → M^{2+} (1680)	7. M^{6+} → M^{7+} (8 500)
3. M^{2+} → M^{3+} (2600)	8. M^{7+} → M^{8+} (10 000)
4. M^{3+} → M^{4+} (3800)	9. M^{8+} → M^{9+} (11 700)
5. M^{4+} → M^{5+} (5500)	10. M^{9+} → M^{10+}

Environmental properties

Biological role	Abundances	Geological data
None	**Sun** (relative to H = 1 × 10^{12}): 7.1	**Chief deposits and sources:** Osiridium [IrOs]; iridiosmium [Os, Ir]; also found with platinum ores
Levels in humans:		
Muscle/p.p.m.: 2×10^{-5}?	**Earth's crust**/p.p.m.: *c.* 3×10^{-6}	
Bone/p.p.m.: n.a.		**World production**/tonnes y^{-1}: 3
Blood/mg dm^{-3}: n.a. but very low	**Seawater**/p.p.m.: n.a. but minute	
Daily dietary intake: n.a. but very low		**Reserves**/tonnes: 950
Toxic intake: low toxicity		
Total mass of element in average (70 kg) person: n.a.		

Fe

Atomic number: 26

Relative atomic mass ($^{12}C = 12.0000$): 55.847

Chemical properties

When pure, iron is lustrous, silvery, and soft (workable). Most important of all metals, used principally as steels. Rusts in damp air, dissolves in dilute acids.

Radii/pm: Fe^{2+} 82; Fe^{3+} 67: atomic (α form) 124.1; covalent 116.5

Electronegativity: 1.83 (Pauling); 1.64 (Allred); 4.06 (absolute)

Effective nuclear charge: 3.75 (Slater); 5.43 (Clementi); 7.40 (Froese-Fischer)

Standard reduction potentials $E^{\ominus}/V$

	VI	III	II	0

Acid solution (pH 0)

$$Fe^{3+} \xrightarrow{\;-0.04\;}$$

$$Fe^{3+} \xrightarrow{\;0.771\;} Fe^{2+} \xrightarrow{\;-0.44\;} Fe$$

$$[Fe(CN)_6]^{3-} \xrightarrow{\;0.361\;} [Fe(CN)_6]^{2-} \xrightarrow{\;-1.16\;} Fe$$

Alkaline solution (pH 14)

$$FeO_4^{2-} \xrightarrow{\;c.0.55\;} FeO_2^{-} \xrightarrow{\;c.-0.69\;} HFeO_2^{-} \xrightarrow{\;c.-0.8\;} Fe$$

Oxidation states

Fe^{-II}	(d^{10})	rare $Fe(CO)_4^{2-}$
Fe^{-I}	(d^{9})	rare $Fe_2(CO)_8^{2-}$
Fe^{0}	(d^{8})	$Fe(CO)_5$
Fe^{I}	(d^{7})	rare $[Fe(NO)(H_2O)_5]^{2+}$
Fe^{II}	(d^{6})	$FeO, FeS_2 (=Fe^{II}S_2^{2-}) Fe(OH)_2, [Fe(H_2O)_6]^{2+}$ (aq), FeF_2, $Fe(C_5H_5)_2$, etc.
Fe^{III}	(d^{5})	$Fe_2O_3, Fe_3O_4 (=Fe^{II}O \cdot Fe_2^{III}O_3), FeF_3, FeCl_3, FeO(OH)$, $[Fe(H_2O)_6]^{3+}$ (aq), etc.
Fe^{IV}	(d^{4})	rare, some complexes
Fe^{V}	(d^{3})	FeO_4^{3-} ?
Fe^{VI}	(d^{2})	FeO_4^{2-}

Physical properties*

*Very much affected by impurities such as carbon

Melting point/K: 1808

Boiling point/K: 3023

ΔH_{fusion}/kJ mol^{-1}: 14.9   **ΔH_{vap}/kJ mol^{-1}:** 351.0

Thermodynamic properties (298.15 K, 0.1 MPa)

State	$\Delta_f H^{\ominus}$/kJ mol^{-1}	$\Delta_f G^{\ominus}$/kJ mol^{-1}	$S^{\ominus}$/J K^{-1} mol^{-1}	C_p/J K^{-1} mol^{-1}
Solid	0	0	27.28	25.10
Gas	416.3	370.7	180.490	25.677

Density/kg m^{-3}: 7874 [293 K]; 7035 [liquid at m.p.]

Thermal conductivity/W m^{-1} K^{-1}: 80.2 [300 K]

Electrical resistivity/Ω m: 9.71×10^{-8} [293 K]

Mass magnetic susceptibility/kg^{-1} m^3: ferromagnetic

Molar volume/cm^3: 7.09

Coefficient of linear thermal expansion/K^{-1}: 12.3×10^{-6}

Crystal structure (cell dimensions/pm), space group

α-Fe b.c.c. ($a = 286.645$), Im3m
β-Fe not true allotrope
γ-Fe c.c.p. ($a = 364.68$), Fm3m
δ-Fe b.c.c. ($a = 293.22$), Im3m

$T(\alpha \rightarrow \gamma) = 1183$ K
$T(\gamma \rightarrow \delta) = 1663$ K

X-ray diffraction: mass absorption coefficients (μ/ρ)/cm^2 g^{-1}: CuK_{α} 308 MoK_{α} 38.5

Known to ancient civilizations

[Anglo-Saxon, *iron*; Latin, *ferrum*]

Iron

Thermal neutron capture cross-section/barns: 2.56
Number of isotopes (including nuclear isomers): 16
Isotope mass range: $49 \rightarrow 63$

Key isotopes

Nuclide	Atomic mass	Natural abundance (%)	Half-life $T_{1/2}$	Decay mode and energy (MeV)	Nuclear spin I	Nuclear magnetic moment μ	Uses
^{52}Fe	51.948 114	0	8.28h	β^+, (2.37); 57%; EC(2.37) 43%; γ	0+		tracer
^{54}Fe	53.939 612	5.82	stable		0+		
^{55}Fe	54.938 296	0	2.7y	EC(0.2314); no γ	3/2−		tracer medical
^{56}Fe	55.934 939	91.18	stable		0+		
^{57}Fe	56.935 396	2.1	stable		1/2−	+0.090 44	NMR
^{58}Fe	57.933 277	0.28	stable		0+		
^{59}Fe	58.934 877	0	44.51d	β^-(1.565); γ	3/2+	0.29	tracer, medical
^{60}Fe	59.934 080	0	$c.\ 10^5$y	β^-(0.243)	0+		

NMR

^{57}Fe

Relative sensitivity (^{1}H = 1.00) 3.37×10^{-5}
Receptivity (^{13}C = 1.00) 4.2×10^{-3}
Magnetogyric ratio/rad T^{-1} s^{-1} 0.8661×10^7
Frequency (^{1}H = 100 MHz; 2.3488 T)/MHz   3.231
Reference: Fe(CO)$_5$

Ground state electron configuration: $[Ar]3d^64s^2$
Term symbol: $^5D_4$
Electron affinity $(M \rightarrow M^-)$/kJ mol^{-1}: 15.7

Main lines in atomic spectrum

Wavelength/nm	Species
248.327 (AA)	I
248.814	I
252.285	I
344.061	I
371.994	I
373.713	I
374.556	I
385.991	I

Ionization energies/kJ mol^{-1}

1. $M \rightarrow M^+$	759.3	6. $M^{5+} \rightarrow M^{6+}$	9 600
2. $M^+ \rightarrow M^{2+}$	1561	7. $M^{6+} \rightarrow M^{7+}$	12 100
3. $M^{2+} \rightarrow M^{3+}$	2957	8. $M^{7+} \rightarrow M^{8+}$	14 575
4. $M^{3+} \rightarrow M^{4+}$	5290	9. $M^{8+} \rightarrow M^{9+}$	22 678
5. $M^{4+} \rightarrow M^{5+}$	7240	10. $M^{9+} \rightarrow M^{10+}$	25 290

Environmental properties

Biological role

Essential to all species
Levels in humans:
Muscle/p.p.m.: 180
Bone/p.p.m.: 3–380
Blood/mg dm^{-3}: 447
Daily dietary intake: 6–40 mg
Toxic intake: 200 mg
Lethal intake: 7–35 g
Total mass of element in average (70 kg) person: 4.2 g

Abundances

Sun (relative to H = 1×10^{12}): 3.16×10^7
Earth's crust/p.p.m.: 41 000
Seawater/p.p.m.:
Atlantic surface: 1×10^{-4}
Atlantic deep: 4×10^{-4}
Pacific surface: 0.1×10^{-4}
Pacific deep: 1×10^{-4}
Residence time/years: 98
Classification: recycled
Oxidation state: III

Geological data

Chief ores: haematite [Fe$_2$O$_3$]; magnetite [Fe$_3$O$_4$]; siderite [FeCO$_3$]
World production/tonnes y^{-1}: 7.16×10^8
Reserves/tonnes: 1.1×10^{11}

Kr

Chemical properties

Colourless, odourless gas. Chemically inert to everything but fluorine. ^{86}Kr has orange-red line in atomic spectrum which is fundamental standard of length: 1 metre = 1 650 763.73 wavelengths.

Radii/pm: covalent 189; van der Waals 198; Kr^+ 169

Electronegativity: n.a. (Pauling); n.a. (Allred); [6.8 eV (absolute)]

Effective nuclear charge: 8.25 (Slater); 9.77 (Clementi); 11.79 (Froese-Fischer)

Standard reduction potentials $E^{\ominus}/V$

n.a. [KrF_2 decomposes in water]

Covalent bonds r/pm E/kJ mol^{-1}

Kr–F	188.9	50

Oxidation states

Kr^0	clathrates $Kr_8(H_2O)_{46}$, Kr (quinol)$_3$
Kr^{II}	KrF_2, $[KrF]^+[AsF_6]^-$

Physical properties

Melting point/K: 116.6
Boiling point/K: 120.85
ΔH_{fusion}/kJ mol^{-1}: 1.64
ΔH_{vap}/kJ mol^{-1}: 9.05

Thermodynamic properties (298.15 K, 0.1 MPa)

State	$\Delta_f H^{\ominus}$/kJ mol^{-1}	$\Delta_f G^{\ominus}$/kJ mol^{-1}	$S^{\ominus}$/J K^{-1} mol^{-1}	C_p/J K^{-1} mol^{-1}
Gas	0	0	164.082	20.786

Density/kg m^{-3}: 2823 [solid, m.p.]; 2413 [liquid b.p.]; 3.7493 [gas, 273 K]
Thermal conductivity/W m^{-1} K^{-1}: 0.009 49 [300 K]$_g$
Mass magnetic susceptibility/kg^{-1} m^3: -4.32×10^{-9} (g)
Molar volume/cm^3: 29.68 [116 K]

Crystal structure (cell dimensions/pm), space group

f.c.c. (80 K) ($a = 572.1$), Fm3m

X-ray diffraction: mass absorption coefficients (μ/ρ)/cm^2 g^{-1}:
CuK$_\alpha$ 108   MoK$_\alpha$ 84.9

Discovered in 1898 by Sir William Ramsay and M. W. Travers at London, UK

[Greek, *kryptos* = hidden]

Krypton

Thermal neutron capture cross-section/barns: 25
Number of isotopes (including nuclear isomers): 27
Isotope mass range: 72→94

Nuclear properties

Key isotopes

Nuclide	Atomic mass	Natural abundance (%)	Half-life $T_{1/2}$	Decay mode and energy (MeV)	Nuclear spin I	Nuclear magnetic moment μ	Uses
^{78}Kr	77.920 400	0.35	stable		0+		
^{80}Kr	79.916 380	2.25	stable		0+		
^{82}Kr	81.913 482	11.6	stable		0+		
^{83}Kr	82.914 135	11.5	stable		9/2+	−0.970	NMR
^{84}Kr	83.911 507	57.0	stable		0+		
^{85}Kr	84.912 531	0	10.72y	β^- (0.687); γ	9/2+	±1.005	tracer
^{86}Kr	85.910 616	17.3	stable		0+		

NMR (few compounds) ^{83}Kr
Relative sensitivity ($^1H = 1.00$) 1.88×10^{-3}
Receptivity ($^{13}C = 1.00$)   1.23
Magnetogyric ratio/rad T^{-1} s^{-1} -1.029×10^7
Quadrupole moment/m^2 0.15×10^{-28}
Frequency ($^1H = 100$ MHz; 2.3488 T)/MHz   3.847

Ground state electron configuration: $[Ar]3d^{10}4s^24p^6$
Term symbol: $^1S_0$
Electron affinity ($M \rightarrow M^-$)/kJ mol^{-1}: −39 (calc.)

Electron shell properties

Main lines in atomic spectrum		Ionization energies/kJ mol^{-1}	
Wavelength/nm	Species		
473.900	II	1. $M \rightarrow M^+$ 1350.7	6. $M^{5+} \rightarrow M^{6+}$ 7570
587.091	I	2. $M^+ \rightarrow M^{2+}$ 2350	7. $M^{6+} \rightarrow M^{7+}$ 10 710
810.436	I	3. $M^{2+} \rightarrow M^{3+}$ 3565	8. $M^{7+} \rightarrow M^{8+}$ 12 200
811.290	I	4. $M^{3+} \rightarrow M^{4+}$ 5070	9. $M^{8+} \rightarrow M^{9+}$ 22 229
829.811	I	5. $M^{4+} \rightarrow M^{5+}$ 6240	10. $M^{9+} \rightarrow M^{10+}$ (28 900)
877.675	I		

Environmental properties

Biological role	Abundances	Geological data
None; non-toxic but could asphyxiate	**Sun** (relative to $H = 1 \times 10^{12}$): n.a.	**Chief resource:** liquid air
Levels in humans: n.a. but very low	**Earth's crust**/p.p.m.: *c.* 1×10^{-5}	**World production**/tonnes y^{-1}: 8
	Seawater/p.p.m.: Concentration/p.p.m.: 8×10^{-5}	**Reserves**/tonnes: 1.7×10^{10} (atmosphere)
	Oxidation state: 0	
	Atmosphere/p.p.m. (by volume): 1.14	

La

Atomic number: 57

Relative atomic mass ($^{12}C = 12.0000$): 138.9055

Chemical properties

Soft, silvery-white metal; rapidly tarnishes in air and burns easily. Reacts with water to give hydrogen gas. Used in optical glass and for flints. La^{3+} is used as a biological tracer for calcium Ca^{2+}.

Radii/pm: La^{3+} 122; atomic 187.7; covalent 169

Electronegativity: 1.10 (Pauling); 1.08 (Allred); 3.1 eV (absolute)

Effective nuclear charge: 2.85 (Slater); 9.31 (Clementi); 10.43 (Froese-Fischer)

Standard reduction potentials $E^{\ominus}/V$

	III		0
Acid solution	La^{3+}	$\xrightarrow{-2.38}$	La
Alkaline solution	$La(OH)_3$	$\xrightarrow{-2.80}$	La

Oxidation states

La^{III} ([Xe])	La_2O_3, $La(OH)_3$, $[La(H_2O)_x]^{3+}$(aq)
	LaF_3, $LaCl_3$ etc., La^{3+} salts,
	$LaOCl$, $[La(NCS)_6]^{3-}$, complexes
	LaH_2–LaH_3 is probably $La^{3+}H^-$

Physical properties

Melting point/K: 1194

Boiling point/K: 3730

ΔH_{fusion}/kJ mol^{-1}: 10.04

ΔH_{vap}/kJ mol^{-1}: 399.6

Thermodynamic properties (298.15 K, 0.1 MPa)

State	$\Delta_f H^{\ominus}$/kJ mol^{-1}	$\Delta_f G^{\ominus}$/kJ mol^{-1}	$S^{\ominus}$/J K^{-1} mol^{-1}	C_p/J K^{-1} mol^{-1}
Solid	0	0	56.9	27.11
Gas	431.0	393.56	182.377	22.753

Density/kg m^{-3}: 6145 [298 K]

Thermal conductivity/W m^{-1} K^{-1}: 13.5 [300 K]

Electrical resistivity/Ω m: 57×10^{-8} [298 K]

Mass magnetic susceptibility/kg^{-1} m^3: $+1.1 \times 10^{-8}$ (s)

Molar volume/cm^3: 22.60

Coefficient of linear thermal expansion/K^{-1}: 4.9×10^{-6}

Crystal structure (cell dimensions/pm), space group

α-La hexagonal ($a = 377.0$, $c = 121.59$), P6$_3$/mmc
β-La f.c.c. ($a = 529.6$), Fm3m
γ-La b.c.c. ($a = 426$), Im3m

$T(\alpha \rightarrow \beta) = 583$ K
$T(b \rightarrow \gamma) = 1137$ K

X-ray diffraction: mass absorption coefficients (μ/ρ)/cm^2 g^{-1}:
CuK$_\alpha$ 341   MoK$_\alpha$ 45.8

Discovered in 1839 by C. G. Mosander at Stockholm, Sweden

[Greek, *lanthanein* = to lie hidden]

Lanthanum

Thermal neutron capture cross-section/barns: 8.98
Number of isotopes (including nuclear isomers): 26
Isotope mass range: 125→149

Key isotopes

Nuclide	Atomic mass	Natural abund. (%)	Half-life $T_{1/2}$	Decay mode and energy (MeV)	Nuclear spin I	Nuclear magnetic moment μ	Uses
^{138}La	137.907 105	0.09	1.0×10^{11}y	$\beta(1.04)$ 34%; EC(1.75) 66%; γ	5+	+3.707	NMR
^{139}La	138.906 346	99.91			7/2+	+2.778	NMR
^{140}La	139.909 471	0	40.28h	$\beta^-(3.761)$; γ	3−	+0.73	tracer

NMR

	$[^{138}$La$]$	^{139}La
Relative sensitivity (^{1}H = 1.00)	9.19×10^{-2}	5.92×10^{-2}
Receptivity (^{13}C = 1.00)	0.43	336
Magnetogyric ratio/rad T^{-1} s^{-1}	3.5295×10^7	3.7787×10^7
Quadrupole moment/m^2	-0.47×10^{-28}	0.21×10^{-28}
Frequency (^{1}H = 100 MHz; 2.3488 T)/MHz	13.193	14.126

References: 0.01M LaCl$_3$

Ground state electron configuration: [Xe]5d^{1}6s^2
Term symbol: $^2D_{3/2}$
Electron affinity (M→M$^-$)/kJ mol^{-1}: *c.* 50

Main lines in atomic spectrum

Wavelength/nm	Species
394.910	II
408.672	II
418.732	II
433.374	II
550.134 (AA)	I

Ionization energies/kJ mol^{-1}

1. M →M$^+$	538.1	6. M^{5+}→M^{6+} (7 600)
2. M$^+$→M^{2+}	1067	7. M^{6+}→M^{7+} (9 600)
3. M^{2+}→M^{3+}	1850	8. M^{7+}→M^{8+} (11 000)
4. M^{3+}→M^{4+}	4819	9. M^{8+}→M^{9+} (12 400)
5. M^{4+}→M^{5+}	(6400)	10. M^{9+}→M^{10+} (15 900)

Environmental properties

Biological role

None

Levels in humans:
Muscle/p.p.m.: 0.0004
Bone/p.p.m.: <0.08
Blood/mg dm^{-3}: n.a.
Daily dietary intake: n.a. but very low
Toxic intake: n.a.
Lethal intake: 720 mg (rats)
Total mass of element in average (70 kg) person: n.a.

Abundances

Sun (relative to H = 1 × 10^{12}): 13.5
Earth's crust/p.p.m.: 32
Seawater/p.p.m.:
Atlantic surface: 1.8×10^{-6}
Atlantic deep: 3.8×10^{-6}
Pacific surface: 2.6×10^{-6}
Pacific deep: 6.9×10^{-6}
Residence time/years: 200
Classification: recycled
Oxidation state: III

Geological data

Chief deposits and sources:
monazite
[(Ce, La, etc.) PO$_4$];
bastnaesite
[(Ce, La, etc.)(CO$_3$)F]
World production/tonnes y^{-1}: 8400
Reserves/tonnes: *c.* 25 × 10^6

Lr

Atomic number: 103

Relative atomic mass (^{12}C = 12.0000): **(260)**

Chemical properties

Radioactive metal which does not occur naturally.

Radii/pm: Lr^{2+} 112; Lr^{3+} 94; Lr^{4+} 83

Electronegativity: 1.3 (Pauling)

Effective nuclear charge: 1.80 (Slater)

Standard reduction potentials $E^{\ominus}$/V

III		0
Lr^{3+}	$\underline{\quad -2.06 \quad}$	Lr

Oxidation states

Lr^{III}	(f^{14})	Lr^{3+} (aq)

Physical properties

Melting point/K: n.a.

Boiling point/K: n.a.

ΔH_{fusion}/kJ mol^{-1}: n.a.

ΔH_{vap}/kJ mol^{-1}: n.a.

Thermodynamic properties (298.15 K, 0.1 MPa)

State	$\Delta_f H^{\ominus}$/kJ mol^{-1}	$\Delta_f G^{\ominus}$/kJ mol^{-1}	$S^{\ominus}$/J K^{-1} mol^{-1}	C_p/J K^{-1} mol^{-1}
Solid	0	0	n.a.	n.a.
Gas	n.a.	n.a.	n.a.	n.a.

Density/kg m^{-3}: n.a.

Thermal conductivity/W m^{-1} K^{-1}: 10 (est.) [300 K]

Electrical resistivity/Ω m: n.a.

Mass magnetic susceptibility/kg^{-1} m^3: n.a.

Molar volume/cm^3: n.a.

Coefficient of linear thermal expansion/K^{-1}: n.a.

Crystal structure (cell dimensions/pm), space group

n.a.

X-ray diffraction: mass absorption coefficients (μ/ρ)/cm^2 g^{-1}: n.a.

Prepared in 1961 by A. Ghiorso, T. Sikkeland, A. E. Larsh, and R. M. Latimer at Berkeley, California, USA

[Named after Ernest O. Lawrence]

Lawrencium

Thermal neutron capture cross-section/barns: n.a.
Number of isotopes (including nuclear isomers): 8
Isotope mass range: $253 \rightarrow 260$

Key isotopes

Nuclide	Atomic mass	Natural abundance (%)	Half-life $T_{1/2}$	Decay mode and energy (MeV)	Nuclear spin I	Nuclear magnetic moment μ	Uses
^{260}Lr	260.105 320	0	3m	$\alpha(8.30)$	n.a.	n.a.	none

Ground state electron configuration: $[Rn]5f^{14}6d^17s^2$
Term symbol: $^2D_{5/2}$
Electron affinity $(M \rightarrow M^-)$/kJ mol^{-1}: n.a.

Main lines in atomic spectrum

Wavelength/nm	Species
n.a.	

Ionization energies/kJ mol^{-1}

1. $M \rightarrow M^+$ n.a.
2. $M^+ \rightarrow M^{2+}$
3. $M^{2+} \rightarrow M^{3+}$
4. $M^{3+} \rightarrow M^{4+}$
5. $M^{4+} \rightarrow M^{5+}$

Environmental properties

Biological role	Abundances	Geological data
None; never encountered, but would be toxic due to radioactivity	**Sun** (relative to $H = 1 \times 10^{12}$): n.a. **Earth's crust**/p.p.m.: nil **Seawater**/p.p.m.: nil	Only a few atoms have ever been made by bombarding ^{252}Cf with boron nuclei

Pb

Atomic number: 82

Relative atomic mass ($^{12}C = 12.0000$): 207.2

Chemical properties

Soft, weak, ductile, dull grey metal. Tarnishes in moist air but stable to oxygen and water, dissolves in nitric acid. Used in batteries, cables, paints, glass, solder, petrol, radiation shielding, etc.

Radii/pm: Pb^{2+} 132; Pb^{4+} 84; atomic 175.0; covalent 154; Pb^{4-} 215

Electronegativity: 2.33 (Pauling); 1.55 (Allred); 3.90 eV (absolute)

Effective nuclear charge: 5.65 (Slater); 12.39 (Clementi); 15.33 (Froese–Fischer)

Standard reduction potentials $E^{\ominus}/V$

	IV		II		0		$-$II
Acid solution	Pb^{4+}	$\underline{1.69}$	Pb^{2+}	$\underline{-0.1251}$	Pb	$\underline{-1.507}$	PbH_2

[Alkaline solutions contain many different forms]

Covalent bonds r/pm $\quad E$/kJ mol^{-1} Oxidation states

	r/pm	E/kJ mol^{-1}
Pb–H	184	180
Pb–C	229	130
Pb–O	192	398
Pb–F	213	314
Pb–Cl	247	244
Pb–Pb	350	100

Pb^{II} PbO, PbF_2, $PbCl_2$ etc., PbOH$^+$(aq), $Pb(H_2O)_n^{2+}$(aq) salts, complexes.

Pb^{IV} PbO_2, Pb_3O_4 ($=2PbO \cdot PbO_2$) PbF_4, $PbCl_4$, $PbBr_4$, $PbCl_6^{2-}$, $Pb(OH)_6^{2-}$(aq) [Pb^{4+} does not exist in water], organo-lead compounds, complexes

Physical properties

Melting point/K: 600.65

Boiling point/K: 2013

ΔH_{fusion}/kJ mol^{-1}: 5.121

ΔH_{vap}/kJ mol^{-1}: 179.4

Thermodynamic properties (298.15 K, 0.1 MPa)

State	$\Delta_f H^{\ominus}$/kJ mol^{-1}	$\Delta_f G^{\ominus}$/kJ mol^{-1}	$S^{\ominus}$/J K^{-1} mol^{-1}	C_p/J K^{-1} mol^{-1}
Solid	0	0	64.81	26.44
Gas	195.0	161.9	175.373	20.786

Density/kg m^{-3}: 11 350 [293 K]; 10 678 [liquid, m.p.]

Thermal conductivity/W m^{-1} K^{-1}: 35.3 [300 K]

Electrical resistivity/Ω m: 20.648×10^{-8} [293 K]

Mass magnetic susceptibility/kg^{-1} m^3: -1.39×10^{-9} (s)

Molar volume/cm^3: 18.26

Coefficient of linear thermal expansion/K^{-1}: 29.1×10^{-9}

Crystal structure (cell dimensions/pm), space group

f.c.c. ($a = 495.00$), Fm3m

X-ray diffraction: mass absorption coefficients (μ/ρ)/cm^2 g^{-1}:
CuK$_\alpha$ 232   MoK$_\alpha$ 120

Lead

Thermal neutron capture cross-section/barns: 0.171

Number of isotopes (including nuclear isomers): 41

Isotope mass range: $184 \rightarrow 214$

Key isotopes

Nuclide	Atomic mass	Natural abund. (%)	Half-life $T_{1/2}$	Decay mode and energy (MeV)	Nuclear spin I	Nuclear magnetic moment μ	Uses
^{204}Pb	203.973 020	1.4	stable		0+		
^{205}Pb	204.974 458	0	1.51×10^7y	EC(0.052); γ			
^{206}Pb	205.974 440	24.1	stable		0+		
^{207}Pb	206.975 872	22.1	stable		1/2−	+0.5926	NMR
^{208}Pb	207.976 627	52.4	stable		0+		
^{210}Pb	209.984 163	trace	22.3y	β^-(0.063) 81%; (0.061) 19%; γ			tracer
^{214}Pb	213.999 798	trace	26.8h	β^-(1.032) 48%) 0+ (0.73) 42%; γ			

NMR

^{207}Pb

Relative sensitivity (^{1}H $= 1.00$) 9.16×10^{-3}

Receptivity (^{13}C $= 1.00$)   11.8

Magnetogyric ratio/rad T^{-1} s^{-1} 5.5797×10^7

Frequency (^{1}H $= 100$ MHz; 2.3488 T)/MHz   20.921

Reference: Pb(CH$_3$)$_4$

Ground state electron configuration: [Xe]4f^{14}5d^{10}6s^{2}6p^2

Term symbol: $^3P_0$

Electron affinity $(M \rightarrow M^-)$/kJ mol^{-1}: 35.1

Main lines in atomic spectrum

Wavelength/nm	Species
217.000 (AA)	I
261.418	I
283.305	I
357.273	I
363.957	I
368.346	I
405.781	I

Ionization energies/kJ mol^{-1}

1.	$M \rightarrow M^+$	715.5	6. $M^{5+} \rightarrow M^{6+}$	(8 100)
2.	$M^+ \rightarrow M^{2+}$	1450.4	7. $M^{6+} \rightarrow M^{7+}$	(9 900)
3.	$M^{2+} \rightarrow M^{3+}$	3081.5	8. $M^{7+} \rightarrow M^{8+}$	(11 800)
4.	$M^{3+} \rightarrow M^{4+}$	4083	9. $M^{8+} \rightarrow M^{9+}$	(13 700)
5.	$M^{4+} \rightarrow M^{5+}$	6640	10. $M^{9+} \rightarrow M^{10+}$	(16 700)

Environmental properties

Biological role

None; carcinogenic; teratogenic

Levels in humans:

Muscle/p.p.m.: 0.23–3.3

Bone/p.p.m.: 3.6 30

Blood/mg dm^{-3}: 0.21

Daily dietary intake: 0.06–0.5 mg

Toxic intake: 1 mg

Lethal intake: 10 g

Total mass of element in average (70 kg) person: 120 mg (stored in skeleton)

Abundances

Sun (relative to H $= 1 \times 10^{12}$): 85.1

Earth's crust/p.p.m.: 14

Seawater/p.p.m.:

Atlantic surface: 30×10^{-6}

Atlantic deep: 4.0×10^{-6}

Pacific surface: 10.0×10^{-6}

Pacific deep: 1×10^{-6}

Residence time/years: 50

Classification: scavenged

Oxidation state: II

Geological data

Chief ores: galena [PbS] which accounts for most lead production; anglesite [PbSO$_4$]; cerussite [PbCO$_3$]; pyromorphite [Pb$_5$(PO$_4$)$_3$Cl]; and mimetesite [Pb$_5$(AsO$_4$)$_3$Cl]

World production/tonnes y^{-1}: 4.1×10^6

Reserves/tonnes: 85×10^6

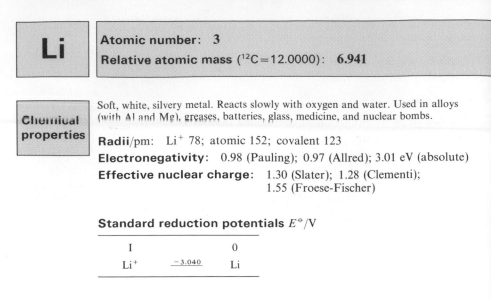

Li	Atomic number: 3
	Relative atomic mass ($^{12}C = 12.0000$): **6.941**

Chemical properties

Soft, white, silvery metal. Reacts slowly with oxygen and water. Used in alloys (with Al and Mg), greases, batteries, glass, medicine, and nuclear bombs.

Radii/pm: Li$^+$ 78; atomic 152; covalent 123

Electronegativity: 0.98 (Pauling); 0.97 (Allred); 3.01 eV (absolute)

Effective nuclear charge: 1.30 (Slater); 1.28 (Clementi); 1.55 (Froese-Fischer)

Standard reduction potentials $E^{\ominus}/V$

$$\begin{array}{ccc} \text{I} & & 0 \\ \text{Li}^+ & \xrightarrow{-3.040} & \text{Li} \end{array}$$

Oxidation states

Li^{-1}	(s^2)	Li solutions in liquid ammonia
Li^{I}	([He])	Li$_2$O, LiOH, LiH, LiAlH$_4$, LiF, LiCl etc., Li(H$_2$O)$_4^+$ (aq), Li$_2$CO$_3$, salts of Li$^+$, some complexes, (LiCH$_3$)$_4$

Physical properties

Melting point/K: 453.69
Boiling point/K: 1620
ΔH_{fusion}/kJ mol^{-1}: 4.60
ΔH_{vap}/kJ mol^{-1}: 134.7

Thermodynamic properties (298.15 K, 0.1 MPa)

State	$\Delta_f H^{\ominus}$/kJ mol^{-1}	$\Delta_f G^{\ominus}$/kJ mol^{-1}	$S^{\ominus}$/J K^{-1} mol^{-1}	C_p/J K^{-1} mol^{-1}
Solid	0	0	29.12	24.77
Gas	159.37	126.66	138.77	20.786

Density/kg m^{-3}: 534 [293 K]; 515 [liquid m.p.]
Thermal conductivity/W m^{-1} K^{-1}: 84.7 [300 K]
Electrical resistivity/Ω m: 8.55 × 10^{-8} [273 K]
Mass magnetic susceptibility/kg^{-1} m^3: +2.56 × 10^{-8} (s)
Molar volume/cm^3: 13.00
Coefficient of linear thermal expansion/K^{-1}: 56 × 10^{-6}

Crystal structure (cell dimensions/pm), space group

α-Li b.c.c. ($a = 351.00$), Im3m
β-Li f.c.c. ($a = 437.9$), Fm3m

α form stable at room temperature; converts to β form at low temperatures

X-ray diffraction: mass absorption coefficients (μ/ρ)/cm^2 g^{-1}:
CuK$_\alpha$ 0.716   MoK$_\alpha$ 0.217

Discovered in 1817 by J. A. Arfvedson at Stockholm, Sweden.
Isolated by W. T. Brande 1821

[Greek, *lithos* = stone]

Lithium

Thermal neutron capture cross-section/barns: 0.045
Number of isotopes (including nuclear isomers): 5
Isotope mass range: $5 \rightarrow 9$

Nuclear
properties

Key isotopes

Nuclide	Atomic mass	Natural abundance (%)	Half-life $T_{1/2}$	Decay mode and energy (MeV)	Nuclear spin I	Nuclear magnetic moment μ	Uses
^{6}Li	6.015 121	7.5	stable		1	+0.822 056	NMR
^{7}Li	7.016 003	92.5	stable		3/2	+3.256 44	NMR

NMR

	[^{6}Li]	^{7}Li
Relative sensitivity (^{1}H = 1.00)	8.50×10^{3}	0.29
Receptivity (^{13}C = 1.00)	3.58	1540
Magnetogyric ratio/rad T^{-1} s^{-1}	3.9366×10^{7}	10.3964×10^{7}
Quadrupole moment/m^{2}	-8×10^{-32}	-4.5×10^{-30}
Frequency (^{1}H = 100 MHz; 2.3488 T)/MHz	14.716	38.863

Reference: LiCl (aq)

Ground state electron configuration: [He]2s^{1}
Term symbol: $^{2}S_{1/2}$
Electron affinity ($M \rightarrow M^{-}$)/kJ mol^{-1}: 59.6

Electron
shell
properties

Main lines in atomic spectrum

Wavelength/nm	Species
323.266	I
548.355	II
548.565	II
610.362	I
670.776	I
670.791 (AA)	I

Ionization energies/kJ mol^{-1}

1. $M \rightarrow M^{+}$ 513.3
2. $M^{+} \rightarrow M^{2+}$ 7298.0
3. $M^{2+} \rightarrow M^{3+}$ 11814.8

Environmental properties

Biological role

None; stimulatory;
  teratogenic; anti-depressant

Levels in humans:
Muscle/p.p.m.: 0.023
Bone/p.p.m.: n.a.
Blood/mg dm^{-3}: 0.004
Daily dietary intake: 0.1–2 mg
Toxic intake: 92–200 mg
Lethal intake: n.a.
Total mass of element in
  average (70 kg) person:
  0.67 mg

Abundances

Sun (relative to H = 1×10^{12}):
  10
Earth's crust/p.p.m.: 20
Seawater/p.p.m.: 0.17
Residence time/years: 2×10^{6}
Classification: accumulating
Oxidation state: I

Geological data

Chief deposits and sources:
  spodumene [LiAlSi$_2$O$_6$];
  lepidolite
  [KLiAl(F, OH)$_2$ Si$_4$O$_{10}$];
  pentalite
  [LiAlSi$_4$O$_{10}$]; amblygonite
  [LiAl(F, OH)PO$_4$]

**World production of
  Li$_2$CO$_3$/tonnes y^{-1}: 39 000

Reserves/tonnes: 7.3×10^{6}

Lu

Atomic number: 71

Relative atomic mass (^{12}C = 12.0000): 174.967

Chemical properties

Hardest, densest, and one of the rarest of the lanthanide (rare earth) metals. Little used except in research.

Radii/pm: Lu^{3+} 85; atomic 173.4; covalent 156

Electronegativity: 1.27 (Pauling); 1.14 (Allred); ≤ 3.0 eV (absolute)

Effective nuclear charge: 3.00 (Slater); 8.80 (Clementi); 12.68 (Froese-Fischer)

Standard reduction potentials $E^{\ominus}$/V

	III		0
Acid solution	Lu^{3+}	$\xrightarrow{-2.30}$	Lu
Alkaline solution	$Lu(OH)_3$	$\xrightarrow{-2.83}$	Lu

Oxidation states

Lu^{III}	(f^{14})	Lu_2O_3, $Lu(OH)_3$, $[Lu(H_2O)_x]^{3+}$ (aq), Lu^{3+} salts, LuF_3, $LuCl_3$ etc., $LuCl_6^{3-}$, complexes

---

Physical properties

Melting point/K: 1936

Boiling point/K: 3668

ΔH_{fusion}/kJ mol^{-1}: 19.2

ΔH_{vap}/kJ mol^{-1}: 428

Thermodynamic properties (298.15 K, 0.1 MPa)

State	$\Delta_f H^{\ominus}$/kJ mol^{-1}	$\Delta_f G^{\ominus}$/kJ mol^{-1}	$S^{\ominus}$/J K^{-1} mol^{-1}	C_p/J K^{-1} mol^{-1}
Solid	0	0	50.96	26.86
Gas	427.6	387.8	184.800	20.861

Density/kg m^{-3}: 9840 [298 K]

Thermal conductivity/W m^{-1} K^{-1}: 16.4 [300 K]

Electrical resistivity/Ω m: 79.0×10^{-8} [298 K]

Mass magnetic susceptibility/kg^{-1} m^3: $+1.3 \times 10^{-9}$ (s)

Molar volume/cm^3: 17.78

Coefficient of linear thermal expansion/K^{-1}: 8.12×10^{-6}

Crystal structure (cell dimensions/pm), space group

α-Lu h.c.p. ($a = 350.31$, $c = 555.09$), P6$_3$/mmc
β-Lu b.c.c. ($a = 390$), Im3m

X-ray diffraction: mass absorption coefficients (μ/ρ)/cm^2 g^{-1}:
CuK$_\alpha$ 153   MoK$_\alpha$ 88.2

Discovered in 1907 by G. Urbain at Paris, France, and independently by C. James at the University of New Hampshire, USA
[Latin, *Lutetia* = Paris]

Lutetium

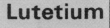

Thermal neutron capture cross-section/barns: 84
Number of isotopes (including nuclear isomers): 41
Isotope mass range: 154→182

Key isotopes

Nuclide	Atomic mass	Natural abundance (%)	Half-life $T_{1/2}$	Decay mode and energy (MeV)	Nuclear spin I	Nuclear magnetic moment μ	Uses
^{175}Lu	174.940 770	97.41	stable		7/2+	+2.2327	NMR
^{176}Lu	175.942 679	2.59	2.2×10^{10}y	β^-(1.02); γ	7−	+3.19	
^{177}Lu	176.943 752	0	6.71d	β^-(0.497); γ	7/2+	+2.239	tracer

NMR (not used)

^{175}Lu

Relative sensitivity (^{1}H = 1.00) 3.12×10^{-2}
Receptivity (^{13}C = 1.00)   156
Magnetogyric ratio/rad T^{-1} s^{-1} 3.05×10^7
Quadrupole moment/m^2 5.68×10^{-28}
Frequency (^{1}H = 100 MHz; 2.3488 T)/MHz   11.407

Ground state electron configuration: [Xe]$4f^{14}5d^16s^2$
Term symbol: $^2D_{3/2}$
Electron affinity (M→M$^-$)/kJ mol^{-1}: ≤50

Main lines in atomic spectrum

Wavelength/nm	Species
261.542	II
291.139	II
328.174	I
331.211	I
335.956 (AA)	I
350.739	II

Ionization energies/kJ mol^{-1}

1. M →M$^+$ 523.5	6. M^{3+}→M^{6+}
2. M$^+$→M^{2+} 1340	7. M^{6+}→M^{7+}
3. M^{2+}→M^{3+} 2022	8. M^{7+}→M^{8+}
4. M^{3+}→M^{4+} 4360	9. M^{8+}→M^{9+}
5. M^{4+}→M^{5+}	10. M^{9+}→M^{10+}

Environmental properties

Biological role	Abundances	Geological data
None; low toxicity' stimulatory	**Sun** (relative to H = 1×10^{12}): 5.8	**Chief deposits and sources:** monazite
Levels in humans: n.a., but low	**Earth's crust**/p.p.m.: 0.51	[(Ce, La, etc.)PO$_4$]; bastnaesite
	Seawater/p.p.m.:	[(Ce, La, etc.) (CO$_3$)F]
	Atlantic surface: 1.4×10^{-7}	**World production**/tonnes y^{-1}:
	Atlantic deep: 2.0×10^{-7}	*c.* 100
	Pacific surface: 0.60×10^{-7}	**Reserves**/tonnes: *c.* 10^5
	Pacific deep: 4.1×10^{-7}	
	Residence time/years: 4000	
	Classification: recycled	
	Oxidation state: III	

Mg

Atomic number: **12**

Relative atomic mass ($^{12}C = 12.0000$): **24.3050**

Chemical properties

Silvery white, lustrous, relatively soft metal. Obtained by electrolysis of fused $MgCl_2$. Burns in air and reacts with hot water. Used as bulk metal and in lightweight alloys with magnesium for engines, also as a sacrificial electrode to protect other metals exposed to seawater and ground water.

Radii/pm: Mg^{2+} 78; atomic 160; covalent 136

Electronegativity: 1.31 (Pauling); 1.23 (Allred); 3.75 eV (absolute)

Effective nuclear charge: 2.85 (Slater); 3.31 (Clementi); 4.15 (Froese-Fischer)

Standard reduction potentials $E^\ominus$/V

	II		I		0
Acid solution	Mg^{2+}	$\frac{-2.054}{-2.356}$	Mg^+	-2.657	Mg

Alkaline solution	$Mg(OH)_2$ ——————— -2.687 ———————	Mg

Oxidation states

Mg^{II}	([Ne])	MgO, MgO_2, $Mg(OH)_2$, $[Mg(H_2O)_6]^{2+}$(aq), MgH_2, $MgCO_3$, Mg^{2+} salts, MgF_2, $MgCl_2$, etc.,CH_3MgI, complexes

Physical properties

Melting point/K: 922.0

Boiling point/K: 1363

ΔH_{fusion}/kJ mol^{-1}: 9.04

ΔH_{vap}/kJ mol^{-1}: 128.7

Thermodynamic properties (298.15 K, 0.1 MPa)

State	$\Delta_f H^\ominus$/kJ mol^{-1}	$\Delta_f G^\ominus$/kJ mol^{-1}	$S^\ominus$/J K^{-1} mol^{-1}	C_p/J K^{-1} mol^{-1}
Solid	0	0	32.68	24.89
Gas	147.70	113.10	148.650	20.786

Density/kg m^{-3}: 1738 [293 K]; 1585 [liquid at m.p.]

Thermal conductivity/W m^{-1} K^{-1}: 156 [300 K]

Electrical resistivity/Ω m: 4.38×10^{-8} [293 K]

Mass magnetic susceptibility/kg^{-1} m^3: $+6.8 \times 10^{-9}$ (s)

Molar volume/cm^3: 13.98

Coefficient of linear thermal expansion/K^{-1}: 26.1×10^{-6}

Crystal structure (cell dimensions/pm), space group

h.c.p. ($a = 320.94$; $c = 521.03$), P6$_3$/mmc

X-ray diffraction: mass absorption coefficients (μ/ρ)/cm^2 g^{-1}:
CuK$_\alpha$ 38.6 MoK$_\alpha$ 4.11

Recognized as an element in 1755 by Joseph Black at Edinburgh, Scotland; isolated by Sir Humphry Davy in 1808

[Greek, *Magnesia*, district of Thessaly]

Magnesium

Key isotopes

Nuclide	Atomic mass	Natural abundance (%)	Half-life $T_{1/2}$	Decay mode and energy (MeV)	Nuclear spin I	Nuclear magnetic moment μ	Uses
^{24}Mg	23.985 042	78.99	stable		0+		
^{25}Mg	24.985 837	10.00	stable		5/2+	$-0.855\,45$	NMR
^{26}Mg	25.982 593	11.01	stable		0+		
^{28}Mg*	27.983 876	0	21.0h	β^-(1.832); γ			

* Longest lived radioactive isotope

NMR

^{25}Mg

Relative sensitivity (^{1}H$=1.00$)	2.67×10^{-3}
Receptivity (^{13}C$=1.00$)	1.54
Magnetogyric ratio/rad T^{-1} s^{-1}	1.6375×10^7
Quadrupole moment/m^2	0.22×10^{-28}
Frequency (^{1}H$=100$ MHz; 2.3488 T)/MHz	6.1195

Reference: MgCl$_2$(aq)

Ground state electron configuration: [Ne]3s^2

Term symbol: ^{1}S$_0$

Electron affinity (M$\rightarrow$M$^-$)/kJ mol^{-1}: -21

Electron shell properties

Main lines in atomic spectrum

Wavelength/nm	Species
279.553	II
280.270	II
285.213 (AA)	I
383.829	I
518.361	I

Ionization energies/kJ mol^{-1}

1. M $\rightarrow$M$^+$	737.7	6. M$^{5+}\rightarrow$M^{6+}	17 995
2. M$^+\rightarrow$M^{2+}	1 450.7	7. M$^{6+}\rightarrow$M^{7+}	21 703
3. M$^{2+}\rightarrow$M^{3+}	7 732.6	8. M$^{7+}\rightarrow$M^{8+}	25 656
4. M$^{3+}\rightarrow$M^{4+}	10 540	9. M$^{8+}\rightarrow$M^{9+}	31 642
5. M$^{4+}\rightarrow$M^{5+}	13 630	10. M$^{9+}\rightarrow$M^{10+}	35 461

Environmental properties

Biological role

Essential to all species

Levels in humans:
Muscle/p.p.m.: 900
Bone/p.p.m.: 700–1800
Blood/mg dm^{-3}: 37.8
Daily dietary intake:
  250–380 mg
Toxic intake: non-toxic
Total mass of element in
  average (70 kg) person: 19 g

Abundances

Sun (relative to H$=1 \times 10^{12}$):
  4.0×10^7

Earth's crust/p.p.m.: 23 000

Seawater/p.p.m.: 1200
Residence time/years: 1×10^7
Classification: accumulating
Oxidation state: II

Geological data

Chief ores and sources:
dolomite
[MgCO$_3$.CaCO$_3$];
magnesite [MgCO$_3$];
carnallite
[KCl.MgCl$_2$.6H$_2$O];
kieserite [MgSO$_4$.H$_2$O];
seawater

World production/tonnes y^{-1}:
325 000

Reserves/tonnes: $>2 \times 10^{10}$
as ores, and $>1 \times 10^{24}$ in
the sea

Mn

Atomic number: 25

Relative atomic mass ($^{12}C = 12.0000$): **54.93805**

Chemical properties

Hard, brittle, silvery metal. Reactive when impure and will burn in oxygen.
Surface oxidation occurs in air; will react with water, dissolves in dilute acids.
Used in steel production; animal feed supplement; fertiliser additives; ceramics.

Radii/pm: Mn^{2+} 91; Mn^{3+} 70; Mn^{4+} 52; atomic 124; covalent 117

Electronegativity: 1.55 (Pauling); 1.60 (Allred); 3.72 eV (absolute)

Effective nuclear charge: 3.60 (Slater); 5.23 (Clementi);
7.17 (Froese-Fischer)

Standard reduction potentials $E^{\ominus}$/V

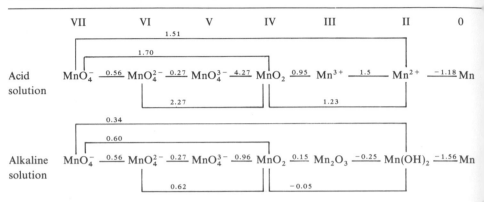

Oxidation states

Mn^{-III}	(d^{10})	$[Mn(NO)_3(CO)]$
Mn^{-II}	(d^9)	some complexes known
Mn^{-I}	(d^8)	$[Mn(CO)_5]^-$
Mn^0	(d^7)	$Mn_2(CO)_{10}$
Mn^I	(d^6)	$[Mn(CN)_6]^-$
Mn^{II}	(d^5)	MnO, $Mn_3O_4 (= Mn^{II}Mn^{III}_2O_4)$,
		$[Mn(H_2O)_6]^{2+}$ (aq), MnF_2,
		$MnCl_2$ etc., salts, complexes

Mn^{III}	(d^4)	$Mn_2O_3 [Mn(H_2O)_6]^{3+}$(aq)
		unstable; MnF_3, $MnCl_5^{2-}$
Mn^{IV}	(d^3)	MnO_2, MnF_4, MnF_6^{2-}
Mn^V	(d^2)	MnO_4^{3-}
Mn^{VI}	(d^1)	MnO_4^{2-}
Mn^{VII}	$(d^0, [Ar])$	Mn_2O_7, MnO_4^-

Physical properties

Melting point/K: 1517

Boiling point/K: 2235

ΔH_{fusion}/kJ mol^{-1}: 14.4 ΔH_{vap}/kJ mol^{-1}: 219.7

Thermodynamic properties (298.15 K, 0.1 MPa)

State	$\Delta_f H^{\ominus}$/kJ mol^{-1}	$\Delta_f G^{\ominus}$/kJ mol^{-1}	$S^{\ominus}$/J K^{-1} mol^{-1}	C_p/J K^{-1} mol^{-1}
Solid	0	0	32.01	26.32
Gas	280.7	238.5	173.70	20.79

Density/kg m^{-3}: 7440 (α) [293 K]; 6430 [liquid at m.p.]

Thermal conductivity/W m^{-1} K^{-1}: 7.82 [300 K]

Electrical resistivity/Ω m: 185.0×10^{-8} [298 K]

Mass magnetic susceptibility/kg^{-1} m^3: $+1.21 \times 10^{-7}$ (s)

Molar volume/cm^3: 7.38

Coefficient of linear thermal expansion/K^{-1}: 22×10^{-6}

Crystal structure (cell dimensions/pm), space group

α-Mn b.c.c. ($a = 891.39$), I$\bar{4}$3m γ-Mn f.c.c. ($a = 386.3$), Fm3m
β-Mn b.c.c. ($a = 631.45$), P4$_1$32 δ-Mn b.c.c. ($a = 308.1$), Im3m

$T(\alpha \rightarrow \beta) = 973$ K; $T(\beta \rightarrow \gamma) = 1352$ K; $T(\gamma \rightarrow \delta) = 1413$ K

X-ray diffraction: mass absorption coefficients (μ/ρ)/cm^2 g^{-1}:
CuK$_\alpha$ 285   MoK$_\alpha$ 34.7

Manganese

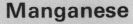

Thermal neutron capture cross-section/barns: 13.3
Number of isotopes (including nuclear isomers): 15
Isotope mass range: $49 \rightarrow 62$

Nuclear properties

Key isotopes

Nuclide	Atomic mass	Natural abundance (%)	Half-life $T_{1/2}$	Decay mode and energy (MeV)	Nuclear spin I	Nuclear magnetic moment μ	Uses
^{53}Mn	52.941 291	0	3.7×10^6y	EC(0.596); no γ	$7/2-$	5.024	
^{54}Mn	53.940 361	0	312d	EC(1.377); γ	$3+$	$+3.2818$	tracer
^{55}Mn	54.938 047	100	stable		$5/2-$	$+3.4687$	NMR
^{56}Mn	55.938 906	0	2.579h	β^-(3.696); γ	$3+$	$+3.2266$	tracer

NMR

^{55}Mn

Relative sensitivity (^{1}H = 1.00) 0.18
Receptivity (^{13}C = 1.00) 994
Magnetogyric ratio/rad T^{-1} s^{-1} 6.6195×10^7
Quadrupole moment/m^2 0.55×10^{-28}
Frequency (^{1}H = 100 MHz; 2.3488 T)/MHz 24.664
Reference: KMnO$_4$(aq)

Ground state electron configuration: [Ar]$3d^5 4s^2$
Term symbol: $^6S_{5/2}$
Electron affinity (M $\rightarrow$ M$^-$)/kJ mol^{-1}: < 0

Electron shell properties

Main lines in atomic spectrum

Wavelength/nm	Species
257.610	I
279.482 (AA)	I
279.827	I
403.076	I
403.307	I
403.449	I

Ionization energies/kJ mol^{-1}

1. M $\rightarrow$ M$^+$ 717.4	6. M$^{5+} \rightarrow$ M^{6+} 9 200
2. M$^+ \rightarrow$ M^{2+} 1509.0	7. M$^{6+} \rightarrow$ M^{7+} 11 508
3. M$^{2+} \rightarrow$ M^{3+} 3248.4	8. M$^{7+} \rightarrow$ M^{8+} 18 956
4. M$^{3+} \rightarrow$ M^{4+} 4940	9. M$^{8+} \rightarrow$ M^{9+} 21 400
5. M$^{4+} \rightarrow$ M^{5+} 6990	10. M$^{9+} \rightarrow$ M^{10+} 23 960

Environmental properties

Biological role

Essential to all species; suspected carcinogenic

Levels in humans:
Muscle/p.p.m.: 0.2–2.3
Bone/p.p.m.: 0.2–100
Blood/mg dm^{-3}: 0.0016–0.075
Daily dietary intake: 0.4 10 mg
Toxic intake: 10–20 mg (rats)
Lethal intake: n.a.
Total mass of element in average (70 kg) person: 12 mg

Abundances

Sun (relative to H = 1×10^{12}): 2.63×10^5
Earth's crust/p.p.m.: 950
Seawater/p.p.m.:
Atlantic surface: 1.0×10^{-4}
Atlantic deep: 0.96×10^{-4}
Pacific surface: 1.0×10^{-4}
Pacific deep: 0.4×10^{-4}
Residence time/years: 50
Classification: scavenged
Oxidation state: II

Geological data

Chief ores: pyrolusite [MnO$_2$]; psilomelane or wad [impure MnO$_2$]; cryptomelane [KMn$_8$O$_{16}$]; manganite [MnO(OH)]; etc.

World production/tonnes y^{-1}: 4.85×10^6 of ferromanganese (*ca.* 80% Mn)

Reserves/tonnes: 3.6×10^9

Md

Atomic number: **101**

Relative atomic mass (^{12}C $=$ 12.0000): **(258)**

Radioactive metal which does not occur naturally.

Radii/pm: Md^{2+} 114; Md^{3+} 96; Md^{4+} 84

Electronegativity: 1.3 (Pauling); n.a. (Allred)

Effective nuclear charge: 1.65 (Slater)

Standard reduction potentials $E^{\ominus}$/V

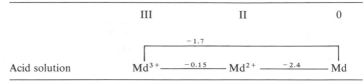

	III	II	0
Acid solution	Md^{3+} —$^{-0.15}$— Md^{2+} —$^{-2.4}$— Md		

-1.7

Oxidation states

Md^{II}	(f^{13})	stable ?
Md^{III}	(f^{12})	[Md(H$_2$O)$_x$]$^{3+}$(aq)

Physical properties

Melting point/K: n.a.

Boiling point/K: n.a.

ΔH_{fusion}/kJ mol^{-1}: n.a.

ΔH_{vap}/kJ mol^{-1}: n.a.

Thermodynamic properties (298.15 K, 0.1 MPa)

State	$\Delta_f H^{\ominus}$/kJ mol^{-1}	$\Delta_f G^{\ominus}$/kJ mol^{-1}	$S^{\ominus}$/J K^{-1} mol^{-1}	C_p/J K^{-1} mol^{-1}
Solid	0	0	n.a.	n.a.
Gas	n.a.	n.a.	n.a.	n.a.

Density/kg m^{-3}: n.a.

Thermal conductivity/W m^{-1} K^{-1}: 10 (est.) [300 K]

Electrical resistivity/Ω m: n.a.

Mass magnetic susceptibility/kg^{-1} m^3: n.a.

Molar volume/cm^3: n.a.

Coefficient of linear thermal expansion/K^{-1}: n.a.

Crystal structure (cell dimensions/pm), space group

n.a.

X-ray diffraction: mass absorption coefficients (μ/ρ)/cm^2 g^{-1}:
n.a.

Prepared in 1955 by A. Ghiorso, B. G. Harvey, G. R. Choppin, S. G. Thompson, and G. T. Seaborg at Berkeley, California, USA
[Named after Dmitri Mendeleyev]

Mendelevium

Thermal neutron capture cross-section/barns: n.a.

Number of isotopes (including nuclear isomers). 13

Isotope mass range: $248 \rightarrow 259$

Key isotopes

Nuclide	Atomic mass	Natural abundance (%)	Half-life $T_{1/2}$	Decay mode and energy (MeV)	Nuclear spin I	Nuclear magnetic moment μ	Uses
^{258}Md	258.098 570	0	56d	$\alpha(6.716)$ 72%; $\alpha(6.79)$ 28%; SF	8−	n.a.	none

Ground state electron configuration: $[Rn]5f^{13}7s^2$

Term symbol: $^2F_{7/2}$

Electron affinity $(M \rightarrow M^-)/kJ \, mol^{-1}$: n.a.

Main lines in atomic spectrum

Wavelength/nm	Species
n.a.	

Ionization energies/kJ mol^{-1}

1. $M \rightarrow M^+$ 635
2. $M^+ \rightarrow M^{2+}$
3. $M^{2+} \rightarrow M^{3+}$
4. $M^{3+} \rightarrow M^{4+}$
5. $M^{4+} \rightarrow M^{5+}$

Environmental properties

Biological role	Abundances	Geological data
None; never encountered, but would be toxic due to radioactivity **Levels in humans:** nil	**Sun** (relative to $H = 1 \times 10^{12}$): n.a. **Earth's crust**/p.p.m.: nil **Seawater**/p.p.m.: nil	**Chief source:** only a few atoms have been made by bombarding ^{253}Es with α particles [^{4}He]

Hg

Atomic number: **80**
Relative atomic mass ($^{12}C = 12.0000$): **200.59**

Chemical properties

Liquid silvery metal. Stable with air and water, unreactive to acids (except conc HNO_3) and alkalis. Used in chlorine and NaOH manufacture, street lights, fungicides, electrical apparatus, etc.

Radii/pm: Hg^+ 127; Hg^{2+} 112; atomic 160; covalent 144

Electronegativity: 2.00 (Pauling); 1.44 (Allred); 4.91 eV (absolute)

Effective nuclear charge: 4.35 (Slater); 11.15 (Clementi); 16.22 (Froese-Fischer)

Standard reduction potentials $E^{\ominus}/V$

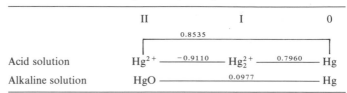

	II	I	0
		0.8535	
Acid solution	Hg^{2+} ——-0.9110——	Hg_2^{2+} ——0.7960——	Hg
Alkaline solution	HgO ——————0.0977	—————————	Hg

Oxidation states

Hg^I	$(d^{10}s^1)$	Hg_2F_2, Hg_2Cl_2 etc., Hg_2^{2+} salts, most are insoluble, except $Hg_2(NO_3)_2 \cdot 2H_2O$
Hg^{II}	(d^{10})	HgO, HgS, HgF_2, $HgCl_2$, etc., Hg^{2+} salts, $[Hg(H_2O)_6]^{2+}$ (aq) HgN(OH), complexes eg $[Hg(SCN)_4]^{2-}$, $Hg(CH_3)_2$, etc.

Physical properties

Melting point/K: 234.28
Boiling point/K: 629.73
ΔH_{fusion}/kJ mol^{-1}: 2.331
ΔH_{vap}/kJ mol^{-1}: 59.15

Thermodynamic properties (298.15 K, 0.1 MPa)

State	$\Delta_f H^{\ominus}$/kJ mol^{-1}	$\Delta_f G^{\ominus}$/kJ mol^{-1}	$S^{\ominus}$/J K^{-1} mol^{-1}	C_p/J K^{-1} mol^{-1}
Solid	0	0	76.02	27.983
Gas	61.317	31.820	174.96	20.786

Density/kg m^{-3}: 13 546 [293 K]
Thermal conductivity/W m^{-1} K^{-1}: 8.34 [300 K]
Electrical resistivity/Ω m: 94.1×10^{-8} [273 K]
Mass magnetic susceptibility/kg^{-1} m^3: -2.095×10^{-9} (l)
Molar volume/cm^3: 14.81
Coefficient of cubical thermal expansion/K^{-1}: 18.1×10^{-5}

Crystal structure (cell dimensions/pm), space group

α-Hg rhombohedral ($a = 299.25$, $\alpha = 70°\ 44.6'$), R$\bar{3}$m
β-Hg tetragonal ($a = 399.5$, $c = 282.5$), I4/mmm
$\alpha \rightarrow \beta$ high pressure

X-ray diffraction: mass absorption coefficients (μ/ρ)/cm^2 g^{-1}:
CuK$_\alpha$ 216   MoK$_\alpha$ 117

Known to ancient civilizations	# Mercury
[Named after planet Mercury. Latin, *hydragyrum* = liquid silver]	

Thermal neutron capture cross-section/barns: 374
Number of isotopes (including nuclear isomers): 37
Isotope mass range: $178 \rightarrow 206$

Key isotopes

Nuclide	Atomic mass	Natural abundance (%)	Half-life $T_{1/2}$	Decay mode and energy (MeV)	Nuclear spin I	Nuclear magnetic moment μ	Uses
^{196}Hg	195.965 807	0.15	stable		0+		
^{197}Hg	196.967 187	0	64.1	EC(0.600); γ	1/2−	+0.5274	tracer, medical
^{198}Hg	197.966 743	10.1	stable		0+		
^{199}Hg	198.968 254	17.0	stable		1/2−	+0.5059	NMR
^{200}Hg	199.968 300	23.1	stable		0+		
^{201}Hg	200.970 277	13.2	stable		3/2−	−0.5602	NMR
^{202}Hg	201.970 617	26.65	stable		0+		
^{203}Hg	202.972 848	0	46.6	β^-(0.492); γ	5/2−	+0.8489	tracer, medical
^{204}Hg	203.973 467	6.85	stable		0+		

NMR

	^{199}Hg	$[^{201}$Hg]
Relative sensitivity (^{1}H = 1.00)	5.67×10^{-3}	1.44×10^{-3}
Receptivity (^{13}C = 1.00)	5.42	1.08
Magnetogyric ratio/rad T^{-1} s^{-1}	4.7912×10^7	-1.7686×10^7
Quadrupole moment/m^2	—	0.5×10^{-28}
Frequency (^{1}H = 100 MHz; 2.3488 T)/MHz	17.827	6.599

Reference: Hg(CH$_3$)$_2$

Ground state electron configuration: [Xe]4f^{14}5d^{10}6s^2
Term symbol: ^{1}S$_0$
Electron affinity (M→M$^-$)/kJ mol^{-1}: −18

Main lines in atomic spectrum

Wavelength/nm	Species
253.652 (AA)	I
365.015	I
404.656	I
435.833	I
1013.975	I

Ionization energies/kJ mol^{-1}

1. M →M$^+$	1007.0	6. M^{5+}→M^{6+} (7 400)
2. M$^+$→M^{2+}	1809.7	7. M^{6+}→M^{7+} (9 100)
3. M^{2+}→M^{3+}	3300	8. M^{7+}→M^{8+} (11 600)
4. M^{3+}→M^{4+}	(4400)	9. M^{8+}→M^{9+} (13 400)
5. M^{4+}→M^{5+}	(5900)	10. M^{9+}→M^{10+} (15 300)

Environmental properties

Biological role	Abundances	Geological data
None; teratogenic; methyl mercury is very toxic	**Sun** (relative to H = 1×10^{12}): <125	**Chief ores:** cinnabar [HgS]
Levels in humans:	**Earth's crust**/p.p.m.: 0.05	**World production**/tonnes y^{-1}: 8400
Muscle/p.p.m.: 0.02–0.7	**Seawater**/p.p.m.:	**Reserves**/tonnes: 590 000
Bone/p.p.m.: 0.45	Atlantic surface: 4.9×10^{-7}	
Blood/mg dm^{-3}: 0.0078	Atlantic deep: 4.9×10^{-7}	
Daily dietary intake: 0.004–0.02 mg	Pacific surface: 3.3×10^{-7}	
Toxic intake: 0.4 mg	Pacific deep: 3.3×10^{-7}	
Lethal intake: 150–300 mg	Residence time/years: n.a.	
Total mass of element in average (70 kg) person: n.a.	Classification: scavenged	
	Oxidation state: II	

Mo

Atomic number: **42**

Relative atomic mass ($^{12}C = 12.0000$): **95.94**

Chemical properties

Metal is lustrous, silvery, and fairly soft when pure. Usually obtained as grey powder. Used in alloys, electrodes, and catalysts.

Radii/pm: Mo^{2+} 92; Mo^{6+} 6.2; atomic 136.2; covalent 129

Electronegativity: 2.16 (Pauling); 1.30 (Allred); 3.9 eV (absolute)

Effective nuclear charge: 3.45 (Slater); 6.98 (Clementi);
9.95 (Froese-Fischer)

Standard reduction potentials $E^{\ominus}/V$

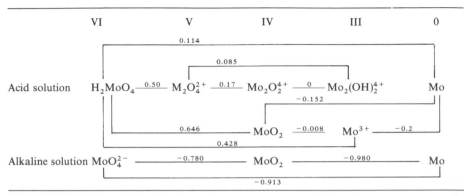

	VI	V	IV	III	0

Acid solution H_2MoO_4 —0.50— $M_2O_4^{2+}$ —0.17— $Mo_2O_2^{4+}$ —0— $Mo_2(OH)_2^{4+}$ Mo

0.114 / 0.085 / −0.152

0.646 / 0.428 MoO_2 —−0.008— Mo^{3+} —−0.2

Alkaline solution MoO_4^{2-} ————−0.780———— MoO_2 ————−0.980———— Mo

−0.913

Oxidation states

Mo^{-II}	(d^8)	rare $[Mo(CO)_5]^{2-}$
Mo^0	(d^6)	rare $Mo(CO)_6$
Mo^I	(d^5)	rare $[Mo(C_6H_6)_2]^+$
Mo^{II}	(d^4)	Mo_6Cl_{12}, $[Mo_2Cl_8]^{4-}$, Mo_2^{4+}(aq)
Mo^{III}	(d^3)	MoF_3, $MoCl_3$ etc., $[Mo(H_2O)_6]^{3+}$ (aq)
Mo^{IV}	(d^2)	MoO_2, MoS_2, MoF_4, $MoCl_4$, etc.
Mo^V	(d^1)	Mo_2O_5, MoF_5, $MoCl_5$
$\mathbf{Mo^{VI}}$	(d^0, [Kr])	MoO_3, MoO_4^{2-}(aq), MoF_6, MoF_8^{2-}, $MoOF_4$

Physical properties

Melting point/K: 2890

Boiling point/K: 4885

ΔH_{fusion}/kJ mol^{-1}: 27.6 ΔH_{vap}/kJ mol^{-1}: 594.1

Thermodynamic properties (298.15 K, 0.1 MPa)

State	$\Delta_f H^{\ominus}$/kJ mol^{-1}	$\Delta_f G^{\ominus}$/kJ mol^{-1}	$S^{\ominus}$/J K^{-1} mol^{-1}	C_p/J K^{-1} mol^{-1}
Solid	0	0	28.66	24.06
Gas	658.1	612.5	181.950	20.786

Density/kg m^{-3}: 10 220 [293 K]; 9330 [liquid at m.p.]

Thermal conductivity/W m^{-1} K^{-1}: 138 [300 K]

Electrical resistivity/Ω m: 5.2×10^{-8} [273 K]

Mass magnetic susceptibility/kg^{-1} m^3: $+1.2 \times 10^{-8}$ (s)

Molar volume/cm^3: 9.39

Coefficient of linear thermal expansion/K^{-1}: 5.43×10^{-6}

Crystal structure (cell dimensions/pm), space group

b.c.c. ($a = 314.700$), Im3m

X-ray diffraction: mass absorption coefficients (μ/ρ)/cm^2 g^{-1}:
CuK_α 162 MoK_α 18.4

Isolated in 1781 by P. J. Hjelm at Uppsala, Sweden

[Greek, *molybdos* = lead]

Molybdenum

Thermal neutron capture cross-section/barns: 2.60
Number of isotopes (including nuclear isomers): 23
Isotope mass range: 88→106

Nuclear
properties

Key isotopes

Nuclide	Atomic mass	Natural abundance (%)	Half-life $T_{1/2}$	Decay mode and energy (MeV)	Nuclear spin I	Nuclear magnetic moment μ	Uses
^{92}Mo	91.906808	14.84	stable		0+		
^{94}Mo	93.905085	9.25	stable		0+		
^{95}Mo	94.905840	15.92	stable		5/2+	−0.9133	NMR
^{96}Mo	95.904678	16.68	stable		0+		
^{97}Mo	96.906020	9.55	stable		5/2+	−0.9335	NMR
^{98}Mo	97.905406	24.13	stable		0+		
^{99}Mo	98.907711	0	65.94h	β^- (1.357); γ	1/2+		tracer
^{100}Mo	99.907477	9.63	stable		0+		

NMR

	^{95}Mo	[^{97}Mo]
Relative sensitivity (^{1}H = 1.00)	3.23×10^{-3}	3.43×10^{-3}
Receptivity (^{13}C = 1.00)	2.88	1.84
Magnetogyric ratio/rad T^{-1} s^{-1}	1.7433×10^7	-1.7799×10^7
Quadrupole moment/m^2	0.12×10^{-28}	1.1×10^{-28}
Frequency (^{1}H = 100 MHz; 2.3488 T)/MHz	6.514	6.652

Reference: MoO_4^{2-} (aq)

Ground state electron configuration: [Kr]$4d^5 5s^1$
Term symbol: $^7S_3$
Electron affinity (M→M$^-$)/kJ mol^{-1}: 72.0

Electron
shell
properties

Main lines in atomic spectrum

Wavelength/nm	Species
201.511	II
202.030	II
203.844	II
313.259 (AA)	I
379.825	I
386.411	I
390.296	I

Ionization energies/kJ mol^{-1}

1. $M \rightarrow M^+$	685.0	6. $M^{5+} \rightarrow M^{6+}$	6560
2. $M^+ \rightarrow M^{2+}$	1558	7. $M^{6+} \rightarrow M^{7+}$	12230
3. $M^{2+} \rightarrow M^{3+}$	2621	8. $M^{7+} \rightarrow M^{8+}$	14800
4. $M^{3+} \rightarrow M^{4+}$	4480	9. $M^{8+} \rightarrow M^{9+}$	(16800)
5. $M^{4+} \rightarrow M^{5+}$	5900	10. $M^{9+} \rightarrow M^{10+}$	(19700)

Environmental properties

Biological role

Essential to all species; teratogenic

Levels in humans:
Muscle/p.p.m.: 0.018
Bone/p.p.m.: <0.7
Blood/mg dm^{-3}: c. 0.001
Daily dietary intake:
  0.05–0.35 mg
Toxic intake: 5 mg
Lethal intake: 50 mg (rats)
Total mass of element in
  average (70 kg) person: n.a.

Abundances

Sun (relative to H = 1×10^{12}):
145
Earth's crust/p.p.m.: 1.5
Seawater/p.p.m.: 0.0100
Residence time/years: 600000
Classification: accumulating
Oxidation state: VI

Geological data

Chief deposit and sources:
molybdenite [MoS_2];
obtained also as a by-product of copper production
World production/tonnes y^{-1}:
80000

Reserves/tonnes: 5×10^6

Nd

Atomic number: 60

Relative atomic mass ($^{12}C = 12.0000$): 144.24

Silvery-white metal of the lanthanide (rare earth) group. Tarnishes in air, reacts slowly with cold water, rapidly with hot. Used in alloys for permanent magnets, lasers, flints, glazes, and glass.

Radii/pm: Nd^{3+} 104; atomic 182.1; covalent 164

Electronegativity: 1.14 (Pauling); 1.07 (Allred); ≤ 3.0 eV (absolute)

Effective nuclear charge: 2.85 (Slater); 9.31 (Clementi); 10.83 (Froese-Fischer)

Standard reduction potentials $E^{\ominus}/V$

	IV		III		II		0
				-2.32			
Acid solution	Nd^{4+}	$\underline{4.9}$	Nd^{3+}	$\underline{-2.6}$ Nd^{2+}	$\underline{-2.2}$	Nd
Alkaline solution	$[NdO_2]$	$\underline{2.5}$	$Nd(OH)_3$	$\underline{-2.78}$		Nd

Oxidation states

Nd^{II}	(f^4)	NdO, $NdCl_2$, NdI_2
Nd^{III}	(f^3)	Nd_2O_3, $Nd(OH)_3$, $[Nd(H_2O)_x]^{3+}$ (aq), NdF_3, $NdCl_3$, etc., Nd^{3+} salts, complexes
Nd^{IV}	(f^2)	Cs_3NdF_7

 **Physical
properties**

Melting point/K: 1294

Boiling point/K: 3341

ΔH_{fusion}/kJ mol^{-1}: 7.113

ΔH_{vap}/kJ mol^{-1}: 283.7

Thermodynamic properties (298.15 K, 0.1 MPa)

State	$\Delta_f H^{\ominus}$/kJ mol^{-1}	$\Delta_f G^{\ominus}$/kJ mol^{-1}	$S^{\ominus}$/J K^{-1} mol^{-1}	C_p/J K^{-1} mol^{-1}
Solid	0	0	71.5	27.45
Gas	327.6	292.4	189.406	22.092

Density/kg m^{-3}: 7007 [293 K]

Thermal conductivity/W m^{-1} K^{-1}: 16.5 [300 K]

Electrical resistivity/Ω m: 64.0×10^{-8} [293 K]

Mass magnetic susceptibility/kg^{-1} m^3: $+4.902 \times 10^{-7}$ (s)

Molar volume/cm^3: 20.59

Coefficient of linear thermal expansion/K^{-1}: 6.7×10^{-6}

Crystal structure (cell dimensions/pm), space group

α-Nd hexagonal ($a = 365.79$, $c = 1179.92$), P6$_3$/mmc
β-Nd b.c.c. ($a = 413$), Im3m

$T(\alpha \rightarrow \beta) = 1135$ K

High pressure form: f.c.c. ($a = 480$), Fm3m

X-ray diffraction: mass absorption coefficients (μ/ρ)/cm^2 g^{-1}:
CuK$_\alpha$ 374   MoK$_\alpha$ 53.2

Neodymium

Thermal neutron capture cross-section/barns: 49

Number of isotopes (including nuclear isomers): 24

Isotope mass range: $133 \rightarrow 154$

Key isotopes

Nuclide	Atomic mass	Natural abundance (%)	Half-life $T_{1/2}$	Decay mode and energy (MeV)	Nuclear spin I	Nuclear magnetic moment μ	Uses
^{142}Nd	141.907 719	27.13	stable		0+		
^{143}Nd	142.909 810	12.18	stable		7/2−	−1.08	NMR
^{144}Nd	143.910 083	23.80	2.1×10^{15}y	$\alpha(1.83)$	0+		
^{145}Nd	144.912 570	8.30	stable		7/2−	−0.66	NMR
^{146}Nd	145.913 113	17.19	stable		0+		
^{147}Nd	146.916 097	0	10.99d	$\beta^-(0.895)$; γ	5/2−	0.59	tracer
^{148}Nd	147.916 889	5.76	stable		0+		
^{150}Nd	149.920 889	5.64	stable		0+		

NMR

	^{143}Nd	^{145}Nd
Relative sensitivity (^{1}H = 1.00)	3.38×10^{-3}	7.86×10^{-4}
Receptivity (^{13}C = 1.00)	2.43	0.393
Magnetogyric ratio/rad T^{-1} s^{-1}	-1.474×10^7	-0.913×10^7
Quadrupole moment/m^2	-0.48×10^{-28}	-0.25×10^{-28}
Frequency (^{1}H = 100 MHz; 2.3488 T)/MHz	5.437	3.346

Ground state electron configuration: $[Xe]4f^46s^2$

Term symbol: $^5I_4$

Electron affinity $(M \rightarrow M^-)$/kJ mol^{-1}: $\leqslant 50$

Main lines in atomic spectrum

Wavelength/nm	Species
386.333	II
395.116	II
401.225	II
406.109	II
430.358	II
495.453 (AA)	I

Ionization energies/kJ mol^{-1}

1. $M \rightarrow M^+$ 520.6
2. $M^+ \rightarrow M^{2+}$ 1035
3. $M^{2+} \rightarrow M^{3+}$ 2130
4. $M^{3+} \rightarrow M^{4+}$ 3899
5. $M^{4+} \rightarrow M^{5+}$
6. $M^{5+} \rightarrow M^{6+}$
7. $M^{6+} \rightarrow M^{7+}$
8. $M^{7+} \rightarrow M^{8+}$
9. $M^{8+} \rightarrow M^{9+}$
10. $M^{9+} \rightarrow M^{10+}$

Environmental properties

Biological role

None; low toxicity, eye irritant

Levels in humans: n.a., but low

Abundances

Sun (relative to H = 1×10^{12}): 17.0

Earth's crust/p.p.m.: 38

Seawater/p.p.m.:
Atlantic surface: 1.8×10^{-6}
Atlantic deep: 3.2×10^{-6}
Pacific surface: 1.8×10^{-6}
Pacific deep: 4.8×10^{-6}
Residence time/years: 500
Classification: recycled
Oxidation state: III

Geological data

Chief deposits and sources: monazite
[(Ce, La, etc.)PO$_4$];
bastnaesite
[(Ce, La, etc.] (CO$_3$)F]

World production/tonnes y^{-1}: 2900

Reserves/tonnes: 10^7

Ne

Chemical properties

Colourless, odourless gas, obtained from liquid air. Chemically inert towards everything including fluorine gas. Used in ornamental lighting ('neon' signs)

Radii/pm: van der Waals 160

Electronegativity: n.a. (Pauling); n.a. (Allred); [10.6 eV (absolute)]

Effective nuclear charge: 5.85 (Slater); 5.76 (Clementi); 5.18 (Froese-Fischer)

Standard reduction potentials $E^{\ominus}/V$

n.a.

Covalent bonds	r/pm	E/kJ mol^{-1}	Oxidation states
forms no bonds			Only Ne^0 as gas

Physical properties

Melting point/K: 24.48

Boiling point/K: 27.10

ΔH_{fusion}/kJ mol^{-1}: 0.324

ΔH_{vap}/kJ mol^{-1}: 1.736

Critical temperature/K: 44.4

Critical pressure/kPa: 2760

Critical volume/cm^3 mol^{-1}: 41.7

Thermodynamic properties (298.15 K, 0.1 MPa)

State	$\Delta_f H^{\ominus}$/kJ mol^{-1}	$\Delta_f G^{\ominus}$/kJ mol^{-1}	$S^{\ominus}$/J K^{-1} mol^{-1}	C_p/J K^{-1} mol^{-1}
Gas	0	0	146.328	20.786

Density/kg m^{-3}: 1444 [solid, m.p.]; 1207.3 [liquid, b.p.]; 0.899 94 [gas, 273 K]

Thermal conductivity/W m^{-1} K^{-1}: 0.0493 [300 K]$_g$

Mass magnetic susceptibility/kg^{-1} m^3: -4.2×10^{-9} (g);

Molar volume/cm^3: 13.97 [24 K]

Crystal structure (cell dimensions/pm), space group

f.c.c. ($a = 445.462$), Fm3m

h.c.p. ($a = 314.5$, $c = 514$), P6$_3$/mmc [3 K]

X-ray diffraction: mass absorption coefficients (μ/ρ)/cm^2 g^{-1}: CuK$_\alpha$ 22.9   MoK$_\alpha$ 2.47

Discovered in 1898 by Sir William Ramsay and M. W. Travers at London, UK

[Greek, *neos* = new]

Neon

Thermal neutron capture cross-section/barns: 0.040
Number of isotopes (including nuclear isomers): 9
Isotope mass range: $17 \rightarrow 25$

Key isotopes

Nuclide	Atomic mass	Natural abundance (%)	Half-life $T_{1/2}$	Decay mode and energy (MeV)	Nuclear spin I	Nuclear magnetic moment μ	Uses
^{20}Ne	19.992 435	90.48	stable		0+		
^{21}Ne	20.993 843	0.27	stable		3/2+	$-0.661\,79$	NMR
^{22}Ne	21.991 383	9.215	stable		0		

NMR (no known compounds) ^{21}Ne

Relative sensitivity (^{1}H = 1.00)	2.50×10^{-3}
Receptivity (^{13}C = 1.00)	0.0359
Magnetogyric ratio/rad T^{-1} s^{-1}	-2.1118×10^7
Quadrupole moment/m^2	9×10^{-30}
Frequency (^{1}H = 100 MHz; 2.3488 T)/MHz	7.894

Ground state electron configuration: [He]$2s^2 2p^6$
Term symbol: $^1S_0$
Electron affinity (M $\rightarrow$ M$^-$)/kJ mol^{-1}: -29 (calc.)

Main lines in atomic spectrum

Wavelength/nm	Species
837.761	I
865.438	I
878.062	I
878.375	I
885.387	I

Ionization energies/kJ mol^{-1}

1. M $\rightarrow$ M$^+$	2 080.6
2. M$^+$ $\rightarrow$ M^{2+}	3 952.2
3. M^{2+} $\rightarrow$ M^{3+}	6 122
4. M^{3+} $\rightarrow$ M^{4+}	9 370
5. M^{4+} $\rightarrow$ M^{5+}	12 177
6. M^{5+} $\rightarrow$ M^{6+}	15 238
7. M^{6+} $\rightarrow$ M^{7+}	19 998
8. M^{7+} $\rightarrow$ M^{8+}	23 069
9. M^{8+} $\rightarrow$ M^{9+}	115 377
10. M^{9+} $\rightarrow$ M^{10+}	131 429

Environmental properties

Biological role	Abundances	Geological data
None; non toxic but can asphyxiate **Levels in humans**: n.a., but very low	**Sun** (relative to H = 1×10^{12}): 3.72×10^7 **Earth's crust**/p.p.m.: 7×10^{-5} **Seawater**/p.p.m.: 2×10^{-4} Residence time/years: n.a. Oxidation state: 0 Atmosphere/p.p.m. (volume): 18	**Chief source**: liquid air **World production**/tonnes y^{-1}: $c.$ 1 **Reserves**/tonnes: 6.5×10^{10} (atmosphere)

Np	Atomic number: 93
	Relative atomic mass ($^{12}C = 12.0000$): **237.0482**

Chemical properties

Radioactive silvery metal which does not occur naturally. Attacked by oxygen, steam, and acids, but not alkalis.

Radii/pm: Np^{3+} 110; Np^{4+} 95; Np^{5+} 88; Np^{6+} 82; atomic 131

Electronegativity: 1.36 (Pauling); 1.22 (Allred)

Effective nuclear charge: 1.80 (Slater)

Standard reduction potentials $E^{\ominus}/V$

	VII		VI		V		IV		III		0

Acid solution NpO_3^+ —2.04— NpO_2^{2+} —1.24— NpO_2^+ —0.66— Np^{4+} —0.18— Np^{3+} —−1.79— Np

          $\lfloor$—0.95—$\rfloor$ $\lfloor$—−1.30—$\rfloor$

Alkaline solution NpO_5^{3-} —0.58— $NpO_2(OH)_2$ —0.6— NpO_2OH —0.3— NpO_2 —−2.1— $Np(OH)_3$ —−2.2— Np

Oxidation states

Np^{II}	$(f^4 d^1)$	NpO
Np^{III}	(f^4)	NpF_3, $NpCl_3$, etc., $[NpCl_6]^{3-}$, $(Np(H_2O)_x)^{3+}$ (aq),
Np^{IV}	(f^3)	NpO_2, $[Np(H_2O)_x]^{4+}$ (aq), NpF_4, $NpCl_4$, $NpBr_4$,
		$[NpCl_6]^{2-}$, complexes
Np^{V}	(f^2)	Np_2O_5, NpF_5, $CsNpF_6$, Na_3NpF_8, NpO_2^+ (aq)
Np^{VI}	(f^1)	$NpO_3 \cdot H_2O$, NpO_2^{2+} (aq), NpF_6
Np^{VII}	$([Rn])$	Li_5NpO_6

Physical properties

Melting point/K: 913

Boiling point/K: 4175

ΔH_{fusion}/kJ mol^{-1}: 9.46

ΔH_{vap}/kJ mol^{-1}: 336.6

Thermodynamic properties (298.15 K, 0.1 MPa)

State	$\Delta_f H^{\ominus}$/kJ mol^{-1}	$\Delta_f G^{\ominus}$/kJ mol^{-1}	$S^{\ominus}$/J K^{-1} mol^{-1}	C_p/J K^{-1} mol^{-1}
Solid	0	0	n.a.	n.a.
Gas	n.a.	n.a.	n.a.	n.a.

Density/kg m^{-3}: 20 250 [293 K]

Thermal conductivity/W m^{-1} K^{-1}: 6.3 [300 K]

Electrical resistivity/Ω m: 122×10^{-8} [293 K]

Mass magnetic susceptibility/kg^{-1} m^3: n.a.

Molar volume/cm^3: 11.71

Coefficient of linear thermal expansion/K^{-1}: 27.5×10^{-6}

Crystal structure (cell dimensions/pm), space group

α-Np orthorhombic ($a = 472.3$, $b = 488.7$, $c = 666.3$), Pmcn
β-Np tetragonal ($a = 489.7$, $c = 338.8$), P42$_1$2
γ-Np cubic ($a = 352$), Im3m

$T(\alpha \rightarrow \beta) = 551$ K
$T(\beta \rightarrow \gamma) = 850$ K

X-ray diffraction: mass absorption coefficients (μ/ρ)/cm^2 g^{-1}:
n.a.

Prepared in 1940 by E. M. McMillan and P. Abelson at Berkeley, California, USA

[Named after planet Neptune]

Neptunium

Thermal neutron capture cross-section/barns: 180 (^{237}Np)
Number of isotopes (including nuclear isomers): 18
Isotope mass range: 228→242

Key isotopes

Nuclide	Atomic mass	Natural abundance (%)	Half-life $T_{1/2}$	Decay mode and energy (MeV)	Nuclear spin I	Nuclear magnetic moment μ	Uses
^{237}Np	237.048 167	0	2.14×10^6y	$\alpha(4.957)$; γ	$5/2+$	$+3.14$	tracer

NMR

^{237}Np

Relative sensitivity (^{1}H $= 1.00$)	—
Receptivity (^{13}C $= 1.00$)	—
Magnetogyric ratio/rad T^{-1} s^{-1}	3.1×10^7
Quadrupole moment/m^2	4.2×10^{-28}
Frequency (^{1}H $= 100$ MHz; 2.3488 T)/MHz	11.25

Ground state electron configuration: [Rn]$5f^4 6d^1 7s^2$
Term symbol: $^6L_{11/2}$
Electron affinity (M →M$^-$)/kJ mol^{-1}: n.a.

Main lines in atomic spectrum

Wavelength/nm	Species
901.618	I
1009.199	I
1081.745	I
1169.515	I
1177.664	I
1214.818	I
1237.742	I
1240.799	I
1383.433	I

Ionization energies/kJ mol^{-1}

1. M →M$^+$	597
2. M$^+$→M^{2+}	
3. M^{2+}→M^{3+}	
4. M^{3+}→M^{4+}	
5. M^{4+}→M^{5+}	

Environmental properties

Biological role	Abundances	Geological data
None; never encountered, but would be toxic due to radioactivity **Levels in humans:** nil	**Sun** (relative to H $= 1 \times 10^{12}$): n.a. **Earth's crust**/p.p.m.: nil **Seawater**/p.p.m.: nil	**Chief source:** obtained in kilogram quantities as ^{237}Np from uranium fuel elements

<table>
<tr><td rowspan="2">**Ni**</td><td>**Atomic number:** **28**</td></tr>
<tr><td>**Relative atomic mass** (^{12}C = 12.0000): **58.69**</td></tr>
</table>

Chemical properties

Silvery-white metal, lustrous, malleable, and ductile. Resists corrosion, soluble in acids, except concentrated HNO_3, unaffected by alkalis. Used in alloys, coins, metal plating, and catalysts.

Radii/pm: Ni^{2+} 78; Ni^{3+} 62; atomic 124.6; covalent 115

Electronegativity: 1.91 (Pauling); 1.75 (Allred); 4.40 eV (absolute)

Effective nuclear charge: 4.05 (Slater); 5.71 (Clementi); 7.86 (Froese-Fischer)

Standard reduction potentials $E^{\ominus}$/V

	VI	IV	II	0

Acid solution: NiO_4^{2-} $\xrightarrow{>1.8}$ NiO_2 $\xrightarrow{1.593}$ Ni^{2+} $\xrightarrow{-0.257}$ Ni (with >1.6 over VI→IV)

Alkaline solution: NiO_4^{2-} $\xrightarrow{>0.4}$ NiO_2 $\xrightarrow{0.490}$ $Ni(OH)_2$ $\xrightarrow{-0.72}$ Ni

Oxidation states

Ni^{-I}	$(d^{10}s^1)$	$[Ni_2(CO)_6]^{2-}$
Ni^0	(d^{10})	$Ni(CO)_4$, $K_4[Ni(CN)_4]$
Ni^I	(d^9)	$[Ni(PPh_3)_3Br]$
Ni^{II}	(d^8)	NiO, $Ni(OH)_2$, $[Ni(H_2O)_6]^{2+}$ (aq), NiF_2, $NiCl_2$, etc., salts, $K_2[Ni(CN)_4]$, $[NiCl_4]^{2-}$, complexes, $[Ni(C_5H_5)_2]$
Ni^{III}	(d^7)	$NiO(OH)$, NiF_3 ?, NiF_6^{3-}
Ni^{IV}	(d^6)	NiO_2 ?, NiF_6^{2-}
Ni^{VI}	(d^4)	K_2NiO_4 ?

Physical properties

Melting point/K: 1726
Boiling point/K: 3005
ΔH_{fusion}/kJ mol^{-1}: 17.6
ΔH_{vap}/kJ mol^{-1}: 371.8

Thermodynamic properties (298.15 K, 0.1 MPa)

State	$\Delta_f H^{\ominus}$/kJ mol^{-1}	$\Delta_f G^{\ominus}$/kJ mol^{-1}	$S^{\ominus}$/J K^{-1} mol^{-1}	C_p/J K^{-1} mol^{-1}
Solid	0	0	29.87	26.07
Gas	429.7	384.5	182.193	23.359

Density/kg m^{-3}: 8902 [298 K]; 7780 [liquid at m.p.]
Thermal conductivity/W m^{-1} K^{-1}: 90.7 [300 K]
Electrical resistivity/Ω m: 6.84×10^{-8} [293 K]
Mass magnetic susceptibility/kg^{-1} m^3: ferromagnetic;
Curie temperature/K: 633
Molar volume/cm^3: 6.59
Coefficient of linear thermal expansion/K^{-1}: 13.3×10^{-6}

Crystal structure (cell dimensions/pm), space group

f.c.c. ($a = 352.38$), Fm3m
'Hexagonal' nickel* ($a = 266$, $c = 432$), P6$_3$/mmc

*Impure form of nickel

X-ray diffraction: mass absorption coefficients (μ/ρ)/cm^2 g^{-1}:
CuK$_\alpha$ 45.7 MoK$_\alpha$ 46.6

Nickel

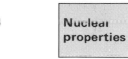

Thermal neutron capture cross-section/barns: 37.2

Number of isotopes (including nuclear isomers): 14

Isotope mass range: $53 \rightarrow 67$

Nuclear properties

Key isotopes

Nuclide	Atomic mass	Natural abundance (%)	Half-life $T_{1/2}$	Decay mode and energy (MeV)	Nuclear spin I	Nuclear magnetic moment μ	Uses
^{58}Ni	57.935 346	68.27	stable		0+		
^{59}Ni	58.934 349	0	7.6×10^4	EC(1.072); no γ	3/2−		
^{60}Ni	59.930 788	26.10	stable		0+		
^{61}Ni	60.931 058	1.13	stable		3/2−	−0.75002	NMR
^{62}Ni	61.928 346	3.59	stable		0+		
^{63}Ni	62.929 669	0	100y	β^-(0.065); no γ	1/2−		tracer
^{64}Ni	63.927 968	0.91	stable		0+		

NMR

^{61}Ni

Relative sensitivity (^{1}H − 1.00) 3.57×10^{-3}

Receptivity (^{13}C = 1.00)   0.242

Magnetogyric ratio/rad T^{-1} s^{-1} -2.3948×10^7

Quadrupole moment/m^2 0.16×10^{-28}

Frequency (^{1}H = 100 MHz; 2.3488 T)/MHz   8.936

Ground state electron configuration: $[Ar]3d^8 4s^2$

Term symbol: $^3F_4$

Electron affinity $(M \rightarrow M^-)$/kJ mol^{-1}: 156

Electron shell properties

Main lines in atomic spectrum

Wavelength/nm	Species
232.003 (AA)	I
341.476	I
349.296	I
351.505	I
352.454	I
361.939	I

Ionization energies/kJ mol^{-1}

1. $M \rightarrow M^+$ 736.7	6. $M^{5+} \rightarrow M^{6+}$ 10 400
2. $M^+ \rightarrow M^{2+}$ 1753.0	7. $M^{6+} \rightarrow M^{7+}$ 12 800
3. $M^{2+} \rightarrow M^{3+}$ 3393	8. $M^{7+} \rightarrow M^{8+}$ 15 600
4. $M^{3+} \rightarrow M^{4+}$ 5300	9. $M^{8+} \rightarrow M^{9+}$ 18 600
5. $M^{4+} \rightarrow M^{5+}$ 7280	10. $M^{9+} \rightarrow M^{10+}$ 21 660

Environmental properties

Biological role

Essential to some species; carcinogenic; stimulatory; nickel carbonyl is very toxic

Levels in humans:

Muscle/p.p.m.: 1–2

Bone/p.p.m.: <0.7

Blood/mg dm^{-3}: 0.01–0.05

Daily dietary intake: 0.3–0.5 mg

Toxic intake: 50 mg (rats)

Lethal intake: n.a.

Total mass of element in average (70 kg) person: 1 mg

Abundances

Sun (relative to H = 1×10^{12}): 1.91×10^6

Earth's crust/p.p.m.: *c.* 80

Seawater/p.p.m.:

Atlantic surface: 1×10^{-4}

Atlantic deep: 4.0×10^{-4}

Pacific surface: 1×10^{-4}

Pacific deep: 5.7×10^{-4}

Residence time/years: 80 000

Classification: recycled

Oxidation state: II

Geological data

Chief ores: garnierite $[(Ni, Mg)_6 Si_4 O_{10}(OH)_2]$; pentlandite $[(Ni,Fe)_9 S_8]$

World production/tonnes y^{-1}: 510 000

Reserves/tonnes: 70×10^6

Nb

Atomic number: 41

Relative atomic mass ($^{12}C = 12.0000$): 92.90638

Chemical properties

Shiny silvery metal, soft when pure. Resists corrosion due to oxide film, attacked by hot, concentrated acids but resists fused alkalis. Used in stainless steels.

Radii/pm: Nb^{4+} 74; Nb^{5+} 69; atomic 142.9; covalent 134

Electronegativity: 1.6 (Pauling); 1.23 (Allred); 4.0 eV (absolute)

Effective nuclear charge: 3.30 (Slater); 6.70 (Clementi); 9.60 (Froese-Fischer)

Standard reduction potentials $E^{\ominus}/V$

	V		III		0
Acid solution	Nb_2O_5	$\xrightarrow{-0.1}$	Nb^{3+}	$\xrightarrow{-1.1}$	Nb
			$\xrightarrow{-0.65}$		

Oxidation states

Nb^{-III}	(d^8)	$[Nb(CO)_5]^{3-}$
Nb^{-I}	(d^6)	$[Nb(CO)_6]^-$
Nb^I	(d^4)	$[(C_5H_5)Nb(CO)_4]$
Nb^{II}	(d^3)	NbO
Nb^{III}	(d^2)	$LiNbO_2$, $NbCl_3$, $NbBr_3$, NbI_3, $[Nb(CN)_8]^{5-}$
Nb^{IV}	(d^1)	NbO_2, NbF_4, $NbCl_4$ etc., $NbOCl_2$
Nb^V	(d^0, f^{14})	Nb_2O_5, $[HNb_6O_{19}]^-$ (aq), NbF_5, $NbCl_5$, etc., NbO_2F, $NbOCl_3$

Physical properties

Melting point/K: 2741

Boiling point/K: 5015

ΔH_{fusion}/kJ mol^{-1}: 27.2

ΔH_{vap}/kJ mol^{-1}: 696.6

Thermodynamic properties (298.15 K, 0.1 MPa)

State	$\Delta_f H^{\ominus}$/kJ mol^{-1}	$\Delta_f G^{\ominus}$/kJ mol^{-1}	$S^{\ominus}$/J K^{-1} mol^{-1}	C_p/J K^{-1} mol^{-1}
Solid	0	0	36.40	24.60
Gas	725.9	681.1	186.256	30.158

Density/kg m^{-3}: 8570 [293 K]; 7830 [liquid at m.p.]

Thermal conductivity/W m^{-1} K^{-1}: 53.7 [300 K]

Electrical resistivity/Ω m: 12.5×10^{-8} [273 K]

Mass magnetic susceptibility/kg^{-1} m^3: $+2.76 \times 10^{-8}$ (s)

Molar volume/cm^3: 10.84

Coefficient of linear thermal expansion/K^{-1}: 7.07×10^{-6}

Crystal structure (cell dimensions/pm), space group

---

b.c.c. ($a = 329.86$), Im3m

X-ray diffraction: mass absorption coefficients (μ/ρ)/cm^2 g^{-1}:
CuK$_\alpha$ 153 MoK$_\alpha$ 17.1

Discovered in 1801 by C. Hatchett at London, UK

[Greek, *Niobe* = daughter of Tantalus]

Niobium

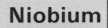

Thermal neutron capture cross-section/barns: 1.15
Number of isotopes (including nuclear isomers): 31
Isotope mass range: 86→103

Key isotopes

Nuclide	Atomic mass	Natural abundance (%)	Half-life $T_{1/2}$	Decay mode and energy (MeV)	Nuclear spin I	Nuclear magnetic moment μ	Uses
^{93}Nb	92.906 377	100	stable		9/2+	+6.1705	NMR
^{94}Nb	93.907 280	0	2.4×10^4y	β^- (2.04); γ	6+		

NMR

^{93}Nb

Relative sensitivity (^{1}H = 1.00)	0.48
Receptivity (^{13}C = 1.00)	2740
Magnetogyric ratio/rad T^{-1} s^{-1}	6.5476×10^7
Quadrupole moment/m^2	-0.2×10^{-28}
Frequency (^{1}H = 100 MHz; 2.3488 T)/MHz	24.442

Reference: NbF$_6^-$ (conc. HF)

Ground state electron configuration: [Kr]4d^{4}5s^1
Term symbol: ^{6}D$_{1/2}$
Electron affinity (M→M$^-$)/kJ mol^{-1}: 86.2

Main lines in atomic spectrum

Wavelength/nm	Species
334.371 (AA)	I
358.027	I
405.894	I
407.973	I
410.092	I
412.381	I

Ionization energies/kJ mol^{-1}

1. M →M$^+$ 664	6. M^{5+}→M^{6+} 9899
2. M$^+$→M^{2+} 1382	7. M^{6+}→M^{7+} 12100
3. M^{2+}→M^{3+} 2416	8. M^{7+}→M^{8+}
4. M^{3+}→M^{4+} 3695	9. M^{8+}→M^{9+}
5. M^{4+}→M^{5+} 4877	10. M^{9+}→M^{10+}

Environmental properties

Biological role

None

Levels in humans:
Muscle/p.p.m.: 0.14
Bone/p.p.m.: <0.07
Blood/mg dm^{-3}: 0.005?
Daily dietary intake:
　0.02–0.6 mg
Toxic intake: n.a., but
　moderately toxic
Total mass of element in
　average (70 kg) person: n.a.

Abundances

Sun (relative to H = 1×10^{12}):
　79

Earth's crust/p.p.m.: 20

Seawater/p.p.m.: 9×10^{-7}

Residence time/years: n.a.

Oxidation state: V

Geological data

Chief deposits and sources:
　columbite
　[(Fe, Mn) Nb$_2$O$_6$];
　obtained as a by-product of
　tin extraction

World production/tonnes y^{-1}:
　c. 15 000

Reserves/tonnes: n.a.

N

Atomic number: 7

Relative atomic mass ($^{12}C = 12.0000$): **14.00674**

Chemical properties

Colourless, odourless gas (N_2). Generally unreactive at room temperature. Extensive inorganic and organic chemistry. Used in fertilizers, acids (HNO_3), explosives, plastics, dyes, etc.

Radii/pm: atomic 71; covalent 70 (single bond); van der Waals 154
Electronegativity: 3.04 (Pauling); 3.07 (Allred); 7.30 eV (absolute)
Effective nuclear charge: 3.90 (Slater); 3.83 (Clementi); 3.46 (Froese-Fischer)

Standard reduction potentials $E^{\ominus}/V$

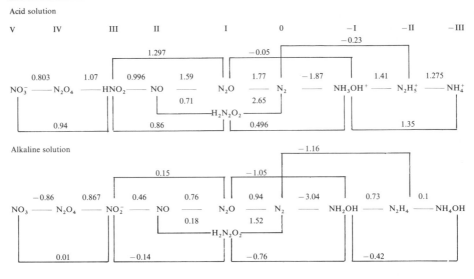

Covalent bonds r/pm E/kJ mol^{-1} Oxidation states

	r/pm	E/kJ mol^{-1}				
N—H	101	390	N^{-III}	NH_3, NH_4^+ (aq)	N^{III}	HNO_2, NO_2^- (aq),
N—N	147	160	N^{-II}	N_2H_4, $N_2H_5^+$ (aq)		NF_3
N=N	125	415	N^{-I}	NH_2OH	N^{IV}	$N_2O_4 \rightleftharpoons 2NO_2$
N≡N	110	946	N^0	N_2	N^V	HNO_3, NO_3^- (aq)
N—Cl	195	193	N^{II}	NO		

Physical properties

Melting point/K: 63.29
Boiling point/K: 77.4
ΔH_{fusion}/kJ mol^{-1}: 0.720
ΔH_{vap}/kJ mol^{-1}: 5.577

Critical temperature/K: 126.2
Critical pressure/kPa: 3390
Critical volume/cm^3 mol^{-1}: 89.5

Thermodynamic properties (298.15 K, 0.1 MPa)

State	$\Delta_f H^{\ominus}$/kJ mol^{-1}	$\Delta_f G^{\ominus}$/kJ mol^{-1}	$S^{\ominus}$/J K^{-1} mol^{-1}	C_p/J K^{-1} mol^{-1}
Gas (N_2)	0	0	191.61	29.125
Gas (atoms)	472.704	455.563	153.298	20.786

Density/kg m^{-3}: 1026 [solid, 21 K]; 880 [liquid, b.p.]; 1.2506 [gas, 273 K]
Thermal conductivity/W m^{-1} K^{-1}: 0.025 98 [300 K]$_g$
Mass magnetic susceptibility/kg^{-1} m^3: -5.4×10^{-9} (g)
Molar volume/cm^3: 13.65 [21 K]

Crystal structure (cell dimensions/pm), space group

α-N_2 cubic ($a = 564.4$), P2$_1$3
β-N_2 h.c.p. ($a = 404.2$, $c = 660.1$), P6$_3$/mmc
$T(\alpha \rightarrow \beta) = 35$ K

X-ray diffraction: mass absorption coefficients (μ/ρ)/cm^2 g^{-1}:
CuK$_\alpha$ 7.52   MoK$_\alpha$ 0.916

Discovered by D. Rutherford in 1772 at Edinburgh, Scotland

[Greek, *nitron genes* = nitre forming]

Nitrogen

Thermal neutron capture cross-section/barns: 1.91
Number of isotopes (including nuclear isomers): 8
Isotope mass range: $12 \rightarrow 18$

Key isotopes

Nuclide	Atomic mass	Natural abundance (%)	Half-life $T_{1/2}$	Decay mode and energy (MeV)	Nuclear spin I	Nuclear magnetic moment μ	Uses
^{14}N	14.003 074	99.63	stable		1+	+0.403 76	NMR
^{15}N	15.000 108	0.37	stable		1/2−	−0.283 19	NMR

No long-lived radioactive isotopes: ^{13}N has $T_{1/2} = 9.97$ m

NMR

	$[^{14}$N$]$	^{15}N
Relative sensitivity (^{1}H = 1.00)	1.01×10^{-3}	1.04×10^{-3}
Receptivity (^{13}C = 1.00)	5.69	0.0219
Magnetogyric ratio/rad T^{-1} s^{-1}	1.9331×10^7	-2.7116×10^7
Quadrupole moment/m^2	1.6×10^{-30}	
Frequency (^{1}H = 100 MHz; 2.3488 T)/MHz	7.224	10.133

Reference: MeNO$_2$ or NO$_3^-$

Ground state electron configuration: [He]$2s^2 2p^3$
Term symbol: $^4S_{3/2}$
Electron affinity (M→M$^-$)/kJ mol^{-1}: −7

Main lines in atomic spectrum

Wavelength/nm	Species
399.500	II
463.054	II
500.515	II
567.956	II
746.831	I
1246.962	I

Ionization energies/kJ mol^{-1}

1. M → M$^+$	1402.3	6. M^{5+} → M^{6+} 53 265.6
2. M$^+$ → M^{2+}	2856.1	7. M^{6+} → M^{7+} 64 358.7
3. M^{2+} → M^{3+}	4578.0	
4. M^{3+} → M^{4+}	7474.9	
5. M^{4+} → M^{5+}	9440.0	

Environmental properties

Biological role

Constituent element of DNA; nitrogen cycle in nature

Levels in humans:
Muscle/p.p.m.: 72 000
Bone/p.p.m.: 43 000
Blood/mg dm^{-3}: n.a.
Daily dietary intake: n.a., but high
Toxic intake: some nitrogen compounds are toxic
Total mass of element in average (70 kg) person: 1.8 kg

Abundances

Sun (relative to H = 1 × 10^{12}): 8.71 × 10^7
Earth's crust/p.p.m.: 25
Seawater/p.p.m.:
Atlantic surface: 0.00008
Atlantic deep: 0.27
Pacific surface: 0.00008
Pacific deep: 0.54
Residence time/years: 6000
Classification: recycled
Oxidation state: V
Atmosphere/p.p.m. (by volume): 780 900

Geological data

Chief resource: liquid air
World production/tonnes y^{-1}: 44 × 10^6
Reserves/tonnes: 3.9 × 10^{15} (atmosphere)

Chemical properties

Radioactive metal, which does not occur naturally.

Radii/pm: No^{2+} 113; No^{3+} 95; No^{4+} 83

Electronegativity: 1.3 (Pauling); n.a. (Allred); n.a. (absolute)

Effective nuclear charge: 1.65 (Slater)

Standard reduction potentials $E^{\ominus}$/V

	III	II	0

Acid solution

$$No^{3+} \xrightarrow{\quad 1.4 \quad} No^{2+} \xrightarrow{\quad -2.5 \quad} No$$

with -1.2 spanning III to 0

Oxidation states

No^{II}	(f^{14})	$[No(H_2O)_x]^{2+}$ (aq)
No^{III}	(f^{13})	$[No(H_2O)_x]^{3+}$ (aq)

Physical properties

Melting point/K: n.a.

Boiling point/K: n.a.

ΔH_{fusion}/kJ mol^{-1}: n.a.

ΔH_{vap}/kJ mol^{-1}: n.a.

Thermodynamic properties (298.15 K, 0.1 MPa)

State	$\Delta_f H^{\ominus}$/kJ mol^{-1}	$\Delta_f G^{\ominus}$/kJ mol^{-1}	$S^{\ominus}$/J K^{-1} mol^{-1}	C_p/J K^{-1} mol^{-1}
Solid	0	0	n.a.	n.a.
Gas	n.a.	n.a.	n.a.	n.a.

Density/kg m^{-3}: n.a.

Thermal conductivity/W m^{-1} K^{-1}: 10 (est.) [300 K]

Electrical resistivity/Ω m: n.a.

Mass magnetic susceptibility/kg^{-1} m^3: n.a.

Molar volume/cm^3: n.a.

Coefficient of linear thermal expansion/K^{-1}: n.a.

Crystal structure (cell dimensions/pm), space group

n.a.

X-ray diffraction: mass absorption coefficients (μ/ρ)/cm^2 g^{-1}:
n.a.

Conclusively identified in 1958 by A. Ghiorso, T. Sikkeland,
J. R. Walton, and G. T. Seaborg at Berkeley, California, USA
[Named after Alfred Nobel]

Nobelium

Thermal neutron capture cross-section/barns: n.a.
Number of isotopes (including nuclear isomers): 11
Isotope mass range: $250 \rightarrow 259$

Nuclear properties

Key isotopes

Nuclide	Atomic mass	Natural abundance (%)	Half-life $T_{1/2}$	Decay mode and energy (MeV)	Nuclear spin I	Nuclear magnetic moment μ	Uses
^{259}No	259.100 931	0	58m	$\alpha(7.794)$ 78%; EC 22%	9/2+		

Ground state electron configuration: $[Rn]5f^{14}7s^2$
Term symbol: $^1S_0$
Electron affinity $(M \rightarrow M^-)/kJ\ mol^{-1}$: n.a.

Electron shell properties

Main lines in atomic spectrum

Wavelength/nm	Species
n.a.	

Ionization energies/kJ mol^{-1}

1. $M \rightarrow M^+$ 642
2. $M^+ \rightarrow M^{2+}$
3. $M^{2+} \rightarrow M^{3+}$
4. $M^{3+} \rightarrow M^{4+}$
5. $M^{4+} \rightarrow M^{5+}$

Environmental properties

Biological role	Abundances	Geological data
None; never encountered, but would be toxic due to radioactivity **Levels in humans:** nil	**Sun** (relative to $H = 1 \times 10^{12}$): n.a. **Earth's crust**/p.p.m.: nil **Seawater**/p.p.m.: nil	**Chief source:** only a few atoms have been made by bombardment of ^{246}Cm with carbon nuclei

Os

Atomic number: 76

Relative atomic mass ($^{12}C=12.0000$): 190.2

Chemical

Lustrous silvery metal of platinum group. Unaffected by air, water, and acids, but dissolves in molten alkalis. Smells, due to formation of volatile OsO_4. Used in alloys and catalysts.

Radii/pm: Os^{2+} 89; Os^{3+} 81; Os^{4+} 67; atomic 135; covalent 126

Electronegativity: 2.2 (Pauling); 1.52 (Allred); 4.9 eV (absolute)

Effective nuclear charge: 3.75 (Slater); 10.32 (Clementi); 14.90 (Froese-Fischer)

Standard reduction potentials $E^\ominus$/V

VIII	IV	III	II	0

$$OsO_4 \xrightarrow{\quad 1.005 \quad} OsO_2 \xrightarrow{\quad 0.687 \quad} \cdots \cdots \cdots \cdots Os$$

with $OsO_4 \xrightarrow{\quad 0.85 \quad}$ branch over OsO_2

$$OsCl_6^{2-} \xrightarrow{\quad 0.45 \quad} OsCl_6^{3-}$$

$$Os(CN)_4(OH)_2^{3-} \xrightarrow{\quad 0.634 \quad} Os(CN)_4(OH)_2^{4-}$$

Oxidation states

Os^{-II}	(d^{10})	$[Os(CO)_4]^{2-}$
Os^0	(d^8)	$Os(CO)_5$, $Os_2(CO)_9$
Os^I	(d^7)	OsI
Os^{II}	(d^6)	$OsCl_2$, OsI_2
Os^{III}	(d^5)	$OsCl_3$, $OsBr_3$, OsI_3, complexes
Os^{IV}	(d^4)	OsO_2, OsO_2 (aq), OsF_4, $OsCl_4$, $OsBr_4$, $OsCl_6^{2-}$, complexes
Os^V	(d^3)	OsF_5, $OsCl_5$
Os^{VI}	(d^2)	OsO_3?, OsF_6
Os^{VII}	(d^1)	OsF_7
Os^{VIII}	(d^0, f^{14})	OsO_4, $[OsO_4(OH)_2]^{2-}$ (aq)

Physical properties

Melting point/K: 3327

Boiling point/K: 5300

ΔH_{fusion}/kJ mol^{-1}: 29.3

ΔH_{vap}/kJ mol^{-1}: 627.6

Thermodynamic properties (298.15 K, 0.1 MPa)

State	$\Delta_f H^\ominus$/kJ mol^{-1}	$\Delta_f G^\ominus$/kJ mol^{-1}	$S^\ominus$/J K^{-1} mol^{-1}	C_p/J K^{-1} mol^{-1}
Solid	0	0	32.6	24.7
Gas	791	745	192.573	20.786

Density/kg m^{-3}: 22 590 [293 K]; 20 100 [liquid at m.p.]

Thermal conductivity/W m^{-1} K^{-1}: 87.6 [300 K]

Electrical resistivity/Ω m: 8.12×10^{-8} [273 K]

Mass magnetic susceptibility/kg^{-1} m^3: $+6.5 \times 10^{-10}$ (s)

Molar volume/cm^3: 8.43

Coefficient of linear thermal expansion/K^{-1}:
4.3×10^{-6} (*a* axis); 6.1×10^{-6} (*b* axis); 6.8×10^{-6} (*c* axis)

Crystal structure (cell dimensions/pm), space group

h.c.p. ($a=273.43$; $c=432.00$), $P6_3/mmc$

X-ray diffraction: mass absorption coefficients (μ/ρ)/cm^2 g^{-1}:
CuK$_\alpha$ 186   MoK$_\alpha$ 106

Discovered in 1803 by S. Tennant at London, UK

[Greek, *osme* = smell]

Osmium

Thermal neutron capture cross-section/barns: 15
Number of isotopes (including nuclear isomers): 37
Isotope mass range: 166→196

Nuclear properties

Key isotopes

Nuclide	Atomic mass	Natural abundance (%)	Half-life $T_{1/2}$	Decay mode and energy (MeV)	Nuclear spin I	Nuclear magnetic moment μ	Uses
^{184}Os	183.952 488	0.02	stable		0+		
^{185}Os	184.954 041	0	9.36d	EC(1.015); γ	1/2−		tracer
^{186}Os	185.953 830	1.58	2×10^{15}y	α	0+		
^{187}Os	186.955 741	1.6	stable		1/2−	+0.0646	NMR
^{188}Os	187.955 860	13.3	stable		0+		
^{189}Os	188.958 137	16.1	stable		3/2+	+0.6599	NMR
^{190}Os	189.958 436	26.4	stable		0+		
^{191}Os	190.960 920	0	15.4d	β^-(0.313); γ	9/2−		tracer
^{192}Os	191.961 476	41.0	stable		0+		

NMR (Only OsO$_4$ studied)	^{187}Os	^{189}Os
Relative sensitivity (^{1}H = 1.00)	1.22×10^{-5}	2.34×10^{-3}
Receptivity (^{13}C = 1.00)	1.14×10^{-3}	2.13
Magnetogyric ratio/rad T^{-1} s^{-1}	0.6105×10^7	2.0773×10^7
Quadrupole moment/rad T^{-1} s^{-1}	—	0.8×10^{-28}
Frequency (^{1}H = 100 MHz; 2.3488 T)/MHz	2.282	7.758

Reference: OsO$_4$

Ground state electron configuration: [Xe]$4f^{14}5d^66s^2$
Term symbol: $^5D_4$
Electron affinity (M→M$^-$)/kJ mol^{-1}: 106

Electron shell properties

Main lines in atomic spectrum

Wavelength/nm	Species
201.015	I
201.814	I
202.026	I
203.444	I
204.536	I
290.906 (AA)	I

Ionization energies/kJ mol^{-1}

1. M →M$^+$ 840	6. M^{5+}→M^{6+} (6600)
2. M$^+$→M^{2+} (1600)	7. M^{6+}→M^{7+} (8100)
3. M^{2+}→M^{3+} (2400)	8. M^{7+}→M^{8+} (9500)
4. M^{3+}→M^{4+} (3900)	9. M^{8+}→M^{9+}
5. M^{4+}→M^{5+} (5200)	10. M^{9+}→M^{10+}

Environmental properties

Biological role	Abundances	Geological data
None; highly toxic especially OsO$_4$	**Sun** (relative to H = 1×10^{12}): 5	**Chief deposits and sources**: found in free state, and as rare osmiridium [Os, Ir] but obtained as a by-product of nickel refining
Levels in humans: n.a., but low	**Earth's crust**/p.p.m.: c. 1×10^{-4}	**World production**/tonnes y^{-1}: 0.06
	Seawater/p.p.m.: n.a., but minute	**Reserves**/tonnes: 200

O

Atomic number: 8

Relative atomic mass ($^{12}C = 12.0000$): **15.9994**

Chemical properties

Colourless, odourless gas. Very reactive and forms oxides of all elements except He, Ne, Ar, and Kr. Moderately soluble in water (30.8 cm³ per dm³) at 293 K. Used in steel making, metal cutting, chemical industry.

Radii/pm: O^+ 22; O^{2-} 132; covalent (single bonds) 66; van der Waals 140

Electronegativity: 3.44 (Pauling); 3.50 (Allred); 7.54 eV (absolute)

Effective nuclear charge: 4.55 (Slater); 4.45 (Clementi); 4.04 (Froese-Fischer)

Standard reduction potentials $E^{\ominus}/V$

	0		−I		−II			

Acid solutions: $O_2 \xrightarrow{0.695} H_2O_2 \xrightarrow{1.763} H_2O$; (1.229 overall) $O_3 \xrightarrow{1.246} O_2$

Alkaline solutions: $O_2 \xrightarrow{-0.0649} HO_2^- \xrightarrow{0.867} OH^-$; (0.401 overall) $O_3 \xrightarrow{2.075} O_2$

Covalent bonds r/pm E/kJ mol⁻¹

Bond	r/pm	E/kJ mol⁻¹
O—O	148	146
O=O (O_2)	120.8	498
N—O	146	200
N=O	115	678
N≡O (NO)	106	1063

For other covalent bonds to oxygen see other elements

Oxidation states

O^{-II}	H_2O, H_3O^+, OH^-, oxides, etc.
O^{-I}	H_2O_2, peroxides
O^0	O_2, O_3
O^I	O_2F_2
O^{II}	OF_2

Physical properties

Melting point/K: 54.8

Boiling point/K: 90.188

ΔH_{fusion}/kJ mol⁻¹: 0.444

ΔH_{vap}/kJ mol⁻¹: 6.82

Critical temperature/K: 154.6

Critical pressure/kPa: 5050

Critical volume/cm³ mol⁻¹: 73.4

Thermodynamic properties (298.15 K, 0.1 MPa)

State	$\Delta_f H^{\ominus}$/kJ mol⁻¹	$\Delta_f G^{\ominus}$/kJ mol⁻¹	$S^{\ominus}$/J K⁻¹ mol⁻¹	C_p/J K⁻¹ mol⁻¹
Gas (O_2)	0	0	205.138	29.355
Gas (atoms)	249.170	231.731	161.055	21.912

Density/kg m⁻³: 2000 [solid, m.p.]; 1140 [liquid, b.p.]; 1.429 [gas, 273 K]

Thermal conductivity/W m⁻¹ K⁻¹: 0.2674 [300 K]

Mass magnetic susceptibility/kg⁻¹ m³: $+1.355 \times 10^{-6}$ (g)

Molar volume/cm³: 8.00 [54 K]

Crystal structure (cell dimensions/pm), space group

α-O_2 Orthorhombic ($a = 540.3$; $b = 342.9$; $c = 508.6$; $\beta = 132.53°$), C2/m
β-O_2 rhombohedral ($a = 330.7$; $c = 1125.6$), R$\bar{3}$m
γ-O_2 cubic ($a = 683$), Pm3n

$T(\alpha \rightarrow \beta) = 23.8$ K
$T(\beta \rightarrow \gamma) = 43.8$ K

X-ray diffraction: mass absorption coefficients (μ/ρ)/cm² g⁻¹: CuK$_\alpha$ 11.5 MoK$_\alpha$ 1.31

Discovered in 1774 by J. Priestley at Leeds, UK, and independently
by C. W. Scheele at Uppsala, Sweden

[Greek, *oxy genes* = acid-forming]

Oxygen

Thermal neutron capture cross-section/barns: 0.28×10^{-3}
Number of isotopes (including nuclear isomers): 8
Isotope mass range: $13 \rightarrow 20$

Key isotopes

Nuclide	Atomic mass	Natural abundance (%)	Half-life $T_{1/2}$	Decay mode and energy (MeV)	Nuclear spin I	Nuclear magnetic moment μ	Uses
^{16}O	15.994915	99.76	stable		0+		
^{17}O	16.999311	0.048	stable		5/2+	-1.89379	NMR
^{18}O	17.999160	0.20	stable		0+		

There are no long-lived radioactive isotopes: ^{15}O is longest lived with $T_{1/2} = 122$ s

NMR

^{17}O

Relative sensitivity ($^1H = 1.00$)	2.91×10^{-2}
Receptivity ($^{13}C = 1.00$)	0.061
Magnetogyric ratio/rad T^{-1} s^{-1}	-3.6264×10^7
Quadrupole moment/m^2	-2.6×10^{-30}
Frequency ($^1H - 100$ MHz; 2.3488 T)/MHz	13.557

Reference: H_2O

Ground state electron configuration: $[He]2s^2 2p^4$
Term symbol: $^3P_2$
Electron affinity ($M \rightarrow M^-$)/kJ mol^{-1}: 141

Main lines in atomic spectrum

Wavelength/nm	Species
777.194	I
777.417	I
844.625	I
844.636	I
844.676	I

Ionization energies/kJ mol^{-1}

1. $M \rightarrow M^+$	1313.9	6. $M^{5+} \rightarrow M^{6+}$ 13326.2
2. $M^+ \rightarrow M^{2+}$	3388.2	7. $M^{6+} \rightarrow M^{7+}$ 71333.3
3. $M^{2+} \rightarrow M^{3+}$	5300.3	8. $M^{7+} \rightarrow M^{8+}$ 84076.3
4. $M^{3+} \rightarrow M^{4+}$	7469.1	
5. $M^{4+} \rightarrow M^{5+}$	10989.3	

Environmental properties

Biological role	Abundances	Geological data
Constituent element of DNA	**Sun** (relative to $H = 1 \times 10^{12}$): 6.92×10^8	**Chief resource:** liquid air
Levels in humans:		**World production**/tonnes y^{-1}: 1×10^8
Muscle/p.p.m.: 160000	**Earth's crust**/p.p.m.: 474000	
Bone/p.p.m.: 285000	**Seawater**/p.p.m.: constituent element of water	**Reserves**/tonnes: 1.2×10^{15} (in atmosphere)
Daily dietary intake: mainly as water	Atmosphere/p.p.m. (by volume): 209500	
Toxic intake: non-toxic as O_2, toxic as O_3		
Total mass of element in average (70 kg) person: 43 kg		

Pd

Atomic number: 46
Relative atomic mass ($^{12}C = 12.0000$): **106.42**

Chemical properties

Silvery-white metal, lustrous, malleable, ductile. Resists corrosion, dissolves in oxidising acids and fused alkalis. Readily absorbs hydrogen gas. Main use is as catalyst.

Radii/pm: Pd^{2+} 86; Pd^{4+} 64; atomic 137.6; covalent 128
Electronegativity: 2.20 (Pauling); 1.35 (Allred); 4.45 eV (absolute)
Effective nuclear charge: 4.05 (Slater); 7.84 (Clementi);
11.11 (Froese-Fischer)

Standard reduction potentials E°/V

	VI		IV		II		0
Acid solution			PdO_2	_1.263_	Pd^{2+}	_0.915_	Pd
Alkaline solution	'PdO_3'	_2.03_	PdO_2	_1.283_	$Pd(OH)_2$	_−0.19_	Pd

Oxidation states

Pd^0	(d^{10})	$[Pd(PPh_3)_3]$, $[Pd(PF_3)_4]$
Pd^{II}	(d^8)	PdO, $[Pd(H_2O)_4]^{2+}$ (aq); PdF_3,
		$PdCl_2$ etc., $PdCl_4^{2-}$, salts, complexes
Pd^{IV}	(d^6)	PdO_2, PdF_4, $PdCl_6^{2-}$

Physical properties

Melting point/K: 1825
Boiling point/K: 3413
ΔH_{fusion}/kJ mol^{-1}: 17.2
ΔH_{vap}/kJ mol^{-1}: 393.3

Thermodynamic properties (298.15 K, 0.1 MPa)

State	$\Delta_f H^\circ$/kJ mol^{-1}	$\Delta_f G^\circ$/kJ mol^{-1}	S°/J K^{-1} mol^{-1}	C_p/J K^{-1} mol^{-1}
Solid	0	0	37.57	25.98
Gas	378.2	339.7	167.05	20.786

Density/kg m^{-3}: 12 020 [293 K]; 10 379 [liquid at m.p.]
Thermal conductivity/W m^{-1} K^{-1}: 71.8 [300 K]
Electrical resistivity/Ω m: 10.8×10^{-8} [293 K]
Mass magnetic susceptibility/kg^{-1} m^3: $+6.702 \times 10^{-8}$ (s)
Molar volume/cm^3: 8.85
Coefficient of linear thermal expansion/K^{-1}: 11.2×10^{-6}

Crystal structure (cell dimensions/pm), space group

f.c.c. ($a = 389.08$), Fm3m

X-ray diffraction: mass absorption coefficients (μ/ρ)/cm^2 g^{-1}:
CuK_α 206 MoK_α 24.1

Discovered in 1803 by W. H. Wollaston at London, UK

[Named after the asteroid Pallas]

Palladium

Thermal neutron capture cross-section/barns: 6.9

Number of isotopes (including nuclear isomers): 25

Isotope mass range: 96→116

Key isotopes

Nuclide	Atomic mass	Natural abundance (%)	Half-life $T_{1/2}$	Decay mode and energy (MeV)	Nuclear spin I	Nuclear magnetic moment μ	Uses
^{102}Pd	101.905 634	1.02	stable		0+		
^{103}Pd	102.906 114	0	16.97d	EC(0.52); γ	5/2+		tracer
^{104}Pd	103.904 029	11.14	stable		0+		
^{105}Pd	104.905 079	22.33	stable		5/2+	−0.642	NMR
^{106}Pd	105.903 478	27.33	stable		0+		
^{108}Pd	107.903 895	26.46	stable		0+		
^{109}Pd	108.905 954	0	13.47h	β^-(1.116); γ	5/2+		tracer
^{110}Pd	109.905 167	11.72	stable		0+		

NMR

^{105}Pd   (Only K_2PdCl_6 recorded)

Relative sensitivity ($^1H = 1.00$) 1.12×10^{-3}

Receptivity ($^{13}C = 1.00$)   1.41

Magnetogyric ratio/rad T^{-1} s^{-1} -0.756×10^7

Quadrupole moment/m^2 $+0.8 \times 10^{-28}$

Frequency ($^1H = 100$ MHz; 2.3488 T)/MHz   4.576

Ground state electron configuration: [Kr]$4d^{10}$

Term symbol: $^1S_0$

Electron affinity (M→M$^-$)/kJ mol^{-1}: 53.7

Main lines in atomic spectrum

Wavelength/nm	Species
247.642 (AA)	I
340.458	I
342.124	I
351.694	I
355.308	I
340.955	I
363.470	I

Ionization energies/kJ mol^{-1}

1. M →M$^+$ 805	6. M^{5+}→M^{6+} (8 700)
2. M$^+$→M^{2+} 1875	7. M^{6+}→M^{7+} (10 700)
3. M^{2+}→M^{3+} 3177	8. M^{7+}→M^{8+} (12 700)
4. M^{3+}→M^{4+} (4700)	9. M^{8+}→M^{9+} (15 000)
5. M^{4+}→M^{5+} (6300)	10. M^{9+}→M^{10+} (17 200)

Environmental properties

Biological role	Abundances	Geological data
None; non-toxic generally **Levels in humans:** n.a., but low	**Sun** (relative to $H = 1 \times 10^{12}$): 32 **Earth's crust**/p.p.m.: c. 6×10^{-4} **Seawater**/p.p.m.: Atlantic surface: n.a. Atlantic deep: n.a. Pacific surface: 1.9×10^{-8} Pacific deep: 6.8×10^{-8} Residence time/years: 50 000 Classification: recycled Oxidation state: II	**Chief deposits and sources:** occurs as one of the platinum group metals; extracted as a by-product from Cu and Zn refining **World production**/tonnes y^{-1}: 24 **Reserves**/tonnes: 24 000

P	Atomic number: **15**
	Relative atomic mass (^{12}C = 12.0000): **30.973 762**

Chemical properties

White phosphorus (P_4) is soft and flammable, red phosphorus is powdery and usually non-flammable. Neither form reacts with water or dilute acid but alkalis react to form phosphine gas. Used in fertilizers, insecticides, metal treatment, detergents, etc.

Radii/pm: P^{3+} 44; atomic 93 (white) 115 (red); covalent 110; van der Waals 190; P^{3-} 212

Electronegativity: 2.19 (Pauling); 2.06 (Allred); 5.62 eV (absolute)

Effective nuclear charge: 4.80 (Slater); 4.89 (Clementi); 5.28 (Froese-Fischer)

Standard reduction potentials $E^{\ominus}$/V

	V	'IV'	III	'I'	0	$-$II	$-$III

Acid solution

$H_3PO_4 \xrightarrow{-0.933} H_4P_2O_6 \xrightarrow{0.380} H_3PO_3 \xrightarrow{-0.499} H_3PO_2 \xrightarrow{-0.365} P \xrightarrow{-0.100} P_2H_4 \xrightarrow{-0.006} PH_3$

with overbars: -0.276 (over H_3PO_4–H_3PO_3); -0.502 (over H_3PO_3–P); -0.063 (over P–PH_3)

Alkaline solution

$PO_4^{3-} \xrightarrow{-1.12} HPO_3^{2-} \xrightarrow{-1.57} H_2PO_2^- \xrightarrow{-2.05} P \xrightarrow{-0.89} PH_3$

overbars: -1.73; -1.18

Covalent bonds r/pm E/kJ mol^{-1}

	r/pm	E/kJ mol^{-1}
P—H	144	328
P—C	185	264
P—O	164	407
P=O	145	560
P—F	157	490
P—Cl	204	319
P—P	222	209

Oxidation states

P^{-III}	PH_3, Ca_3P_2	P^V	P_4O_{10}, H_3PO_4 (aq),
P^{-II}	P_2H_4		$H_2PO_4^-$ (aq) etc.,
P^0	P_4		PF_5, PCl_5, $POCl_3$
P^I	H_3PO_2 (aq), $H_2PO_2^-$ (aq)		phosphates
P^{II}	P_2I_4		
P^{III}	P_4O_6, H_3PO_3 (aq), PF_3, PCl_3, etc.		

Physical properties

Melting point/K: 317.3 (P_4); 683 (red) under pressure
Boiling point/K: 553 (P_4)
ΔH_{fusion}/kJ mol^{-1}: 2.51 (P_4)
ΔH_{vap}/kJ mol^{-1}: 51.9 (P_4)

Thermodynamic properties (298.15 K, 0.1 MPa)

State	$\Delta_f H^{\ominus}$/kJ mol^{-1}	$\Delta_f G^{\ominus}$/kJ mol^{-1}	$S^{\ominus}$/J K^{-1} mol^{-1}	C_p/J K^{-1} mol^{-1}
Solid (P_4)	0	0	41.09	23.840
Solid (red)	-17.6	-12.1	22.80	21.21
Gas	314.64	278.25	163.193	20.786

Density/kg m^{-3}: 1820 (P_4); 2200 (red); 2690 (black) [293 K];
Thermal conductivity/W m^{-1} K^{-1}: 0.235 (P_4); 12.1 (black) [300 K]
Electrical resistivity/Ω m: 1×10^9 (P_4) [293 K]
Mass magnetic susceptibility/kg^{-1} m^3: -1.1×10^{-8} (P_4); -8.4×10^{-9} (red)
Molar volume/cm^3: 17.02 (P_4)
Coefficient of linear thermal expansion/K^{-1}: 124.5×10^{-6} (P_4)

Crystal structure (cell dimensions/pm), space group

α-P_4 white, cubic ($a = 1851$), I$\bar{4}$3m
β-P_4 white, rhombohedral ($a = 337.7$; $c = 880.6$), R$\bar{3}$m [high pressure form]
γ-P_4 white, cubic ($a = 237.7$), Pm3m [high pressure form]
Red, cubic ($a = 1131$) Pm3m or P$\bar{4}$3
Hittorf's phosphorus (purple), monoclinic ($a = 921$; $b = 915$; $c = 2260$; $\beta = 106.1°$), P2/c
Black, orthorhombic ($a = 331.36$; $b = 1047.8$; $c = 437.63$), Cmca

X-ray diffraction: mass absorption coefficients (μ/ρ)/cm^2 g^{-1}:
CuK$_\alpha$ 74.1   MoK$_\alpha$ 7.89

Discovered in 1669 by Hennig Brandt at Hamburg, Germany

Phosphorus

[Greek, *phosphoros* = bringer of light]

Thermal neutron capture cross-section/barns: 0.180
Number of isotopes (including nuclear isomers): 10
Isotope mass range: $26 \rightarrow 36$

Key isotopes

Nuclide	Atomic mass	Natural abundance (%)	Half-life $T_{1/2}$	Decay mode and energy (MeV)	Nuclear spin I	Nuclear magnetic moment μ	Uses
^{31}P	30.973 762	100	stable		1/2+	+1.13160	NMR
^{32}P	31.973 907	0	14.23d	β^-(1.710); no γ	1+	−0.2524	tracer, medical
^{33}P	32.971 725	0	25.3d	β^-(0.249); no γ	1/2+		

NMR

	^{31}P
Relative sensitivity (^{1}H = 1.00)	6.63×10^{-2}
Receptivity (^{13}C = 1.00)	377
Magnetogyric ratio/rad T^{-1} s^{-1}	10.8289×10^7
Frequency (^{1}H = 100 MHz; 2.3488 T)/MHz	40.481

Reference: 85% H_3PO_4

Ground state electron configuration: [Ne]$3s^2 3p^3$
Term symbol: $^4S_{3/2}$
Electron affinity (M→M$^-$)/kJ mol^{-1}: 72.0

Main lines in atomic spectrum

Wavelength/nm	Species
213.618 (AA)	I
952.573	I
956.344	I
979.685	I
1648.292	I

Ionization energies/kJ mol^{-1}

1. M $\rightarrow$ M$^+$ 1011.7	6. M$^{5+}\rightarrow$M^{6+} 21 268
2. M$^+$ $\rightarrow$ M^{2+} 1903.2	7. M$^{6+}\rightarrow$M^{7+} 25 397
3. M$^{2+}\rightarrow$M^{3+} 2912	8. M$^{7+}\rightarrow$M^{8+} 29 854
4. M$^{3+}\rightarrow$M^{4+} 4956	9. M$^{n}\rightarrow$M^{n} 33 867
5. M$^{4+}\rightarrow$M^{5+} 6273	10. M$^{9+}\rightarrow$M^{10+} 40 958

Environmental properties

Biological role

Constituent of DNA; phosphate cycle in nature; P_4 and many phosphorus compounds highly toxic

Levels in humans:
Muscle/p.p.m.: 3000–8500
Bone/p.p.m.: 67 000–71 000
Blood/mg dm^{-3}: 345
Daily dietary intake: 900–1900 mg
Toxic intake: phosphates non-toxic
Lethal intake: 60 mg as P_4
Total mass of element in average (70 kg) person: 780 g

Abundances

Sun (relative to H = 1×10^{12}): 3.16×10^5

Earth's crust/p.p.m.: 1000

Seawater/p.p.m.:
Atlantic surface: 0.0015
Atlantic deep: 0.042
Pacific surface: 0.0015
Pacific deep: 0.084
Residence time/years: 100 000
Classification: recycled
Oxidation state: V

Geological data

Chief ores: fluorapatite [Ca$_5$(PO$_4$)$_3$F] occurs as vast deposits

World production of phosphate rock/tonnes y^{-1}: 153×10^6

World production of P$_4$/tonnes y^{-1}: 1.2×10^6

Reserves/tonnes: 5.7×10^9

Pt

Atomic number: **78**
Relative atomic mass ($^{12}C = 12.0000$): **195.08**

Chemical properties

Silvery-white metal, lustrous, malleable, ductile. Unaffected by oxygen and water, only dissolves in aqua-regia and fused alkalis. Used in jewellery, drugs, catalysts.

Radii/pm: Pt^{2+} 85; Pt^{4+} 70; atomic 138; covalent 129
Electronegativity: 2.28 (Pauling); 1.44 (Allred); 5.6 eV (absolute)
Effective nuclear charge: 4.05 (Slater); 10.75 (Clementi);
15.65 (Froese-Fischer)

Standard reduction potentials $E^{\ominus}/V$

VI		IV		II		0
PtO_3	$\underline{\quad 2.0 \quad}$	PtO_2	$\underline{\quad 1.045 \quad}$	PtO	$\underline{\quad 0.980 \quad}$	Pt
		PtO_2	$\underline{\quad 0.837 \quad}$	Pt^{2+}	$\underline{\quad 1.188 \quad}$	Pt
		$PtCl_6^{2-}$	$\underline{\quad 0.726 \quad}$	$PtCl_4^{2-}$	$\underline{\quad 0.758 \quad}$	Pt

Oxidation states

Pt^0	(d^{10})	$[Pt(PPh_3)_3]$ $[Pt(PF_3)_4]$
Pt^{II}	(d^8)	PtO, $PtCl_2$, $PrBr_3$, PtI_2, $PtCl_4^{2-}$, $[Pt(CN)_4]^{2-}$, complexes
$\mathbf{Pt^{IV}}$	(d^6)	PtO_2, $[Pt(OH)_6]^{2-}$ (aq), PtF_4, $PtCl_4$ etc., $PtCl_6^{2-}$ complexes
Pt^V	(d^5)	$(PtF_5)_4$, PtF_6^-
Pt^{VI}	(d^4)	PtO_3, PtF_6

Physical properties

Melting point/K: 2045
Boiling point/K: 4100 ± 100
ΔH_{fusion}/kJ mol^{-1}: 19.7
ΔH_{vap}/kJ mol^{-1}: 510.5

Thermodynamic properties (298.15 K, 0.1 MPa)

State	$\Delta_f H^{\ominus}$/kJ mol^{-1}	$\Delta_f G^{\ominus}$/kJ mol^{-1}	$S^{\ominus}$/J K^{-1} mol^{-1}	C_p/J K^{-1} mol^{-1}
Solid	0	0	41.63	25.86
Gas	565.3	520.5	192.406	25.531

Density/kg m^{-3}: 21 450 [293 K]
Thermal conductivity/W m^{-1} K^{-1}: 71.6 [300 K]
Electrical resistivity/Ω m: 10.6×10^{-8} [293 K]
Mass magnetic susceptibility/kg^{-1} m^3: $+1.301 \times 10^{-8}$ (s)
Molar volume/cm^3: 9.10
Coefficient of linear thermal expansion/K^{-1}: 9.0×10^{-6}

Crystal structure (cell dimensions/pm), space group

f.c.c. ($a = 392.40$), Fm3m

X-ray diffraction: mass absorption coefficients (μ/ρ)/cm^2 g^{-1}:
CuK$_\alpha$ 200 MoK$_\alpha$ 113

Known to pre-Columbian South Americans and taken to Europe about 1750

[Spanish, *platina* = silver]

Platinum

Thermal neutron capture cross-section/barns: 10
Number of isotopes (including nuclear isomers):   36
Isotope mass range: 172→201

Nuclear properties

Key isotopes

Nuclide	Atomic mass	Natural abundance (%)	Half-life $T_{1/2}$	Decay mode and energy (MeV)	Nuclear spin I	Nuclear magnetic moment μ	Uses
^{190}Pt	189.959 917	0.01	6.9×10^{11}y	α (3.18)	0+		
^{192}Pt	191.961 019	0.79	$c.\ 10^{15}$y	α	0+		
^{194}Pt	193.962 655	32.9	stable		0+		
^{195m}Pt		0	4.02d	IT(0.2592); γ	13/2+	0.597	tracer
^{195}Pt	194.964 766	33.8	stable		1/2−	+0.6095	NMR
^{196}Pt	195.9650	25.3	stable		0+		
^{197}Pt	196.967 315	0	18.3h	β^- (0.719); γ	1/2−	−0.51	tracer
^{198}Pt	197.967 869	7.2	stable		0+		

NMR

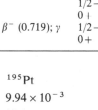

^{195}Pt

Relative sensitivity (^{1}H = 1.00) 9.94×10^{-3}
Receptivity (^{13}C = 1.00)   19.1
Magnetogyric ratio/rad T^{-1} s^{-1} 5.7412×10^7
Frequency (^{1}H = 100 MHz; 2.3488 T)/MHz   21.499
Reference: $[Pt(CN)_6]^{2-}$

Ground state electron configuration: [Xe]4f^{14}5d^{9}6s^1
Term symbol: $^3D_3$
Electron affinity (M→M$^-$)/kJ mol^{-1}:   205.3

Electron shell properties

Main lines in atomic spectrum

Wavelength/nm	Species
204.937	I
208.459	I
214.432	I
265.945 (AA)	I
270.240	I
299.767	I
306.471	I

Ionization energies/kJ mol^{-1}

1. M →M$^+$ 870	6. M^{5+}→M^{6+} (7 200)
2. M$^+$→M^{2+} 1791	7. M^{6+}→M^{7+} (8 900)
3. M^{2+}→M^{3+} (2800)	8. M^{7+}→M^{8+} (10 500)
4. M^{3+}→M^{4+} (3900)	9. M^{8+}→M^{9+} (12 300)
5. M^{4+}→M^{3+} (5300)	10. M^{9+}→M^{10+} (14 100)

Environmental properties

Biological role	Abundances	Geological data
None; generally non-toxic **Levels in humans:** n.a., but low	**Sun** (relative to H = 1 × 10^{12}): 56.2 **Earth's crust**/p.p.m.: *c.* 0.001 **Seawater**/p.p.m.: Atlantic surface: n.a. Atlantic deep: n.a. Pacific surface: 1.1 × 10^{-7} Pacific deep: 2.7 × 10^{-7} Residence time/years: n.a. Oxidation state: II	**Chief deposits and sources**: platinum ores; extracted as a by-product of Cu and Ni refining **World production**/tonnes y^{-1}: 30 **Reserves**/tonnes: 27 000

<table>
<tr><td rowspan="2">**Pu**</td><td>**Atomic number: 94**</td></tr>
<tr><td>**Relative atomic mass** ($^{12}C = 12.0000$): **(244)**</td></tr>
</table>

Radioactive silvery metal. Attacked by oxygen, steam, and acids, but not alkalis. Used as compact energy source, nuclear fuel, and for nuclear weapons.

Radii/pm: Pu^{3+} 108; Pu^{4+} 93; Pu^{5+} 87; Pu^{6+} 81; atomic 151 (α form)

Electronegativity: 1.28 (Pauling); 1.22 (Allred)

Effective nuclear charge: 1.65 (Slater)

Standard reduction potentials $E^{\ominus}/V$

	VII	VI	V	IV	III	0

Acid solution

$$PuO_2^{2+} \xrightarrow{1.02} PuO_2^{+} \xrightarrow{1.04} Pu^{4+} \xrightarrow{1.01} Pu^{3+} \xrightarrow{1.584} Pu$$

with $\overset{1.03}{\overline{\phantom{PuO_2^{2+}\quad PuO_2^{+}}}}$ over PuO_2^{2+}–PuO_2^{+} and $\overset{-1.25}{\overline{\phantom{Pu^{4+}\quad Pu^{3+}}}}$ over Pu^{4+}–Pu^{3+}

Alkaline solution

$$PuO_5^{3-} \xrightarrow{0.95} Pu_2(OH)_3^{-} \xrightarrow{0.3} PuO_2(OH) \xrightarrow{0.9} PuO_2 \xrightarrow{-1.4} Pu(OH)_3 \xrightarrow{2.46} Pu$$

Oxidation states

Pu^{II}	(f^6)	PuO, PuH_2
Pu^{III}	(f^5)	Pu_2O_3, PuF_3 $PuCl_3$ etc., $[Pu(H_2O)_x]^{3+}$ (aq), Pu^{3+} salts, complexes
Pu^{IV}	(f^4)	PuO_2, PuF_4, $[PuCl_6]^{2-}$, $[Pu(H_2O)_x]^{4+}$ (aq) unstable, complexes
Pu^{V}	(f^3)	PuO_2^{+} (aq) unstable, $CsPuF_6$
Pu^{VI}	(f^2)	PuO_2^{2+} (aq), PuF_6
Pu^{VII}	(f^1)	Li_5PuO_6, $[PuO_5]^{3-}$ (aq)

Physical properties

Melting point/K: 914 ΔH_{fusion}/kJ mol^{-1}: 2.8

Boiling point/K: 3505 ΔH_{vap}/kJ mol^{-1}: 343.5

Thermodynamic properties (298.15 K, 0.1 MPa)

State	$\Delta_f H^{\ominus}$/kJ mol^{-1}	$\Delta_f G^{\ominus}$/kJ mol^{-1}	$S^{\ominus}$/J K^{-1} mol^{-1}	C_p/J K^{-1} mol^{-1}
Solid	0	0	n.a.	n.a.
Gas	n.a.	n.a.	n.a.	n.a.

Density/kg m^{-3}: 19 840 (α) [298 K]; 16 623 [liquid at m.p.]

Thermal conductivity/W m^{-1} K^{-1}: 6.74 [300 K]

Electrical resistivity/Ω m: 146×10^{-8} [273 K]

Mass magnetic susceptibility/kg^{-1} m^3: $+3.17 \times 10^{-8}$ (s)

Molar volume/cm^3: 12.3

Coefficient of linear thermal expansion/K^{-1}: 55×10^{-6}

Crystal structure (cell dimensions/pm), space group

α-Pu monoclinic ($a = 618.3$; $b = 482.2$; $c = 1096.3$; $\beta = 101.79°$), P2$_1$/m
β-Pu monoclinic ($a = 928.4$; $b = 1046.3$; $c = 785.9$; $\beta = 92.13°$), I2/m
γ-Pu orthorhombic ($a = 315.87$; $b = 576.82$; $c = 1016.2$), Fddd
δ-Pu f.c.c. ($a = 463.71$), Fm3m
δ'-Pu tetragonal ($a = 333.9$; $c = 444.6$), I4/mmm
ε-Pu b.c.c. ($a = 363.48$), Im3m
$T(\alpha \rightarrow \beta) = 395$ K; $(\beta \rightarrow \gamma) = 473$ K; $(\gamma \rightarrow \delta) = 583$ K; $(\delta \rightarrow \delta') = 725$ K; $(\delta' \rightarrow \varepsilon) = 753$ K

X-ray diffraction: mass absorption coefficients (μ/ρ)/cm^2 g^{-1}: n.a.

Plutonium

Thermal neutron capture cross-section/barns: 1.7 (^{244}Pu)

Number of isotopes (including nuclear isomers): 15

Isotope mass range: 232→246

Key isotopes

Nuclide	Atomic mass	Natural abundance (%)	Half-life $T_{1/2}$	Decay mode and energy (MeV)	Nuclear spin I	Nuclear magnetic moment μ	Uses
^{239}Pu	239.052 157	0	2.411×10^4y	α(5.244), γ	1/2+	+0.203	NMR
^{242}Pu	242.058 737	0	3.76×10^5y	α(4.983); γ	0+		
^{244}Pu	244.064 199	0	8.2×10^7y	α(4.665), 99%; SF 0.1%; γ	0+		

NMR

	^{239}Pu
Relative sensitivity (^{1}H = 1.00)	—
Receptivity (^{13}C = 1.00)	—
Magnetogyric ratio/rad T^{-1} s^{-1}	0.972×10^7
Quadrupole moment/m^2	—
Frequency (^{1}H = 100 MHz; 2.3488 T)/MHz	3.63

Ground state electron configuration: [Rn]$5f^6 7s^2$

Term symbol: $^7F_0$

Electron affinity (M→M$^-$)/kJ mol^{-1}: n.a.

Main lines in atomic spectrum*

Wavelength/nm	Species
321.508	I
324.416	I
325.208	I
327.524	I
329.256	I
329.361	I
329.691	I

*First seven lines positively identified as arising from neutral atom species

Ionization energies/kJ mol^{-1}

1. M → M$^+$ 585
2. M$^+$ → M^{2+}
3. M^{2+} → M^{3+}
4. M^{3+} → M^{4+}
5. M^{4+} → M^{5+}

Environmental properties

Biological role	Abundances	Geological data
None; never encountered, but would be toxic due to radioactivity Levels in humans: n.a., and probably nil	Sun (relative to H = 1×10^{12}): n.a. Earth's crust/p.p.m.: traces in uranium ores Seawater/p.p.m.: nil	Chief source: obtained in tonne quantities from uranium fuel elements

Po

Atomic number: **84**

Relative atomic mass ($^{12}C=12.0000$): **(209)**

Chemical properties

Radioactive silver-grey metal. Soluble in dilute acids. Used as heat source in space equipment and as source of α radiation for research.

Radii/pm: Po^{4+} 65; atomic 167; covalent 153; Po^{2-} 230

Electronegativity: 2.0 (Pauling); 1.76 (Allred); 5.16 eV (absolute)

Effective nuclear charge: 6.95 (Slater); 14.22 (Clementi); 18.31 (Froese-Fischer)

Standard reduction potentials $E^{\ominus}/V$

	VI		IV		II		0		$-II$

Acid solution:
$$PoO_3 \xrightarrow{1.51} PoO_2 \xrightarrow{1.1} Po^{2+} \xrightarrow{0.37} Po \xrightarrow{c.\ -1.0} H_2Po$$
(1.3 spanning PoO$_3$ to Po^{2+}; 0.73 spanning PoO$_2$ to Po)

Alkaline solution:
$$PoO_3 \xrightarrow{1.48} PoO_3^{2-} \xrightarrow{-0.5} Po \xrightarrow{c.\ -1.4} Po^{2-}$$
(0.16 spanning PoO$_3$ to PoO$_3^{2-}$)

Covalent bonds r/pm E/kJ mol^{-1}

	r/pm	E/kJ mol^{-1}
Po–Cl	238	n.a.
Po–Po	335	n.a.

Oxidation states

Po^{-II}	H_2Po, Na_2Po
Po^{II}	PoO, $PoCl_2$, $PoBr_2$
Po^{IV}	PoO_2, PoO_3^{2-}(aq), $PoCl_4$, $PoBr_4$, PoI_4, PoI_6^{2-}
Po^{VI}	PoO_3 ? PoF_6

Physical properties

Melting point/K: 527

Boiling point/K: 1235

ΔH_{fusion}/kJ mol^{-1}: 10

ΔH_{vap}/kJ mol^{-1}: 100.8

Thermodynamic properties (298.15 K, 0.1 MPa)

State	$\Delta_f H^{\ominus}$/kJ mol^{-1}	$\Delta_f G^{\ominus}$/kJ mol^{-1}	$S^{\ominus}$/J K^{-1} mol^{-1}	C_p/J K^{-1} mol^{-1}
Solid	0	0	n.a.	26.1
Gas	146?	n.a.	n.a.	n.a.

Density/kg m^{-3}: 9320 (α) [293 K]

Thermal conductivity/W m^{-1} K^{-1}: 20 [300 K]

Electrical resistivity/Ω m: 140×10^{-8} [293 K]

Mass magnetic susceptibility/kg^{-1} m^3: n.a.

Molar volume/cm^3: 22.4

Coefficient of linear thermal expansion/K^{-1}: 23.0×10^{-6}

Crystal structure (cell dimensions/pm), space group

α-Po cubic ($a=335.2$), Pm3m
β-Po rhombohedral ($a=336.6$, $\alpha=98°13'$), R$\bar{3}$m

$T(\alpha \rightarrow \beta) = 309$ K

X-ray diffraction: mass absorption coefficients (μ/ρ)/cm^2 g^{-1}: n.a.

Polonium

Thermal neutron capture cross-section/barns: <0.5 (^{210}Po)
Number of isotopes (including nuclear isomers): 33
Isotope mass range: $194 \rightarrow 218$

Nuclear properties

Key isotopes

Nuclide	Atomic mass	Natural abundance (%)	Half-life $T_{1/2}$	Decay mode and energy (MeV)	Nuclear spin I	Nuclear magnetic moment μ	Uses
^{209}Po	208.982 404	0	105y	$\alpha(4.976)$; γ	$1/2-$	$+0.77$	
^{210}Po	209.982 848	trace	138.4d	$\alpha(5.407)$; γ	$0+$		tracer, fuel
^{211}Po	210.986 627	trace	0.52s	$\alpha(7.594)$; γ	$9/2+$		
^{216}Po	216.001 889	trace	0.15s	$\alpha(6.906)$; no γ	$0+$		
^{218}Po	218.0089	trace	3.11m	$\alpha(6.114)$; no γ	$0+$		

Ground state electron configuration: [Xe]$4f^{14}5d^{10}6s^26p^4$
Term symbol: $^3P_2$
Electron affinity $(M \rightarrow M^-)$/kJ mol^{-1}: 183

Electron shell properties

Main lines in atomic spectrum

Wavelength/nm	Species
245.008	I
255.801	I
300.321	I
417.052	I

Ionization energies/kJ mol^{-1}

1. $M \rightarrow M^+$ 812	6. $M^{5+} \rightarrow M^{6+}$ (7 000)
2. $M^+ \rightarrow M^{2+}$ (1800)	7. $M^{6+} \rightarrow M^{7+}$ (10 800)
3. $M^{2+} \rightarrow M^{3+}$ (2700)	8. $M^{7+} \rightarrow M^{8+}$ (12 700)
4. $M^{3+} \rightarrow M^{4+}$ (3700)	9. $M^{8+} \rightarrow M^{9+}$ (14 900)
5. $M^{4+} \rightarrow M^{5+}$ (5900)	10. $M^{9+} \rightarrow M^{10+}$ (17 000)

Environmental properties

Biological role	Abundances	Geological data
None; never encountered, but would be toxic due to radioactivity **Levels in humans:** nil	**Sun** (relative to $H = 1 \times 10^{12}$): n.a. **Earth's crust**/p.p.m.: traces in uranium ores **Seawater**/p.p.m.: nil	**Chief source**: produced in gram quantities from neutron bombardment of bismuth

Chemical properties

Soft white metal, silvery when cut but reacts rapidly with oxygen and vigorously with water. Metal obtained from $Na + KCl$ at 1100 K. Used in fertilizers, chemicals, and glass.

Radii/pm: K^+ 133; atomic 227; covalent 203; van der Waals 231

Electronegativity: 0.82 (Pauling); 0.91 (Allred); 2.42 e V (absolute)

Effective nuclear charge: 2.20 (Slater); 3.50 (Clementi); 4.58 (Froese-Fischer)

Standard reduction potentials $E^{\ominus}/V$

I   0

K^+ $\xrightarrow{-2.924}$ K

Oxidation states

K^{-1}	(s^2)	solution in liquid ammonia
K^{I}	([Ar])	K_2O, K_2O_2 (peroxide)
		KO_2 (superoxide), KO_3 (ozonide),
		KOH, $[K(H_2O)_4]^+$ (aq),
		KH, KF, KCl etc.,
		K^+ salts, K_2CO_3, complexes

Physical properties

Melting point/K: 336.80

Boiling point/K: 1047

ΔH_{fusion}/kJ mol^{-1}: 2.40

ΔH_{vap}/kJ mol^{-1}: 77.53

Thermodynamic properties (298.15 K, 0.1 MPa)

State	$\Delta_f H^{\ominus}$/kJ mol^{-1}	$\Delta_f G^{\ominus}$/kJ mol^{-1}	$S^{\ominus}$/J K^{-1} mol^{-1}	C_p/J K^{-1} mol^{-1}
Solid	0	0	64.18	29.58
Gas	89.24	60.59	160.336	20.786

Density/kg m^{-3}: 862 [293 K]; 828 [liquid at m.p.]

Thermal conductivity/W m^{-1} K^{-1}: 102.4 [300 K]

Electrical resistivity/Ω m: 6.15×10^{-8} [273 K]

Mass magnetic susceptibility/kg^{-1} m^3: $+6.7 \times 10^{-9}$ (s)

Molar volume/cm^3: 45.36

Coefficient of linear thermal expansion/K^{-1}: 83×10^{-6}

Crystal structure (cell dimensions/pm), space group

b.c.c. ($a = 533.4$), Im3m

X-ray diffraction: mass absorption coefficients (μ/ρ)/cm^2 g^{-1}:

CuK$_\alpha$ 143   MoK$_\alpha$ 15.8

Discovered in 1807 by Sir Humphry Davy at London, UK

[English, *potash*; Latin *kalium*]

Potassium

Thermal neutron capture cross-section/barns: 2.1
Number of isotopes (including nuclear isomers): 18
Isotope mass range: $35 \rightarrow 51$

Key isotopes

Nuclide	Atomic mass	Natural abundance (%)	Half-life $T_{1/2}$	Decay mode and energy (MeV)	Nuclear spin I	Nuclear magnetic moment μ	Uses
^{39}K	38.963 707	93.2581	stable		3/2+	+0.391 46	NMR
^{40}K	39.963 999	0.012	1.25×10^9y	β^-(1.32); EC; γ	4−	−1.298	
^{41}K	40.961 825	6.7302	stable		3/2+	+0.214 87	NMR
^{42}K	41.962 402	0	12.36h	β^-(3.532); γ	2−	−1.1425	tracer, medical
^{43}K	42.960 717	0	22.3h	β^-(1.82); γ	3/2+	+0.163	

NMR

	^{39}K	[^{41}K]
Relative sensitivity (^{1}H = 1.00)	5.08×10^{-4}	8.40×10^{-5}
Receptivity (^{13}C = 1.00)	2.69	3.28×10^{-2}
Magnetogyric ratio/rad T^{-1} s^{-1}	1.2483×10^7	0.6851×10^7
Quadrupole moment /m^2	5.5×10^{-30}	6.7×10^{-30}
Frequency (^{1}H = 100 MHz; 2.3488 T)/MHz	4.667	2.561

Reference: K$^+$ (aq)

Ground state electron configuration: [Ar]4s^1
Term symbol: $^2S_{1/2}$
Electron affinity (M$\rightarrow$M$^-$)/kJ mol^{-1}: 48.4

Main lines in atomic spectrum

Wavelength/nm	Species
404.414	I
691.108	I
693.877	I
766.491	I
769.896	I

Ionization energies/kJ mol^{-1}

1. M $\rightarrow$M$^+$	418.8	6. M$^{5+}\rightarrow$M^{6+} 9 649
2. M$^+\rightarrow$M^{2+}	3051.4	7. M$^{6+}\rightarrow$M^{7+} 11 343
3. M$^{2+}\rightarrow$M^{3+}	4411	8. M$^{7+}\rightarrow$M^{8+} 14 942
4. M$^{3+}\rightarrow$M^{4+}	5877	9. M$^{8+}\rightarrow$M^{9+} 16 964
5. M$^{4+}\rightarrow$M^{5+}	7975	10. M$^{9+}\rightarrow$M^{10+} 48 575

Environmental properties

Biological role

Essential to all living things
Levels in humans:
Muscle/p.p.m.: 16 000
Bone/p.p.m.: 2100
Blood/mg dm^{-3}: 1620
Daily dietary intake:
  1400–7400 mg
Toxic intake: 6 g
Lethal intake: 14 g
Total mass of element in
  average (70 kg) person:
  140 g

Abundances

Sun (relative to H = 1×10^{12}):
  1.45×10^5
Earth's crust/p.p.m.: 21 000
Seawater/p.p.m.: 379
Residence time/years: 5×10^6
Classification: accumulating
Oxidation state: I

Geological data

Chief ores: sylvite [KCl];
  sylvinite [NaCl . KCl];
  carnallite
  [KCl . MgCl$_2$. 6H$_2$O]
**World production of
  potassium salts**/tonnes y^{-1}:
  51×10^6
Reserves/tonnes: vast, $> 10^{10}$
**World production of
  potassium metal**/tonnes
  y^{-1}: 200

Pr

Atomic number: 59

Relative atomic mass ($^{12}C = 12.0000$): 140.90765

Soft, malleable, silvery metal of the lanthanide (rare earth) group. Reacts slowly with oxygen, rapidly with water. Used in alloys for permanent magnets, flints, yellow glass for eye protection for welders, etc.

Radii/pm: Pr^{3+} 106; Pr^{4+} 92; atomic 182.8; covalent 165

Electronegativity: 1.13 (Pauling); 1.07 (Allred); ≤ 3.0 eV (absolute)

Effective nuclear charge: 2.85 (Slater); 7.75 (Clementi); 10.70 (Froese-Fischer)

Standard reduction potentials $E^{\ominus}$/V

	IV		III		0
Acid solution	Pr^{4+}	—3.2—	Pr^{3+}	—−2.35—	Pr
Alkaline solution	PrO_2	—0.8—	$Pr(OH)_3$	—−2.79—	Pr

Oxidation states

Pr^{III}	(f^2)	P_2O_3, $Pr(OH)_3$, $[Pr(H_2O)_x]^{3+}$ (aq), Pr^{3+} salts, PrF_3, $PrCl_3$ etc., complexes
Pr^{IV}	(f^1)	PrO_2, PrF_4, Na_2PrF_6

Physical properties

Melting point/K: 1204
Boiling point/K: 3785
ΔH_{fusion}/kJ mol^{-1}: 11.3
ΔH_{vap}/kJ mol^{-1}: 332.6

Thermodynamic properties (298.15 K, 0.1 MPa)

State	$\Delta_f H^{\ominus}$/kJ mol^{-1}	$\Delta_f G^{\ominus}$/kJ mol^{-1}	$S^{\ominus}$/J K^{-1} mol^{-1}	C_p/J K^{-1} mol^{-1}
Solid	0	0	73.2	27.20
Gas	355.6	320.9	189.808	21.359

Density/kg m^{-3}: 6773 [293 K]
Thermal conductivity/W m^{-1} K^{-1}: 12.5 [300 K]
Electrical resistivity/Ω m: 68×10^{-8} [298 K]
Mass magnetic susceptibility/kg^{-1} m^3: $+4.47 \times 10^{-7}$ (s)
Molar volume/cm^3: 20.80
Coefficient of linear thermal expansion/K^{-1}: 6.79×10^{-6}

Crystal structure (cell dimensions/pm), space group

α-Pr h.c.p. ($a = 367.25$, $c = 1183.5$), P6$_3$/mmc
β-Pr b.c.c. ($a = 413$), Im3m

$T(\alpha \rightarrow \beta) = 1065$ K

X-ray diffraction: mass absorption coefficients (μ/ρ)/cm^2 g^{-1}: CuK$_\alpha$ 363   MoK$_\alpha$ 50.7

Praseodymium

Thermal neutron capture cross-section/barns: 11.4
Number of isotopes (including nuclear isomers): 26
Isotope mass range: $132 \rightarrow 152$

Nuclear properties

Key isotopes

Nuclide	Atomic mass	Natural abund. (%)	Half-life $T_{1/2}$	Decay mode and energy (MeV)	Nuclear spin I	Nuclear magnetic moment μ	Uses
^{141}Pr	140.907647	100	stable		5/2+	+4.3	NMR
^{142}Pr	141.910039	0	19.13h	β^- (2.160); γ	2	−0.26	tracer
^{143}Pr	142.910814	0	13.58d	β^- (0.934); weak γ	7/2+		tracer

NMR

	^{141}Pr
Relative sensitivity (^{1}H = 1.00)	0.29
Receptivity (^{13}C = 1.00)	1.62×10^3
Magnetogyric ratio/rad T^{-1} s^{-1}	7.765×10^7
Quadrupole moment /m^2	-5.9×10^{-30}
Frequency (^{1}H = 100 MHz; 2.3488 T)/MHz	29.291

Ground state electron configuration: [Xe]$4f^3 6s^2$
Term symbol: $^4I_{9/2}$
Electron affinity (M→M$^-$)/kJ mol^{-1}: $\leqslant 50$

Electron shell properties

Main lines in atomic spectrum

Wavelength/nm	Species
406.282	II
410.072	II
417.939	II
422.293	II
422.535	II
495.137 (AA)	I

Ionization energies/kJ mol^{-1}

1. M → M$^+$	523.1
2. M$^+$ → M^{2+}	1018
3. M^{2+} → M^{3+}	2086
4. M^{3+} → M^{4+}	3761
5. M^{4+} → M^{5+}	5543

Environmental properties

Biological role	Abundances	Geological data
None; low toxicity; stimulatory	**Sun** (relative to H = 1×10^{12}): 4.6	**Chief deposits and sources:** monazite [(Ce, La, etc.)PO$_4$]; bastnaesite [(Ce, La, etc.)(CO$_3$)F]
Levels in humans: n.a., but low	**Earth's crust**/p.p.m.: 9.5	
	Seawater/p.p.m.:	**World production**/tonnes y^{-1}: 1000
	Atlantic surface: 4×10^{-7}	
	Atlantic deep: 7×10^{-7}	**Reserves**/tonnes: 4×10^6
	Pacific surface: 4.4×10^{-7}	
	Pacific deep: 10×10^{-7}	
	Residence time/years: n.a.	
	Oxidation state: III	

Pm

Atomic number: 61

Relative atomic mass ($^{12}C = 12.0000$): **(145)**

 Chemical properties

Radioactive metal of the lanthanide (rare earth) group. Used in specialized miniature batteries.

Radii/pm: Pm^{3+} 106; atomic 181.0

Electronegativity: n.a. (Pauling); 1.07 (Allred);
≤ 3.0 eV (absolute)

Effective nuclear charge: 2.85 (Slater); 9.40 (Clementi);
10.94 (Froese-Fischer)

Standard reduction potentials $E^{\ominus}/V$

	III		0
Acid solution	Pm^{3+}	$\underline{-2.29}$	Pm
Alkaline solution	$Pm(OH)_3$	$\underline{-2.76}$	Pm

Oxidation states

Pm^{III}	(f^4)	Pm_2O_3, $Pm(OH)_3$, $[Pm(H_2O)_x]^{3+}$ (aq), PmF_3, some complexes

Physical properties

Melting point/K: 1441
Boiling point/K: *c.* 3000
ΔH_{fusion}/kJ mol^{-1}: 12.6
ΔH_{vap}/kJ mol^{-1}: n.a.

Thermodynamic properties (298.15 K, 0.1 MPa)

State	$\Delta_f H^{\ominus}$/kJ mol^{-1}	$\Delta_f G^{\ominus}$/kJ mol^{-1}	$S^{\ominus}$/J K^{-1} mol^{-1}	C_p/J K^{-1} mol^{-1}
Solid	0	0	n.a.	26.8
Gas	n.a.	n.a.	187.101	24.255

Density/kg m^{-3}: 7220 [298 K]
Thermal conductivity/W m^{-1} K^{-1}: 17.9 (est.) [300 K]
Electrical resistivity/Ω m: 50×10^{-8} (est.) [273 K]
Mass magnetic susceptibility/kg^{-1} m^3: n.a.
Molar volume/cm^3: 20.1
Coefficient of linear thermal expansion/K^{-1}: n.a.

Crystal structure (cell dimensions/pm), space group

Hexagonal

X-ray diffraction: mass absorption coefficients (μ/ρ)/cm^2 g^{-1}:
CuK$_\alpha$ 386   MoK$_\alpha$ 55.9

Produced in 1945 by J. A. Marinsky, L. E. Glendenin, and C. D.
Coryell at Oak Ridge, Tennessee, USA

[Greek, *Prometheus*, who stole fire from the gods]

Promethium

Thermal neutron capture cross-section/barns: 8000 (^{146}Pm)

Number of isotopes (including nuclear isomers). 27

Isotope mass range: 134→155

Nuclear properties

Key isotopes

Nuclide	Atomic mass	Natural abund. (%)	Half-life $T_{1/2}$	Decay mode and energy (MeV)	Nuclear spin I	Nuclear magnetic moment μ	Uses
^{145}Pm	144.912 743	0	17.7y	EC(0.161); γ	5/2+		
^{146}Pm	145.914 708	0	5.53y	EC(1.48) 63%; β^-(1.542); 37% γ	3−		
^{147}Pm	146.915 135	0	2.6234y	β^-(0.224); weak γ	7/2+	+2.7	tracer
^{149}Pm	148.918 332	0	53.1h	β^-(1.073); γ	7/2+	±3.3	} tracer
^{151}Pm	150.921 203	0	28.4h	β^-(1.187); γ	5/2+	±1.8	} pair

NMR

^{147}Pm

Relative sensitivity (^{1}H = 1.00) —

Receptivity (^{13}C = 1.00) —

Magnetogyric ratio/rad T^{-1} s^{-1} 3.613×10^7

Quadrupole moment /m^2 0.67×10^{-28}

Frequency (^{1}H = 100 MHz; 2.3488 T)/MHz   13.51

Ground state electron configuration: [Xe]4f^{5}6s^2

Term symbol: ^{6}H$_{5/2}$

Electron affinity (M→M$^-$)/kJ mol^{-1}: ≤ 50

Electron shell properties

Main lines in atomic spectrum*

Wavelength/nm	Species
389.215	II
391.026	II
391.910	II
395.774	II
399.896	II
441.796	II

*All of equal intensity

Ionization energies/kJ mol^{-1}

1. M → M$^+$ 535.9
2. M$^+$ → M^{2+} 1052
3. M^{2+} → M^{3+} 2150
4. M^{3+} → M^{4+} 3970
5. M^{4+} → M^{5+}

Environmental properties

Biological role	Abundances	Geological data
None; never encountered, but would be toxic due to radioactivity **Levels in humans**: nil	**Sun** (relative to H = 1 × 10^{12}): n.a. **Earth's crust**/p.p.m.: traces in uranium ores **Seawater**/p.p.m.: nil	**Chief source**: obtained in kilogram quantities from the fission products of nuclear reactors

Pa

Atomic number: 91

Relative atomic mass ($^{12}C = 12.0000$): 231.03588

Radioactive, silvery metal found naturally in uranium ores. Attacked by oxygen, steam, and acids, but not by alkalis. Little used.

Radii/pm: Pa^{3+} 113; Pa^{4+} 98; Pa^{5+} 89; atomic 160.6

Electronegativity: 1.5 (Pauling); 1.14 (Allred)

Effective nuclear charge: 1.80 (Slater)

Standard reduction potentials $E^{\ominus}/V$

	V	IV	0
		−1.19	
Acid solution	$PaO(OH)^{2+}$ —$^{−0.1}$— Pa^{4+} —$^{−1.46}$— Pa		

Oxidation states

Pa^{III}	(f^2)	PaI_3
Pa^{IV}	(f^1)	PaO_2, $[Pa(H_2O)_x]^{4+}$ (aq),
		PaF_4, $PaCl_4$, etc.
$\mathbf{Pa^V}$	$(f^0, [Rn])$	Pa_2O_5, PaO_2^+ (compounds),
		Pa^V (aq) unstable, PaF_5, $PaCl_5$, etc.,
		$[PaF_6]^-$, $[PaF_7]^{2-}$, $[PaF_8]^{3-}$

Physical properties

Melting point/K: 2113

Boiling point/K: c. 4300

ΔH_{fusion}/kJ mol^{-1}: 16.7

ΔH_{vap}/kJ mol^{-1}: 481

Thermodynamic properties (298.15 K, 0.1 MPa)

State	$\Delta_f H^{\ominus}$/kJ mol^{-1}	$\Delta_f G^{\ominus}$/kJ mol^{-1}	$S^{\ominus}$/J K^{-1} mol^{-1}	C_p/J K^{-1} mol^{-1}
Solid	0	0	51.9	28
Gas	607	563	198.05	22.93

Density/kg m^{-3}: 15 370 (est.)

Thermal conductivity/W m^{-1} K^{-1}: 47 (est.) [300 K]

Electrical resistivity/Ω m: 17.7×10^{-8} [273 K]

Mass magnetic susceptibility/kg^{-1} m^3: n.a.

Molar volume/cm^3: 15.0

Coefficient of linear thermal expansion/K^{-1}: 7.3×10^{-6}

Crystal structure (cell dimensions/pm), space group

Tetragonal ($a = 393.2$, $c = 323.8$). I4/mmm

X-ray diffraction: mass absorption coefficients (μ/ρ)/cm^2 g^{-1}: n.a.

Discovered in 1917 by Otto Hahn and Lise Meitner at Berlin, by
K. Fajans at Karlsruhe, Germany, and by F. Soddy,
J. A. Cranston, and A. Fleck at Glasgow, Scotland
[Greek, *protos* = first]

Protactinium

Thermal neutron capture cross-section/barns: 500 (^{232}Pa)

Number of isotopes (including nuclear isomers):   21

Isotope mass range: 216→238

Nuclear properties

Key isotopes

Nuclide	Atomic mass	Natural abundance (%)	Half-life $T_{1/2}$	Decay mode and energy (MeV)	Nuclear spin I	Nuclear magnetic moment μ	Uses
^{231}Pa	231.035 880	trace	3.27×10^4y	$\alpha(5.148)$; γ	3/2−	±2.01	
^{232}Pa	232.038 565	0	1.31d	$\beta^-(1.34)$; γ	3/2−	+3.5	tracer
^{233}Pa	233.040 242	0	27.0d	$\beta^-(0.572)$; γ	3/2−	+3.5	tracer
^{234}Pa	234.043 303	trace	6.70h	$\beta^-(2.199)$; γ	4+		

Ground state electron configuration: [Rn]$5f^2 6d^1 7s^2$

Term symbol: $^4K_{11/2}$

Electron affinity (M→M$^-$)/kJ mol^{-1}:   n.a.

Electron shell properties

Main lines in atomic spectrum*

Wavelength/nm	Species
363.652	I
398.223	I
694.572	I
711.489	I
736.825	I
740.315	I
760.820	I

*First seven lines identified as arising from neutral atom species

Ionization energies/kJ mol^{-1}

1. M   →M$^+$ 568
2. M$^+$→M^{2+}
3. M^{2+}→M^{3+}
4. M^{3+}→M^{4+}
5. M^{4+}→M^{5+}

Environmental properties

Biological role

None; never encountered, but would be toxic due to radioactivity

Levels in humans: nil

Abundances

Sun (relative to H = 1 × 10^{12}):
n.a.

Earth's crust/p.p.m.: traces in uranium ores

Seawater/p.p.m.: 2×10^{-11}

Geological data

Chief source: produced in gram quantities from uranium fuel elements

Ra

Atomic number: 88

Relative atomic mass ($^{12}C = 12.0000$): 226.0254

Chemical properties

Radioactive element found naturally in uranium ores. Silvery, lustrous, soft. Annual production c. 100 g. Formerly used in cancer therapy and for luminous paint; both uses now rare. Reacts with oxygen and water.

Radii/pm: Ra^{2+} 152; atomic 223

Electronegativity: 0.89 (Pauling); 0.97 (Allred)

Effective nuclear charge: 1.65 (Slater)

Standard reduction potentials $E^{\ominus}/V$

II		0
Ra^{2+}	$\xrightarrow{-2.916}$	Ra
RaO	$\xrightarrow{-1.319}$	Ra

Oxidation states

Ra^{II} ([Rn])	RaO, $Ra(OH)_2$, $[Ra(H_2O)_x]^{2+}$ (aq), Ra^{2+} salts

Physical properties

Melting point/K: 973

Boiling point/K: 1413

ΔH_{fusion}/kJ mol^{-1}: 7.15

ΔH_{vap}/kJ mol^{-1}: 136.8

Thermodynamic properties (298.15 K, 0.1 MPa)

State	$\Delta_f H^{\ominus}$/kJ mol^{-1}	$\Delta_f G^{\ominus}$/kJ mol^{-1}	$S^{\ominus}$/J K^{-1} mol^{-1}	C_p/J K^{-1} mol^{-1}
Solid	0	0	71	27.1
Gas	159	130	176.47	20.79

Density/kg m^{-3}: c. 5000 [293 K]

Thermal conductivity/W m^{-1} K^{-1}: 18.6 (est.) [300 K]

Electrical resistivity/Ω m: 100×10^{-8} [273 K]

Mass magnetic susceptibility/kg^{-1} m^3: n.a.

Molar volume/cm^3: 45.2

Coefficient of linear thermal expansion/K^{-1}: 20.2×10^{-6}

Crystal structure (cell dimensions/pm), space group

b.c.c. ($a = 515$)

X-ray diffraction: mass absorption coefficients (μ/ρ)/cm^2 g^{-1}:
CuK$_\alpha$ 304   MoK$_\alpha$ 172

Radium

Thermal neutron capture cross-section/barns: 20 (^{226}Ra)

Number of isotopes (including nuclear isomers): 25

Isotope mass range: 213→230

Nuclear properties

Key isotopes

Nuclide	Atomic mass	Natural abundance (%)	Half-life $T_{1/2}$	Decay mode and energy (MeV)	Nuclear spin I	Nuclear magnetic moment μ	Uses
^{223}Ra	223.018 501	some	11.43d	α(5.979); γ	1/2+		
^{224}Ra	224.020 186	some	3.66d	α(5.789); γ	0+		
^{226}Ra	226.025 402	some	1600y	α(4.780); γ	0+		tracer, medical
^{228}Ra	228.031 064	some	5.75y	β^-(0.045); no γ	0+		

Ground state electron configuration: [Rn]$7s^2$

Term symbol: $^1S_0$

Electron affinity (M→M$^-$)/kJ mol^{-1}: n.a.

Electron shell properties

Main lines in atomic spectrum

Wavelength/nm	Species
364.955	II
381.442	II
434.064	II
468.228	II
482.591	I

Ionization energies/kJ mol^{-1}

1. M →M$^+$	509.3	6. M^{5+}→M^{6+} (7 300)
2. M$^+$→M^{2+}	979.0	7. M^{6+}→M^{7+} (8 600)
3. M^{2+}→M^{3+} (3300)		8. M^{7+}→M^{8+} (9 900)
4. M^{3+}→M^{4+} (4400)		9. M^{8+}→M^{9+} (13 500)
5. M^{4+}→M^{5+} (5700)		10. M^{9+}→M^{10+} (15 100)

Environmental properties

Biological role	Abundances	Geological data
None; toxic due to radioactivity	**Sun** (relative to H = 1×10^{12}): n.a.	**Chief sources:** found naturally in uranium ores
Levels in humans: Muscle/p.p.m.: 0.23×10^{-9} Bone/p.p.m.: 4×10^{-9} Blood/mg dm^{-3}: 6.6×10^{-9} Daily dietary intake: 2×10^{-9} mg Total mass of element in average (70 kg) person: 31×10^{-9} mg	**Earth's crust**/p.p.m.: 6×10^{-7} **Seawater**/p.p.m.: 2×10^{-11} Oxidation state: II	

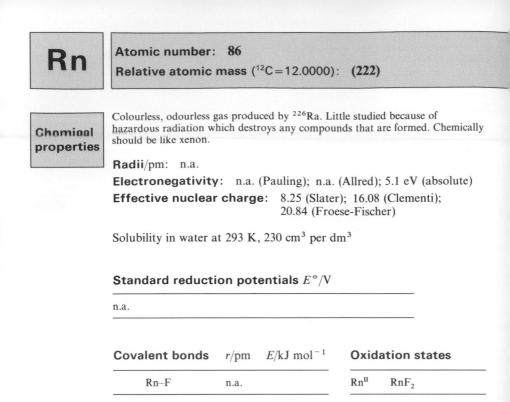

Rn

Atomic number: **86**

Relative atomic mass ($^{12}C=12.0000$): **(222)**

Chemical properties

Colourless, odourless gas produced by ^{226}Ra. Little studied because of hazardous radiation which destroys any compounds that are formed. Chemically should be like xenon.

Radii/pm: n.a.

Electronegativity: n.a. (Pauling); n.a. (Allred); 5.1 eV (absolute)

Effective nuclear charge: 8.25 (Slater); 16.08 (Clementi); 20.84 (Froese-Fischer)

Solubility in water at 293 K, 230 cm^3 per dm^3

Standard reduction potentials $E^{\ominus}$/V

n.a.

Covalent bonds	r/pm	E/kJ mol^{-1}	Oxidation states	
Rn–F		n.a.	Rn^{II}	RnF$_2$

Physical properties

Melting point/K: 202
Boiling point/K: 211.4
ΔH_{fusion}/kJ mol^{-1}: 2.7 (est.)
ΔH_{vap}/kJ mol^{-1}: 18.1

Thermodynamic properties (298.15 K, 0.1 MPa)

State	$\Delta_f H^{\ominus}$/kJ mol^{-1}	$\Delta_f G^{\ominus}$/kJ mol^{-1}	$S^{\ominus}$/J K^{-1} mol^{-1}	C_p/J K^{-1} mol^{-1}
Gas	0	0	176.21	20.786

Density/kg m^{-3}: n.a. [solid]; 4400 [liquid, b.p.]; 9.73 [gas, 273 K]
Thermal conductivity/W m^{-1} K^{-1}: 0.003 64 (est.) [300 K]$_g$
Mass magnetic susceptibility/kg^{-1} m^3: n.a.
Molar volume/cm^3: 50.5 [211 K]

Crystal structure (cell dimensions/pm)

f.c.c.

X-ray diffraction: mass absorption coefficients (μ/ρ)/cm^2 g^{-1}: n.a.

Radon

Thermal neutron capture cross-section/barns: 0.7 (^{222}Rn)
Number of isotopes (including nuclear isomers): 28
Isotope mass range: $200 \rightarrow 226$

Nuclear properties

Key isotopes

Nuclide	Atomic mass	Natural abundance (%)	Half-life $T_{1/2}$	Decay mode and energy (MeV)	Nuclear spin I	Nuclear magnetic moment μ	Uses
^{219}Rn	219.009 479	trace	3.96s	α(6.946); γ	5/2+		
^{220}Rn	220.011 368	trace	55.6s	α(6.404); γ	0+		
^{222}Rn	222.017 570	trace	3.82d	α(5.590); γ	0+		tracer, medical

Ground state electron configuration: $[Xe]4f^{14}5d^{10}6s^26p^6$
Term symbol: $^1S_0$
Electron affinity $(M \rightarrow M^-)$/kJ mol^{-1}: -41 (calc.)

Electron shell properties

Main lines in atomic spectrum

Wavelength/nm	Species
434.960	I
705.542	I
726.811	I
745.000	I
780.982	I
809.951	I
827.096	I
860.007	I

Ionization energies/kJ mol^{-1}

1. $M \rightarrow M^+$ 1037
2. $M^+ \rightarrow M^{2+}$
3. $M^{2+} \rightarrow M^{3+}$
4. $M^{3+} \rightarrow M^{4+}$
5. $M^{4+} \rightarrow M^{5+}$

Environmental properties

Biological role

None; toxic due to radioactivity; worrying levels in indoor air in certain localities

Levels in humans: nil

Abundances

Sun (relative to $H = 1 \times 10^{12}$): n.a.

Earth's crust/p.p.m.: traces

Seawater/p.p.m.: $c.\ 10^{-14}$
Oxidation state: 0

Atmosphere/p.p.m. by volume: trace

Geological data

Chief sources: obtained from ^{226}Ra

Re

Atomic number: 75
Relative atomic mass ($^{12}C = 12.0000$): **186.207**

Chemical properties

Silvery metal, usually obtained as grey powder. Resists corrosion and oxidation but slowly tarnishes in moist air. Dissolves in nitric and sulfuric acids. Used in filaments, thermistors, and catalysts.

Radii/pm: Re^{4+} 72; Re^{6+} 61; Re^{7+} 60; atomic 137.0; covalent 128

Electronegativity: 1.9 (Pauling); 1.46 (Allred); 4.02 eV (absolute)

Effective nuclear charge: 3.60 (Slater); 10.12 (Clementi); 14.62 (Froese-Fischer)

Standard reduction potentials $E^{\ominus}$/V

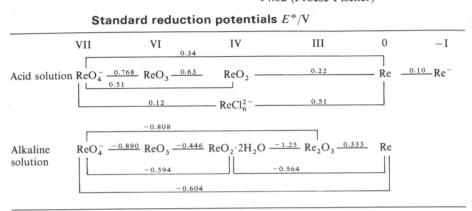

Oxidation states

Re^{-III}	(d^{10})	$[Re(CO)_4]^{3-}$
Re^{-I}	(d^8)	$[Re(CO)_5]^{-}$
Re^0	(d^7)	$Re_2(CO)_{10}$
Re^{I}	(d^6)	$Re(CO)Cl$, $K_5Re(CN)_6$
Re^{II}	(d^5)	ReF_2, $ReCl_2$ etc.
Re^{III}	(d^4)	$Re_2O_3 \cdot xH_2O$, Re_3Cl_9, Re_3Br_9, Re_3I_9, $Re_2Cl_8^{2-}$, $[Re(CN)_7]^{4-}$, complexes

Re^{IV}	(d^3)	ReO_2, ReF_4, $ReCl_4$, etc., complexes
Re^{V}	(d^2)	Re_2O_5, ReF_5, $ReCl_5$, $ReBr_5$, $ReOF_3$, complexes
Re^{VI}	(d^1)	ReO_3, ReF_6, $ReCl_6$, ReF_8^{2-}, $ReOCl_4$, complexes
		Re_2O_7, ReF_7, ReO_3F, $ReOF_5$,
Re^{VII}	(d^0, f^{14})	Re_2O_7, ReF_7, ReO_3F, $ReOF_5$, ReO_4^- (aq), $[ReH_9]^{2-}$, complexes

---

Physical properties

Melting point/K: 3453
Boiling point/K: 5900

ΔH_{fusion}/kJ mol^{-1}: 33.1
ΔH_{vap}/kJ mol^{-1}: 707.1

Thermodynamic properties (298.15 K, 0.1 MPa)

State	$\Delta_f H^{\ominus}$/kJ mol^{-1}	$\Delta_f G^{\ominus}$/kJ mol^{-1}	$S^{\ominus}$/J K^{-1} mol^{-1}	C_p/J K^{-1} mol^{-1}
Solid	0	0	36.86	25.48
Gas	769.9	724.6	188.938	20.786

Density/kg m^{-3}: 21 020 [293 K]; 18 900 [liquid at m.p.]
Thermal conductivity/W m^{-1} K^{-1}: 47.9 [300 K]
Electrical resistivity/Ω m: 19.3×10^{-8} [293 K]
Mass magnetic susceptibility/kg^{-1} m^3: $+4.56 \times 10^{-9}$ (s)
Molar volume/cm^3: 8.86
Coefficient of linear thermal expansion/K^{-1}: 6.63×10^{-6}

Crystal structure (cell dimensions/pm), space group

---

h.c.p. ($a = 276.09$; $c = 445.76$), P6$_3$/mmc

X-ray diffraction: mass absorption coefficients (μ/ρ)/cm^2 g^{-1}:
CuK$_{\alpha}$ 179   MoK$_{\alpha}$ 103

Rhenium

Thermal neutron capture cross-section/barns: 90
Number of isotopes (including nuclear isomers): 34
Isotope mass range: $162 \rightarrow 192$

Nuclear properties

Key isotopes

Nuclide	Atomic mass	Natural abundance (%)	Half-life $T_{1/2}$	Decay mode and energy (MeV)	Nuclear spin I	Nuclear magnetic moment μ	Uses
^{185}Re	184.952 951	37.40	stable		$5/2+$	$+3.172$	NMR
^{186}Re	185.954 984	0	88.9h	β^- (1.071) 92%; EC 8%; γ	$1-$	$+1.739$	tracer
^{187}Re	186.955 744	62.60	4.5×10^{10}y	β^- (0.0025)	$5/2+$	$+3.2197$	NMR
^{188}Re	187.958 106	0	16.98h	β^- (2.10); γ	$1-$	$+1.788$	tracer

NMR

	$[^{185}\text{Re}]$	^{187}Re
Relative sensitivity (^{1}H = 1.00)	0.13	0.13
Receptivity (^{13}C = 1.00)	280	490
Magnetogyric ratio/rad T^{-1} s^{-1}	6.0255×10^7	6.0862×10^7
Quadrupole moment/m^2	2.8×10^{-28}	2.6×10^{-28}
Frequency (^{1}H = 100 MHz; 2.3488 T)/MHz	22.513	22.744
Reference: NaReO$_4$ (aq)		

Ground state electron configuration: [Xe]4f^{14}5d^{2}6s^2
Term symbol: $^6S_{5/2}$
Electron affinity (M $\rightarrow$ M$^-$)/kJ mol^{-1}: 14

Electron shell properties

Main lines in atomic spectrum

Wavelength/nm	Species
200.353	I
204.908	I
345.188	I
346.046 (AA)	I
346.473	I

Ionization energies/kJ mol^{-1}

1. M $\rightarrow$ M$^+$	760	6. M$^{5+} \rightarrow$ M^{6+} (6300)
2. M$^+ \rightarrow$ M^{2+}	1260	7. M$^{6+} \rightarrow$ M^{7+} (7600)
3. M$^{2+} \rightarrow$ M^{3+}	2510	8. M$^{7+} \rightarrow$ M^{8+}
4. M$^{3+} \rightarrow$ M^{4+}	3640	9. M$^{8+} \rightarrow$ M^{9+}
5. M$^{4+} \rightarrow$ M^{5+} (4900)		10. M$^{9+} \rightarrow$ M^{10+}

Environmental properties

Biological role	Abundances	Geological data
None; low toxicity	**Sun** (relative to H = 1×10^{12}): < 2	**Chief sources:** extracted from flue dusts of molybdenum smelters
Levels in humans: n.a., but low	**Earth's crust**/p.p.m.: 4×10^{-4}	
	Seawater/p.p.m.: 4×10^{-6}	**World production**/tonnes y^{-1}: c. 1
	Oxidation state: III	**Reserves**/tonnes: n.a.

Rh

Atomic number: 45

Relative atomic mass ($^{12}C = 12.0000$): **102.90550**

Chemical properties

Rare; lustrous, silvery, hard metal of the platinum group. Stable in air up to 875 K; inert to all acids; attacked by fused alkalis. Used as a catalyst.

Radii/pm: Rh^{2+} 86; Rh^{3+} 75; Rh^{4+} 67; atomic 134.5; covalent 125

Electronegativity: 2.28 (Pauling); 1.45 (Allred); 4.30 eV (absolute)

Effective nuclear charge: 3.90 (Slater); 7.64 (Clementi); 10.85 (Froese-Fischer)

Standard reduction potentials $E^{\ominus}$/V

III		0
Rh^{3+}	$\underline{\quad 0.76 \quad}$	Rh

Oxidation states

Rh^{-I}	(d^{10})	$[Rh(CO)_4]^-$
Rh^0	(d^9)	$[Rh_4(CO)_{12}]$
Rh^I	(d^8)	$[RhCl(PPh_3)_3]$
Rh^{II}	(d^7)	RhO
Rh^{III}	(d^6)	Rh_2O_3 RhF_3, $RhCl_3$ etc., $[RhCl_6]^{3-}$
		$[Rh(H_2O)_x]^{3+}$ (aq)
Rh^{IV}	(d^5)	RhO_2, RhF_4, $[RhCl_6]^{2-}$
Rh^V	(d^4)	$[RhF_5]_4$, $[RhF_6]^-$
Rh^{VI}	(d^3)	RhF_6

Physical properties

Melting point/K: 2239
Boiling point/K: 4000
ΔH_{fusion}/kJ mol^{-1}: 21.55
ΔH_{vap}/kJ mol^{-1}: 495.4

Thermodynamic properties (298.15 K, 0.1 MPa)

State	$\Delta_f H^{\ominus}$/kJ mol^{-1}	$\Delta_f G^{\ominus}$/kJ mol^{-1}	$S^{\ominus}$/J K^{-1} mol^{-1}	C_p/J K^{-1} mol^{-1}
Solid	0	0	31.51	24.98
Gas	556.9	510.8	185.808	21.012

Density/kg m^{-3}: 12 410 [293 K]; 10 650 [liquid at m.p.]
Thermal conductivity/W m^{-1} K^{-1}: 150 [300 K]
Electrical resistivity/Ω m: 4.51×10^{-8} [293 K]
Mass magnetic susceptibility/kg^{-1} m^3: $+1.36 \times 10^{-8}$ (s)
Molar volume/cm^3: 8.29
Coefficient of linear thermal expansion/K^{-1}: 8.40×10^{-6}

Crystal structure (cell dimensions/pm), space group

f.c.c. ($a = 380.36$), Fm3m

X-ray diffraction: mass absorption coefficients (μ/ρ)/cm^2 g^{-1}:
CuK$_\alpha$ 194 MoK$_\alpha$ 22.6

Rhodium

Thermal neutron capture cross-section/barns: 145
Number of isotopes (including nuclear isomers): 34
Isotope mass range: 94m→112

Key isotopes

Nuclide	Atomic mass	Natural abundance (%)	Half-life $T_{1/2}$	Decay mode and energy (MeV)	Nuclear spin I	Nuclear magnetic moment μ	Uses
^{103}Rh	102.905 500	100	stable		$1/2-$	-0.0884	NMR
^{105}Rh	104.905 686	0	35.4h	β^- (0.57); γ	$7/2+$	$+4.428$	tracer

NMR

^{103}Rh

Relative sensitivity (^{1}H $= 1.00$)	3.11×10^{-5}
Receptivity (^{13}C $= 1.00$)	0.177
Magnetogyric ratio/rad T^{-1} s^{-1}	-0.8520×10^7
Frequency (^{1}H $= 100$ MHz; 2.3488 T)/MHz	3.172

Reference: mer-[RhCl$_3$(SMe$_2$)$_3$]

Ground state electron configuration: [Kr]$4d^8 5s^1$
Term symbol: $^4F_{9/2}$
Electron affinity (M→M$^-$)/kJ mol^{-1}: 109.7

Main lines in atomic spectrum

Wavelength/nm	Species
343.489 (4.4)	I
350.252	I
352.802	I
365.799	I
369.236	I
370.091	I

Ionization energies/kJ mol^{-1}

1. M →M$^+$	720	6. M^{5+}→M^{6+} (8 200)
2. M$^+$→M^{2+}	1744	7. M^{6+}→M^{7+} (10 100)
3. M^{2+}→M^{3+}	2997	8. M^{7+}→M^{8+} (12 200)
4. M^{3+}→M^{4+}	(4400)	9. M^{8+}→M^{9+} (14 200)
5. M^{4+}→M^{5+}	(6500)	10. M^{9+}→M^{10+} (22 000)

Environmental properties

Biological role	Abundances	Geological data
None; suspected carcinogen; toxicity data n.a.	**Sun** (relative to H $= 1 \times 10^{12}$): 25.1	**Chief sources**: certain copper and nickel ores contain up to 0.1% Rh
Levels in humans: n.a., but low	**Earth's crust**/p.p.m.: c. 2×10^{-4}	**World production**/tonnes y^{-1}: 3
	Seawater/p.p.m.: n.a., but minute	**Reserves**/tonnes: 3000

Rb

Atomic number: 37
Relative atomic mass ($^{12}C = 12.0000$): **85.4678**

Chemical properties

Very soft metal with silvery white lustre when cut. Ignites in air and reacts violently with water. Finds little use outside research.

Radii/pm: Rb^+ 1.49; atomic 247.5; van der Waals 244
Electronegativity: 0.82 (Pauling); 0.89 (Allred); 2.34 eV (absolute)
Effective nuclear charge: 2.20 (Slater); 4.98 (Clementi); 6.66 (Froese-Fischer)

Standard reduction potentials $E^\oplus$/V

$$\begin{array}{cc} \text{I} & 0 \\ Rb^+ \xrightarrow{\ -2.924\ } & Rb \end{array}$$

Oxidation states

Rb^{-1}	(s^2)	solution of metal in liquid ammonia
Rb^I	([Kr])	Rb_2O, Rb_2O_2 (peroxide),
		RbO_2 (superoxide),
		RbOH, RbH, RbF, RbCl etc.,
		$[Rb(H_2O)_x]^+$ (aq),
		Rb_2CO_3, many salts,
		some complexes

Physical properties

Melting point/K: 312.2
Boiling point/K: 961
ΔH_{fusion}/kJ mol^{-1}: 2.20
ΔH_{vap}/kJ mol^{-1}: 69.2

Thermodynamic properties (298.15 K, 0.1 MPa)

State	$\Delta_f H^\oplus$/kJ mol^{-1}	$\Delta_f G^\oplus$/kJ mol^{-1}	$S^\oplus$/J K^{-1} mol^{-1}	C_p/J K^{-1} mol^{-1}
Solid	0	0	76.78	31.062
Gas	80.88	53.06	170.089	20.786

Density/kg m^{-3}: 1532 [293 K]; 1475 [liquid at m.p.]
Thermal conductivity/W m^{-1} K^{-1}: 58.2 [300 K]
Electrical resistivity/Ω m: 12.5×10^{-8} [293 K]
Mass magnetic susceptibility/kg^{-1} m^3: $+2.49 \times 10^{-9}$ (s)
Molar volume/cm^3: 55.79
Coefficient of linear thermal expansion/K^{-1}: 90×10^{-6}

Crystal structure (cell dimensions/pm), space group

b.c.c. ($a = 562$), Im3m

X-ray diffraction: mass absorption coefficients (μ/ρ)/cm^2 g^{-1}:
CuK_α 117 MoK_α 90.0

Rubidium

Thermal neutron capture cross-section/barns: 0.38

Number of isotopes (including nuclear isomers): 30

Isotope mass range: 75→98

Nuclear properties

Key isotopes

Nuclide	Atomic mass	Natural abund. (%)	Half-life $T_{1/2}$	Decay mode and energy (MeV)	Nuclear spin I	Nuclear magnetic moment μ	Uses
^{83}Rb	82.915 144	0	86.2d	EC(0.86); γ	5/2−	+1.43	tracer
^{85}Rb	84.911 794	72.17	stable		5/2−	+1.353 02	NMR
^{86}Rb	85.911 172	0	18.63d	β^-(1.774); γ	2−	−1.6920	tracer
^{87}Rb	86.909 187	27.83	4.9×10^{10}y	β^-(0.273); no γ	3/2−	+2.7512	NMR

NMR

	[^{85}Rb]	^{87}Rb
Relative sensitivity (^{1}H = 1.00)	1.05×10^{-2}	0.17
Receptivity (^{13}C = 1.00)	43	277
Magnetogyric ratio/rad T^{-1} s^{-1}	2.5828×10^7	8.7532×10^7
Quadrupole moment/m^2	0.25×10^{-28}	0.12×10^{-28}
Frequency (^{1}H = 100 MHz; 2.3488 T)/MHz	9.655	32.721

Reference: RbCl (aq)

Ground state electron configuration: [Kr]5s^1

Term symbol: $^2S_{1/2}$

Electron affinity (M→M$^-$)/kJ mol^{-1}: 46.9

Electron shell properties

Main lines in atomic spectrum

Wavelength/nm	Species
214.383	II
247.220	II
424.440	II
477.595	II
780.027 (AA)	I
794.760	I

Ionization energies/kJ mol^{-1}

1. M → M$^+$	403.0	6. M^{5+}→M^{6+} 8140
2. M$^+$→M^{2+} 2632		7. M^{6+}→M^{7+} 9570
3. M^{2+}→M^{3+} 3900		8. M^{7+}→M^{8+} 13 100
4. M^{3+}→M^{4+} 5080		9. M^{8+}→M^{9+} 14 800
5. M^{4+}→M^{5+} 6850		10. M^{9+}→M^{10+} 26 740

Environmental properties

Biological role	Abundances	Geological data
None; stimulatory	**Sun** (relative to H = 1×10^{12}): 400	**Chief sources:** present in minerals such as lepidolite, pollucite, and carnallite
Levels in humans:		
Muscle/p.p.m.: 20–70	**Earth's crust**/p.p.m.: 90	
Bone/p.p.m.: 0.1–5	**Seawater**/p.p.m.: 0.12	**World production**/tonnes y^{-1}: n.a.
Blood/mg dm^{-3}: 2.49	Residence time/years: 800 000	
Daily dietary intake: 1.5–6 mg	Classification: accumulating	**Reserves**/tonnes: n.a.
Toxic intake: n.a., but relatively non-toxic	Oxidation state: I	
Lethal intake: n.a.		
Total mass of element in average (70 kg) person: 680 mg		

Ru

Atomic number: 44
Relative atomic mass (^{12}C = 12.0000): 101.07

Chemical properties

Lustrous, silvery metal of the platinum group. Unaffected by air, water and acids but dissolves in molten alkali. Used to harden Pt and Pd, and as catalyst.

Radii/pm: Ru^{3+} 77; Ru^{4+} 65; Ru^{8+} 54; atomic 134; covalent 124

Electronegativity: 2.2 (Pauling); 1.42 (Allred); 4.5 eV (absolute)

Effective nuclear charge: 3.75 (Slater); 7.45 (Clementi); 10.57 (Froese-Fischer)

Standard reduction potentials $E^{\ominus}$/V

VIII	VII	VI	IV	III	II	0

$$\text{RuO}_4 \xrightarrow{0.99} \text{RuO}_4^- \xrightarrow{0.593} \text{RuO}_4^{2-} \xrightarrow{2.0} \text{RuO}_2 \xrightarrow{0.86} \text{Ru}^{3+} \xrightarrow{0.249} \text{Ru}^{2+} \xrightarrow{n.a.} \text{Ru}$$

(1.04 overall; 1.533; 1.40; 0.68)

Oxidation states

Ru^{-II}	(d^{10})	rare [Ru(CO)$_4$]$^{2-}$
Ru	(d^8)	rare Ru(CO)$_5$
Ru^{I}	(d^7)	some complexes
Ru^{II}	(d^6)	[Ru(H$_2$O)$_6$]$^{2+}$ (aq), RuCl$_2$, RuBr$_2$, RuI$_2$, [Ru(CN)$_6$]$^{2-}$, complexes
Ru^{III}	(d^5)	Ru$_2$O$_3$, [Ru(H$_2$O)$_6$]$^{3+}$ (aq), RuF$_3$, RuCl$_3$, etc., RuCl$_6^{3-}$
Ru^{IV}	(d^4)	RuO$_2$, RuF$_4$, RuCl$_6^{2-}$
Ru^{V}	(d^3)	RuF$_5$, RuF$_6^-$
Ru^{VI}	(d^2)	RuO$_3$, RuO$_4^{2-}$ (aq), RuF$_6$
Ru^{VII}	(d^1)	RuO$_4^-$ (aq)
Ru^{VIII}	(d^0, [Kr])	RuO$_4$

Physical properties

Melting point/K: 2583
Boiling point/K: 4173
ΔH_{fusion}/kJ mol^{-1}: 23.7
ΔH_{vap}/kJ mol^{-1}: 567.8

Thermodynamic properties (298.15 K, 0.1 MPa)

State	$\Delta_f H^{\ominus}$/kJ mol^{-1}	$\Delta_f G^{\ominus}$/kJ mol^{-1}	$S^{\ominus}$/J K^{-1} mol^{-1}	C_p/J K^{-1} mol^{-1}
Solid	0	0	28.53	24.06
Gas	642.7	595.8	186.507	21.522

Density/kg m^{-3}: 12 370 [293 K]; 10 900 [liquid at m.p.]
Thermal conductivity/W m^{-1} K^{-1}: 117 [300 K]
Electrical resistivity/Ω m: 7.6 × 10^{-8} [273 K]
Mass magnetic susceptibility/kg^{-1} m^3: +5.37 × 10^{-9} (s)
Molar volume/cm^3: 8.14
Coefficient of linear thermal expansion/K^{-1}: 9.1 × 10^{-6}

Crystal structure (cell dimensions/pm), space group

h.c.p. (a = 270.58; c = 428.11), P6$_3$/mmc

X-ray diffraction: mass absorption coefficients (μ/ρ)/cm^2 g^{-1}:
CuK$_\alpha$ 183   MoK$_\alpha$ 21.1

Discovered in 1808 by J. A. Sniadecki at University of Vilno, Poland; rediscovered in 1828 by G. W. Osann at University of Tartu, Russia
[Latin, *Ruthenia* = Russia]

Ruthenium

Thermal neutron capture cross-section/barns: 2.6

Number of isotopes (including nuclear isomers): 20

Isotope mass range: $92 \rightarrow 110$

Key isotopes

Nuclide	Atomic mass	Natural abundance (%)	Half-life $T_{1/2}$	Decay mode and energy (MeV)	Nuclear spin I	Nuclear magnetic moment μ	Uses
^{96}Ru	95.907 599	5.53	stable		0+		
^{97}Ru	96.907 556	0	2.89d	EC(1.12); γ	5/2+	0.687	tracer
^{98}Ru	97.905 287	1.87	stable		0+		
^{99}Ru	98.905 939	12.7	stable		5/2+	-6.413	NMR
^{100}Ru	99.904 219	12.6	stable		0+		
^{101}Ru	100.905 582	17.1	stable		5/2+	-0.7188	NMR
^{102}Ru	101.904 348	31.6	stable		0+		
^{103}Ru	102.906 323	0	39.24d	$\beta^-(0.767)$; γ	5/2+	0.67	tracer
^{104}Ru	103.905 424	18.6	stable		0+		
^{106}Ru	105.907 321	0	372.6d	$\beta^-(0.039)$; no γ	0+		tracer, medical

NMR

	^{99}Ru	^{101}Ru
Relative sensitivity (^{1}H = 1.00)	1.95×10^{-4}	1.41×10^{-3}
Receptivity (^{13}C = 1.00)	0.83	1.56
Magnetogyric ratio/rad T^{-1} s^{-1}	-1.2343×10^7	-1.3834×10^7
Quadrupole moment/m^2	0.076×10^{-28}	0.44×10^{-28}
Frequency (^{1}H = 100 MHz, 2.3488 T)/MHz	3.389	4.941

Reference: RuO$_4$

Ground state electron configuration: $[Kr]4d^7 5s^1$

Term symbol: $^5F_5$

Electron affinity (M$\rightarrow$M$^-$)/kJ mol^{-1}: 101

Main lines in atomic spectrum		Ionization energies/kJ mol^{-1}	

Wavelength/nm	Species
349.894	I
372.693	I
372.803 (AA)	I
379.890	I
379.935	I
419.990	I

1. M $\rightarrow$M$^+$	711	6. M$^{5+}\rightarrow$M^{6+} (7800)
2. M$^+\rightarrow$M^{2+}	1617	7. M$^{6+}\rightarrow$M^{7+} (9600)
3. M$^{2+}\rightarrow$M^{3+}	2747	8. M$^{7+}\rightarrow$M^{8+} (11500)
4. M$^{3+}\rightarrow$M^{4+}	(4500)	9. M$^{8+}\rightarrow$M^{9+} (18700)
5. M$^{4+}\rightarrow$M^{5+}	(6100)	10. M$^{9+}\rightarrow$M^{10+} (20900)

Environmental properties

Biological role	Abundances	Geological data
None; RuO$_4$ highly toxic Levels in humans: n.a., but low	Sun (relative to H = 1×10^{12}): 67.6 Earth's crust/p.p.m.: *c.* 0.001 Seawater/p.p.m.: n.a., but minute	Chief deposits and sources: found in free state, but obtained from the wastes of Ni refining World production/tonnes y^{-1}: 0.12 Reserves/tonnes: 5000

Sm

Atomic number: 62

Relative atomic mass ($^{12}C = 12.0000$): 150.36

Chemical properties

Silvery white metal of the lanthanide (rare earth) group. Relatively stable in dry air but in moist air an oxide coating forms. Used in permanent magnets, organic reagents, special glass, catalysts, ceramics, and electronics.

Radii/pm: Sm^{2+} 111; Sm^{3+} 100; atomic 180.2; covalent 166

Electronegativity: 1.17 (Pauling); 1.07 (Allred); ≤ 3.1 eV (absolute)

Effective nuclear charge: 2.85 (Slater); 8.01 (Clementi); 11.06 (Froese-Fischer)

Standard reduction potentials $E^{\ominus}$/V

	III	II	0
Acid solution	Sm^{3+} —-1.55—	Sm^{2+} —-2.67—	Sm
Alkaline solution	$Sm(OH)_3$	—-2.80—	Sm

(Acid solution III → 0 overall: -2.30)

Oxidation states

Sm^{II}	(f^6)	SmO, SmS, SmF_2, $SmCl_2$, etc.
Sm^{III}	(f^5)	Sm_2O_3, $Sm(OH)_3$, SmF_3, $SmCl_3$ etc., $[Sm(H_2O)_x]^{3+}$ (aq), Sm^{3+} salts, complexes

Physical properties

Melting point/K: 1350
Boiling point/K: 2064
ΔH_{fusion}/kJ mol^{-1}: 10.9
ΔH_{vap}/kJ mol^{-1}: 191.6

Thermodynamic properties (298.15 K, 0.1 MPa)

State	$\Delta_f H^{\ominus}$/kJ mol^{-1}	$\Delta_f G^{\ominus}$/kJ mol^{-1}	$S^{\ominus}$/J K^{-1} mol^{-1}	C_p/J K^{-1} mol^{-1}
Solid	0	0	69.58	29.54
Gas	206.7	172.8	183.042	30.355

Density/kg m^{-3}: 7520 [293 K]
Thermal conductivity/W m^{-1} K^{-1}: 13.3 [300 K]
Electrical resistivity/Ω m: 94.0×10^{-8} [298 K]
Mass magnetic susceptibility/kg^{-1} m^3: $+1.52 \times 10^{-7}$ (s)
Molar volume/cm^3: 20.00
Coefficient of linear thermal expansion/K^{-1}: 10.4×10^{-6}

Crystal structure (cell dimensions/pm), space group

α-Sm rhombohedral ($a = 899.6$, $\alpha = 23°13'$), R$\bar{3}$m
β-Sm cubic ($a = 407$), Im3m

$T(\alpha \rightarrow \beta) = 1190$ K

High pressure form: h.c.p. ($a = 361.8$, $c = 1166$), P6$_3$/mmc

X-ray diffraction: mass absorption coefficients (μ/ρ)/cm^2 g^{-1}:
CuK$_\alpha$ 397   MoK$_\alpha$ 58.6

Discovered by P.-E. Lecoq de Boisbaudran in 1879 at Paris, France

[Named after the mineral Samarskite]

Samarium

Thermal neutron capture cross-section/barns: 5900

Number of isotopes (including nuclear isomers): 24

Isotope mass range: $138 \rightarrow 158$

Nuclear properties

Key isotopes

Nuclide	Atomic mass	Natural abundance (%)	Half-life $T_{1/2}$	Decay mode and energy (MeV)	Nuclear spin I	Nuclear magnetic moment μ	Uses
^{144}Sm	143.911 998	3.1	stable				
^{146}Sm	145.913 059	0	1.03×10^8y	$\alpha(2.50)$			
^{147}Sm	146.914 895	15.0	1.08×10^{11}y	$\alpha(2.23)$	$7/2-$	-0.813	NMR
^{148}Sm	147.914 820	11.3	7×10^{15}y	$\alpha(1.96)$			
^{149}Sm	148.917 181	13.8	10^{16}y	α	$7/2-$	-0.670	NMR
^{150}Sm	149.917 273	7.4	stable				
^{152}Sm	151.919 729	26.6	stable				
^{153}Sm	152.922 094	0	46.7h	$\beta^-(0.810); \gamma$	$3/2+$	-0.0217	tracer
^{154}Sm	153.922 206	22.6	stable				

NMR

	^{147}Sm	^{149}Sm
Relative sensitivity (^{1}H = 1.00)	1.48×10^{-3}	7.47×10^{-4}
Receptivity (^{13}C = 1.00)	1.28	0.665
Magnetogyric ratio/rad T^{-1} s^{-1}	-1.1124×10^7	-0.9175×10^7
Quadrupole moment/m^2	-0.208×10^{-28}	6×10^{-30}
Frequency (^{1}H = 100 MHz; 2.3488 T)/MHz	4.128	3.289

Ground state electron configuration: $[Xe]4f^66s^2$

Term symbol: $^7F_0$

Electron affinity (M$\rightarrow$M$^-$)/kJ mol^{-1}: $\leqslant 50$

Electron shell properties

Main lines in atomic spectrum

Wavelength/nm	Species
356.827	II
359.260	II
363.429	II
373.912	II
388.529	II
429.674 (AA)	I

Ionization energies/kJ mol^{-1}

1. M $\rightarrow$ M$^+$ 543.3	6. M$^{5+} \rightarrow$ M^{6+}	
2. M$^+ \rightarrow$ M^{2+} 1068	7. M$^{6+} \rightarrow$ M^{7+}	
3. M$^{2+} \rightarrow$ M^{3+} 2260	8. M$^{7+} \rightarrow$ M^{8+}	
4. M$^{3+} \rightarrow$ M^{4+} 3990	9. M$^{8+} \rightarrow$ M^{9+}	
5. M$^{4+} \rightarrow$ M^{5+}	10. M$^{9+} \rightarrow$ M^{10+}	

Environmental properties

Biological role	Abundances	Geological data
None; low toxicity; stimulatory	**Sun** (relative to H = 1×10^{12}): 5.2	**Chief deposits and sources:** monazite [(Ce, La, etc.)PO$_4$]
Levels in humans: n.a., but low	**Earth's crust**/p.p.m.: 7.9	**World production**/tonnes y^{-1}: c. 100
	Seawater/p.p.m.:	**Reserves**/tonnes: c. 10^5
	Atlantic surface: 4.0×10^{-7}	
	Atlantic deep: 6.4×10^{-7}	
	Pacific surface: 4.0×10^{-7}	
	Pacific deep: 10×10^{-7}	
	Residence time/years: 200	
	Classification: recycled	
	Oxidation state: III	

Sc

Atomic number: **21**
Relative atomic mass ($^{12}C = 12.0000$): **44.955910**

Chemical properties

Soft, silvery-white metal. Tarnishes in air and burns easily. Reacts with water to form hydrogen gas. Forms salts with acids. Little used.

Radii/pm: Sc^{3+} 83; atomic 160.6; covalent 144

Electronegativity: 1.36 (Pauling); 1.20 (Allred); 3.34 eV (absolute)

Effective nuclear charge: 3.00 (Slater); 4.63 (Clementi); 6.06 (Froese-Fischer)

Standard reduction potentials $E^{\ominus}/V$

III		0
Sc^{3+}	$\xrightarrow{-2.03}$	Sc

Oxidation states

Sc^{II}	(d^1)	$CsScCl_3$
Sc^{III}	$([Ar])$	Sc_2O_3, $ScO.OH$,
		'$Sc(OH)_3$', $Sc(OH)_6^{3-}$,
		ScF_3, $ScCl_3$, etc.,
		ScF_6^{3-}, complexes

[ScH_2 is probably $Sc^{III}H^-$ with complex bonding]

Physical properties

Melting point/K: 1814
Boiling point/K: 3104
ΔH_{fusion}/kJ mol^{-1}: 15.9
ΔH_{vap}/kJ mol^{-1}: 304.8

Thermodynamic properties (298.15 K, 0.1 MPa)

State	$\Delta_f H^{\ominus}$/kJ mol^{-1}	$\Delta_f G^{\ominus}$/kJ mol^{-1}	$S^{\ominus}$/J K^{-1} mol^{-1}	C_p/J K^{-1} mol^{-1}
Solid	0	0	34.64	25.52
Gas	377.8	336.03	174.79	22.09

Density/kg m^{-3}: 2989 [273 K]
Thermal conductivity/W m^{-1} K^{-1}: 15.8 [300 K]
Electrical resistivity/Ω m: 61.0×10^{-8} [295 K]
Mass magnetic susceptibility/kg^{-1} m^3: $+8.8 \times 10^{-8}$ (s)
Molar volume/cm^3: 15.04
Coefficient of linear thermal expansion/K^{-1}: 10.0×10^{-6}

Crystal structure (cell dimensions/pm), space group

α-Sc h.c.p. ($a = 330.90$, $c = 527.3$), P6$_3$/mmc
β-Sc cubic, Im3m

$T(\alpha \rightarrow \beta) = 1223$ K

X-ray diffraction: mass absorption coefficients (μ/ρ)/cm^2 g^{-1}:
CuK$_\alpha$ 184   MoK$_\alpha$ 21.1

Scandium

Thermal neutron capture cross-section/barns: 27.2
Number of isotopes (including nuclear isomers): 15
Isotope mass range: $40 \rightarrow 51$

Key isotopes

Nuclide	Atomic mass	Natural abundance (%)	Half-life $T_{1/2}$	Decay mode and energy (MeV)	Nuclear spin I	Nuclear magnetic moment μ	Uses
^{44}Sc	43.959 404	0	3.93h	β^- (3.655); γ	$0+$	$+2.56$	tracer
^{45}Sc	44.955 910	100	stable		$7/2-$	$+4.756$	NMR
^{46}Sc	45.955 170	0	83.8d	β^- (2.367); γ	$4+$	$+3.03$	tracer
^{47}Sc	46.952 408	0	3.42d	β^- (0.601); γ	$7/2-$	$+5.34$	tracer

NMR

^{45}Sc

Relative sensitivity (^{1}H = 1.00)	0.30
Receptivity (^{13}C = 1.00)	1710
Magnetogyric ratio/rad T^{-1} s^{-1}	6.4982×10^7
Quadrupole momentm^2	-0.22×10^{-28}
Frequency (^{1}H = 100 MHz; 2.3488 T)/MHz	24.290

Reference: $Sc(ClO_4)_3$ (aq)

Ground state electron configuration: $[Ar]3d^14s^2$
Term symbol: $^2D_{3/2}$
Electron affinity ($M \rightarrow M^-$)/kJ mol^{-1}: 18.1

Main lines in atomic spectrum

Wavelength/nm	Species
361.384	I
363.075	II
390.749	I
391.181 (AA)	I
402.040	I
402.369	I

Ionization energies/kJ mol^{-1}

1. $M \rightarrow M^+$ 631	6. $M^{5+} \rightarrow M^{6+}$ 10 720
2. $M^+ \rightarrow M^{2+}$ 1235	7. $M^{6+} \rightarrow M^{7+}$ 13 320
3. $M^{2+} \rightarrow M^{3+}$ 2389	8. $M^{7+} \rightarrow M^{8+}$ 15 310
4. $M^{3+} \rightarrow M^{4+}$ 7089	9. $M^{8+} \rightarrow M^{9+}$ 17 369
5. $M^{4+} \rightarrow M^{5+}$ 8844	10. $M^{9+} \rightarrow M^{10+}$ 21 740

Environmental properties

Biological role	Abundances	Geological data
None; suspected carcinogen	**Sun** (relative to H = 1×10^{12}): 1100	**Chief mineral:** thortveitite [(Sc,Y)$_2$Si$_2$O$_7$] (rare)
Levels in humans:	**Earth's crust**/p.p.m.: 16	**World production**/tonnes y^{-1}: 0.05
Muscle/p.p.m.: n.a.	**Seawater**/p.p.m.:	**Reserves**/tonnes: n.a.
Bone/p.p.m.: *c.* 0.001	Atlantic surface: 6.1×10^{-7}	
Blood/mg dm^{-3}: *c.* 0.008	Atlantic deep: 8.8×10^{-7}	
Daily dietary intake:	Pacific surface: 3.5×10^{-7}	
c. 0.00005 mg	Pacific deep: 7.9×10^{-7}	
Toxic intake: low toxicity	Residence time/years: 5000	
Total mass of element in	Classification: recycled	
average (70 kg) person: n.a.	Oxidation state: III	

Se

Atomic number: 34
Relative atomic mass ($^{12}C = 12.0000$): 78.96

Obtained as silvery metallic allotrope or red amorphous powder, which is less stable. Burns in air, unaffected by water, dissolves in concentrated nitric acid and alkalis. Used in photoelectric cells, photocopiers, solar cells, and semiconductors.

Radii/pm: Se^{4+} 69; atomic 215.2 (grey); covalent 117; van der Waals 200; Se^{2-} 191

Electronegativity: 2.55 (Pauling); 2.48 (Allred); 5.89 eV (absolute)

Effective nuclear charge: 6.95 (Slater); 8.29 (Clementi); 9.96 (Froese-Fischer)

Standard reduction potentials $E^{\ominus}/V$

	VI		IV		0		−II
Acid solution	SeO_4^{2-}	—1.1—	H_2SeO_3	—0.74—	Se	—−0.11—	H_2Se
Alkaline solution	SeO_4^{2-}	—0.03—	SeO_3^{2-}	—−0.36—	Se	—−0.67—	Se^{2-}

Covalent bonds

	r/pm	E/kJ mol^{-1}
Se–H	146	305
Se–C	198	245
Se–O	161	343
Se–F	170	285
Se–Cl	220	245
Se–Se (Se_8)	232	330

Oxidation states

Se^{-II}	H_2Se
Se^{0-I}	Se cluster cations, e.g. Se_4^{2+}, Se_8^{2+}
Se^I	Se_2Cl_2, Se_2Br_2
Se^{II}	?
Se^{IV}	SeO_2, H_2SeO_3, SeO_3^{2-} (aq), $SeOF_2$, $SeOCl_4$, $SeOBr_2$, SeF_4, $SeCl_4$, $SeBr_4$, $SeBr_6^{2-}$
Se^{VI}	SeO_3 ? H_2SeO_4, SeO_4^{2-} (aq), SeO_2F_2, SeO_2Cl_2, SeF_6

Melting point/K: 490
Boiling point/K: 958.1
ΔH_{fusion}/kJ mol^{-1}: 5.1
ΔH_{vap}/kJ mol^{-1}: 26.32

Thermodynamic properties (298.15 K, 0.1 MPa)

State	$\Delta_f H^{\ominus}$/kJ mol^{-1}	$\Delta_f G^{\ominus}$/kJ mol^{-1}	$S^{\ominus}$/J K^{-1} mol^{-1}	C_p/J K^{-1} mol^{-1}
Solid (α)	0	0	42.442	25.363
Gas	227.07	187.03	176.72	20.820

Density/kg m^{-3}: 4790 (grey) [293 K]; 3987 [liquid at m.p.]
Thermal conductivity/W m^{-1} K^{-1}: 2.04 [300 K]
Electrical resistivity/Ω m: 0.01 [293 K]
Mass magnetic susceptibility/kg^{-1} m^3: -4.0×10^{-9} (s)
Molar volume/cm^3: 16.48
Coefficient of linear thermal expansion/K^{-1}: 36.9×10^{-6}

Crystal structure (cell dimensions/pm), space group

Grey hexagonal ($a = 436.56$, $c = 495.90$), P3$_1$21, metallic form
α-Se monoclinic ($a = 906.4$, $b = 907.2$, $c = 115.6$, $\beta = 90°52'$), P2$_1$/a, Se$_8$
β-Se monoclinic ($a = 1285$, $b = 807$, $c = 931$, $\beta = 93°8'$), P2$_1$/a, Se$_8$
α'-Se cubic ($a = 297.0$), Pm3m
β'-Se cubic ($a = 604$), Fd3m

X-ray diffraction: mass absorption coefficients (μ/ρ)/cm^2 g^{-1}:
CuK$_\alpha$ 91.4   MoK$_\alpha$ 74.7

Selenium

Thermal neutron capture cross-section/barns: 11.7
Number of isotopes (including nuclear isomers): 26
Isotope mass range: 69→89

Nuclear properties

Key isotopes

Nuclide	Atomic mass	Natural abundance (%)	Half-life $T_{1/2}$	Decay mode and energy (MeV)	Nuclear spin I	Nuclear magnetic moment μ	Uses
^{74}Se	73.922 475	0.9	stable		0		
^{75}Se	74.922 521	0	118.5d	β^-(0.864); γ	5/2+	0.67	tracer, medical
^{76}Se	75.919 212	9.2	stable		0+		
^{77}Se	76.919 912	7.6	stable		1/2−	+0.535 506	NMR
^{78}Se	77.9173	23.7	stable		0+		
^{80}Se	79.916 520	49.8	stable		0+		
^{82}Se	81.916 698	8.8	stable		0+		

NMR

^{77}Se

Relative sensitivity (^{1}H = 1.00) 6.93×10^{-3}
Receptivity (^{13}C = 1.00) 2.98
Magnetogyric ratio/rad T^{-1} s^{-1} 5.1018×10^7
Frequency (^{1}H = 100 MHz; 2.3488 T)/MHz 19.092
Reference: S(CH$_3$)$_2$

Ground state electron configuration: [Ar]3d^{10}4s^{2}4p^4
Term symbol: ^{3}P$_2$
Electron affinity (M→M$^-$)/kJ mol^{-1}: 195.0

Electron shell properties

Main lines in atomic spectrum

Wavelength/nm	Species
196.026 (AA)	I
241.35	I
1032.726	I
1038.636	I
2144.256	I

Ionization energies/kJ mol^{-1}

1. M →M$^+$	940.9	6. M^{5+}→M^{6+}	7 883
2. M$^+$→M^{2+}	2044	7. M^{6+}→M^{7+}	14 990
3. M^{2+}→M^{3+}	2974	8. M^{7+}→M^{8+}	(19 500)
4. M^{3+}→M^{4+}	4144	9. M^{8+}→M^{9+}	(23 300)
5. M^{4+}→M^{5+}	6590	10. M^{9+}→M^{10+}	(27 200)

Environmental properties

Biological role

Essential to some species, including humans; stimulatory; carcinogenic; teratogenic
Levels in humans:
Muscle/p.p.m.: 0.42–1.9
Bone/p.p.m.: 1–9
Blood/mg dm^{-3}: 0.171
Daily dietary intake: 0.006–0.2 mg
Toxic intake: 5 mg
Lethal intake: n.a.
Total mass of element in average (70 kg) person: 7 mg

Abundances

Sun (relative to H = 1 × 10^{12}): n.a.
Earth's crust/p.p.m.: 0.05
Seawater/p.p.m.:
Atlantic surface: 0.46×10^{-7}
Atlantic deep: 1.8×10^{-7}
Pacific surface: 0.15×10^{-7}
Pacific deep: 1.65×10^{-7}
Residence time/years: 3000
Classification: recycled
Oxidation state: IV and VI, mainly VI

Geological data

Chief sources: traces in certain sulfide ores; obtained as a by-product in electro-refining of Cu
World production/tonnes y^{-1}: 1650
Reserves/tonnes: n.a.

Si

Atomic number: 14

Relative atomic mass ($^{12}C = 12.0000$): 28.0855

Chemical properties

Black amorphous Si obtained by reduction of sand (SiO_2) with carbon; ultrapure semiconductor grade crystals are blue–grey metallic. Bulk Si unreactive towards oxygen, water, acids (except HF), but dissolves in hot alkali. Used in semiconductors, alloys, polymers.

Radii/pm: Si^{4+} 26; atomic 117; covalent 117; van der Waals 200; Si^{4-} 271

Electronegativity: 1.90 (Pauling); 1.74 (Allred); 4.77 eV (absolute)

Effective nuclear charge: 4.15 (Slater); 4.29 (Clementi); 4.48 (Froese-Fischer)

Standard reduction potentials $E^{\ominus}/V$

	IV		II		0		$-IV$
Acid solution	SiO_2	$\xrightarrow{-0.967}$	'SiO'	$\xrightarrow{-0.808}$	Si	$\xrightarrow{-0.143}$	SiH_4

[Alkaline solutions contain many different forms]

Covalent bonds	r/pm	E/kJ mol^{-1}
Si–H	148.0	326
Si–C	187	301
Si–O	151	452
Si–F	155	582
Si–Cl	202	391
Si–Si	232	226

Oxidation states

Si^{II} SiF_2 (gas)

Si^{IV} SiO_2, 'H_4SiO_4', silicates, zeolites etc., SiH_4 etc., SiF_4, $SiCl_4$ etc., SiF_6^{2-}, metal silicides, e.g. Ca_2Si, CaSi, organosilicon compounds

Physical properties

Melting point/K: 1683

Boiling point/K: 2628

ΔH_{fusion}/kJ mol^{-1}: 39.6

ΔH_{vap}/kJ mol^{-1}: 383.3

Thermodynamic properties (298.15 K, 0.1 MPa)

State	$\Delta_f H^{\ominus}$/kJ mol^{-1}	$\Delta_f G^{\ominus}$/kJ mol^{-1}	$S^{\ominus}$/J K^{-1} mol^{-1}	C_p/J K^{-1} mol^{-1}
Solid	0	0	18.83	20.00
Gas	455.6	411.3	167.97	22.251

Density/kg m^{-3}: 2329 [293 K]; 2525 [liquid at m.p.]

Thermal conductivity/W m^{-1} K^{-1}: 148 [300 K]

Electrical resistivity/Ω m: 0.001 [273 K]

Mass magnetic susceptibility/kg^{-1} m^3: -1.8×10^{-9} (s)

Molar volume/cm^3: 12.06

Coefficient of linear thermal expansion/K^{-1}: 4.2×10^{-6}

Crystal structure (cell dimensions/pm), space group

Cubic ($a = 543.07$), Fd3m, diamond structure

High pressure forms: ($a = 468.6$, $c = 258.5$), I4$_1$/amd

                    ($a = 664$), Ia3

                    ($a = 380$, $c = 628$) P6$_3$mc

X-ray diffraction: mass absorption coefficients (μ/ρ)/cm^2 g^{-1}: CuK$_\alpha$ 60.6   MoK$_\alpha$ 6.44

Silicon

Thermal neutron capture cross-section/barns: 171
Number of isotopes (including nuclear isomers): 11
Isotope mass range: 24→34

Nuclear properties

Key isotopes

Nuclide	Atomic mass	Natural abundance (%)	Half-life $T_{1/2}$	Decay mode and energy (MeV)	Nuclear spin I	Nuclear magnetic moment μ	Uses
^{28}Si	27.976927	92.23	stable		0+		
^{29}Si	28.976495	4.67	stable		1/2+	−0.5553	NMR
^{30}Si	29.973770	3.10	stable		0+		
^{32}Si	31.974148	0	*c.* 100y	β^- (0.227); no γ	0+		tracer

NMR

^{29}Si

Relative sensitivity (^{1}H = 1.00)	7.84×10^{-3}
Receptivity (^{13}C = 1.00)	2.09
Magnetogyric ratio/rad T^{-1} s^{-1}	-5.3146×10^7
Frequency (^{1}H = 100 MHz; 2.3488 T)/MHz	19.865

Reference: Si(CH$_3$)$_4$

Ground state electron configuration: [Ne]$3s^2 3p^2$
Term symbol: $^3P_0$
Electron affinity (M→M$^-$)/kJ mol^{-1}: 133.6

Electron shell properties

Main lines in atomic spectrum

Wavelength/nm	Species
251.611 (AA)	I
288.156	I
504.103	II
505.598	II
566.956	II
634.710	II
637.136	II

Ionization energies/kJ mol^{-1}

1.	M → M$^+$	786.5	6.	M^{5+} → M^{6+}	19 784
2.	M$^+$ → M^{2+}	1577.1	7.	M^{6+} → M^{7+}	23 786
3.	M^{2+} → M^{3+}	3231.4	8.	M^{7+} → M^{8+}	29 252
4.	M^{3+} → M^{4+}	4355.5	9.	M^{8+} → M^{9+}	33 876
5.	M^{4+} → M^{5+}	16 091	10.	M^{9+} → M^{10+}	38 732

Environmental properties

Biological role

Essential to some species and possibly humans; some silicates are carcinogenic

Levels in humans:
Muscle/p.p.m.: 100–200
Bone/p.p.m.: 17
Blood/mg dm^{-3}: 3.9
Daily dietary intake:
18–1200 mg
Toxic intake: non-toxic
Total mass of element in average (70 kg) person: n.a.

Abundances

Sun (relative to H = 1 × 10^{12}):
4.47 × 10^7
Earth's crust/p.p.m.: 277 000
Seawater/p.p.m.:
Atlantic surface: 0.03
Atlantic deep: 0.82
Pacific surface: 0.03
Pacific deep: 4.09
Residence time/years: 30 000
Classification: recycled
Oxidation state: IV

Geological data

Chief deposits and sources: quartz [SiO$_2$]; many and varied silicates

World production of ferrosilicon/tonnes y^{-1}: 3.4 × 10^6

World production of metallurgical grade silicon/tonnes y^{-1}: 480 000

World production of electronic grade, i.e. pure, silicon/tonnes y^{-1}: 5000

Reserves/tonnes: unlimited

Ag

Atomic number: 47
Relative atomic mass ($^{12}C = 12.0000$): **107.8682**

Chemical properties

Soft, malleable metal with characteristic silver sheen. Stable to water and oxygen but attacked by sulfur compounds in air to form black sulfide layer. Dissolves in sulfuric and nitric acid. Used in photography, silverware, jewellery, electrical industry, and glass (mirrors).

Radii/pm: Ag^+ 113; Ag^{2+} 89; atomic 144.4; covalent 134
Electronegativity: 1.93 (Pauling); 1.42 (Allred); 4.44 eV (absolute)
Effective nuclear charge: 4.20 (Slater); 8.03 (Clementi); 11.35 (Froese-Fischer)

Standard reduction potentials $E^{\ominus}$/V

	III	II	I	0

Acid solution
$$Ag_2O_3 \xrightarrow{1.670} Ag^{2+}$$
$$Ag_2O_3 \xrightarrow[1.569]{1.360} Ag^{2+} \xrightarrow{1.980} Ag^+ \xrightarrow{0.7991} Ag$$
$$AgO \xrightarrow{1.772} $$
$$AgO \xrightarrow{1.398} Ag_2O \xrightarrow{1.173}$$

Alkaline solution
$$Ag_2O_3 \xrightarrow{0.793} AgO \xrightarrow{0.604} Ag_2O \xrightarrow{0.342} Ag$$
$$Ag_2O_3 \xrightarrow{1.757} Ag^+$$
$$\xrightarrow{1.711} Ag_2O_2$$

Oxidation states

Ag^0	$(d^{10}s^1)$	rare $Ag(CO)_3$ at 10 K
Ag^I	(d^{10})	Ag_2O, $Ag(OH)_2^-$ (aq), $Ag(H_2O)_4^+$ (aq), AgF, $AgCl$ etc., Ag^+ salts, e.g. $AgNO_3$, Ag_2S, $Ag(CN)_2^-$, and other complexes
Ag^{II}	(d^9)	AgF_2, $[Ag(C_5H_5N)_2]^+$, AgO is not Ag^{II} but $Ag^IAg^{III}O_2$
Ag^{III}	(d^8)	rare AgF_4^-, AgF_6^{3-}

Physical properties

Melting point/K: 1235.08
Boiling point/K: 2485
ΔH_{fusion}/kJ mol^{-1}: 11.3
ΔH_{vap}/kJ mol^{-1}: 255.1

Thermodynamic properties (298.15 K, 0.1 MPa)

State	$\Delta_f H^{\ominus}$/kJ mol^{-1}	$\Delta_f G^{\ominus}$/kJ mol^{-1}	$S^{\ominus}$/J K^{-1} mol^{-1}	C_p/J K^{-1} mol^{-1}
Solid	0	0	42.55	25.351
Gas	284.55	245.65	172.997	20.786

Density/kg m^{-3}: 10 500 [293 K]; 9345 [liquid at m.p.]
Thermal conductivity/W m^{-1} K^{-1}: 429 [300 K]
Electrical resistivity/Ω m: 1.59×10^{-8} [293 K]
Mass magnetic susceptibility/kg^{-1} m^3: -2.27×10^{-9} (s)
Molar volume/cm^3: 10.27
Coefficient of linear thermal expansion/K^{-1}: 19.2×10^{-6}

Crystal structure (cell dimensions/pm), space group

f.c.c. ($a = 408.626$), Fm3m)

X-ray diffraction: mass absorption coefficients (μ/ρ)/cm^2 g^{-1}:
CuK$_\alpha$ 218   MoK$_\alpha$ 25.8

Thermal neutron capture cross-section/barns: 63.6
Number of isotopes (including nuclear isomers): 46
Isotope mass range: 96→122

Key isotopes

Nuclide	Atomic mass	Natural abundance (%)	Half-life $T_{1/2}$	Decay mode and energy (MeV)	Nuclear spin I	Nuclear magnetic moment μ	Uses
^{107}Ag	106.905 092	51.84	stable		$1/2-$	-0.1135	NMR
^{109}Ag	108.904 757	48.16	stable		$1/2-$	-0.1305	NMR
^{110m}Ag	109.906 111	0	249.8d	β^- (c. 3) 99%, IT 1%; γ	$6+$	$+3.6047$	tracer
^{111}Ag	110.905 295	0	7.47d	β^- (1.037); γ	$1/2$	-0.146	tracer

NMR

	^{107}Ag	^{109}Ag
Relative sensitivity (^{1}H = 1.00)	6.62×10^{-5}	1.01×10^{-4}
Receptivity (^{13}C = 1.00)	0.195	0.276
Magnetogyric ratio/rad T^{-1} s^{-1}	-1.0828×10^7	-1.2448×10^7
Frequency (^{1}H = 100 MHz; 2.3488 T)/MHz	4.046	4.652

Reference: Ag^+(aq)

Ground state electron configuration: $[Kr]4d^{10}5s^1$
Term symbol: $^2S_{1/2}$
Electron affinity (M→M$^-$)/kJ mol^{-1}: 125.7

Main lines in atomic spectrum

Wavelength/nm	Species
328.068 (AA)	I
338.289	I
520.908	I
546.550	I
827.352	I

Ionization energies/kJ mol^{-1}

1. M →M$^+$	731.0	
2. M$^+$→M^{2+}	2073	
3. M^{2+}→M^{3+}	3361	
4. M^{3+}→M^{4+}	(5000)	
5. M^{4+}→M^{5+}	(6700)	
6. M^{5+}→M^{6+}	(8 600)	
7. M^{6+}→M^{7+}	(11 200)	
8. M^{7+}→M^{8+}	(13 400)	
9. M^{8+}→M^{9+}	(15 600)	
10. M^{9+}→M^{10+}	(18 000)	

Environmental properties

Biological role

None; suspected carcinogen; toxic to lower organisms

Levels in humans:
Muscle/p.p.m.: 0.009–0.28
Bone/p.p.m.: 0.01–0.44
Blood/mg dm^{-3}: <0.003
Daily dietary intake: 0.0014–0.08 mg
Toxic intake: 60 mg
Lethal intake: 1.3–6.2 g
Total mass of element in average (70 kg) person: n.a.

Abundances

Sun (relative to H = 1 × 10^{12}): 7.1

Earth's crust/p.p.m.: 0.07

Seawater/p.p.m.:
Atlantic surface: n.a.
Atlantic deep: n.a.
Pacific surface: 1 × 10^{-7}
Pacific deep: 24 × 10^{-7}
Residence time/years: 5000
Classification: recycled
Oxidation state: I

Geological data

Chief sources: argentite (silver glance) [Ag$_2$S]; also obtained as a by-product of other metals such as copper

World production/tonnes y^{-1}: 9950

Reserves/tonnes: c. 10^6

<table>
<tr><td>**Na**</td><td>Atomic number: **11**
Relative atomic mass ($^{12}C = 12.0000$): **22.989 768**</td></tr>
</table>

Chemical properties

Soft, silvery white metal which oxidizes rapidly when cut. Reacts vigorously with water. Produced in large quantities and used as metal in heat exchangers in atomic reactors. NaCl is key industrial chemical, used to make Cl_2, NaOH, etc.

Radii/pm: Na^+ 98; atomic 153.7; van der Waals 231
Electronegativity: 0.93 (Pauling); 1.01 (Allred); 2.85 eV (absolute)
Effective nuclear charge: 2.20 (Slater); 2.51 (Clementi); 3.21 (Froese-Fischer)

Standard reduction potentials $E^{\ominus}/V$

$$
\begin{array}{ccc}
I & & 0 \\
Na^+ & \underline{\quad -2.713 \quad} & Na
\end{array}
$$

Oxidation states

Na^{-I} (s^2)   Na metal solutions in liquid NH_3
Na^I ([Ne]) Na_2O, Na_2O_2 (peroxide),
NaOH, NaH, NaF,
NaCl etc., $[Na(H_2O)_4]^+$ (aq),
$NaHCO_3$, Na_2CO_3,
Na^+ salts, some complexes

Physical properties

Melting point/K: 370.96
Boiling point/K: 1156.1
ΔH_{fusion}/kJ mol^{-1}: 2.64
ΔH_{vap}/kJ mol^{-1}: 89.04

Thermodynamic properties (298.15 K, 0.1 MPa)

State	$\Delta_f H^{\ominus}$/kJ mol^{-1}	$\Delta_f G^{\ominus}$/kJ mol^{-1}	$S^{\ominus}$/J K^{-1} mol^{-1}	C_p/J K^{-1} mol^{-1}
Solid	0	0	51.21	28.24
Gas	107.32	76.761	153.712	20.786

Density/kg m^{-3}: 971 [293 K]; 928 [liquid at m.p.]
Thermal conductivity/W m^{-1} K^{-1}: 141 [300 K]
Electrical resistivity/Ω m: 4.2×10^{-8} [273 K]
Mass magnetic susceptibility/kg^{-1} m^3: $+8.8 \times 10^{-9}$ (s)
Molar volume/cm^3: 23.68
Coefficient of linear thermal expansion/K^{-1}: 70.6×10^{-6}

Crystal structure (cell dimensions/pm), space group

α-Na hexagonal ($a = 376.7$, $c = 615.4$), P6$_3$/mmc
β-Na b.c.c. ($a = 429.06$), Im3m
T(b.c.c.$\rightarrow$hexagonal) $= 5$ K

X-ray diffraction: mass absorption coefficients (μ/ρ)/cm^2 g^{-1}:
CuK$_\alpha$ 30.1   MoK$_\alpha$ 3.21

Isolated by Sir Humphry Davy in 1807 at the Royal Institution, London, UK

[English, soda; Latin, *natrium*]

Sodium

Thermal neutron capture cross-section/barns: 0.53
Numbor of isotopes (including nuclear isomers): 14
Isotope mass range: 19→31

Nuclear properties

Key isotopes

Nuclide	Atomic mass	Natural abundance (%)	Half-life $T_{1/2}$	Decay mode and energy (MeV)	Nuclear spin I	Nuclear magnetic moment μ	Uses
^{22}Na	21.994 434	0	2.605y	β^+ (2.842) 90%, EC 10%; γ	3+	+1.746	tracer
^{23}Na	22.989 767	100	stable		3/2+	+2.217 52	NMR
^{24}Na	23.990 961	0	14.97y	β^- (5.514); γ	4+	+1.6903	tracer, medical

NMR

^{23}Na

Relative sensitivity (^{1}H = 1.00) 9.25×10^{-2}
Receptivity (^{13}C = 1.00)   525
Magnetogyric ratio/rad T^{-1} s^{-1} 7.0761×10^7
Quadrupole moment/m^2 0.12×10^{-28}
Frequency (^{1}H = 100 MHz; 2.3488 T)/MHz   26.451
Reference: NaCl (aq)

Ground state electron configuration: [Ne]3s^1
Term symbol: ^{2}S$_{1/2}$
Electron affinity (M→M$^-$)/kJ mol^{-1}: 52.9

Electron shell properties

Main lines in atomic spectrum

Wavelength/nm	Species
313.548	II
588.995 (AA)	I
589.592	I
818.326	I
819.482	I

Ionization energies/kJ mol^{-1}

1.	M → M$^+$	495.8	6 M^{5+} → M^{6+}	16 610
2.	M$^+$ → M^{2+}	4 562.4	7. M^{6+} → M^{7+}	20 114
3.	M^{2+} → M^{3+}	6 912	8. M^{7+} → M^{8+}	25 490
4.	M^{3+} → M^{4+}	9 543	9. M^{8+} → M^{9+}	28 933
5.	M^{4+} → M^{5+}	13 353	10. M^{9+} → M^{10+}	141 360

Environmental properties

Biological role

Essential to most species including humans

Levels in humans:
Muscle/p.p.m.: 2600–7800
Bone/p.p.m.: 10 000
Blood/mg dm^{-3}: 1970
Daily dietary intake: 2–15 g
Toxic intake: non-toxic
Total mass of element in average (70 kg) person: 100 g

Abundances

Sun (relative to H = 1 × 10^{12}): 1.91 × 10^6
Earth's crust/p.p.m.: 23 000
Seawater/p.p.m.: 10 500
Residence time/years: 1 × 10^8
Classification: accumulating
Oxidation state: I

Geological data

Chief deposits and sources:
halite (rock salt) [NaCl];
trona
[Na$_3$(CO$_3$) (HCO$_3$) . 2H$_2$O]
World production of salt/tonnes y^{-1}: 168 × 10^6
World production of sodium carbonate/tonnes y^{-1}: 29 × 10^6
World production of metal/tonnes y^{-1}: c. 200 000
Reserves/tonnes: almost unlimited

Sr

Atomic number: 38
Relative atomic mass ($^{12}C = 12.0000$): 87.62

Chemical properties

Silvery white, soft metal obtained by high temperature reduction of SrO with Al. Protected as bulk metal by oxide film but will burn in air and reacts with water. Used in special glass for TV and VDUs, in fireworks and flares to give red colour.

Radii/pm: Sr^{2+} 127; atomic 215.1 (α form); covalent 192
Electronegativity: 0.95 (Pauling); 0.99 (Allred); 2.0 eV (absolute)
Effective nuclear charge: 2.85 (Slater); 6.07 (Clementi); 8.09 (Froese-Fischer)

Standard reduction potentials $E^{\ominus}/V$

```
         II              0            -II
              -1.085
         ┌─────────────────────┐
   Sr²⁺    -2.89    Sr   0.718   SrH₂*
  SrO(hyd)  -2.047        │
         └─────────────────┘
                        -0.665
```

Also SrO_2^* $\xrightarrow{2.333}$ Sr^{2+}
        SrO_2 $\xrightarrow{1.492}$ SrO (hyd)

*See oxidation states

Oxidation states

Sr^{II} ([Kr]) SrO, SrO_2 (peroxide), $Sr(OH)_2$, $[Sr(H_2O)_x]^{2+}$ (aq), Sr^{2+} salts, SrF_2, $SrCl_2$ etc., $SrCO_3$, some complexes
SrH_2 is $Sr^{2+}2H^-$

Physical properties

Melting point/K: 1042
Boiling point/K: 1657
ΔH_{fusion}/kJ mol^{-1}: 9.16
ΔH_{vap}/kJ mol^{-1}: 138.91

Thermodynamic properties (298.15 K, 0.1 MPa)

State	$\Delta_f H^{\ominus}$/kJ mol^{-1}	$\Delta_f G^{\ominus}$/kJ mol^{-1}	$S^{\ominus}$/J K^{-1} mol^{-1}	C_p/J K^{-1} mol^{-1}
Solid	0	0	52.3	26.4
Gas	164.4	130.9	164.62	20.786

Density/kg m^{-3}: 2540 [293 K]; 2375 [liquid at m.p.]
Thermal conductivity/W m^{-1} K^{-1}: 35.3 [300 K]
Electrical resistivity/Ω m: 23.0×10^{-8} [293 K]
Mass magnetic susceptibility/kg^{-1} m^3: $+1.32 \times 10^{-8}$ (s)
Molar volume/cm^3: 34.50
Coefficient of linear thermal expansion/K^{-1}: 23×10^{-6}

Crystal structure (cell dimensions/pm), space group

α-Sr f.c.c. ($a = 608.49$), Fm3m
β-Sr h.c.p. ($a = 432$, $c = 706$), P6$_3$/mmc
γ-Sr b.c.c. ($a = 485$), Im3m
$T(\alpha \rightarrow \beta) = 506$ K
$T(\beta \rightarrow \gamma) = 813$ K

X-ray diffraction: mass absorption coefficients (μ/ρ)/cm^2 g^{-1}:
CuK$_\alpha$ 125   MoK$_\alpha$ 95.0

Recognized as an element in 1790 by A. Crawford at Edinburgh, Scotland. Isolated in 1808 by Sir Humphry Davy at London, UK

[Named after Strontian, Scotland]

Strontium

Thermal neutron capture cross-section/barns: 1.2
Number of isotopes (including nuclear isomers): 23
Isotope mass range: 79→98

Key isotopes

Nuclide	Atomic mass	Natural abundance (%)	Half-life $T_{1/2}$	Decay mode and energy (MeV)	Nuclear spin I	Nuclear magnetic moment μ	Uses
^{82}Sr	81.918 414	0	25.6d	EC(0.21)	0+		tracer
^{84}Sr	83.913 430	0.56	stable				
^{85}Sr	84.912 937	0	64.8d	EC(1.08); γ	9/2+		tracer medical
^{86}Sr	85.909 267	9.86	stable		0+		
^{87}Sr	86.908 884	7.00	stable		9/2+	-1.093	NMR
^{88}Sr	87.905 619	82.58	stable		0+		
^{89}Sr	88.907 450	0	50.52d	β^-(1.492); γ	5/2+		
^{90}Sr	89.907 738	0	29y	β^-(0.546); no γ	0+		tracer, medical

NMR

^{87}Sr

Relative sensitivity (^{1}H$=1.00$) 2.69×10^{-3}
Receptivity (^{13}C$=1.00$) 1.07
Magnetogyric ratio/rad T^{-1} s^{-1} -1.1593×10^7
Quadrupole moment/m^2 0.36×10^{-28}
Frequency (^{1}H$=100$ MHz; 2.3488 T)/MHz 4.333
Reference: Sr^{2+}(aq)

Ground state electron configuration: [Kr]5s^2
Term symbol: $^1S_0$
Electron affinity (M→M$^-$)/kJ mol^{-1}: -146

Main lines in atomic spectrum

Wavelength/nm	Species
407.771	II
421.552	II
460.733 (AA)	I
496.226	I
548.084	I
640.847	I

Ionization energies/kJ mol^{-1}

1. M $\to$M$^+$	549.5	6. M$^{5+}\to$M^{6+} 8 760
2. M$^+\to$M^{2+}	1064.2	7. M$^{6+}\to$M^{7+} 10 200
3. M$^{2+}\to$M^{3+}	4210	8. M$^{7+}\to$M^{8+} 11 800
4. M$^{3+}\to$M^{4+}	5500	9. M$^{8+}\to$M^{9+} 15 600
5. M$^{4+}\to$M^{5+}	6910	10. M$^{9+}\to$M^{10+} 17 100

Environmental properties

Biological role

None; can mimic calcium
Levels in humans:
Muscle/p.p.m.: 0.12–0.35
Bone/p.p.m.: 36–140
Blood/mg dm^{-3}: 0.031
Daily dietary intake: 0.8–5 mg
Toxic intake: non-toxic
Total mass of element in average (70 kg) person: 320 mg

Abundances

Sun (relative to H$=1 \times 10^{12}$): 790
Earth's crust/p.p.m.: 370
Seawater/p.p.m.:
Atlantic surface: 7.6
Atlantic deep: 7.7
Pacific surface: 7.6
Pacific deep: 7.7
Residence time/years: 4×10^6
Classification: recycled
Oxidation state: II

Geological data

Chief sources: celestite [SrSO$_4$]; strontianite [SrCO$_3$]
World production of Sr ores/tonnes y^{-1}: 137 000
Reserves/tonnes: n.a.

S Atomic number: **16**
Relative atomic mass ($^{12}C = 12.0000$): **32.066**

Chemical properties

Several allotropes, of which orthorhombic S_8 is most stable. Stable to air and water but burns if heated. Attacked by oxidizing acids. Recovered from H_2S in natural gas. Key industrial chemical.

Radii/pm: S^{4+} 37; S^{6+} 29; atomic 104 (S_8); covalent 104: S^{2-} 184; van der Waals 185

Electronegativity: 2.58 (Pauling); 2.44 (Allred); 6.22 eV (absolute)

Effective nuclear charge: 5.45 (Slater); 5.48 (Clementi); 6.04 (Froese-Fischer)

Standard reduction potentials $E^{\ominus}$/V

	VI	V	IV	III	II*	0	−II

Acid solution: $SO_4^{2-} \xrightarrow{-0.07} S_2O_6^{2-} \xrightarrow{0.57} H_2SO_3 \xrightarrow{-0.07} HS_2O_4^- \xrightarrow{0.87} S_2O_3^{2-} \xrightarrow{0.60} S \xrightarrow{0.14} H_2S$

(with $\xrightarrow{0.16}$ over V–IV, $\xrightarrow{0.40}$ over III, $\xrightarrow{0.50}$ below)

Also: $S_2O_8^{2-} \xrightarrow{2.01} SO_4^{2-}$

Alkaline solution: $SO_4^{2-} \xrightarrow{-0.94} SO_3^{2-} \xrightarrow{-0.58} S_2O_3^{2-} \xrightarrow{-0.74} S \xrightarrow{-0.45} S^{2-}$

(with $\xrightarrow{-0.66}$ over III–II)

*Average oxidation state

Covalent bonds r/pm E/kJ mol^{-1}

	r/pm	E/kJ mol^{-1}
S—H	133.5	347
S—C	182	272
S=C	155	476
S—O	150	265
S=O	144	c. 525
S—F	156	284
S—Cl	207	255
S—S	208	226

Oxidation states

S^{-II}	H_2S, S^{2-}	polysulphides S_n^{2-}
S^{-I}	H_2S_2, etc.	
S^0	S_6, S_8, etc.	
S^I	S_2O?, S_2F_2, S_2Cl_2	
S^{II}	SF_2, SCl_2	
S^{III}	$Na_2S_2O_4$	
S^{IV}	SO_2, SO_3^{2-} (aq), SF_4, SCl_4, $SOCl_2$	
S^V	$Na_2S_2O_6$, S_2F_{10}	
S^{VI}	SO_3, H_2SO_4, SO_4^{2-} (aq), etc., SF_6, HSO_3F, SO_2Cl_2	

Physical properties

Melting point/K: 386.0 (α) 392.2 (β) 380.0 (γ)

Boiling point/K: 717.824

ΔH_{fusion}/kJ mol^{-1}: 1.23 $\qquad \Delta H_{vap}$/kJ mol^{-1}: 9.62

Thermodynamic properties (298.15 K, 0.1 MPa)

State	$\Delta_f H^{\ominus}$/kJ mol^{-1}	$\Delta_f G^{\ominus}$/kJ mol^{-1}	$S^{\ominus}$/J K^{-1} mol^{-1}	C_p/J K^{-1} mol^{-1}
Solid (α)	0	0	31.80	22.64
Solid (β)	0.33	n.a.	n.a.	n.a.
Gas	278.805	238.250	167.821	23.673

Density/kg m^{-3}: 2070 (α), 1957 (β) [293 K]; 1819 [liquid, 393 K]

Thermal conductivity/W m^{-1} K^{-1}: 0.269 (α).[300 K]

Electrical resistivity/Ω m: 2×10^{15} [293 K]

Mass magnetic susceptibility/kg^{-1} m^3: -6.09×10^{-9} (α); -5.83×10^{-9} (β)

Molar volume/cm^3: 15.49

Coefficient of linear thermal expansion/K^{-1}: 74.33×10^{-6}

Crystal structure (cell dimensions/pm), space group

α-S_8 orthorhombic ($a = 1046.46$, $b = 1286.60$, $c = 2448.60$), Fddd
β-S_8 monoclinic ($a = 1102$, $b = 1096$, $c = 1090$, $\alpha = 96.7°$), P2$_1$/c
γ-S_8 monoclinic ($a = 857$, $b = 1305$, $c = 823$, $\alpha = 112°54'$), P2/c
ε-S_6 rhombohedral ($a = 646$, $\alpha = 115°18'$), R$\bar{3}$
In addition to the above ring forms there are also S_7, S_{9-12}, S_{18} and S_{20} rings.
Plastic sulfur is long chains of S_n also known in several forms χ, ψ, φ, μ and ω.
$T(\alpha \rightarrow \beta) = 366.7$ K

X-ray diffraction: mass absorption coefficients (μ/ρ)/cm^2 g^{-1}: CuK$_\alpha$ 89.1 MoK$_\alpha$ 9.55

Sulfur

Thermal neutron capture cross-section/barns: 0.52
Number of isotopes (including nuclear isomers): 11
Isotope mass range: 29→39

Nuclear
properties

Key isotopes

Nuclide	Atomic mass	Natural abund. (%)	Half-life $T_{1/2}$	Decay mode and energy (MeV)	Nuclear spin I	Nuclear magnetic moment μ	Uses
^{32}S	31.972 070	95.02	stable		0+		
^{33}S	32.971 456	0.75	stable		3/2+	+0.64382	NMR
^{34}S	33.967 866	4.21	stable		0+		
^{35}S	34.969 031	0	8.72d	β^- (0.1674); no γ	3/2+	+1.00	tracer
^{36}S	35.967 080	0.02	stable		0+		

NMR

^{33}S

Relative sensitivity ($^1H = 1.00$) 2.26×10^{-3}
Receptivity ($^{13}C = 1.00$)   0.0973
Magnetogyric ratio/rad T^{-1} s^{-1} 2.0534×10^7
Quadrupole moment/m^2 -0.05×10^{-28}
Frequency ($^1H = 100$ MHz; 2.3488 T)/MHz   7.670
Reference: CS_2

Ground state electron configuration: $[Ne]3s^2 3p^4$
Term symbol: $^3P_2$
Electron affinity ($M \to M^-$)/kJ mol^{-1}: 200.4

Electron
shell
properties

Main lines in atomic spectrum

Wavelength/nm	Species
545.38	II
547.36	II
550.97	II
560.61	II
565.99	II
792.40	I
964.99	I

Ionization energies/kJ mol^{-1}

1. $M \to M^+$ 999.6	6. $M^{5+} \to M^{6+}$ 8495
2. $M^+ \to M^{2+}$ 2251	7. $M^{6+} \to M^{7+}$ 27 106
3. $M^{2+} \to M^{3+}$ 3361	8. $M^{7+} \to M^{8+}$ 31 669
4. $M^{3+} \to M^{4+}$ 4564	9. $M^{8+} \to M^{9+}$ 36 578
5. $M^{4+} \to M^{5+}$ 7013	10. $M^{9+} \to M^{10+}$ 43 138

Environmental properties

Biological role

Essential to all living things

Levels in humans:

Muscle/p.p.m.: 5000–11 000
Bone/p.p.m.: 500–2400
Blood/mg dm^{-3}: 1800
Daily dietary intake:
   850–930 mg
Toxic intake: non-toxic
Total mass of element in
   average (70 kg) person:
   140 g

Abundances

Sun (relative to H = 1×10^{12}):
   1.6×10^7

Earth's crust/p.p.m.: 260

Seawater/p.p.m.: 870

Residence time/years: 8×10^6

Classification: accumulating

Oxidation state: VI

Geological data

Chief ores and sources: native
   sulfur, metal sulfide ores,
   e.g. pyrites [FeS_2]

World production/tonnes y^{-1}:
   54×10^6

Reserves/tonnes: 2.5×10^9

Ta

Atomic number: 73

Relative atomic mass ($^{12}C = 12.0000$): 180.9479

Chemical properties

Shiny, silvery metal, soft when pure. Very corrosion resistant due to oxide film; attacked by HF and fused alkalis. Used in electronics, cutting tools, chemical plants and surgery.

Radii/pm: Ta^{3+} 72; Ta^{4+} 68; Ta^{5+} 64; atomic 143; covalent 134

Electronegativity: 1.5 (Pauling); 1.33 (Allred); 4.11 eV (absolute)

Effective nuclear charge: 3.30 (Slater); 9.53 (Clementi); 13.78 (Froese-Fischer)

Standard reduction potentials $E^{\ominus}$/V

V		0
Ta_2O_5	$\xrightarrow{-0.81}$	Ta

Oxidation states

Ta^{-III}	(d^8)	$[Ta(CO)_5]^{3-}$
Ta^{-I}	(d^6)	$[Ta(CO)_6]^-$
Ta^I	(d^4)	$[(C_5H_5)Ta(CO)_4]$
Ta^{II}	(d^3)	TaO?
Ta^{III}	(d^2)	TaF_3, $TaCl_3$, $TaBr_3$
Ta^{IV}	(d^1)	TaO_2, $TaCl_4$, $TaBr_4$, TaI_4
Ta^V	(d^0, f^{14})	Ta_2O_5, $[Ta_6O_{19}]^{8-}$ (aq), TaF_5, $TaCl_5$, TaF_6^-, TaF_7^{2-}, $TaOF_3$, TaO_2F

Physical properties

Melting point/K: 3269

Boiling point/K: 5698 ± 100

ΔH_{fusion}/kJ mol^{-1}: 31.4

ΔH_{vap}/kJ mol^{-1}: 753.1

Thermodynamic properties (298.15 K, 0.1 MPa)

State	$\Delta_f H^{\ominus}$/kJ mol^{-1}	$\Delta_f G^{\ominus}$/kJ mol^{-1}	$S^{\ominus}$/J K^{-1} mol^{-1}	C_p/J K^{-1} mol^{-1}
Solid	0	0	41.51	25.36
Gas	782.0	739.3	185.214	20.857

Density/kg m^{-3}: 16 654 [293 K]; 15 000 [liquid at m.p.]

Thermal conductivity/W m^{-1} K^{-1}: 57.5 [300 K]

Electrical resistivity/Ω m: 12.45×10^{-8} [298 K]

Mass magnetic susceptibility/kg^{-1} m^3: $+1.07 \times 10^{-8}$ (s)

Molar volume/cm^3: 10.87

Coefficient of linear thermal expansion/K^{-1}: 6.6×10^{-6}

Crystal structure (cell dimensions/pm), space group

b.c.c. ($a = 330.29$), Im3m

X-ray diffraction: mass absorption coefficients (μ/ρ)/cm^2 g^{-1}: CuK$_\alpha$ 166   MoK$_\alpha$ 95.4

Discovered in 1802 by A. G. Ekeberg at Uppsala, Sweden

[Greek, *Tantalos* = father of Niobe]

Tantalum

Nuclear
properties

Thermal neutron capture cross-section/barns: 20.5
Number of isotopes (including nuclear isomers): 28
Isotope mass range: 159→186

Key isotopes

Nuclide	Atomic mass	Natural abundance (%)	Half-life $T_{1/2}$	Decay mode and energy (MeV)	Nuclear spin I	Nuclear magnetic moment μ	Uses
^{180}Ta	179.947 462	0.012			9−		
^{181}Ta	180.947 992	99.988	stable		7/2+	+2.370	NMR
^{182}Ta	181.950 149	0	114.5d	β^- (1.811); γ	3−	2.6	tracer

NMR

	^{181}Ta
Relative sensitivity (^{1}H = 1.00)	3.60×10^{-2}
Receptivity (^{13}C = 1.00)	204
Magnetogyric ratio/rad T^{-1} s^{-1}	3.2073×10^7
Quadrupole moment /m^2	3×10^{-28}
Frequency (^{1}H = 100 MHz; 2.3488 T)/MHz	11.970

Reference: TaF$_6^-$ (aq)

Electron
shell
properties

Ground state electron configuration: [Xe]4f^{14}5d^{3}6s^2
Term symbol: ^{4}F$_{3/2}$
Electron affinity (M→M$^-$)/kJ mol^{-1}: 14

Main lines in atomic spectrum

Wavelength/nm	Species
240.063	II
264.747	I
265.327	I
271.467 (AA)	I
285.098	I
301.254	II

Ionization energies/kJ mol^{-1}

1.	M → M$^+$ 761	6.	M^{5+}→M^{6+}
2.	M$^+$→M^{2+} (1500)	7.	M^{6+}→M^{7+}
3.	M^{2+}→M^{3+} (2100)	8.	M^{7+}→M^{8+}
4.	M^{3+}→M^{4+} (3200)	9.	M^{8+}→M^{9+}
5.	M^{4+}→M^{5+} (4300)	10.	M^{9+}→M^{10+}

Environmental properties

Biological role	Abundances	Geological data
None	**Sun** (relative to H = 1×10^{12}): n.a.	**Chief deposits and sources:** tantalite [(Fe, Mn)Ta$_2$O$_6$]; obtained mostly as a by-product of tin extraction
Levels in humans:	**Earth's crust**/p.p.m.: 2	
Muscle/p.p.m.: n.a., but low	**Seawater**/p.p.m.: 2×10^{-6}	**World production**/tonnes y^{-1}: 840
Bone/p.p.m.: c. 0.03	Residence time/years: n.a.	
Blood/mg dm^{-3}: n.a., but low	Oxidation state: V	**Reserves**/tonnes: n.a.
Daily dietary intake: 0.001 mg		
Toxic intake: n.a.		
Lethal intake: 300 mg (rats)		
Total mass of element in average (70 kg) person: n.a., but low		

Tc

Atomic number: 43

Relative atomic mass ($^{12}C = 12.0000$): 98.9062

Chemical properties

Radioactive metal which does not occur naturally. Silvery as metal but usually obtained as grey powder. Resists oxidation, slowly tarnishes in moist air, burns in oxygen, dissolves in nitric and sulfuric acids.

Radii/pm: Tc^{2+} 95; Tc^{4+} 72; Tc^{7+} 56; atomic 135.8

Electronegativity: 1.9 (Pauling); 1.36 (Allred); 3.91 eV (absolute)

Effective nuclear charge: 3.60 (Slater); 7.23 (Clementi); 10.28 (Froese-Fischer)

Standard reduction potentials E°/V

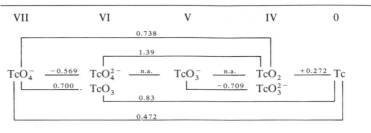

Oxidation states

Tc^{-I}	(d^8)	$[Tc(CO)_5]^-$
Tc^0	(d^7)	$Tc_2(CO)_{10}$
Tc^{IV}	(d^3)	TcO_2, TcO_3^{2-} (aq), $TcCl_4$, complexes
Tc^V	(d^2)	TcO_3^- (aq), $TcCl_5$, complexes
Tc^{VI}	(s^1)	TcO_3 ?, TcF_6, $TcOCl_4$, complexes
Tc^{VII}	$(d^0, [Kr])$	Tc_2O_7, TcO_4^- (aq), TcO_3Cl, complexes

Physical properties

Melting point/K: 2445

Boiling point/K: 5150

ΔH_{fusion}/kJ mol^{-1}: 23.81

ΔH_{vap}/kJ mol^{-1}: 585.22

Thermodynamic properties (298.15 K, 0.1 MPa)

State	$\Delta_f H^{\circ}$/kJ mol^{-1}	$\Delta_f G^{\circ}$/kJ mol^{-1}	S°/J K^{-1} mol^{-1}	C_p/J K^{-1} mol^{-1}
Solid	0	0	n.a.	25
Gas	678	n.a.	181.07	20.79

Density/kg m^{-3}: 11 500 (est.) [293 K]

Thermal conductivity/W m^{-1} K^{-1}: 50.6 [300 K]

Electrical resistivity/Ω m: 22.6×10^{-8} [393 K]

Mass magnetic susceptibility/kg^{-1} m^3: $+3.1 \times 10^{-8}$ (s)

Molar volume/cm^3: 8.6 (est.)

Coefficient of linear thermal expansion/K^{-1}: 8.06×10^{-6}

Crystal structure (cell dimensions/pm), space group

h.c.p. ($a = 274.3$, $c = 440.0$), P6$_3$/mmc

X-ray diffraction: mass absorption coefficients (μ/ρ)/cm^2 g^{-1}:
CuK$_\alpha$ 172   MoK$_\alpha$ 19.7

Discovered in 1937 by C. Perrier and E. G. Segré at Palermo, Italy

Technetium

[Greek, *technikos* = artificial]

Thermal neutron capture cross-section/barns: 22 (^{99}Tc)
Number of isotopes (including nuclear isomers): 25
Isotope mass range: $90 \rightarrow 108$

Key isotopes

Nuclide	Atomic mass	Natural abundance (%)	Half-life $T_{1/2}$	Decay mode and energy (MeV)	Nuclear spin I	Nuclear magnetic moment μ	Uses
^{97}Tc	96.906 364	0	2.6×10^6y	EC(0.32)	9/2+		
^{98}Tc	97.907 215	0	4.2×10^6y	β^-(1.79); γ	6+		
^{99}Tc	98.906 254	0	2.13×10^5y	β^-(0.293); no γ	9/2+	+5.6847	NMR
^{99m}Tc	98.906 254	0	6.01h	IT(0.142); γ	1/2−		tracer, medical

NMR

^{99}Tc

Relative sensitivity (^{1}H = 1.00)	—
Receptivity (^{13}C = 1.00)	—
Magnetogyric ratio/rad T^{-1} s^{-1}	6.0503×10^7
Quadrupole moment /m^2	-0.13×10^{-28}
Frequency (^{1}H = 100 MHz; 2.3488 T)/MHz	22.508

Reference: TcO$_4^-$ (aq)

Ground state electron configuration: [Kr]4d^{5}5s^2
Term symbol: ^{6}S$_{5/2}$
Electron affinity (M$\rightarrow$M$^-$)/kJ mol^{-1}: 96

Main lines in atomic spectrum

Wavelength/nm	Species
403.163	I
409.567	I
426.227	I
429.706	I
485.359	I

Ionization energies/kJ mol^{-1}

1. M $\rightarrow$M$^+$	702	6. M$^{5+}\rightarrow$M^{6+}	(7 300)
2. M$^+\rightarrow$M^{2+}	1472	7. M$^{6+}\rightarrow$M^{7+}	(9 100)
3. M$^{2+}\rightarrow$M^{3+}	2850	8. M$^{7+}\rightarrow$M^{8+}	(15 600)
4. M$^{3+}\rightarrow$M^{4+}	(4100)	9. M$^{8+}\rightarrow$M^{9+}	(17 800)
5. M$^{4+}\rightarrow$M^{5+}	(5700)	10. M$^{9+}\rightarrow$M^{10+}	(19 900)

Environmental properties

Biological role	Abundances	Geological data
None; never normally encountered, but would be toxic due to radioactivity	**Sun** (relative to H = 1×10^{12}): n.a.	**Chief sources**: produced in tonne quantities from fission of nuclear fuel
Levels in humans: nil	**Earth's crust**/p.p.m.: nil	
	Seawater/p.p.m.: nil	

Te

Atomic number: 52

Relative atomic mass ($^{12}C = 12.0000$): 127.60

Chemical properties

Silvery white, metallic looking in bulk but usually obtained as dark grey powder. Semi-metal. Burns in air or oxygen. Unaffected by water or HCl but dissolves in HNO_3. Used in alloys to improve machinability; chemicals, catalysts, electronics.

Radii/pm: Te^{4+} 97; Te^{6+} 56; atomic 143.2; covalent 137; van der Waals 220; Te^{2-} 211

Electronegativity: 2.1 (Pauling); 2.01 (Allred); 5.49 eV (absolute)

Effective nuclear charge: 6.95 (Slater); 10.81 (Clementi); 13.51 (Froese-Fischer)

Standard reduction potentials $E^{\ominus}/V$

	VI	IV	0	−I	−II
Acid solution	H_2TeO_4 $\xrightarrow{0.93}$	Te^{4+} $\xrightarrow{0.57}$	Te $\xrightarrow{-0.74}$	Te_2^{2-} $\xrightarrow{-0.64}$	H_2Te
	$\xrightarrow{1.00}$	TeO_2 $\xrightarrow{0.53}$			
Alkaline solution	TeO_4^{2-} $\xrightarrow{0.07}$	TeO_3^{2-} $\xrightarrow{-0.42}$	Te $\xrightarrow{-1.14}$		Te^{2-}

Covalent bonds r/pm E/kJ mol^{-1}

	r/pm	E/kJ mol^{-1}
Te–H	c. 170	c. 240
Te–C	205	
Te–O	200	268
Te–F	185	335
Te–Cl	231	251
Te–Te	286	235

Oxidation states

Te^{-II}	H_2Te, Te^{2-}
Te^{-I}	Te_2^{2-}
Te^{0-I}	cluster cations Te_4^{2+}, Te_6^{4+}
Te^{II}	TeO, $TeCl_2$, $TeBr_2$
Te^{IV}	TeO_2, H_2TeO_3, TeO_3^{2-} (aq), TeF_4, $TeCl_4$, TeF_5^-
Te^{V}	Te_2F_{10}
Te^{VI}	TeO_3, H_2TeO_4, TeO_4^{2-} (aq), H_6TeO_6, TeF_6, TeF_8^{2-}

Physical properties

Melting point/K: 722.7

Boiling point/K: 1263.0

ΔH_{fusion}/kJ mol^{-1}: 13.5   **ΔH_{vap}/kJ mol^{-1}:** 50.63

Thermodynamic properties (298.15 K, 0.1 MPa)

State	$\Delta_f H^{\ominus}$/kJ mol^{-1}	$\Delta_f G^{\ominus}$/kJ mol^{-1}	$S^{\ominus}$/J K^{-1} mol^{-1}	C_p/J K^{-1} mol^{-1}
Solid	0	0	49.71	25.73
Gas	196.73	157.08	182.74	20.786

Density/kg m^{-3}: 6240 [293 K]; 5797 [liquid at m.p.]

Thermal conductivity/W m^{-1} K^{-1}: 2.35 [300 K]

Electrical resistivity/Ω m: 4.36×10^{-3} [298 K]

Mass magnetic susceptibility/kg^{-1} m^3: -3.9×10^{-9} (s)

Molar volume/cm^3: 20.45

Coefficient of linear thermal expansion/K^{-1}: 16.75×10^{-6}

Crystal structure (cell dimensions/pm), space group

Hexagonal ($a = 445.65$, $c = 592.68$), P3$_1$21 or P3$_2$21
High pressure forms: ($a = 420.8$, $c = 1203.6$), R$\bar{3}$m
($a = 460.3$, $c = 382.2$), R$\bar{3}$m

X-ray diffraction: mass absorption coefficients (μ/ρ)/cm^2 g^{-1}:
CuK$_\alpha$ 282   MoK$_\alpha$ 35.0

Discovered in 1783 by Baron Franz Joseph Müller von Reichenstein at Sibiu, Romania

[Latin, *tellus* = earth]

Tellurium

Thermal neutron capture cross-section/barns: 5.4

Number of isotopes (including nuclear isomers): 39

Isotope mass range: $108 \rightarrow 137$

Key isotopes

Nuclide	Atomic mass	Natural abundance (%)	Half-life $T_{1/2}$	Decay mode and energy (MeV)	Nuclear spin I	Nuclear magnetic moment μ	Uses
^{120}Te	119.904 048	0.009	stable		0+		
^{122}Te	121.903 054	2.57	stable		0+		
^{123}Te	122.904 271	0.89	1.3×10^{13}y	EC(0.052); no γ	1/2+	−0.7359	NMR
^{124}Te	123.902 823	4.76	stable		0+		
^{125m}Te	124.904 433	0	58d	IT (0.145); γ	11/2	+0.7	tracer
^{125}Te	124.904 433	7.10	stable		1/2+	−0.8871	NMR
^{126}Te	125.903 314	18.89	stable		0+		
^{127}Te	126 905 227	0	9.5h	β^-(0.697); γ	3/2+		tracer
^{128}Te	127.904 463	31.73	stable		0+		
^{130}Te	129.906 229	33.97	2.4×10^{21}y		0		

NMR

	$[^{123}\text{Te}]$	^{125}Te
Relative sensitivity (^{1}H = 1.00)	1.80×10^{-2}	3.15×10^{-2}
Receptivity (^{13}C = 1.00)	0.89	12.5
Magnetogyric ratio/rad T^{-1} s^{-1}	-7.0006×10^7	-8.4398×10^7
Frequency (^{1}H = 100 MHz; 2.3488 T)/MHz	26.207	31.596

Reference: $Te(CH_3)_2$

Ground state electron configuration: $[\text{Kr}]4d^{10}5s^25p^4$

Term symbol: $^3P_2$

Electron affinity $(M \rightarrow M^-)$/kJ mol^{-1}: 190.2

Main lines in atomic spectrum

Wavelength/nm	Species
200.202	I
214.281 (AA)	I
972.274	I
1005.141	I
1108.956	I
1148.723	I

Ionization energies/kJ mol^{-1}

1. $M \rightarrow M^+$	869.2		6. $M^{5+} \rightarrow M^{6+}$	6822
2. $M^+ \rightarrow M^{2+}$	1795		7. $M^{6+} \rightarrow M^{7+}$	13 200
3. $M^{2+} \rightarrow M^{3+}$	2698		8. $M^{7+} \rightarrow M^{8+}$	(15 800)
4. $M^{3+} \rightarrow M^{4+}$	3610		9. $M^{8+} \rightarrow M^{9+}$	(18 500)
5. $M^{4+} \rightarrow M^{5+}$	5668		10. $M^{9+} \rightarrow M^{10+}$	(21 200)

Environmental properties

Biological role

None: teratogenic

Levels in humans:
Muscle/p.p.m.: 0.017?
Bone/p.p.m.: n.a.
Blood/mg dm^{-3}: 0.0055?
Daily dietary intake: <0.1 mg
Toxic intake: 0.25 mg
Lethal intake: 2 g
Total mass of element in average (70 kg) person: n.a.

Abundances

Sun (relative to H = 1×10^{12}): n.a.

Earth's crust/p.p.m.: *c.* 0.005

Seawater/p.p.m.:
Atlantic surface: 1.6×10^{-7}
Atlantic deep: 0.7×10^{-7}
Pacific surface: 1.9×10^{-7}
Pacific deep: 1.7×10^{-7}
Residence time/years: n.a.
Classification: scavenged
Oxidation state: IV and VI; mainly VI

Geological data

Chief deposits and sources:
some rare minerals, e.g. tellurite [TeO_2]; obtained from anode slime in copper refining

World production/tonnes y^{-1}: 215

Reserves/tonnes: n.a.

Tb

Atomic number: 65

Relative atomic mass ($^{12}C = 12.0000$): 158.92534

Chemical properties

Silvery white metal, rare member of the lanthanide (rare earth) group. Slowly oxidized by air, reacts with cold water. Used in solid state devices and lasers.

Radii/pm: Tb^{3+} 93; Tb^{4+} 81; atomic 178.2; covalent 159

Electronegativity: n.a. (Pauling); 1.10 (Allred); ≤ 3.2 eV (absolute)

Effective nuclear charge: 2.85 (Slater); 8.30 (Clementi); 11.39 (Froese-Fischer)

Standard reduction potentials $E^{\ominus}/V$

	IV		III		0
Acid solution	Tb^{4+}	—3.1—	Tb^{3+}	—−2.31—	Tb
Alkaline solution	TbO_2	—0.9—	$Tb(OH)_3$	—−2.82—	Tb

Oxidation states

Tb^{III}	(f^8)	Tb_2O_3, $Tb(OH)_3$, $[Tb(H_2O)_x]^{3+}$ (aq), TbF_3, $TbCl_3$, etc., Tb^{3+} salts, complexes
Tb^{IV}	(f^7)	TbO_2, TbF_4

Physical properties

Melting point/K: 1629
Boiling point/K: 3396
ΔH_{fusion}/kJ mol^{-1}: 16.3
ΔH_{vap}/kJ mol^{-1}: 391

Thermodynamic properties (298.15 K, 0.1 MPa)

State	$\Delta_f H^{\ominus}$/kJ mol^{-1}	$\Delta_f G^{\ominus}$/kJ mol^{-1}	$S^{\ominus}$/J K^{-1} mol^{-1}	C_p/J K^{-1} mol^{-1}
Solid	0	0	73.22	28.91
Gas	388.7	349.7	203.58	24.56

Density/kg m^{-3}: 8229 [293 K]
Thermal conductivity/W m^{-1} K^{-1}: 11.1 [300 K]
Electrical resistivity/Ω m: 114×10^{-8} [298 K]
Mass magnetic susceptibility/kg^{-1} m^3: $+1.15 \times 10^{-5}$ (s)
Molar volume/cm^3: 19.31
Coefficient of linear thermal expansion/K^{-1}: 7.0×10^{-6}

Crystal structure (cell dimensions/pm), space group

Tb Orthorhombic ($a = 359.0$, $b = 626.0$, $c = 571.5$), Cmcm
α-Tb h.c.p. ($a = 360.10$, $c = 569.36$), P6$_3$/mmc
β-Tb b.c.c. ($a = 402$), Im3m
$T(\alpha \rightarrow \text{Orthorhombic}) = 220$ K
$T(\alpha \rightarrow \beta) = 1590$ K

X-ray diffraction: mass absorption coefficients (μ/ρ)/cm^2 g^{-1}:
CuK$_\alpha$ 273   MoK$_\alpha$ 67.5

Terbium

Thermal neutron capture cross-section/barns: 23

Number of Isotopes (Including nuclear isomers): 31

Isotope mass range: 145→165

Key isotopes

Nuclide	Atomic mass	Natural abundance (%)	Half-life $T_{1/2}$	Decay mode and energy (MeV)	Nuclear spin I	Nuclear magnetic moment μ	Uses
^{159}Tb	158.925 342	100	stable		3/2+	+1.95	NMR
^{160}Tb	159.927 163	0	72.4d	β^- (1.834); γ	3−		tracer

NMR

^{159}Tb

Relative sensitivity (^{1}H = 1.00)	5.83×10^{-2}
Receptivity (^{13}C = 1.00)	3.94×10^2
Magnetogyric ratio/rad T^{-1} s^{-1}	6.4306×10^7
Quadrupole moment/m^2	1.3×10^{-28}
Frequency (^{1}H = 100 MHz; 2.3488 T)/MHz	22.678

Ground state electron configuration: [Xe]4f^{9}6s^2

Term symbol: $^6H_{15/2}$

Electron affinity (M→M$^-$)/kJ mol^{-1}: $\leqslant 50$

Main lines in atomic spectrum

Wavelength/nm	Species
332.440	II
350.917	II
356.852	II
367.635	II
370.286	II
384.873	II
387.417	II
432.643 (AA)	I

Ionization energies/kJ mol^{-1}

1. M $\rightarrow$M$^+$	564.6	6. M$^{5+}\rightarrow$M^{6+}
2. M$^+\rightarrow$M^{2+}	1112	7. M$^{6+}\rightarrow$M^{7+}
3. M$^{2+}\rightarrow$M^{3+}	2114	8. M$^{7+}\rightarrow$M^{8+}
4. M$^{3+}\rightarrow$M^{4+}	3839	9. M$^{8+}\rightarrow$M^{9+}
5. M$^{4+}\rightarrow$M^{5+}		10. M$^{9+}\rightarrow$M^{10+}

Environmental properties

Biological role

None; low toxicity

Levels in humans: n.a., but low

Abundances

Sun (relative to H = 1×10^{12}): n.a.

Earth's crust/p.p.m.: 1.1

Seawater/p.p.m.:
Atlantic surface: 1×10^{-7}
Atlantic deep: 1.5×10^{-7}
Pacific surface: 0.8×10^{-7}
Pacific deep: 2.5×10^{-7}
Residence time/years: n.a.
Classification: recycled
Oxidation state: III

Geological data

Chief deposits and sources:
monazite
[Ce, La, etc.)PO$_4$]

World production/tonnes y^{-1}:
c. 100

Reserves/tonnes: c. 10^5

Tl

Atomic number: 81
Relative atomic mass ($^{12}C = 12.0000$): 204.3833

Chemical properties

Soft, silvery-grey metal. Tarnishes readily in moist air and with steam reacts to form TlOH. Attacked by acids, rapidly by HNO_3. Little used because of its toxicity, but still employed in special glass.

Radii/pm: Tl^+ 149; Tl^{3+} 105; atomic 170.4 (α form); covalent 155

Electronegativity: 1.62 (Tl^I) 2.04 (Tl^{III}) (Pauling); 1.44 (Allred); 3.2 eV (absolute)

Effective nuclear charge: 5.00 (Slater); 12.25 (Clementi); 13.50 (Froese-Fischer)

Standard reduction potentials $E^{\ominus}/V$

	III		I		0
Acid solution	Tl^{3+}	_1.25_	Tl^+	_−0.3363_	Tl

0.72

Covalent bonds r/pm E/kJ mol^{-1}

	r/pm	E/kJ mol^{-1}
Tl^I–H	187.0	185
Tl^{III}–C	230	125
Tl^{III}–O	226	375
Tl^{III}–F	195	460
Tl^{III}–Cl	248	368
Tl–Tl	340.8	$c.$ 63

Oxidation states

Tl^{-I} (s^2) Tl_2O, TlOH, Tl_2CO_3, $[Tl(H_2O)_6]^+$ (aq), Tl^+ salts, TlF, TlCl, etc.

Tl^{III} (d^{10}) Tl_2O_3, $[Tl(H_2O)_6]^{3+}$ (aq), TlF_3, $TlCl_3$, $TlBr_3$, $(CH_3)_2Tl^+$ (aq), $TlCl_6^{3-}$

Physical properties

Melting point/K: 576.7
Boiling point/K: 1730
ΔH_{fusion}/kJ mol^{-1}: 4.31
ΔH_{vap}/kJ mol^{-1}: 162.1

Thermodynamic properties (298.15 K, 0.1 MPa)

State	$\Delta_f H^{\ominus}$/kJ mol^{-1}	$\Delta_f G^{\ominus}$/kJ mol^{-1}	$S^{\ominus}$/J K^{-1} mol^{-1}	C_p/J K^{-1} mol^{-1}
Solid	0	0	64.18	26.32
Gas	182.21	147.41	180.963	20.786

Density/kg m^{-3}: 11 850 [293 K]; 11 290 [liquid at m.p.]
Thermal conductivity/W m^{-1} K^{-1}: 46.1 [300 K]
Electrical resistivity/Ω m: 18.0×10^{-8} [273 K]
Mass magnetic susceptibility/kg^{-1} m^3: -3.13×10^{-9} (s)
Molar volume/cm^3: 17.24
Coefficient of linear thermal expansion/K^{-1}: 28×10^{-6}

Crystal structure (cell dimensions/pm), space group

α-Tl hexagonal ($a = 345.6$, $c = 552.5$), P6$_3$/mmc
β-Tl cubic ($a = 388.2$), Im3m
γ-Tl f.c.c. ($a = 485.1$), Fm3m
$T(\alpha \rightarrow \beta) = 503$ K

X-ray diffraction: mass absorption coefficients (μ/ρ)/cm^2 g^{-1}:
CuK$_\alpha$ 224 MoK$_\alpha$ 119

Discovered in 1861 by W. Crookes at London, UK; isolated in 1862 by C.-A. Lamy at Paris, France

[Greek, *thallos* = green twig]

Thallium

Thermal neutron capture cross-section/barns: 3.4
Number of isotopes (including nuclear isomers): 41
Isotope mass range: 184→210

Key isotopes

Nuclide	Atomic mass	Natural abund. (%)	Half-life $T_{1/2}$	Decay mode and energy (MeV)	Nuclear spin I	Nuclear magnetic moment μ	Uses
^{203}Tl	202.972 320	29.52	stable		$1/2+$	$+1.6222$	NMR
^{204}Tl		0	3.78y	β^- (0.763) 97%; EC(0.345) 3%; γ	$2-$	-0.06	tracer
^{205}Tl	204.974 401	70.48	stable		$1/2+$	$+1.6382$	NMR
^{208}Tl	207.981 988	trace	3.052m	β^- (4.994); γ	$5+$		

NMR

	$[^{203}\text{Tl}]$	^{205}Tl
Relative sensitivity (^{1}H = 1.00)	0.18	0.19
Receptivity (^{13}C = 1.00)	289	769
Magnetogyric ratio/rad T^{-1} s^{-1}	15.3078×10^7	15.4584×10^7
Frequency (^{1}H = 100 MHz; 2.3488 T)/MHz	57.149	57.708

Reference: $TlNO_3$ (aq)

Ground state electron configuration: $[Xe]4f^{14}5d^{10}6s^26p^1$
Term symbol: $^2P_{1/2}$
Electron affinity $(M \rightarrow M^-)$/kJ mol^{-1}: c. 20

Main lines in atomic spectrum

Wavelength/nm	Species
276.787 (AA)	I
291.832	I
351.924	I
352.943	I
377.572	I
535.046	I

Ionization energies/kJ mol^{-1}

1. $M \rightarrow M^+$ 589.3	6. $M^{5+} \rightarrow M^{6+}$ (8 300)
2. $M^+ \rightarrow M^{2+}$ 1971.0	7. $M^{6+} \rightarrow M^{7+}$ (9 500)
3. $M^{2+} \rightarrow M^{3+}$ 2878	8. $M^{7+} \rightarrow M^{8+}$ (11 300)
4. $M^{3+} \rightarrow M^{4+}$ (4900)	9. $M^{8+} \rightarrow M^{9+}$ (14 000)
5. $M^{4+} \rightarrow M^{5+}$ (6100)	10. $M^{9+} \rightarrow M^{10+}$ (16 000)

Environmental properties

Biological role

None; teratogenic
Levels in humans:
Muscle/p.p.m.: 0.07
Bone/p.p.m.: 0.002
Blood/mg dm^{-3}: 0.00048
Daily dietary intake:
  0.0015 mg
Toxic intake: n.a.
Lethal intake: 600 mg
Total mass of element in
  average (70 kg) person: n.a.

Abundances

Sun (relative to $H = 1 \times 10^{12}$):
  8.0
Earth's crust/p.p.m.: 0.6
Seawater/p.p.m.: 1.4×10^{-5}
Residence time/years: 10 000
Classification: accumulating
Oxidation state: I

Geological data

Chief sources: rare; dispersed
  in potash, feldspar and
  pollucite; by-product of
  zinc and lead smelting
World production/tonnes y^{-1}:
  30
Reserves/tonnes: n.a.

Th

Atomic number: **90**

Relative atomic mass ($^{12}C = 12.0000$): **232.0381**

Chemical properties

Radioactive silvery metal. Metal protected by oxide coating. Attacked by steam and slowly by acids. Metal itself is soft and ductile but alloys can be very strong. Used in refractory materials, nuclear fuel elements, and incandescent gas mantles.

Radii/pm: Th^{3+} 101; Th^{4+} 99; atomic 179.8

Electronegativity: 1.3 (Pauling); 1.11 (Allred)

Effective nuclear charge: 1.95 (Slater)

Standard reduction potentials $E^{\ominus}$/V

	IV		0
Acid solution	Th^{4+}	$\xrightarrow{-1.83}$	Th
Alkaline solution	ThO_2	$\xrightarrow{-2.56}$	Th

Oxidation states

Th^{II}	(d^2)	ThO, ThH_2
Th^{III}	(d^1)	ThI_3
Th^{IV}	([Rn])	ThO_2, $[Th(H_2O)_x]^{4+}$(aq), ThF_4, $ThCl_4$ etc., ThF_7^{3-}, Th^{4+} salts, complexes

Physical properties

Melting point/K: 2023

Boiling point/K: $c.$ 5060

ΔH_{fusion}/kJ mol^{-1}: <19.2

ΔH_{vap}/kJ mol^{-1}:   543.9

Thermodynamic properties   (298.15 K, 0.1 MPa)

State	$\Delta_f H^{\ominus}$/kJ mol^{-1}	$\Delta_f G^{\ominus}$/kJ mol^{-1}	$S^{\ominus}$/J K^{-1} mol^{-1}	C_p/J K^{-1} mol^{-1}
Solid	0	0	53.39	27.32
Gas	598.3	557.53	190.15	20.79

Density/kg m^{-3}:   11 720 [293 K]

Thermal conductivity/W m^{-1} K^{-1}:   54.0 [300 K]

Electrical resistivity/Ω m: 13.0×10^{-8} [273 K]

Mass magnetic susceptibility/kg^{-1} m^3: $+7.2 \times 10^{-9}$ (s)

Molar volume/cm^3:   19.80

Coefficient of linear thermal expansion/K^{-1}: 12.5×10^{-6}

Crystal structure (cell dimensions/pm), space group

α-Th f.c.c. ($a = 508.42$). Fm3m

β-Th b.c.c. ($a = 411$). Im3m

$T(\alpha \rightarrow \beta) = 1673$ K

X-ray diffraction: mass absorption coefficients (μ/ρ)/cm^2 g^{-1}:

CuK_α 327 MoK_α 143

Discovered in 1829 by J. J. Berzelius at Stockholm, Sweden

[Called after Thor, Scandanavian god of war]

Thorium

Thermal neutron capture cross-section/barns: 7.4
Number of isotopes (including nuclear isomers): 25
Isotope mass range: 212→236

Key isotopes

Nuclide	Atomic mass	Natural abundance (%)	Half-life $T_{1/2}$	Decay mode and energy (MeV)	Nuclear spin I	Nuclear magnetic moment μ	Uses
^{228}Th	228.028 715	trace	1.913y	$\alpha(5.520)$; γ	0+		
^{229}Th	229.031 755	0	7300y	$\alpha(5.168)$; γ	5/2+	+0.46	NMR
^{230}Th	230.033 127	trace	75 400y	$\alpha(4.771)$; γ	0+		
^{231}Th	231.036 298	trace	25.5h	$\beta^-(0.389)$; γ	5/2+		
^{232}Th	232.038 054	100	1.4×10^{10}y	$\alpha(4.081)$; γ	0+		tracer
^{234}Th	234.036 593	trace	24.1d	$\beta^-(0.270)$; γ	0+		

NMR

^{229}Th

Relative sensitivity (^{1}H $= 1.00$)	—
Receptivity (^{13}C $= 1.00$)	—
Magnetogyric ratio/rad T^{-1} s^{-1}	0.40×10^7
Quadrupole moment/m^2	4.4×10^{-28}
Frequency (^{1}H $= 100$ MHz; 2.3488 T)/MHz	1.5

Ground state electron configuration: [Rn]$6d^2 7s^2$
Term symbol: $^3F_2$
Electron affinity (M→M$^-$)/kJ mol^{-1}: n.a.

Main lines in atomic spectrum

Wavelength/nm	Species
339.204	II
346.992	II
374.118	II
401.914	II
438.186	II

Ionization energies/kJ mol^{-1}

1. M → M$^+$ 507	6. M^{5+} → M^{6+}
2. M$^+$ → M^{2+} 1110	7. M^{6+} → M^{7+}
3. M^{2+} → M^{3+} 1978	8. M^{7+} → M^{8+}
4. M^{3+} → M^{4+} 2780	9. M^{8+} → M^{9+}
5. M^{4+} → M^{5+}	10. M^{9+} → M^{10+}

Environmental properties

Biological role

None; slightly dangerous due to radioactivity

Levels in humans:
Muscle/p.p.m.: n.a.
Bone/p.p.m.: 0.002–0.012
Blood/mg dm^{-3}: 0.000 16
Daily dietary intake:
 0.000 05–0.003 mg
Toxic intake: low toxicity
Lethal intake: n.a.
Total mass of element in
 average (70 kg) person: n.a.

Abundances

Sun (relative to H $= 1 \times 10^{12}$):
 $c.$ 2
Earth's crust/p.p.m.: 12
Seawater/p.p.m.: 9.2×10^{-6}
Residence time/years: 50
Classification: scavenged
Oxidation state: IV

Geological data

Chief deposits and sources:
 monazite sand
 [(Ce, La, Nd, Th)PO$_4$];
 dispersed on pegmatites,
 zircon, and sphene
**World production of thorium
 concentrate**/tonnes y^{-1}:
 31 000
Reserves/tonnes: 3.3×10^6

Tm

Chemical properties

Silvery metal, rarest member of the lanthanide group (rare earths). Tarnishes in air and reacts with water. Few uses but some employed as radiation source in portable X-ray equipment.

Radii/pm: Tm^{3+} 87; Tm^{4+} 94; atomic 174.6; covalent 156

Electronegativity: 1.25 (Pauling); 1.11 (Allred); ≤ 3.4 eV (absolute)

Effective nuclear charge: 2.85 (Slater); 8.58 (Clementi); 11.80 (Froese-Fischer)

Standard reduction potentials $E^{\ominus}/V$

	III	II	0
Acid solution	Tm^{3+}	$\xrightarrow{-2.3}$ Tm^{2+}	$\xrightarrow{-2.3}$ Tm
Alkaline solution	$Tm(OH)_3$	$\xrightarrow{\hspace{1cm}-2.83\hspace{1cm}}$	Tm

(III to 0: -2.32)

Oxidation states

Tm^{II}	(f^{13})	$TmCl_2$, $TmBr_2$, TmI_2
Tm^{III}	(f^{12})	Tm_2O_3, $Tm(OH)_3$, $[Tm(H_2O)_x]^{3+}$ (aq), Tm^{3+} salts, TmF_3, $TmCl_3$ etc., complexes

Physical properties

Melting point/K: 1818

Boiling point/K: 2220

ΔH_{fusion}/kJ mol^{-1}: 18.4

ΔH_{vap}/kJ mol^{-1}: 247

Thermodynamic properties (298.15 K, 0.1 MPa)

State	$\Delta_f H^{\ominus}$/kJ mol^{-1}	$\Delta_f G^{\ominus}$/kJ mol^{-1}	$S^{\ominus}$/J K^{-1} mol^{-1}	C_p/J K^{-1} mol^{-1}
Solid	0	0	74.01	27.03
Gas	232.2	197.5	190.113	20.786

Density/kg m^{-3}: 9321 [293 K]

Thermal conductivity/W m^{-1} K^{-1}: 16.8 [300 K]

Electrical resistivity/Ω m: 79.0×10^{-8} [298 K]

Mass magnetic susceptibility/kg^{-1} m^3: $+1.90 \times 10^{-6}$ (s)

Molar volume/cm^3: 18.12

Coefficient of linear thermal expansion/K^{-1}: 13.3×10^{-6}

Crystal structure (cell dimensions/pm), space group

h.c.p. ($a = 353.75$; $c = 555.46$), P6$_3$/mmc

X-ray diffraction: mass absorption coefficients (μ/ρ)/cm^2 g^{-1}: CuK$_\alpha$ 140 MoK$_\alpha$ 80.8

Thulium

Thermal neutron capture cross-section/barns: 105
Number of isotopes (including nuclear isomers): 28
Isotope mass range: 152→176

**Nuclear
properties**

Key isotopes

Nuclide	Atomic mass	Natural abund. (%)	Half-life $T_{1/2}$	Decay mode and energy (MeV)	Nuclear spin I	Nuclear magnetic moment μ	Uses
^{169}Tm	168.934 212	100	stable		1/2+	−0.2316	NMR
^{170}Tm	169.935 198	0	128.6	β^- (0.968) 99.8%; EC(0.314) 0.2%; γ	1−	0.2476	tracer

NMR

^{169}Tm

Relative sensitivity (^{1}H $= 1.00$) 5.66×10^{-4}
Receptivity (^{13}C $= 1.00$)   3.21
Magnetogyric ratio/rad T^{-1} s^{-1} -2.21×10^7
Frequency (^{1}H $= 100$ MHz; 2.3488 T)/MHz   8.271

Ground state electron configuration: [Xe]$4f^{13}6s^2$
Term symbol: $^2F_{7/2}$
Electron affinity $(M \rightarrow M^-)$/kJ mol^{-1}: $\leqslant 50$

**Electron
shell
properties**

Main lines in atomic spectrum

Wavelength/nm	Species
346.220	II
371.791 (AA)	I
384.802	II
409.419	I
410.584	I
418.762	I

Ionization energies/kJ mol^{-1}

1. $M \rightarrow M^+$ 596.7	6. $M^{5+} \rightarrow M^{6+}$	
2. $M^+ \rightarrow M^{2+}$ 1163	7. $M^{6+} \rightarrow M^{7+}$	
3. $M^{2+} \rightarrow M^{3+}$ 2285	8. $M^{7+} \rightarrow M^{8+}$	
4. $M^{3+} \rightarrow M^{4+}$ 4119	9. $M^{8+} \rightarrow M^{9+}$	
5. $M^{4+} \rightarrow M^{5+}$	10. $M^{9+} \rightarrow M^{10+}$	

Environmental properties

Biological role	Abundances	Geological data
None; low toxicity; stimulatory	**Sun** (relative to H $= 1 \times 10^{12}$): 1.8	**Chief deposits and sources**: monazite [(Ce, La, etc.)PO$_4$];
Levels in humans: n.a., but low	**Earth's crust**/p.p.m.: 0.48	bastnaesite [(Ce, La, etc.)(CO$_3$)F]
	Seawater/p.p.m.: Atlantic surface: 1.3×10^{-7} Atlantic deep: 1.6×10^{-7} Pacific surface: 0.7×10^{-7} Pacific deep: 3.3×10^{-7} Residence time/years: n.a. Classification: recycled Oxidation state: III	**World production**/tonnes y^{-1}: *c.* 100 **Reserves**/tonnes: *c.* 10^5

Sn | Atomic number: **50**
Relative atomic mass ($^{12}C = 12.0000$): **118.710**

Chemical properties

Soft, pliable, silvery-white metal. Unreactive to oxygen (protected by oxide film) and water but dissolves in acids and bases. Used in solders, alloys, tinplate, polymer additives and anti-fouling paints.

Radii/pm: Sn^{2+} 93; Sn^{4+} 74; atomic 140.5; covalent 140; Sn^{4+} 294

Electronegativity: 1.96 (Pauling); 1.72 (Allred); 4.30 eV (absolute)

Effective nuclear charge: 5.65 (Slater); 9.10 (Clementi); 11.11 (Froese-Fischer)

Standard reduction potentials $E^{\ominus}$/V

	IV		II		0		−IV
Acid solution	SnO_2	$\xrightarrow{-0.088}$	SnO	$\xrightarrow{-0.104}$	Sn	$\xrightarrow{-1.071}$	SnH_4
	Sn^{4+}	$\xrightarrow{0.15}$	Sn^{2+}	$\xrightarrow{-0.137}$			

[Alkaline solutions contain many different forms]

Covalent bonds r/pm E/kJ mol^{-1}

	r/pm	E/kJ mol^{-1}
Sn–H	170.1	<314
Sn–C	217	225
Sn^{II}–O	195	557
Sn^{IV}–F	188	322
Sn^{IV}–Cl	231	315
Sn–Sn (α)	281	195

Oxidation states

Sn^{II} SnO, SnF_2, $SnCl_2$, etc., $[Sn(OH)]^+$ (aq), $[Sn_3(OH)_4]^{2+}$ (aq), Sn^{2+} salts

Sn^{IV} SnO_2, SnF_4, $SnCl_4$, etc., $[SnCl_6]^{2-}$ (aq HCl), $[Sn(OH)_6]^{2-}$ (aq base), organotin compounds

---

Physical properties

Melting point/K: 505.118
Boiling point/K: 2543
ΔH_{fusion}/kJ mol^{-1}: 7.20
ΔH_{vap}/kJ mol^{-1}: 290.4

Thermodynamic properties (298.15 K, 0.1 MPa)

State	$\Delta_f H^{\ominus}$/kJ mol^{-1}	$\Delta_f G^{\ominus}$/kJ mol^{-1}	$S^{\ominus}$/J K^{-1} mol^{-1}	C_p/J K^{-1} mol^{-1}
Solid (α)	−2.09	0.13	44.14	25.77
Solid (β)	0	0	51.55	26.99
Gas	302.1	267.3	168.486	21.259

Density/kg m^{-3}: 5750 (α); 7310 (β) [293 K]; 6973 [liquid at m.p.]
Thermal conductivity/W m^{-1} K^{-1}: 66.6 (α) [300 K]
Electrical resistivity/Ω m: 11.0×10^{-8} (α) [273 K]
Mass magnetic susceptibility/kg^{-1} m^3: -4.0×10^{-9} (α); $+3.3 \times 10^{-10}$ (β)

Molar volume/cm^3: 16.24 (β)
Coefficient of linear thermal expansion/K^{-1}: 5.3×10^{-6} (α); 21.2×10^{-6} (β)

Crystal structure (cell dimensions/pm), space group

α-Sn (grey) cubic ($a = 648.92$), Fd3m
β–Sn (white) tetragonal ($a = 583.16$, $c = 318.13$), I4$_2$/amd
$T(\alpha \rightarrow \beta) = 286.4$ K [β form at room temperatures]

X-ray diffraction: mass absorption coefficients (μ/ρ)/cm^2 g^{-1}:
CuK$_\alpha$ 256   MoK$_\alpha$ 31.1

Thermal neutron capture cross-section/barns: 0.63

Number of isotopes (including nuclear isomers): 37

Isotope mass range: $106 \rightarrow 132$

Key isotopes

Nuclide	Atomic mass	Natural abundance (%)	Half-life $T_{1/2}$	Decay mode and energy (MeV)	Nuclear spin I	Nuclear magnetic moment μ	Uses
^{112}Sn	111.904826	0.97	stable		0+		
^{113}Sn	112.905176	0	115d	EC(1.02); γ	1/2+		tracer
^{114}Sn	113.902784	0.65	stable		0+		
^{115}Sn	114.903348	0.36	stable		1/2+	−0.918	NMR
^{116}Sn	115.901747	14.53	stable		0+		
^{117}Sn	116.902956	7.68	stable		1/2+	−1.000	NMR
^{118}Sn	117.901609	24.22	stable		0+		
^{119}Sn	118.903310	8.58	stable		1/2+	−1.046	NMR
^{120}Sn	119.902220	32.59	stable		0+		
^{121}Sn	120.904238	0	27.0h	β^-(0.388); no γ	3/2+	0.70	tracer
^{122}Sn	121.903440	4.63	stable		0+		
^{124}Sn	123.905274	5.79	stable		0+		

NMR

	$[^{115}$Sn$]$	$[^{117}$Sn$]$	^{119}Sn
Relative sensitivity (^{1}H = 1.00)	3.5×10^{-7}	4.52×10^{-2}	5.18×10^{-2}
Receptivity (^{13}C = 1.00)	0.693	19.54	25.2
Magnetogyric ratio/rad T^{-1} s^{-1}	-8.7475×10^7	-9.5319×10^7	-9.9756×10^7
Frequency (^{1}H = 100 MHz; 2.3488 T)/MHz	32.699	35.625	37.272

Reference: $Sn(CH_3)_4$

Ground state electron configuration: $[Kr]4d^{10}5s^25p^2$

Term symbol: $^3P_0$

Electron affinity $(M \rightarrow M^-)$/kJ mol^{-1}: 116

Main lines in atomic spectrum

Wavelength/nm	Species
224.605 (AA)	I
235.484	I
242.949	I
283.999	I
286.333	I
303.412	I

Ionization energies/kJ mol^{-1}

1. $M \rightarrow M^+$ 708.6	6. $M^{5+} \rightarrow M^{6+}$ (9900)
2. $M^+ \rightarrow M^{2+}$ 1411.8	7. $M^{6+} \rightarrow M^{7+}$ (12200)
3. $M^{2+} \rightarrow M^{3+}$ 2943.0	8. $M^{7+} \rightarrow M^{8+}$ (14600)
4. $M^{3+} \rightarrow M^{4+}$ 3930.2	9. $M^{8+} \rightarrow M^{9+}$ (17000)
5. $M^{4+} \rightarrow M^{5+}$ 6974	10. $M^{9+} \rightarrow M^{10+}$ (20600)

Environmental properties

Biological role

May be essential to some organisms, including humans

Levels in humans:
Muscle/p.p.m.: 0.33–2.4
Bone/p.p.m.: 1.4
Blood/mg dm^{-3}: c. 0.38
Daily dietary intake: 0.2–3.5 mg
Toxic intake: 2 g
Lethal intake: n.a. some organotin compounds are very toxic
Total mass of element in average (70 kg) person: 14 mg

Abundances

Sun (relative to $H = 1 \times 10^{12}$): 100

Earth's crust/p.p.m.: 2.2

Seawater/p.p.m.:
Atlantic surface: 2.3×10^{-6}
Atlantic deep: 5.8×10^{-6}
Residence time/years: n.a.
Classification: scavenged
Oxidation state: IV

Geological data

Chief ore: cassiterite $[SnO_2]$

World production/tonnes y^{-1}: 165 000

Reserves/tonnes: 4.5×10^6

Ti

Atomic number: 22

Relative atomic mass ($^{12}C = 12.0000$): 47.88

Chemical properties

Hard, lustrous, silvery metal. Resists corrosion due to oxide layer, but powdered metal burns in air. Unaffected by many acids, (except HF H_3PO_4 and concentrated H_2SO_4), and alkalis. White TiO_2 used in paints. Metal used in chemical plants, lightweight alloys, hip replacement joints, etc.

Radii/pm: Ti^{2+} 80; Ti^{3+} 69; atomic 144.8; covalent 132

Electronegativity: 1.54 (Pauling); 1.32 (Allred); 3.45 eV (absolute)

Effective nuclear charge: 3.15 (Slater); 4.82 (Clementi); 6.37 (Froese-Fischer)

Standard reduction potentials $E^{\ominus}/V$

	IV	III	II	0

Acid solution

$$TiO^{2+} \xrightarrow{0.1} Ti^{3+} \xrightarrow{-0.37} Ti^{2+} \xrightarrow{-1.63} Ti$$
$$TiO_2 \xrightarrow{-0.56} Ti_2O_3 \xrightarrow{-1.23} TiO \xrightarrow{-1.31}$$

top bracket -0.86; -1.21

Alkaline solution

$$TiO_2 \xrightarrow{-1.38} Ti_2O_3 \xrightarrow{-1.95} TiO \xrightarrow{-2.13} Ti$$

Oxidation states

Ti^{-I}	(d^5)	rare $[Ti(bipyridyl)_3]^-$
Ti^0	(d^4)	rare $[Ti(bipyridyl)_3]$
Ti^{II}	(d^2)	TiO, $TiCl_2$, $TiBr_2$, TiI_2, no solution chemistry (reduces H_2O); complexes
Ti^{III}	(d^1)	Ti_2O_3, $[Ti(H_2O)_6]^{3+}$ (aq), TiF_3, $TiCl_3$ etc., complexes
Ti^{IV}	$([Ar])$	TiO_2, TiO^{2+} (aq), $[Ti(OH)_3]^{2+}$ (aq), TiF_4, $TiCl_4$ etc., titanates (TiO_4^{4-}, TiO_3^{2-}), complexes

Physical properties

Melting point/K: 1933
Boiling point/K: 3560
ΔH_{fusion}/kJ mol^{-1}: 20.9
ΔH_{vap}/kJ mol^{-1}: 428.9

Thermodynamic properties (298.15 K, 0.1 MPa)

State	$\Delta_f H^{\ominus}$/kJ mol^{-1}	$\Delta_f G^{\ominus}$/kJ mol^{-1}	$S^{\ominus}$/J K^{-1} mol^{-1}	C_p/J K^{-1} mol^{-1}
Solid	0	0	30.63	25.02
Gas	469.9	425.1	180.298	24.430

Density/kg m^{-3}: 4540 [293 K]; 4110 [liquid at m.p.]
Thermal conductivity/W m^{-1} K^{-1}: 21.9 [300 K]
Electrical resistivity/Ω m: 42.0×10^{-8} [293 K]
Mass magnetic susceptibility/kg^{-1} m^3: $+4.01 \times 10^{-8}$ (s)
Molar volume/cm^3: 10.55
Coefficient of linear thermal expansion/K^{-1}: 8.35×10^{-6}

Crystal structure (cell dimensions/pm), space group

α-Ti h.c.p. ($a = 295.11$, $c = 468.43$), P6$_3$/mmc
β-Ti b.c.c. ($a = 330.65$), Im3m
$T(\alpha \rightarrow \beta) = 1155$ K
High pressure form: ($a = 462.5$; $c = 281.3$), P$\bar{3}$m1

X-ray diffraction: mass absorption coefficients (μ/ρ)/cm^2 g^{-1}:
CuK$_\alpha$ 208   MoK$_\alpha$ 24.2

Discovered in 1791 by Rev. W. Gregor at Creed, Cornwall, UK, and independently by M. H. Klaproth in 1795 at Berlin, Germany
[Called after the Titans, sons of the Earth goddess]

Titanium

Thermal neutron capture cross-section/barns: 6.1

Number of isotopes (including nuclear isomers). 13

Isotope mass range: $41 \rightarrow 53$

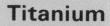
Nuclear properties

Key isotopes

Nuclide	Atomic mass	Natural abundance (%)	Half-life $T_{1/2}$	Decay mode and energy (MeV)	Nuclear spin I	Nuclear magnetic moment μ	Uses
^{44}Ti	43.959 689	0	47y	EC(0.265); γ	0+		tracer
^{46}Ti	45.952 629	8.0	stable		0+		
^{47}Ti	45.951 764	7.43	stable		5/2−	−0.7885	NMR
^{48}Ti	45.947 947	73.8	stable		0+		
^{49}Ti	45.947 871	5.5	stable		7/2−	−1.0417	NMR
^{50}Ti	49.944 792	5.4	stable		0+		

NMR

	^{47}Ti	^{49}Ti
Relative sensitivity (^{1}H = 1.00)	2.09×10^{-3}	3.76×10^{-3}
Receptivity (^{13}C = 1.00)	0.864	1.18
Magnetogyric ratio/rad T^{-1} s^{-1}	1.5084×10^7	1.5080×10^7
Quadrupole moment/m^2	$+0.29 \times 10^{-28}$	$+0.24 \times 10^{-28}$
Frequency (^{1}H = 100 MHz; 2.3488 T)/MHz	5.637	5.638

Reference: TiF_6^{2-} (conc. HF)

Ground state electron configuration: $[Ar]3d^2 4s^2$

Term symbol: $^3F_2$

Electron affinity (M→M$^-$)/kJ mol^{-1}: 7.6

Electron shell properties

Main lines in atomic spectrum

Wavelength/nm	Species
323.452	II
334.941	II
336.121	II
364.268	I
365.350 (AA)	I
399.864	I

Ionization energies/kJ mol^{-1}

1. M → M$^+$	658	6. M^{5+} → M^{6+} 11 516
2. M$^+$ → M^{2+}	1310	7. M^{6+} → M^{7+} 13 590
3. M^{2+} → M^{3+}	2652	8. M^{7+} → M^{8+} 16 260
4. M^{3+} → M^{4+}	4175	9. M^{8+} → M^{9+} 18 640
5. M^{4+} → M^{5+}	9573	10. M^{9+} → M^{10+} 20 830

Environmental properties

Biological role

None; stimulatory; suspected carcinogen

Levels in humans:
Muscle/p.p.m.: 0.9–2.2
Bone/p.p.m.: n.a.
Blood/mg dm^{-3}: 0.054
Daily dietary intake: 0.8 mg
Toxic intake: low toxicity
Total mass of element in average (70 kg) person: n.a.

Abundances

Sun (relative to H = 1 × 10^{12}):
1.12 × 10^5
Earth's crust/p.p.m.: 5600
Seawater/p.p.m.: 4.8 × 10^{-4}
Residence time/years: n.a.
Oxidation state: IV

Geological data

Chief ores: ilmenite [FeTiO$_3$]; rutile [TiO$_2$]; titanite [CaTiSiO$_5$]

World production of TiO$_2$/tonnes y^{-1}: 3 × 10^6

World production of Ti metal/tonnes y^{-1}: 99 000

Reserves/tonnes: 440 × 10^6

Atomic number: 74

Relative atomic mass ($^{12}C = 12.0000$): 183.85

Chemical properties

Obtained as dull grey powder, difficult to melt. Metal is lustrous and silvery white. Resists attack by oxygen, acids, and alkalis. Used in alloys, light bulb filaments, and cutting tools.

Radii/pm: W^{4+} 68; W^{6+} 62; atomic 137.0; covalent 130

Electronegativity: 2.36 (Pauling); 1.40 (Allred); 4.40 eV (absolute)

Effective nuclear charge: 4.35 (Slater); 9.85 (Clementi); 14.22 (Froese-Fischer)

Standard reduction potentials $E^{\ominus}/V$

	VI		V		IV		0

Acid solution:

$WO_3 \xrightarrow{-0.029} W_2O_5 \xrightarrow{-0.031} WO_2 \xrightarrow{-0.119} W$

with $WO_3 \xrightarrow{-0.090} W_2O_5$

Alkaline solution:

$WO_4^{2-} \xrightarrow{-1.259} WO_2 \xrightarrow{-0.982} W$

with $WO_4^{2-} \xrightarrow{-1.074} WO_2$

Oxidation states

W^{-IV}	(d^{10})	$[W(CO)_4]^{4-}$
W^{-II}	(d^8)	$[W(CO)_5]^{2-}$
W^{-I}	(d^7)	$[W_2(CO)_{10}]^{2-}$
W^0	(d^6)	$W(CO)_6$
W^{II}	(d^4)	WCl_2, WBr_2, WI_2, complexes
W^{III}	(d^3)	WCl_3, WBr_3, WI_3, complexes
W^{IV}	(d^2)	WO_2, WF_4, WCl_4, etc. WS_2, complexes
W^V	(d^1)	W_2O_5, WF_5, WCl_5, WF_6^-, complexes
W^{VI}	(d^0, f^{14})	WO_3, WO_4^{2-}, WF_6, WCl_6, $WOCl_4$, polytungstates, complexes

NB. There are no aqua ions of W in any oxidation state.

Physical properties

Melting point/K: 3680 ± 20

Boiling point/K: 5930

ΔH_{fusion}/kJ mol^{-1}: 35.2

ΔH_{vap}/kJ mol^{-1}: 799.1

Thermodynamic properties (298.15 K, 0.1 MPa)

State	$\Delta_f H^{\ominus}$/kJ mol^{-1}	$\Delta_f G^{\ominus}$/kJ mol^{-1}	$S^{\ominus}$/J K^{-1} mol^{-1}	C_p/J K^{-1} mol^{-1}
Solid	0	0	32.64	24.27
Gas	849.4	807.1	173.950	21.309

Density/kg m^{-3}: 19 300 [293 K]; 17 700 [liquid at m.p.]

Thermal conductivity/W m^{-1} K^{-1}: 174 [300 K]

Electrical resistivity/Ω m: 5.65×10^{-8} [300 K]

Mass magnetic susceptibility/kg^{-1} m^3: $+4.0 \times 10^{-9}$ (s)

Molar volume/cm^3: 9.53

Coefficient of linear thermal expansion/K^{-1}: 4.59×10^{-6}

Crystal structure (cell dimensions/pm), space group

b.c.c. ($a = 316.522$), Im3m

X-ray diffraction: mass absorption coefficients (μ/ρ)/cm^2 g^{-1}:
CuK$_\alpha$ 172   MoK$_\alpha$ 99.1

Tungsten (Wolfram)

Thermal neutron capture cross-section/barns: 18.4
Number of isotopes (including nuclear isomers): 29
Isotope mass range: 160→190

Key isotopes

Nuclide	Atomic mass	Natural abundance (%)	Half-life $T_{1/2}$	Decay mode and energy (MeV)	Nuclear spin I	Nuclear magnetic moment μ	Uses
^{180}W	179.946 701	0.12	stable		0+		
^{182}W	181.948 202	26.3	stable		0+		
^{183}W	182.950 220	14.28	stable		1/2−	+0.117 78	NMR
^{184}W	183.950 928	30.7	stable		0+		
^{185}W	184.953 416	0	74.8d	β^-(0.433); γ	3/2−		tracer
^{186}W	185.954 357	28.6	stable		0		
^{187}W	186.957 153	0	23.9h	β^-(1.312); γ	3/2−	0.688	tracer

NMR

	^{183}W
Relative sensitivity (^{1}H = 1.00)	7.20×10^{-4}
Receptivity (^{13}C = 1.00)	0.0589
Magnetogyric ratio/rad T^{-1} s^{-1}	1.1145×10^7
Frequency (^{1}H = 100 MHz; 2.3488 T)/MHz	4.161
Reference: WF$_6$	

Ground state electron configuration: [Xe]4f^{14}5d^{4}6s^2
Term symbol: ^{5}D$_0$
Electron affinity (M → M$^-$)/kJ mol^{-1}: 78.6

Main lines in atomic spectrum

Wavelength/nm	Species
202.998	II
207.911	II
255.135 (AA)	I
400.875	I
407.436	I
429.461	I

Ionization energies/kJ mol^{-1}

1. M → M$^+$	770	6. M^{5+} → M^{6+}	(5900)
2. M$^+$ → M^{2+}	(1700)	7. M^{6+} → M^{7+}	
3. M^{2+} → M^{3+}	(2300)	8. M^{7+} → M^{8+}	
4. M^{3+} → M^{4+}	(3400)	9. M^{8+} → M^{9+}	
5. M^{4+} → M^{5+}	(4600)	10. M^{9+} → M^{10+}	

Environmental properties

Biological role

None proved
Levels in humans:
Muscle/p.p.m.: n.a.
Bone/p.p.m.: 0.000 25
Blood/mg dm^{-3}: 0.001
Daily dietary intake:
   0.001–0.015 mg
Toxic intake: n.a.
Lethal intake: >30 mg (rats)
Total mass of element in
   average (70 kg) person: n.a.

Abundances

Sun (relative to H = 1×10^{12}):
   50
Earth's crust/p.p.m.: 1
Seawater/p.p.m.: 9.2×10^{-5}
Residence time/years: n.a.
Oxidation state: VI

Geological data

Chief sores: scheelite
   [CaWO$_4$]; wolframite
   [(Fe, Mn)WO$_4$]
World production/tonnes y^{-1}:
   45 100
Reserves/tonnes: 1.5×10^6

Unp

Atomic number: 105

Relative atomic mass ($^{12}C = 12.0000$): **262**

Chemical properties

Radioactive metal which does not occur naturally.

Radii/pm: n.a.

Electronegativity: n.a.

Effective nuclear charge: n.a.

Standard reduction potentials $E^{\ominus}/V$

n.a.

Oxidation states

Unp^V?

Physical properties

Melting point/K: n.a.

Boiling point/K: n.a.

ΔH_{fusion}/kJ mol^{-1}: n.a.

ΔH_{vap}/kJ mol^{-1}: n.a.

Thermodynamic properties (298.15 K, 0.1 MPa)

State	$\Delta_f H^{\ominus}$/kJ mol^{-1}	$\Delta_f G^{\ominus}$/kJ mol^{-1}	$S^{\ominus}$/J K^{-1} mol^{-1}	C_p/J K^{-1} mol^{-1}
Solid	0	0	n.a.	n.a.
Gas	n.a.	n.a.	n.a.	n.a.

Density/kg m^{-3}: n.a.

Thermal conductivity/W cm^{-1} K^{-1}: n.a.

Electrical resistivity/Ωm: n.a.

Mass magnetic susceptibility/kg^{-1} m^3: n.a.

Molar volume/cm^3: n.a.

Coefficient of linear thermal expansion/K^{-1}: n.a.

Crystal structure (cell dimensions/Å)

n.a.

X-ray diffraction: mass absorption coefficients (μ/ρ)/cm^2 g^{-1}: n.a. CuK$_\alpha$ MoK$_\alpha$

Isotopes 260 and 261 were reported in 1967 by a group of scientists at Dubna (USSR) but the element was not given a name. The claim was disputed in 1970 by a group of scientists led by A. Ghiorso at Berkeley, California, who reported isotope-260 and named it *hahnium* after Otto Hahn. IUPAC has proposed the name un-nil-pentium, derived from the Greek and Latin terms for 1-0-5

Unnilpentium

Thermal neutron capture cross-section/barns: n.a.

Number of isotopes (including nuclear isomers): 6

Isotope mass range: $257 \rightarrow 262$

Nuclear properties

Key isotopes

Nuclide	Atomic mass	Natural abundance (%)	Half-life $T_{1/2}$	Decay mode and energy (MeV)	Nuclear spin I	Nuclear magnetic moment μ	Uses
^{258}Unp	258.109 020	0	4s	$\alpha(9.02)$	n.a.	n.a.	
^{262}Unp	262.113 760	0	34s	SF; $\alpha(8.45)$	n.a.	n.a.	

Ground state electron configuration: $[Rn]5f^{14}6d^37s^2$?

Term symbol: $^3F_{3/2}$?

Electron affinity $(M \rightarrow M^-)$/kJ mol^{-1}: n.a.

Electron shell properties

Main lines in atomic spectrum		Ionization energies/kJ mol^{-1}
Wavelength/nm	Species	1 $M \rightarrow M^+$ n.a.
n.a.		

Environmental properties

Biological role	Abundances	Geological data
None; never encountered, but would be toxic due to radioactivity	**Sun** (relative to $H = 1 \times 10^{12}$): n.a.	**Chief source**: several atoms have been made from ^{249}Cf by bombarding it with ^{15}N nuclei
Levels in humans: nil	**Earth's crust**/p.p.m.: nil	
	Seawater/p.p.m.: nil	

Unq

Atomic number: **104**

Relative atomic mass ($^{12}C = 12.0000$): **261**

Chemical properties

Radioactive metal which does not occur naturally.

Radii/pm: n.a.

Electronegativity: n.a.

Effective nuclear charge: n.a.

Standard reduction potentials $E^{\ominus}/V$

n.a.

Oxidation states

Unq^{IV}?

Physical properties

Melting point/K: n.a.

Boiling point/K: n.a.

ΔH_{fusion}/kJ mol^{-1}: n.a.

ΔH_{vap}/kJ mol^{-1}: n.a.

Thermodynamic properties (298.15 K, 0.1 MPa)

State	$\Delta_f H^{\ominus}$/kJ mol^{-1}	$\Delta_f G^{\ominus}$/kJ mol^{-1}	$S^{\ominus}$/J K^{-1} mol^{-1}	C_p/J K^{-1} mol^{-1}
Solid	0	0	n.a.	n.a.
Gas	n.a.	n.a.	n.a.	n.a.

Density/kg m^{-3}: n.a.

Thermal conductivity/W m^{-1} K^{-1}: n.a.

Electrical resistivity/Ωm: n.a.

Mass magnetic susceptibility/kg^{-1} m^3: n.a.

Molar volume/cm^3: n.a.

Coefficient of linear thermal expansion/K^{-1}: n.a.

Crystal structure (cell dimensions/Å)

n.a.

X-ray diffraction: mass absorption coefficients (μ/ρ)/cm^2 g^{-1}:
n.a. CuK$_\alpha$ MoK$_\alpha$

Isotope-260 was reported in 1964 by a group of scientists at Dubna (USSR) and named *kurchatovium* after Igor Kurchatov. The claim was disputed in 1969 by a group of scientists led by A. Ghiorso at Berkeley, California, who reported isotope-257 and named it *rutherfordium* after E. R. Rutherford. IUPAC has proposed the name un-nil-quadium, derived from the Greek and Latin terms for 1-0-4

Unnilquadium

Thermal neutron capture cross-section/barns: n.a.

Number of isotopes (including nuclear isomers): 6

Isotope mass range: $257 \rightarrow 262$

Nuclear properties

Key isotopes

Nuclide	Atomic mass	Natural abundance (%)	Half-life $T_{1/2}$	Decay mode and energy (MeV)	Nuclear spin I	Nuclear magnetic moment μ	Uses
^{257}Unq	257.102 950	0	4.8s	$\alpha(9.20)$	n.a.	n.a.	
^{259}Unq	259.105 530	0	c. 3.1s	$\alpha(9.20)$	n.a.	n.a.	
^{261}Unq	261.108 690	0	c. 65s	$\alpha(8.60)$	n.a.	n.a.	

Ground state electron configuration: $[Rn]5f^{14}6d^27s^2$?

Term symbol: $^3F_2$?

Electron affinity $(M \rightarrow M^-)$/kJ mol^{-1}: n.a.

Electron shell properties

Main lines in atomic spectrum

Wavelength/nm	Species
n.a.	

Ionization energies/kJ mol^{-1}

1. $M \rightarrow M^+$ n.a.

Environmental properties

Biological role	Abundances	Geological data
None; never encountered, but would be toxic due to radioactivity **Levels in humans:** nil	**Sun** (relative to $H = 1 \times 10^{12}$): n.a. **Earth's crust**/p.p.m.: nil **Seawater**/p.p.m.: nil	**Chief source:** several thousand atoms have been made from ^{249}Cf by bombarding it with ^{12}C nuclei

Atomic number: 92

Relative atomic mass ($^{12}C=12.0000$): 238.0289

Chemical properties

Radioactive silvery metal. Malleable, ductile, and tarnishes in air. Attacked by steam and acids but not by alkalis. Used as nuclear fuel and in nuclear weapons.

Radii/pm: U^{3+} 103; U^{4+} 97; U^{5+} 89; U^{6+} 80; atomic 138.5

Electronegativity: 1.38 (Pauling); 1.22 (Allred)

Effective nuclear charge: 1.80 (Slater)

Standard reduction potentials $E^{\ominus}$/V

	VI		V		IV		III		0
			−0.027				−1.38		
Acid solution	UO_2^{2+}	0.16	UO_2^+	−0.38	U^{4+}	−0.52	U^{3+}	−1.66	U
Alkaline solution	$UO_2(OH)_2$		−0.3		UO_2	−2.6	$U(OH)_3$	−2.10	U

Oxidation states

U^{II}	$(f^3 d^1)$	UO?
U^{III}	(f^3)	$[U(H_2O)_x]^{3+}$ (aq) unstable, UF_3, UCl_3 etc., $[U(C_5H_5)_3]$
U^{IV}	(f^2)	UO_2, $[U(H_2O)_x]^{4+}$ (aq), salts, UF_4, UCl_4 etc., $[UCl_6]^{2-}$
U^V	(f^1)	U_2O_5, UO_2^+ (aq) unstable, UF_5, UCl_5, UBr_5, UF_6^-, UF_7^{2-}, UF_8^{3-}
U^{VI}	$(f^0, [Rn])$	UO_3 (U_3O_8), UO_2^{2+} (aq), salts, UF_6, UCl_6, complexes

---

Physical properties

Melting point/K: 1405.5

Boiling point/K: 4018

ΔH_{fusion}/kJ mol^{-1}: 15.5

ΔH_{vap}/kJ mol^{-1}: 422.6

Thermodynamic properties (298.15 K, 0.1 MPa)

State	$\Delta_f H^{\ominus}$/kJ mol^{-1}	$\Delta_f G^{\ominus}$/kJ mol^{-1}	$S^{\ominus}$/J K^{-1} mol^{-1}	C_p/J K^{-1} mol^{-1}
Solid	0	0	50.21	27.665
Gas	535.6	491.2	199.77	23.694

Density/kg m^{-3}: 18 950 [293 K]; 17 907 [liquid at m.p.]

Thermal conductivity/W m^{-1} K^{-1}: 27.6 [300 K]

Electrical resistivity/Ω m: 30.8×10^{-8} [273 K]

Mass magnetic susceptibility/kg^{-1} m^3: $+2.16 \times 10^{-8}$ (s)

Molar volume/cm^3: 12.56

Coefficient of linear thermal expansion/K^{-1}: 12.6×10^{-6}

Crystal structure (cell dimensions/pm), space group

α-U orthorhombic ($a=284.785$, $b=585.801$, $c=494.553$), Cmcm
β-U tetragonal ($a=1076.0$, $c=565.2$), P4$_2$/mnm or P4$_2$nm
γ-U b.c.c. ($a=352.4$), Im3m

$T(\alpha \rightarrow \beta)=941$ K
$T(\beta \rightarrow \gamma)=1047$ K

X-ray diffraction: mass absorption coefficients (μ/ρ)/cm^2 g^{-1}:
CuK$_\alpha$ 352 MoK$_\alpha$ 153

Discovered in 1789 by M. H. Klaproth at Berlin, Germany;
isolated in 1841 by E.-M. Peligot at Paris, France

[Named after the planet Uranus]

Uranium

Thermal neutron capture cross-section/barns: 7.57
Number of isotopes (including nuclear isomers): 17
Isotope mass range: 226→242

Key isotopes

Nuclide	Atomic mass	Natural abundance (%)	Half-life $T_{1/2}$	Decay mode and energy (MeV)	Nuclear spin I	Nuclear magnetic moment μ	Uses
^{234}U	234.040 946	0.005	2.45×10^5y	$\alpha(4.856)$; γ	$0+$		
^{235}U	235.043 924	0.720	7.04×10^8y	$\alpha(4.6793)$; γ	$7/2-$	-0.35	NMR
^{236}U	236.045 562	0	2.34×10^7y	$\alpha(4.569)$; γ	$0+$		
^{238}U	238.050 784	99.275	4.46×10^9y	$\alpha(4.039)$; γ	$0+$		

NMR

^{235}U

Relative sensitivity (^{1}H $= 1.00$)	1.21×10^{-4}
Receptivity (^{13}C $= 1.00$)	5.4×10^{-3}
Magnetogyric ratio/rad T^{-1} s^{-1}	-0.4926×10^7
Quadrupole moment/m^2	4.55×10^{-28}
Frequency (^{1}H $= 100$ MHz; 2.3488 T)/MHz	1.790

Reference: UF_6

Ground state electron configuration: $[Rn]5f^36d^17s^2$
Term symbol: $^5L_6$
Electron affinity $(M \rightarrow M^-)$/kJ mol^{-1}: n.a.

Main lines in atomic spectrum

Wavelength/nm	Species
356.659 (AA)	I
358.488	I
367.007	II
385.958	II
389.036	II
409.013	II

Ionization energies/kJ mol^{-1}

1. $M \rightarrow M^+$ 584	6. $M^{5+} \rightarrow M^{6+}$
2. $M^+ \rightarrow M^{2+}$ 1420	7. $M^{6+} \rightarrow M^{7+}$
3. $M^{2+} \rightarrow M^{3+}$	8. $M^{7+} \rightarrow M^{8+}$
4. $M^{3+} \rightarrow M^{4+}$	9. $M^{8+} \rightarrow M^{9+}$
5. $M^{4+} \rightarrow M^{5+}$	10. $M^{9+} \rightarrow M^{10+}$

Environmental properties

Biological role

None; dangerous due to
   radioactivity

Levels in humans:
Muscle/p.p.m.: 9×10^{-4}
Bone/p.p.m.:
   $(0.016-70) \times 10^{-3}$
Blood/mg dm^{-3}: 5×10^{-4}
Daily dietary intake:
   0.001-0.002 mg
Toxic intake: n.a.
Lethal intake: 36 mg (rats)
Total mass of element in
   average (70 kg) person:
   0.09 mg

Abundances

Sun (relative to H $= 1 \times 10^{12}$):
   <4
Earth's crust/p.p.m.: 2.4
Seawater/p.p.m.: 3.13×10^{-3}
Residence time/years: 300 000
Classification: accumulating
Oxidation state: VI

Geological data

Chief ores: uraninite [U_3O_8];
   carnotite
   [$K_2(UO_2)_2(VO_4)_2 \cdot 2H_2O$]
World production/tonnes y^{-1}:
35 000
Reserves/tonnes: 3.5×10^6
   plus 6.3×10^6 in phosphate
   ores

V

Atomic number: 23
Relative atomic mass ($^{12}C = 12.0000$): **50.9415**

Chemical properties

Shiny, silvery metal, soft when pure. Resists corrosion due to protective oxide film. Attacked by concentrated acids but not by fused alkalis. Used mainly as alloys and in steel.

Radii/pm: V^{2+} 72; V^{3+} 65; V^{4+} 61; V^{5+} 59; atomic 132.1

Electronegativity: 1.63 (Pauling); 1.45 (Allred); 3.6 eV (absolute)

Effective nuclear charge: 3.30 (Slater); 4.98 (Clementi); 6.65 (Froese-Fischer)

Standard reduction potentials $E^{\ominus}/V$

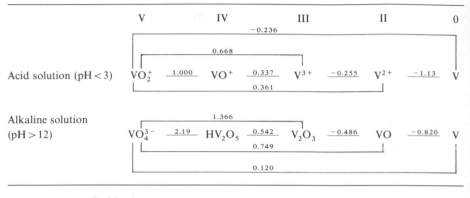

Acid solution (pH < 3)

Alkaline solution (pH > 12)

Oxidation states

V^{-III}	(d^8)	rare $[V(CO)_5]^{3-}$
V^{-I}	(d^6)	$[V(CO)_6]^-$
V^0	(d^5)	$[V(CO)_6]$
V^{I}	(d^4)	$[V(bipyridyl)_3]^+$
V^{II}	(d^3)	VO, $[V(H_2O)_6]^{2+}$ (aq), VF_2, VCl_2, complexes
V^{III}	(d^2)	V_2O_3, $[V(H_2O)_6]^{3+}$ (aq), VF_3, VCl_3, $[VCl_4]^-$
V^{IV}	(d^1)	VO_2, VO^{2+} (aq), VF_4, VCl_4, complexes
V^{V}	(d^0, [Ar])	V_2O_5, VO_2^+ (aq), VO_4^{3-} (aq, alkali), VF_5, VF_6^-, complexes

---

Physical properties

Melting point/K: 2160
Boiling point/K: 3650
ΔH_{fusion}/kJ mol^{-1}: 17.6
ΔH_{vap}/kJ mol^{-1}: 458.6

Thermodynamic properties (298.15 K, 0.1 MPa)

State	$\Delta_f H^{\ominus}$/kJ mol^{-1}	$\Delta_f G^{\ominus}$/kJ mol^{-1}	$S^{\ominus}$/J K^{-1} mol^{-1}	C_p/J K^{-1} mol^{-1}
Solid	0	0	28.91	24.89
Gas	514.21	754.43	182.298	26.012

Density/kg m^{-3}: 6110 [292 K]; 5550 [liquid at m.p.]
Thermal conductivity/W m^{-1} K^{-1}: 30.7 [300 K]
Electrical resistivity/K: 24.8×10^{-8} [293 K]
Mass magnetic susceptibility/kg^{-1} m^3: $+6.28 \times 10^{-8}$ (s)
Molar volume/cm^3: 8.34
Coefficient of linear thermal expansion/K^{-1}: 8.3×10^{-6}

Crystal structure (cell dimensions/pm), space group

b.c.c. ($a = 302.40$), Im3m

X-ray diffraction: mass absorption coefficients (μ/ρ)/cm^2 g^{-1}:
CuK$_\alpha$ 233   MoK$_\alpha$ 27.5

Discovered in 1801 by A. M. del Rio at Mexico City, Mexico;
rediscovered in 1831 by N. G. Selfström at Falun, Sweden

[Named after *Vanadis*, Scandinavian goddess]

Vanadium

Thermal neutron capture cross-section/barns: 5.06
Number of isotopes (including nuclear isomers): 11
Isotope mass range: $44 \rightarrow 55$

Key isotopes

Nuclide	Atomic mass	Natural abund. (%)	Half-life $T_{1/2}$	Decay mode and energy (MeV)	Nuclear spin I	Nuclear magnetic moment μ	Uses
^{48}V	47.952257	0	15.98d	$\beta^+(4.015)$; γ	4+	1.63	tracer
^{49}V	48.948517	0	331d	EC(0.601); no γ	7/2−	4.47	tracer
^{50}V	49.947161	0.25	$>3.9 \times 10^{17}$y	EC, β^-	6+	3.34745	NMR
^{51}V	50.943962	99.75	stable		7/2−	+5.1574	NMR

NMR

	[^{50}V]	^{51}V
Relative sensitivity (^{1}H = 1.00)	5.55×10^{-2}	0.38
Receptivity (^{13}C = 1.00)	0.755	2150
Magnetogyric ratio/rad T^{-1} s^{-1}	2.6491×10^7	7.0362×10^7
Quadrupole moment/m^2	$+0.21 \times 10^{-28}$	-0.052×10^{-28}
Frequency (^{1}H = 100 MHz; 2.3488 T)/MHz	9.970	26.289

Reference: VOCl$_3$

Ground state electron configuration: [Ar]3d^{3}4s^2
Term symbol: $^4F_{3/2}$
Electron affinity (M$\rightarrow$M$^-$)/kJ mol^{-1}: 50.7

Main lines in atomic spectrum

Wavelength/nm	Species
318.398	I
318.540 (AA)	I
411.178	I
437.924	I
438.472	I

Ionization energies/kJ mol^{-1}

1. M $\rightarrow$ M$^+$	650	6. M$^{5+}\rightarrow$M^{6+} 12362
2. M$^+\rightarrow$M^{2+}	1414	7. M$^{6+}\rightarrow$M^{7+} 14489
3. M$^{2+}\rightarrow$M^{3+}	2828	8. M$^{7+}\rightarrow$M^{8+} 16760
4. M$^{3+}\rightarrow$M^{4+}	4507	9. M$^{8+}\rightarrow$M^{9+} 19860
5. M$^{4+}\rightarrow$M^{5+}	6294	10. M$^{9+}\rightarrow$M^{10+} 22240

Environmental properties

Biological role

Essential to some species
  including humans;
  stimulatory
Levels in humans:
Muscle/p.p.m.: 0.02
Bone/p.p.m.: 0.0035
Blood/mg dm^{-3}: <0.0002
Daily dietary intake: 0.04 mg
Toxic intake: 0.25 mg
Lethal intake: 2–4 mg
Total mass of element in
  average (70 kg) person:
  0.11 mg

Abundances

Sun (relative to H = 1 $\times$ 10^{12}):
  1.05 $\times$ 10^4
Earth's crust/p.p.m.: 160
Seawater/p.p.m.:
Atlantic surface: 1.1 $\times$ 10^{-3}
Atlantic deep: n.a.
Pacific surface: 1.6 $\times$ 10^{-3}
Pacific deep: 1.8 $\times$ 10^{-3}
Residence time/years: 50000
Classification: recycled
Oxidation state: V

Geological data

Chief sources: patronite
  [VS$_4$] vanadinite
  [Pb$_5$(VO$_4$)$_3$Cl]; obtained
  as a by-product of other
  ores and Venezuelan oils
World production/tonnes y^{-1}:
  7000
Reserves/tonnes: n.a.

Xe

Chemical properties

Colourless, odourless gas obtained from liquid air. Inert towards most other chemicals but reacts with fluorine gas to form xenon fluorides. Oxides, acids and salts known. Little used outside research.

Radii/pm: Xe^+ 190; atomic 218; covalent 209; van der Waals 216

Electronegativity: 2.6 (Pauling); n.a. (Allred); 5.85 eV (absolute)

Effective nuclear charge: 8.25 (Slater); 12.42 (Clementi); 15.61 (Froese-Fischer)

Standard reduction potentials $E^\ominus/V$

	VIII		IV		II		I		0

Acid solution

$$H_4XeO_6 \xrightarrow{2.42} XeO_3 \xrightarrow{2.12} Xe$$

(over: 2.18)

$$XeF_2 \xrightarrow{0.9} XeF \xrightarrow{3.4}$$

(under XeF_2–XeF: 2.32)

Alkaline solution

$$HXeO_6^{3-} \xrightarrow{0.99} HXeO_4^- \xrightarrow{1.24} Xe$$

(under $HXeO_6^{3-}$: 1.18)

Covalent bonds

	r/pm	E/kJ mol^{-1}
Xe–O (XeO_3)	176	84
Xe–F	194	133

Oxidation states

Xe^0	clathrates: $Xe_8(H_2O)_{46}$, Xe (quinol)$_3$
Xe^{II}	XeF_2, $[XeF]^+[AsF_6]^-$
Xe^{IV}	XeF_4
Xe^{VI}	XeO_3, $XeOF_4$, XeO_2F_2, XeF_6, XeF_7^-, XeF_8^{2-}, $[XeF_5]^+[AsF_6]^-$
Xe^{VIII}	XeO_4, XeO_3F_2, Ba_2XeO_6, XeO_6^{4-} (aq)

Physical properties

Melting point/K: 161.3

Boiling point/K: 166.1

ΔH_{fusion}/kJ mol^{-1}: 3.10

ΔH_{vap}/kJ mol^{-1}: 12.65

Critical temperature/K: 289.7

Critical pressure/kPa: 5840

Critical volume/cm^3 mol^{-1}: 118

Thermodynamic properties (298.15 K, 0.1 MPa)

State	$\Delta_f H^\ominus$/kJ mol^{-1}	$\Delta_f G^\ominus$/kJ mol^{-1}	$S^\ominus$/J K^{-1} mol^{-1}	C_p/J K^{-1} mol^{-1}
Gas	0	0	169.683	20.786

Density/kg m^{-3}: 3540 [solid, m.p.]; 2939 [liquid, b.p.]; 5.8971 [gas, 273 K]

Thermal conductivity/W m^{-1} K^{-1}: 0.005 69 [300 K]$_g$

Mass magnetic susceptibility/kg^{-1} m^3: -4.20×10^{-9} (g)

Molar volume/cm^3: 37.09 [161 K]

Crystal structure (cell dimensions/pm), space group

f.c.c. (88 K) ($a = 619.7$), Fm3m

X-ray diffraction: mass absorption coefficients (μ/ρ)/cm^2 g^{-1}:

CuK_α 306 MoK_α 39.2

Discovered in 1898 by Sir William Ramsay and M. W. Travers at London, UK

[Greek, *xenos* = stranger]

Xenon

Thermal neutron capture cross-section/barns: 25
Number of isotopes (including nuclear isomers): 35
Isotope mass range: 114→142

Key isotopes

Nuclide	Atomic mass	Natural abundance (%)	Half-life $T_{1/2}$	Decay mode and energy (MeV)	Nuclear spin I	Nuclear magnetic moment μ	Uses
^{124}Xe	123.905 894	0.10	stable		0+		
^{126}Xe	125.904 281	0.09	stable		0+		
^{127}Xe	126.905 182	0	36.3d	EC(0.66); γ	1/2+		tracer
^{128}Xe	127.903 531	1.91	stable		0+		
^{129}Xe	128.904 780	26.4	stable		1/2+	−0.7768	NMR
^{130}Xe	129.903 509	4.1	stable		0+		
^{131}Xe	130.905 072	21.2	stable		3/2+		NMR
^{132}Xe	131.904 144	26.9	stable		0+		
^{133}Xe	132.905 888	0	5.25d	β^-(0.427); γ	3/2+		tracer, medical
^{134}Xe	133.905 395	10.4	stable		0+		
^{136}Xe	135.907 214	8.9	stable		0+		

NMR

	^{129}Xe	[^{131}Xe]
Relative sensitivity (^{1}H = 1.00)	2.12×10^{-2}	2.76×10^{-3}
Receptivity (^{13}C = 1.00)	31.8	3.31
Magnetogyric ratio/rad T^{-1} s^{-1}	-7.4003×10^7	2.1939×10^7
Quadrupole moment/m^2	—	-0.12×10^{-28}
Frequency (^{1}H = 100 MHz; 2.3488 T)/MHz	27.660	8.199

Reference: XeOF$_4$

Ground state electron configuration: [Kr]$4d^{10}5s^25p^6$
Term symbol: $^1S_0$
Electron affinity (M→M$^-$)/kJ mol^{-1}: −41 (calc.)

Main lines in atomic spectrum

Wavelength/nm Sensitivity	Species
823.164	I
828.012	I
881.941	I
3106.923	I
3507.025	I

Ionization energies/kJ mol^{-1}

1.	M →M$^+$	1170.4	6.	M^{5+}→M^{6+}	(6 600)
2.	M$^+$→M^{2+}	2046	7.	M^{6+}→M^{7+}	(9 300)
3.	M^{2+}→M^{3+}	3097	8.	M^{7+}→M^{8+}	(10 600)
4.	M^{3+}→M^{4+}	(4300)	9.	M^{8+}→M^{9+}	(19 800)
5.	M^{4+}→M^{5+}	(5500)	10.	M^{9+}→M^{10+}	(23 000)

Environmental properties

Biological role	Abundances	Geological data
None; non-toxic **Levels in humans:** n.a., but low	**Sun** (relative to H = 1×10^{12}): n.a. **Earth's crust**/p.p.m.: 2×10^{-6} **Seawater**/p.p.m.: 1×10^{-4} Residence time/years: n.a. Oxidation state: 0 Atmosphere (volume)/p.p.m. 0.086	**Chief sources:** liquid air **World production**/tonnes y^{-1}: c. 0.6 **Reserves**/tonnes: 2×10^9 (atmosphere)

Yb

Atomic number: **70**
Relative atomic mass ($^{12}C = 12.0000$): **173.04**

Chemical properties

Soft, silvery-white metal of the lanthanide (rare earth) group. Slowly oxidized by air, reacts with water. Some used in stress gauges.

Radii/pm: Yb^{2+} 113; Yb^{3+} 86; atomic 194; covalent 170

Electronegativity: n.a. (Pauling); 1.06 (Allred); ≤ 3.5 eV (absolute)

Effective nuclear charge: 2.85 (Slater); 8.59 (Clementi); 11.90 (Froese–Fischer)

Standard reduction potentials $E^{\ominus}/V$

	III	II	0
		−2.22	
Acid solution	Yb^{3+}	$\xrightarrow{-1.05}$ Yb^{2+}	$\xrightarrow{-2.8}$ Yb
Alkaline solution	$Yb(OH)_3$	$\xrightarrow{\hspace{2cm}-2.74\hspace{2cm}}$	Yb

Oxidation states

Yb^{II}	(f^{14})	YbO, YbS, YbF_2, $YbCl_2$ etc.
Yb^{III}	(f^{13})	Yb_2O_3, $Yb(OH)_3$, $[Yb(H_2O)_x]^{3+}$ (aq), Yb^{3+} salts, YbF_3, $YbCl_3$, etc. $YbCl_6^{3-}$, complexes

Physical properties

Melting point/K: 1097
Boiling point/K: 1466
ΔH_{fusion}/kJ mol^{-1}: 9.20
ΔH_{vap}/kJ mol^{-1}: 159

Thermodynamic properties (298.15 K, 0.1 MPa)

State	$\Delta_f H^{\ominus}$/kJ mol^{-1}	$\Delta_f G^{\ominus}$/kJ mol^{-1}	$S^{\ominus}$/J K^{-1} mol^{-1}	C_p/J K^{-1} mol^{-1}
Solid	0	0	59.87	26.74
Gas	152.3	118.4	173.126	20.786

Density/kg m^{-3}: 6965 [293 K]
Thermal conductivity/W m^{-1} K^{-1}: 34.9 [300 K]
Electrical resistivity/Ω m: 29.0×10^{-8} [293 K]
Mass magnetic susceptibility/kg^{-1} m^3: $+1.81 \times 10^{-8}$ (s)
Molar volume/cm^3: 24.84
Coefficient of linear thermal expansion/K^{-1}: 25.0×10^{-6}

Crystal structure (cell dimensions/pm), space group

α-Yb f.c.c. ($a = 548.62$), Fm3m
β-Yb b.c.c. ($a = 444$), Im3m
$T(\alpha \rightarrow \beta) = 1073$ K

X-ray diffraction: mass absorption coefficients (μ/ρ)/cm^2 g^{-1}:
CuK$_\alpha$ 146 MoK$_\alpha$ 84.5

Ytterbium

Thermal neutron capture cross-section/barns: 35

Number of isotopes (including nuclear isomers):   29

Isotope mass range: 154→179

Key isotopes

Nuclide	Atomic mass	Natural abundance (%)	Half-life $T_{1/2}$	Decay mode and energy (MeV)	Nuclear spin I	Nuclear magnetic moment μ	Uses
^{168}Yb	167.933 894	0.13	stable		0+		
^{169}Yb	168.935 186	0	32.02d	EC(0.908); γ	7/2+		tracer, medical
^{170}Yb	169.934 759	3.05	stable		0+		
^{171}Yb	170.936 323	14.3	stable		1/2−	+0.4919	NMR
^{172}Yb	171.936 378	21.9	stable		0+		
^{173}Yb	172.938 208	16.12	stable		5/2−	−0.6776	NMR
^{174}Yb	173.938 859	31.8	stable		0+		
^{175}Yb	174.941 273	0	4.19d	β^-(0.467); γ	(7/2)	±0.3	tracer
^{176}Yb	175.942 564	12.7	stable		0+		

NMR (rarely studied)

	^{171}Yb	^{173}Yb
Relative sensitivity (^{1}H = 1.00)	5.46×10^{-3}	1.33×10^{-3}
Receptivity (^{13}C = 1.00)	4.05	1.14
Magnetogyric ratio/rad T^{-1} s^{-1}	4.718×10^7	1.310×10^7
Quadrupole moment/m^2	—	$0.4–3.9 \times 10^{-28}$
Frequency (^{1}H = 100 MHz; 2.3488 T)/MHz	17.613	4.852

Ground state electron configuration: $[Xe]4f^{14}6s^2$

Term symbol: $^1S_0$

Electron affinity $(M \rightarrow M^-)$/kJ mol^{-1}: $\leqslant 50$

Main lines in atomic spectrum

Wavelength/nm	Species
289.138	II
328.937	II
346.437	I
369.420	II
398.799 (AA)	I
555.647	I

Ionization energies/kJ mol^{-1}

1. $M \rightarrow M^+$ 603.4	6. $M^{5+} \rightarrow M^{6+}$
2. $M^+ \rightarrow M^{2+}$ 1176	7. $M^{6+} \rightarrow M^{7+}$
3. $M^{2+} \rightarrow M^{3+}$ 2415	8. $M^{7+} \rightarrow M^{8+}$
4. $M^{3+} \rightarrow M^{4+}$ 4220	9. $M^{8+} \rightarrow M^{9+}$
5. $M^{4+} \rightarrow M^{5+}$	10. $M^{9+} \rightarrow M^{10+}$

Environmental properties

Biological role	Abundances	Geological data
None; low toxicity; stimulatory	**Sun** (relative to H = 1×10^{12}): 8	**Chief sources**: euxenite and xenotime contain Yb
Levels in humans: n.a., but low	**Earth's crust**/p.p.m.: 3.3	**World production**/tonnes y^{-1}: c. 100
	Seawater/p.p.m.:	**Reserves**/tonnes: c. 10^5
	Atlantic surface: 5×10^{-7}	
	Atlantic deep: 7.5×10^{-7}	
	Pacific surface: 3.7×10^{-7}	
	Pacific deep: 22×10^{-7}	
	Residence time/years: 400	
	Classification: recycled	
	Oxidation state: III	

Y

Atomic number: 39

Relative atomic mass ($^{12}C = 12.0000$): **88.90585**

Chemical properties

Soft, silvery-white metal. Stable in air due to formation of oxide film. Burns easily. Reacts with water to form hydrogen, H_2. Used as yttrium phosphors to give red colours in television screens; in X-ray filters; superconductors; superalloys.

Radii/pm: Y^{3+} 106; atomic 181; covalent 162

Electronegativity: 1.22 (Pauling); 1.11 (Allred); 3.19 eV (absolute)

Effective nuclear charge: 3.00 (Slater); 6.26 (Clementi); 8.72 (Froese-Fischer)

Standard reduction potentials $E^{\ominus}$/V

	III		0
Acid solution	Y^{3+}	$\underline{-2.37}$	Y
Alkaline solution	$Y(OH)_3$	$\underline{-2.85}$	Y

Oxidation states

Y^{III} ([Kr]) Y_2O_3, $Y(OH)_3$, $[Y(H_2O)_x]^{3+}$ (aq), Y^{3+} salts, $Y_2(CO_3)_3$, YF_3, YCl_3 etc., YOCl, some complexes [YH_2–YH_3 consists of $Y^{3+}H^-$, complex bonding]

Physical properties

Melting point/K: 1795

Boiling point/K: 3611

ΔH_{fusion}/kJ mol^{-1}: 17.2

ΔH_{vap}/kJ mol^{-1}: 393.3

Thermodynamic properties (298.15 K, 0.1 MPa)

State	$\Delta_f H^{\ominus}$/kJ mol^{-1}	$\Delta_f G^{\ominus}$/kJ mol^{-1}	$S^{\ominus}$/J K^{-1} mol^{-1}	C_p/J K^{-1} mol^{-1}
Solid	0	0	44.43	26.53
Gas	421.3	381.1	1179.48	25.86

Density/kg m^{-3}: 4469 [293 K]

Thermal conductivity/W m^{-1} K^{-1}: 17.2 [300 K]

Electrical resistivity/Ω m: 57.0×10^{-8} [298 K]

Mass magnetic susceptibility/kg^{-1} m^3: $+2.70 \times 10^{-8}$ (s)

Molar volume/cm^3: 19.89

Coefficient of linear thermal expansion/K^{-1}: 10.6×10^{-6}

Crystal structure (cell dimensions/pm), space group

α-Y h.c.p. (a = 364.74; c = 573.06), P6$_3$/mmc
β-Y b.c.c. (a = 411), Im3m
$T(\alpha \rightarrow \beta) = 1763$ K

X-ray diffraction: mass absorption coefficients (μ/ρ)/cm^2 g^{-1}: CuK$_{\alpha}$ 134   MoK$_{\alpha}$ 100

Yttrium

Thermal neutron capture cross-section/barns: 1.28
Number of isotopes (including nuclear isomers): 32
Isotope mass range: $80 \rightarrow 99$

Nuclear properties

Key isotopes

Nuclide	Atomic mass	Natural abundance (%)	Half-life $T_{1/2}$	Decay mode and energy (MeV)	Nuclear spin I	Nuclear magnetic moment μ	Uses
^{88}Y	87.909 508	0	106.6d	EC(3.623)99%, β^+0.2%; γ	4−		tracer
^{89}Y	88.905 849	100	stable		1/2−	−0.1373	NMR
^{90}Y	89.907 152	0	64h	β^-(2.283) ; no γ	2−	−1.630	tracer

NMR

	^{89}Y
Relative sensitivity (^{1}H = 1.00)	1.18×10^{-4}
Receptivity (^{13}C = 1.00)	0.668
Magnetogyric ratio/rad T^{-1} s^{-1}	-1.3108×10^7
Frequency (^{1}H = 100 MHz; 2.3488 T)/MHz	4.899

Reference: Y(NO$_3$)$_3$ (aq)

Ground state electron configuration: [Kr]$4d^1 5s^2$
Term symbol: $^2D_{3/2}$
Electron affinity (M$\rightarrow$M$^-$)/kJ mol^{-1}: 29.6

Electron shell properties

Ionization energies/kJ mol^{-1}

Main lines in atomic spectrum

Wavelength/nm	Species
360.073	II
371.030	I
377.433	II
407.738	I
410.238 (AA)	I
437.494	II

Ionization energies/kJ mol^{-1}

1. M $\rightarrow$ M$^+$	616	
2. M$^+ \rightarrow$ M^{2+}	1181	
3. M$^{2+} \rightarrow$ M^{3+}	1980	
4. M$^{3+} \rightarrow$ M^{4+}	5963	
5. M$^{4+} \rightarrow$ M^{5+}	7430	
6. M$^{5+} \rightarrow$ M^{6+}	8970	
7. M$^{6+} \rightarrow$ M^{7+}	11 200	
8. M$^{7+} \rightarrow$ M^{8+}	12 400	
9. M$^{8+} \rightarrow$ M^{9+}	14 137	
10. M$^{9+} \rightarrow$ M^{10+}	18 400	

Environmental properties

Biological role	Abundances	Geological data
None; suspected carcinogen	**Sun** (relative to H = 1×10^{12}): 125	**Chief sources:** xenotime (YPO$_4$)
Levels in humans:	**Earth's crust**/p.p.m.: 30	**World production**/tonnes y^{-1}: 5
Muscle/p.p.m.: 0.02	**Seawater**/p.p.m.: 9×10^{-6}	
Bone/p.p.m.: 0.07	Residence time/years: n.a.	**Reserves**/tonnes: n.a.
Blood/mg dm^{-3}: 0.0047	Oxidation state: III	
Daily dietary intake: 0.016 mg		
Toxic intake: low toxicity		
Total mass of element in average (70 kg) person: n.a.		

Zn

Atomic number: 30

Relative atomic mass ($^{12}C = 12.0000$): **65.39**

Chemical properties

Bluish-white metal, brittle when cast. Tarnishes in air, reacts with acids and alkalis. Used for galvanizing iron, in alloys, e.g. brass, in batteries, as ZnO in rubber, and as polymer stabilizer.

Radii/pm: Zn^{2+} 83; atomic 133.2; covalent 125

Electronegativity: 1.65 (Pauling); 1.66 (Allred); 4.45 eV (absolute)

Effective nuclear charge: 4.35 (Slater); 5.97 (Clementi); 8.28 (Froese-Fischer)

Standard reduction potentials $E^{\ominus}/V$

	II		0
Acid solution	Zn^{2+}	$\xrightarrow{-0.7626}$	Zn
Alkaline solution	$Zn(OH)_4^{2-}$	$\xrightarrow{-1.285}$	Zn
	$Zn(OH)_2$	$\xrightarrow{-1.246}$	Zn

Oxidation states

Zn^I	$(d^{10}s^1)$	rare Zn_2^{2+} in $Zn/ZnCl_2$ glass
$\mathbf{Zn^{II}}$	(d^{10})	ZnO, ZnS, $Zn(OH)_2$, $[Zn(H_2O)_6]^{2+}$ (aq), $[Zn(OH)_4]^{2-}$ (aq alkali) Zn^{2+} salts, ZnF_2, $ZnCl_2$ etc., many complexes

Physical properties

Melting point/K: 692.73
Boiling point/K: 1180
ΔH_{fusion}/kJ mol^{-1}: 6.67
ΔH_{vap}/kJ mol^{-1}: 115.3

Thermodynamic properties (298.15 K, 0.1 MPa)

State	$\Delta_f H^{\ominus}$/kJ mol^{-1}	$\Delta_f G^{\ominus}$/kJ mol^{-1}	$S^{\ominus}$/J K^{-1} mol^{-1}	C_p/J K^{-1} mol^{-1}
Solid	0	0	41.63	25.40
Gas	130.729	95.145	160.984	20.786

Density/kg m^{-3}: 7133 [293 K]; 6577 [liquid at m.p.]
Thermal conductivity/W m^{-1} K^{-1}: 116 [300 K]
Electrical resistivity/Ω m: 5.916×10^{-8} [293 K]
Mass magnetic susceptibility/kg^{-1} m^3: -2.20×10^{-9} (s)
Molar volume/cm^3: 9.17
Coefficient of linear thermal expansion/K^{-1}: 25.0×10^{-6}

Crystal structure (cell dimensions/pm), space group

h.c.p. ($a = 266.47$; $c = 494.69$), P6$_3$/mmc

X-ray diffraction: mass absorption coefficients (μ/ρ)/cm^2 g^{-1}: CuK$_\alpha$ 60.3   MoK$_\alpha$ 55.4

Known in India and China before 1500

[German, *zink*]

Zinc

Thermal neutron capture cross-section/barns: 1.1
Number of isotopes (including nuclear isomers): 23
Isotope mass range: $57 \rightarrow 78$

Key isotopes

Nuclide	Atomic mass	Natural abundance (%)	Half-life $T_{1/2}$	Decay mode and energy (MeV)	Nuclear spin I	Nuclear magnetic moment μ	Uses
^{64}Zn	63.929 145	48.6			0+		
^{65}Zn	64.929 243	0	243.8d	β^+(1.352)98%; EC 1.5%; γ	5/2−	+0.7690	tracer
^{66}Zn	65.926 034	27.9	stable		0+		
^{67}Zn	66.927 129	4.1	stable		5/2−	+0.875 15	NMR
^{68}Zn	67.924 846	18.8	stable		0+		
^{69m}Zn	68.926 552	0	13.8h	IT(0.439); γ	9/2+		tracer
^{70}Zn	69.925 325	0.6	stable		0+		

NMR

^{67}Zn

Relative sensitivity (^{1}H = 1.00) 2.85×10^{-3}
Receptivity (^{13}C = 1.00)   0.665
Magnetogyric ratio/rad T^{-1} s^{-1} 1.6737×10^7
Quadrupole moment/m^2 0.15×10^{-28}
Frequency (^{1}H = 100 MHz; 2.3488 T)/MHz   6.254
References: Zn(ClO$_4$)$_2$ (aq)

Ground state electron configuration: [Ar]3d^{10}4s^2
Term symbol: ^{1}S$_0$
Electron affinity (M→M$^-$)/kJ mol^{-1}: 9

Main lines in atomic spectrum

Wavelength/nm	Species
213.856 (AA)	I
250.199	II
255.795	II
330.259	I
334.502	I
491.162	II
636.234	I

Ionization energies/kJ mol^{-1}

1. M → M$^+$	906.4	6. M^{5+} → M^{6+} 10 400
2. M$^+$ → M^{2+}	1733.3	7. M^{6+} → M^{7+} 12 900
3. M^{2+} → M^{3+}	3832.6	8. M^{7+} → M^{8+} 16 800
4. M^{3+} → M^{4+}	5730	9. M^{8+} → M^{9+} 19 600
5. M^{4+} → M^{5+}	7970	10. M^{9+} → M^{10+} 23 000

Environmental properties

Biological role

Essential for all species; may be carcinogenic

Levels in humans:
Muscle/p.p.m.: 240
Bone/p.p.m.: 75–170
Blood/mg dm^{-3}: 7.0
Daily dietary intake: 5–40 mg
Toxic intake: 150–600 mg
Lethal intake: 6 g
Total mass of element in average (70 kg) person: 2.3 g

Abundances

Sun (relative to H = 1×10^{12}): 2.82×10^4

Earth's crust/p.p.m.: 75

Seawater/p.p.m.:
Atlantic surface: 0.5×10^{-4}
Atlantic deep: 1.0×10^{-4}
Pacific surface: 0.5×10^{-4}
Pacific deep: 5.2×10^{-4}
Residence time/years: 5000
Classification: recycled
Oxidation state: II

Geological data

Chief ores: zinc blende [ZnS], calamine (smithsonite) [ZnCO$_3$]; sphalerite [(Zn, Fe)S]

World production/tonnes y^{-1}: 4.9×10^6

Reserves/tonnes: 120×10^6

Zr

Atomic number: 40

Relative atomic mass ($^{12}C = 12.0000$): 91.224

Chemical properties

Hard, lustrous, silvery metal. Very corrosion-resistant due to oxide layer, but will burn in air. Unaffected by acids, (except HF), and alkalis. Metal used in alloys, coloured glazes, and nuclear reactors. Oxides used in foundry crucibles, bricks, ceramics, and abrasives.

Radii/pm: Zr^{2+} 109; Zr^{4+} 87; atomic 160; covalent 145

Electronegativity: 1.33 (Pauling); 1.22 (Allred); 3.64 eV (absolute)

Effective nuclear charge: 3.15 (Slater); 6.45 (Clementi); 9.20 (Froese-Fischer)

Standard reduction potentials $E^{\ominus}$/V

IV		0
Zr^{4+}	$\underline{\quad -1.55 \quad}$	Zr

Oxidation states

Zr^{-II}	(d^2)	$[Zr(CO)_6]^{2-}$
Zr^0	(d^4)	$[Zr(bipyridyl)_3]$,
		$[Zr(CO)_5(Me_2PCH_2CH_2PMe_2)]$
Zr^I	(d^3)	ZrCl?
Zr^{II}	(d^2)	ZrO? $ZrCl_2$
Zr^{III}	(d^1)	$ZrCl_3$, $ZrBr_3$, ZrI_3, Zr^{3+} reduces H_2O
Zr^{IV}	([Kr])	ZrO_2, $Zr(OH)^{3+}$ (aq), ZrF_4,
		$ZrCl_4$ etc., ZrF_6^{2-}, ZrF_7^{3-}, ZrF_8^{4-},
		zirconates, complexes

Physical properties

Melting point/K: 2125

Boiling point/K: 4650

ΔH_{fusion}/kJ mol^{-1}: 23.0

ΔH_{vap}/kJ mol^{-1}: 581.6

Thermodynamic properties (298.15 K, 0.1 MPa)

State	$\Delta_f H^{\ominus}$/kJ mol^{-1}	$\Delta_f G^{\ominus}$/kJ mol^{-1}	$S^{\ominus}$/J K^{-1} mol^{-1}	C_p/J K^{-1} mol^{-1}
Solid	0	0	38.99	25.36
Gas	608.8	566.5	181.36	26.65

Density/kg m^{-3}: 6506 [293 K]; 5800 [liquid at m.p.]

Thermal conductivity/W m^{-1} K^{-1}: 22.7 [300 K]

Electrical resistivity/Ω m: 42.1×10^{-8} [293 K]

Mass magnetic susceptibility/kg^{-1} m^3: $+1.68 \times 10^{-8}$ (s)

Molar volume/cm^3: 14.02

Coefficient of linear thermal expansion/K^{-1}: 5.78×10^{-6}

Crystal structure (cell dimensions/pm), space group

α-Zr h.c.p. ($a = 323.21$; $b = 514.77$), P6$_3$/mmc

β-Zr b.c.c. ($a = 361.6$), Im3m

$T(\alpha \rightarrow \beta) = 1135$ K

High pressure form: ($a = 503.6$; $c = 310.9$), P$\bar{3}$m1

X-ray diffraction: mass absorption coefficients (μ/ρ)/cm^2 g^{-1}:

CuK$_\alpha$ 143 MoK$_\alpha$ 15.9

Discovered by M. H. Klaproth in 1789 at University of Berlin, Germany; isolated in 1824 by J. J. Berzelius at Stockholm, Sweden

[Arabic, *zargun*, = gold colour]

Zirconium

Thermal neutron capture cross-section/barns: 0.184
Number of isotopes (including nuclear isomers): 25
Isotope mass range: 82→101

Nuclear properties

Key isotopes

Nuclide	Atomic mass	Natural abundance (%)	Half-life $T_{1/2}$	Decay mode and energy (MeV)	Nuclear spin I	Nuclear magnetic moment μ	Uses
^{90}Zr	89.904 703	51.45	stable				
^{91}Zr	90.905 644	11.22	stable		$5/2+$	-1.303	NMR
^{92}Zr	91.905 039	17.15	stable				
^{94}Zr	93.906 314	17.38	stable				
^{95}Zr	94.908 042	0	64.03d	β^-(1.121); γ	$5/2+$		tracer
^{96}Zr	95.908 275	2.80	$>3.6 \times 10^{17}$y				
^{97}Zr	96.910 950	0	16.8h	β^-(2.658); γ	$1/2-$		tracer

NMR
^{91}Zr

Relative sensitivity (^{1}H = 1.00)	9.48×10^{-3}
Receptivity (^{13}C = 1.00)	6.04
Magnetogyric ratio/rad T^{-1} s^{-1}	-2.4868×10^7
Quadrupole moment/m^2	-0.21×10^{-28}
Frequency (^{1}H = 100 MHz; 2.3488 T)/MHz	9.330

Reference: no agreed standard

Ground state electron configuration: $[Kr]4d^2 5s^2$
Term symbol: $^3F_2$
Electron affinity (M→M$^-$)/kJ mol^{-1}: 41.1

Electron shell properties

Main lines in atomic spectrum

Wavelength/nm	Species
339.198	II
343.823	II
349.621	II
360.119 (AA)	I
389.032	I

Ionization energies/kJ mol^{-1}

1. M $\rightarrow$ M$^+$	660	6. M$^{5+}\rightarrow$M^{6+}	(9 500)
2. M$^+\rightarrow$M^{2+}	1267	7. M$^{6+}\rightarrow$M^{7+}	(11 200)
3. M$^{2+}\rightarrow$M^{3+}	2218	8. M$^{7+}\rightarrow$M^{8+}	(13 800)
4. M$^{3+}\rightarrow$M^{4+}	3313	9. M$^{8+}\rightarrow$M^{9+}	(15 700)
5. M$^{4+}\rightarrow$M^{5+}	7860	10. M$^{9+}\rightarrow$M^{10+}	(17 500)

Environmental properties

Biological role
None

Levels in humans:
Muscle/p.p.m.: 0.08
Bone/p.p.m.: <0.1
Blood/mg dm^{-3}: 0.011
Daily dietary intake:
   c. 0.05 mg
Toxic intake: non-toxic
Total mass of element in
   average (70 kg) person:
   1 mg

Abundances
Sun (relative to H = 1×10^{12}):
   560
Earth's crust/p.p.m.: 190
Seawater/p.p.m.: 9×10^{-6}
Residence time/years: n.a.
Oxidation state: IV

Geological data
Chief ores: zircon [ZrSiO$_4$];
   baddeleyite [ZrO$_2$]
World production of
   zircon/tonnes y^{-1}: 7×10^5
World production of
   zirconium metal/tonnes:
   7000
Reserves/tonnes: $>10^9$

Tables of properties of the elements in order of element, and in ranking order of property

Table 1   Discovery of the elements

		Year	Discoverer	Place
1	Hydrogen	1766	Cavendish	London
2	Helium	1895	Ramsay	London
3	Lithium	1817	Arfvedson	Stockholm
4	Beryllium	1797	Vauquelin	Paris
5	Boron	1808	{ Lussac and Thenard	Paris
			Davy	London
6	Carbon	pre-history	–	–
7	Nitrogen	1772	Rutherford	Edinburgh
8	Oxygen	1774	{ Priestley	Leeds
			Scheele	Uppsala
9	Fluorine	1886	Moissan	Paris
10	Neon	1898	Ramsay and Travers	London
11	Sodium	1807	Davy	London
12	Magnesium	1755	Black	Edinburgh
13	Aluminium	1825	Oersted	Copenhagen
14	Silicon	1824	Berzelius	Stockholm
15	Phosphorus	1669	Brandt, H.	Hamburg
16	Sulfur	pre-history	–	–
17	Chlorine	1774	Scheele	Uppsala
18	Argon	1894	Rayleigh and Ramsay	London and Bristol
19	Potassium	1807	Davy	London
20	Calcium	1808	Davy	London
21	Scandium	1879	Nilson	Uppsala
22	Titanium	1791	{ Gregor	Creed, Cornwall
			Klaproth	Berlin
23	Vanadium	1801	delRio	Mexico
24	Chromium	1780	Vauquelin	Paris
25	Manganese	1774	Grahn	Stockholm
26	Iron	c. 2500 BC	–	–
27	Cobalt	1735	Brandt, G.	Stockholm
28	Nickel	1751	Cronstedt	Stockholm
29	Copper	c. 5000 BC	–	–
30	Zinc	pre- 1500*	–	–
31	Gallium	1875	de Boisbaudran	Paris
32	Germanium	1886	Winkler	Freiberg
33	Arsenic	c. 1250	Magnus	Germany
34	Selenium	1817	Berzelius	Stockholm
35	Bromine	1826	{ Balard	Montpellier
			Löwig	Heidelberg
36	Krypton	1898	Ramsay and Travers	London
37	Rubidium	1861	Bunsen and Kirchhoff	Heidelberg
38	Strontium	1808	Crawford	Edinburgh
39	Yttrium	1794	Gadolin	Åbo, Finland
40	Zirconium	1789	Klaproth	Berlin
41	Niobium	1801	Hatchett	London
42	Molybdenum	1781	Hjelm	Uppsala
43	Technetium	1937	Perrier and Segré	Palermo
44	Ruthenium	1808	Sniadecki	Vilno, Poland

*Zinc was known as the copper–zinc alloy, brass, around 20 BC.

Table 1 Continued

		Year	Discoverer	Place
45	Rhodium	1803	Wollaston	London
46	Palladium	1803	Wollaston	London
47	Silver	c. 3000 BC	–	–
48	Cadmium	1817	Davy	London
49	Indium	1863	Reich and Richter	Freiberg
50	Tin	c. 2100 BC	–	–
51	Antimony	c. 1600 BC	–	–
52	Tellurium	1783	von Reichenstein	Sibiu, Romania
53	Iodine	1811	Courtois	Paris
54	Xenon	1898	Ramsay and Travers	London
55	Caesium	1860	Bunsen and Kirchhoff	Heidelberg
56	Barium	1808	Davy	London
57	Lanthanum	1839	Mosander	Stockholm
58	Cerium	1803	Berzelius and Hisinger	Vestmandland, Sweden
59	Praseodymium	1885	von Welsbach	Vienna
60	Neodymium	1885	von Welsbach	Vienna
61	Promethium	1945	Marinsky, Glendenin, and Coryell	Oak Ridge, USA
62	Samarium	1879	de Boisbaudran	Paris
63	Europium	1901	Demarçay	Paris
64	Gadolinium	1880	deMarignac	Geneva
65	Terbium	1843	Mosander	Stockholm
66	Dysprosium	1886	de Boisbaudran	Paris
67	Holmium	1878	{ Cleve / Delafontaine and Soret	Uppsala / Geneva
68	Erbium	1842	Mosander	Stockholm
69	Thulium	1879	Cleve	Uppsala
70	Ytterbium	1878	deMarignac	Geneva
71	Lutetium	1907	{ Urbain / James	Paris / New Hampshire, USA
72	Hafnium	1923	Coster and Hevesey	Copenhagen
73	Tantalum	1802	Ekeberg	Uppsala
74	Tungsten	1783	Elhuijar and Elhuijar	Vergara, Spain
75	Rhenium	1925	Noddack, Tacke, and Berg	Berlin
76	Osmium	1803	Tennant	London
77	Iridium	1803	Tennant	London
78	Platinum	Pre-1700	–	–
79	Gold	c. 3000 BC	–	–
80	Mercury	c. 1500 BC	–	–
81	Thallium	1861	Crookes	London
82	Lead	c. 1000 BC	–	–
83	Bismuth	c. 1500	–	–
84	Polonium	1898	Curie (Marie)	Paris
85	Astatine	1940	Corson, Mackenzie, and Segré	Berkeley, California
86	Radon	1900	Dorn	Halle
87	Francium	1939	Perey	Paris
88	Radium	1898	Curie and Curie	Paris
89	Actinium	1899	Debierne	Paris
90	Thorium	1829	Berzelius	Stockholm

Table 1   Continued

		Year	Discoverer	Place
91	Protactinium	1917	Hahn and Meitner	Berlin
			Fajans	Karlsruhe
			Soddy, Cranston, and Fleck	Glasgow
92	Uranium	1789	Klaproth	Berlin
93	Neptunium	1940	McMillan and Abelson	Berkeley, California
94	Plutonium	1940	Seaborg, Wahl, and Kennedy	Berkeley, California
95	Americium	1944	Seaborg, James, Morgan, and Ghiorso	Chicago, Illinois
96	Curium	1944	Seaborg, James, and Ghiorso	Berkeley, California
97	Berkelium	1949	Thompson, Ghiorso, and Seaborg	Berkeley, California
98	Californium	1950	Thompson, Street, Ghiorso, and Seaborg	Berkeley, California
99	Einsteinium	1952	Choppin, Thompson, Ghiorso, and Harvey	Berkeley, California
100	Fermium	1952	Choppin, Thompson, Ghiorso, and Harvey	Berkeley, California
101	Mendelevium	1955	Ghiorso, Harvey, Choppin, Thompson, and Seaborg	Berkeley, California
102	Nobelium	1958	Ghiorso, Sikkeland, Walton, and Seaborg	Berkeley, California
103	Lawrencium	1961	Ghiorso, Sikkeland, and Larsh	Berkeley, California
104	Unnilquadium	1964?	disputed	
105	Unnilpentium	1967?	disputed	

Table 2 Discovery of the elements in chronological order

Year	Element	Discoverer	Place
pre-history	Carbon	–	–
pre-history	Sulfur	–	–
c. 5000 BC	Copper	–	–
c. 3000 BC	Silver	–	–
c. 3000 BC	Gold	–	
c. 2500 BC	Iron	–	–
c. 2100 BC	Tin	–	
c. 1600 BC	Antimony	–	–
c. 1500 BC	Mercury	–	–
c. 1000 BC	Lead	–	–
c. 1250	Arsenic	Magnus	Germany
pre-1500*	Zinc	–	–
c. 1500	Bismuth	–	–
1669	Phosphorus	Brandt, H.	Hamburg
pre-1700	Platinum	–	–
1735	Cobalt	Brandt, G.	Stockholm
1751	Nickel	Cronstedt	Stockholm
1755	Magnesium	Black	Edinburgh
1766	Hydrogen	Cavendish	London
1772	Nitrogen	Rutherford	Edinburgh
1774	Oxygen	Priestley / Scheele	Leeds / Uppsala
1774	Chlorine	Scheele	Uppsala
1774	Manganese	Grahn	Stockholm
1780	Chromium	Vauquelin	Paris
1781	Molybdenum	Hjelm	Uppsala
1783	Tellurium	von Reichenstein	Sibiu, Romania
1783	Tungsten	Elhujar and Elhuijar	Vegara, Spain
1789	Zirconium	Klaproth	Berlin
1789	Uranium	Klaproth	Berlin
1791	Titanium	Gregor / Klaproth	Creed, Cornwall / Berlin
1794	Yttrium	Gadolin	Åbo, Finland
1797	Beryllium	Vauquelin	Paris
1801	Vanadium	del Rio	Mexico
1801	Niobium	Hatchett	London
1802	Tantalum	Ekeberg	Uppsala
1803	Rhodium	Wollaston	London
1803	Palladium	Wollaston	London
1803	Osmium	Tennant	London
1803	Iridium	Tennant	London
1803	Cerium	Berzelius and Hisinger	Vestmanland, Sweden
1807	Potassium	Davy	London
1807	Sodium	Davy	London
1808	Boron	Lussac and Thenard / Davy	Paris / London
1808	Calcium	Davy	London
1808	Strontium	Crawford	Edinburgh
1808	Ruthenium	Sniadecki	Vilno, Poland

*Zinc was known as the copper–zinc alloy, brass, around 20 BC.

Table 2 Continued

Year	Element	Discoverer	Place
1808	Barium	Davy	London
1811	Iodine	Courtois	Paris
1815	Thorium	Berzelius	Stockholm
1817	Lithium	Arfvedson	Stockholm
1817	Selenium	Berzelius	Stockholm
1817	Cadmium	Davy	London
1824	Silicon	Berzelius	Stockholm
1825	Aluminium	Oersted	Copenhagen
1826	Bromine	{ Balard	Montpellier
		{ Lowig	Heidelberg
1839	Lanthanum	Mosander	Stockholm
1842	Erbium	Mosander	Stockholm
1843	Terbium	Mosander	Stockholm
1860	Caesium	Bunsen and Kirchhoff	Heidelberg
1861	Rubidium	Bunsen and Kirchhoff	Heidelberg
1861	Thallium	Crookes	London
1863	Indium	Reich and Richter	Freiberg
1875	Gallium	de Boisbaudran	Paris
1878	Holmium	{ Cleve	Uppsala
		{ Delafontaine and Soret	Geneva
1878	Ytterbium	de Marignac	Geneva
1879	Scandium	Nilsdon	Uppsala
1879	Samarium	de Boisbaudran	Paris
1879	Thulium	Cleve	Uppsala
1880	Gadolinium	de Marignac	Geneva
1885	Praesodymium	von Welsbach	Vienna
1885	Neodymium	von Welsbach	Vienna
1886	Germanium	Winkler	Freiberg
1886	Fluorine	Moissan	Paris
1886	Dysprosium	de Boisbaudran	Paris
1894	Argon	Rayleigh and Ramsay	London and Bristol
1895	Helium	Ramsay	London
1898	Krypton	Ramsay and Travers	London
1898	Neon	Ramsay and Travers	London
1898	Xenon	Ramsay and Travers	London
1898	Polonium	Curie (Marie)	Paris
1898	Radium	Curie and Curie	Paris
1899	Actinium	Debierne	Paris
1900	Radon	Dorn	Halle
1901	Europium	Demarçay	Paris
1907	Lutetium	{ Urbain	Paris
		{ James	New Hampshire, USA
1917	Protactinium	{ Hahn and Meitner	Berlin
		{ Fajans	Karlsruhe
		{ Soddy, Cranston, and Fleck	Glasgow
1923	Hafnium	Coster and Hevesey	Copenhagen
1925	Rhenium	Noddack, Tacke, and Berg	Berlin
1937	Technetium	Perrier and Segré	Palermo
1939	Francium	Perey	Paris

Table 2 Continued

Year	Element	Discoverer	Place
1940	Neptunium	McMillan and Abelson	Berkeley, California
1940	Astatine	Corson, Mackenzie, and Segré	Berkeley, California
1940	Plutonium	Seaborg, Wahl, and Kennedy	Berkeley, California
1944	Americium	Seaborg, James, Morgan, and Ghiorso	Chicago
1944	Curium	Seaborg, James, and Ghiorso	Berkeley,. California
1945	Promethium	Marinsky, Glendenin, and Coryell	Oak Ridge, Tenn., USA
1949	Berkelium	Thomspon, Ghiorso, and Seaborg	Berkeley, California
1950	Californium	Thompson, Street, Ghiorso, and Seaborg	Berkeley, California
1952	Einsteinium	Choppin, Thompson, Ghiorso, and Harvey	Berkeley, California
1952	Fermium	Choppin, Thompson, Ghiorso, and Harvey	Berkeley, California
1955	Mendelevium	Ghiorso, Harvey, Choppin, Thompson, and Seaborg	Berkeley, California
1958	Nobelium	Ghiorso, Sikkeland, Walton, and Seaborg	Berkeley, California
1961	Lawrencium	Ghiorso, Sikkeland, and Larsh	Berkeleley, California
1964?	Unnilquadium	disputed	
1967?	Unnilpentium	disputed	

Table 3 Melting points of the elements/K

1	Hydrogen	14.01	54	Xenon	161.3	
2	Helium	0.95	55	Caesium	301.6	
3	Lithium	453.69	56	Barium	1002	
4	Beryllium	1551	57	Lanthanum	1194	
5	Boron	2573	58	Cerium	1072	
6	Carbon (diam.)	3820	59	Praseodymium	1204	
7	Nitrogen	63.29	60	Neodymium	1294	
8	Oxygen	54.8	61	Promethium	1441	
9	Fluorine	53.53	62	Samarium	1350	
10	Neon	24.48	63	Europium	1095	
11	Sodium	370.96	64	Gadolinium	1586	
12	Magnesium	922.0	65	Terbium	1629	
13	Aluminium	933.5	66	Dysprosium	1685	
14	Silicon	1683	67	Holmium	1747	
15	Phosphorus (P_4)	317.3	68	Erbium	1802	
16	Sulfur (α)	386.0	69	Thulium	1818	
17	Chlorine	172.2	70	Ytterbium	1097	
18	Argon	83.8	71	Lutetium	1936	
19	Potassium	336.8	72	Hafnium	2503	
20	Calcium	1112	73	Tantalum	3269	
21	Scandium	1814	74	Tungsten	3680	
22	Titanium	1933	75	Rhenium	3453	
23	Vanadium	2160	76	Osmium	3327	
24	Chromium	2130	77	Iridium	2683	
25	Manganese	1517	78	Platinum	2045	
26	Iron	1808	79	Gold	1337.58	
27	Cobalt	1768	80	Mercury	234.28	
28	Nickel	1726	81	Thallium	576.6	
29	Copper	1356.6	82	Lead	600.65	
30	Zinc	692.73	83	Bismuth	544.5	
31	Gallium	302.93	84	Polonium	527	
32	Germanium	1210.6	85	Astatine	575 (est.)	
33	Arsenic	1090	86	Radon	202	
34	Selenium	490	87	Francium	300	
35	Bromine	265.9	88	Radium	973	
36	Krypton	116.6	89	Actinium	1320	
37	Rubidium	312.2	90	Thorium	2023	
38	Strontium	1042	91	Protactinium	2113	
39	Yttrium	1795	92	Uranium	1405.5	
40	Zirconium	2125	93	Neptunium	913	
41	Niobium	2741	94	Plutonium	914	
42	Molybdenum	2890	95	Americium	1267	
43	Technetium	2445	96	Curium	n.a.	
44	Ruthenium	2583	97	Berkelium	n.a.	
45	Rhodium	2239	98	Californium	n.a.	
46	Palladium	1825	99	Einsteinium	n.a.	
47	Silver	1235.1	100	Fermium	n.a.	
48	Cadmium	594.1	101	Mendelevium	n.a.	
49	Indium	429.32	102	Nobelium	n.a.	
50	Tin (β)	505.118	103	Lawrencium	n.a.	
51	Antimony	903.9	104	Unnilquadium	n.a.	
52	Tellurium	722.7	105	Unnilpentium	n.a.	
53	Iodine	386.7				

Table 4 Melting points of the elements in order of temperature/K

6	Carbon (diam.)	3820	38	Strontium	1042
74	Tungsten	3680	56	Barium	1002
75	Rhenium	3453	88	Radium	973
76	Osmium	3327	13	Aluminium	933.5
73	Tantalum	3269	12	Magnesium	922.0
42	Molybdenum	2890	94	Plutonium	914
41	Niobium	2741	93	Neptunium	913
77	Iridium	2683	51	Antimony	903.9
44	Ruthenium	2583	52	Tellurium	722.7
5	Boron	2573	30	Zinc	692.73
72	Hafnium	2503	82	Lead	600.65
43	Technetium	2445	48	Cadmium	594.1
45	Rhodium	2239	81	Thallium	576.6
23	Vanadium	2160	85	Astatine	575 (est.)
24	Chromium	2130	83	Bismuth	544.5
40	Zirconium	2125	84	Polonium	527
91	Protactinium	2113	50	Tin (β)	505.118
78	Platinum	2045	34	Selenium	490
90	Thorium	2023	3	Lithium	453.69
71	Lutetium	1936	49	Indium	429.32
22	Titanium	1933	53	Iodine	386.7
46	Palladium	1825	16	Sulfur (α)	386.0
69	Thulium	1818	11	Sodium	370.96
21	Scandium	1814	19	Potassium	336.8
26	Iron	1808	15	Phosphorus (P_4)	317.31
68	Erbium	1802	37	Rubidium	312.2
39	Yttrium	1795	31	Gallium	302.93
27	Cobalt	1768	55	Caesium	301.6
67	Holmium	1747	87	Francium	300
28	Nickel	1726	35	Bromine	265.9
66	Dysprosium	1685	80	Mercury	234.28
14	Silicon	1683	86	Radon	202
65	Terbium	1629	17	Chlorine	172.2
64	Gadolinium	1586	54	Xenon	161.3
4	Beryllium	1551	36	Krypton	116.6
25	Manganese	1517	18	Argon	83.8
61	Promethium	1441	7	Nitrogen	63.29
92	Uranium	1405.5	8	Oxygen	54.8
29	Copper	1356.6	9	Fluorine	53.53
62	Samarium	1350	10	Neon	24.48
79	Gold	1337.58	1	Hydrogen	14.01
89	Actinium	1320	2	Helium	0.95
60	Neodymium	1294			
95	Americium	1267	96	Curium	n.a.
47	Silver	1235.1	97	Berkelium	n.a.
32	Germanium	1210.6	98	Californium	n.a.
59	Praseodymium	1204	99	Einsteinium	n.a.
57	Lanthanum	1194	100	Fermium	n.a.
20	Calcium	1112	101	Mendelevium	n.a.
70	Ytterbium	1097	102	Nobelium	n.a.
63	Europium	1095	103	Lawrencium	n.a.
33	Arsenic	1090	104	Unnilquadium	n.a.
58	Cerium	1072	105	Unnilpentium	n.a.

Table 5 Boiling points of the elements/K

1	Hydrogen	20.28	54	Xenon	166.1
2	Helium	4.216	55	Caesium	951.6
3	Lithium	1620	56	Barium	1910
4	Beryllium	3243	57	Lanthanum	3730
5	Boron	3931	58	Cerium	3699
6	Carbon	5100 (subl.)	59	Praseodymium	3785
7	Nitrogen	77.4	60	Neodymium	3341
8	Oxygen	90.19	61	Promethium	c. 3000
9	Fluorine	85.01	62	Samarium	2064
10	Neon	27.10	63	Europium	1870
11	Sodium	1156.1	64	Gadolinium	3539
12	Magnesium	1363	65	Terbium	3396
13	Aluminium	2740	66	Dysprosium	2835
14	Silicon	2628	67	Holmium	2968
15	Phosphorus (P_4)	553	68	Erbium	3136
16	Sulfur	717.824	69	Thulium	2220
17	Chlorine	238.6	70	Ytterbium	1466
18	Argon	87.3	71	Lutetium	3668
19	Potassium	1047	72	Hafnium	5470
20	Calcium	1757	73	Tantalum	5698
21	Scandium	3104	74	Tungsten	5930
22	Titanium	3560	75	Rhenium	5900
23	Vanadium	3650	76	Osmium	5300
24	Chromium	2945	77	Iridium	4403
25	Manganese	2235	78	Platinum	4100
26	Iron	3023	79	Gold	3080
27	Cobalt	3143	80	Mercury	629.73
28	Nickel	3005	81	Thallium	1730
29	Copper	2840	82	Lead	2013
30	Zinc	1180	83	Bismuth	1883
31	Gallium	2676	84	Polonium	1235
32	Germanium	3103	85	Astatine	610 (est.)
33	Arsenic	889 (subl.)	86	Radon	211.4
34	Selenium	958.1	87	Francium	950
35	Bromine	331.9	88	Radium	1413
36	Krypton	120.85	89	Actinium	3470
37	Rubidium	961	90	Thorium	5060
38	Strontium	1657	91	Protactinium	c. 4300
39	Yttrium	3611	92	Uranium	4018
40	Zirconium	4650	93	Neptunium	4175
41	Niobium	5015	94	Plutonium	3505
42	Molybdenum	4885	95	Americium	2880
43	Technetium	5150	96	Curium	n.a.
44	Ruthenium	4173	97	Berkelium	n.a.
45	Rhodium	4000	98	Californium	n.a.
46	Palladium	3413	99	Einsteinium	n.a.
47	Silver	2485	100	Fermium	n.a.
48	Cadmium	1038	101	Mendelevium	n.a.
49	Indium	2353	102	Nobelium	n.a.
50	Tin	2543	103	Lawrencium	n.a.
51	Antimony	1908	104	Unnilquadium	n.a.
52	Tellurium	1263	105	Unnilpentium	n.a.
53	Iodine	457.50			

Table 6 Boiling points of the elements in order of temperature/K

74	Tungsten	5930		69	Thulium	2220
75	Rhenium	5900		62	Samarium	2064
73	Tantalum	5698		82	Lead	2013
72	Hafnium	5470		56	Barium	1910
76	Osmium	5300		51	Antimony	1908
43	Technetium	5150		63	Europium	1870
6	Carbon	5100 (subl.)		83	Bismuth	1833
90	Thorium	5060		20	Calcium	1757
41	Niobium	5015		81	Thallium	1730
42	Molybdenum	4885		38	Strontium	1657
40	Zirconium	4650		3	Lithium	1620
77	Iridium	4403		70	Ytterbium	1466
91	Protactinium	c. 4300		88	Radium	1413
93	Neptunium	4175		12	Magnesium	1363
44	Ruthenium	4173		52	Tellurium	1263
78	Platinum	4100		84	Polonium	1235
92	Uranium	4018		30	Zinc	1180
45	Rhodium	4000		11	Sodium	1156.1
5	Boron	3931		19	Potassium	1047
59	Praseodymium	3785		48	Cadmium	1038
57	Lanthanum	3730		37	Rubidium	961
58	Cerium	3699		34	Selenium	958.1
71	Lutetium	3668		55	Caesium	951.6
23	Vanadium	3650		87	Francium	950
39	Yttrium	3611		33	Arsenic	889 (subl.)
22	Titanium	3560		16	Sulfur	717.824
64	Gadolinium	3539		80	Mercury	629.73
94	Plutonium	3505		85	Astatine	610 (est)
89	Actinium	3470		15	Phosphorus (P$_4$)	553
46	Palladium	3413		53	Iodine	457.50
65	Terbium	3396		35	Bromine	331.9
60	Neodymium	3341		17	Chlorine	238.6
4	Beryllium	3243		00	Radon	211.4
27	Cobalt	3143		54	Xenon	166.1
68	Erbium	3136		36	Krypton	120.85
21	Scandium	3104		8	Oxygen	90.19
32	Germanium	3103		18	Argon	87.3
79	Gold	3080		9	Fluorine	85.01
26	Iron	3023		7	Nitrogen	77.4
28	Nickel	3005		10	Neon	27.10
61	Promethium	c. 3000		1	Hydrogen	20.28
67	Holmium	2968		2	Helium	4.216
24	Chromium	2945				
95	Americium	2880		96	Curium	n.a.
29	Copper	2840		97	Berkelium	n.a.
66	Dysprosium	2835		98	Californium	n.a.
13	Aluminium	2740		99	Einsteinium	n.a.
31	Gallium	2676		100	Fermium	n.a.
14	Silicon	2628		101	Mendelevium	n.a.
50	Tin	2543		102	Nobelium	n.a.
47	Silver	2485		103	Lawrencium	n.a.
49	Indium	2353		104	Unnilquadium	n.a.
25	Manganese	2235		105	Unnilpentium	n.a.

Table 7 Enthalpies of vaporization of the elements $\Delta H_{vap}/kJ\ mol^{-1}$

1	Hydrogen	0.46	54	Xenon	12.65
2	Helium	0.082	55	Caesium	66.5
3	Lithium	147.7	56	Barium	150.9
4	Beryllium	308.8	57	Lanthanum	402.1
5	Boron	504.5	58	Cerium	398
6	Carbon	710.9	59	Praseodymium	357
7	Nitrogen	5.58	60	Neodymium	328
8	Oxygen	6.82	61	Promethium	n.a.
9	Fluorine	3.26	62	Samarium	164.8
10	Neon	1.736	63	Europium	176
11	Sodium	99.2	64	Gadolinium	301
12	Magnesium	127.6	65	Terbium	391
13	Aluminium	290.8	66	Dysprosium	293
14	Silicon	383.3	67	Holmium	303
15	Phosphorus (P_4)	51.9	68	Erbium	280
16	Sulfur	9.62	69	Thulium	247
17	Chlorine	20.42	70	Ytterbium	159
18	Argon	6.53	71	Lutetium	428
19	Potassium	79.1	72	Hafnium	570.7
20	Calcium	150.6	73	Tantalum	758.22
21	Scandium	376.1	74	Tungsten	824.2
22	Titanium	425.5	75	Rhenium	704.25
23	Vanadium	459.7	76	Osmium	738.06
24	Chromium	341.8	77	Iridium	612.1
25	Manganese	220.5	78	Platinum	469
26	Iron	340.2	79	Gold	343.1
27	Cobalt	382.4	80	Mercury	59.11
28	Nickel	374.8	81	Thallium	166.1
29	Copper	306.7	82	Lead	177.8
30	Zinc	114.2	83	Bismuth	179.1
31	Gallium	270.3	84	Polonium	100.8
32	Germanium	327.6	85	Astatine	n.a.
33	Arsenic	31.9	86	Radon	18.1
34	Selenium	90	87	Francium	n.a.
35	Bromine	30.5	88	Radium	136.7
36	Krypton	9.05	89	Actinium	293
37	Rubidium	75.7	90	Thorium	513.7
38	Strontium	154.4	91	Protactinium	481
39	Yttrium	367.4	92	Uranium	417.1
40	Zirconium	566.7	93	Neptunium	336.6
41	Niobium	680.19	94	Plutonium	343.5
42	Molybdenum	589.9	95	Americium	238.5
43	Technetium	585.2	96	Curium	n.a.
44	Ruthenium	567	97	Berkelium	n.a.
45	Rhodium	494.3	98	Californium	n.a.
46	Palladium	361.5	99	Einsteinium	n.a.
47	Silver	257.7	100	Fermium	n.a.
48	Cadmium	100.0	101	Mendelevium	n.a.
49	Indium	231.8	102	Nobelium	n.a.
50	Tin	296.2	103	Lawrencium	n.a.
51	Antimony	165.8	104	Unnilquadium	n.a.
52	Tellurium	104.6	105	Unnilpentium	n.a.
53	Iodine	41.67			

Table 8 Enthalpies of vaporization of the elements ΔH_{vap} in order of $\Delta H_{vap}/kJ\ mol^{-1}$

74	Tungsten	824.2		**83**	Bismuth	179.1
73	Tantalum	758.22		**82**	Lead	177.8
76	Osmium	738.06		**63**	Europium	176
6	Carbon	710.9		**81**	Thallium	166.1
75	Rhenium	704.25		**51**	Antimony	165.8
41	Niobium	680.19		**62**	Samarium	164.8
77	Iridium	612.1		**70**	Ytterbium	159
42	Molybdenum	589.9		**38**	Strontium	154.4
43	Technetium	585.2		**56**	Barium	150.9
72	Hafnium	570.7		**20**	Calcium	150.6
44	Ruthenium	567		**3**	Lithium	147.7
40	Zirconium	566.7		**88**	Radium	136.7
90	Thorium	513.7		**12**	Magnesium	127.6
5	Boron	504.5		**30**	Zinc	114.2
45	Rhodium	494.3		**52**	Tellurium	104.6
91	Protactinium	481		**84**	Polonium	100.8
78	Platinum	469		**48**	Cadmium	100.0
23	Vanadium	459.7		**11**	Sodium	99.2
71	Lutetium	428		**34**	Selenium	90
22	Titanium	425.5		**19**	Potassium	79.1
92	Uranium	417.1		**37**	Rubidium	75.7
57	Lanthanum	402.1		**55**	Caesium	66.5
58	Cerium	398		**80**	Mercury	59.11
65	Terbium	391		**15**	Phosphorus (P_4)	51.9
14	Silicon	383.3		**53**	Iodine	41.67
27	Cobalt	382.4		**33**	Arsenic	31.9
21	Scandium	376.1		**35**	Bromine	30.5
28	Nickel	374.8		**17**	Chlorine	20.42
39	Yttrium	367.4		**86**	Radon	18.1
46	Palladium	361.5		**54**	Xenon	12.65
59	Praseodymium	357		**16**	Sulfur	9.62
94	Plutonium	343.5		**36**	Krypton	9.05
70	Gold	343.1		**8**	Oxygen	6.82
24	Chromium	341.8		**18**	Argon	6.53
26	Iron	340.2		**7**	Nitrogen	5.58
93	Neptunium	336.6		**9**	Fluorine	3.26
60	Neodymium	328		**10**	Neon	1.736
32	Germanium	327.6		**1**	Hydrogen	0.46
4	Beryllium	308.8		**2**	Helium	0.082
29	Copper	306.7				
67	Holmium	303		**61**	Promethium	n.a.
64	Gadolinium	301		**85**	Astatine	n.a.
50	Tin	296.2		**87**	Francium	n.a.
66	Dysprosium	293		**96**	Curium	n.a.
89	Actinium	293		**97**	Berkelium	n.a.
13	Aluminium	290.8		**98**	Californium	n.a.
68	Erbium	280		**99**	Einsteinium	n.a.
31	Gallium	270.3		**100**	Fermium	n.a.
47	Silver	257.7		**101**	Mendelevium	n.a.
69	Thulium	247		**102**	Nobelium	n.a.
95	Americium	238.5		**103**	Lawrencium	n.a.
49	Indium	231.8		**104**	Unnilquadium	n.a.
25	Manganese	220.5		**105**	Unnilpentium	n.a.

Table 9 Enthalpy of formation of gaseous atoms of the elements $\Delta H_f^{\ominus}/\text{kJ mol}^{-1}$ at 298.15 K and 0.1 MPa

1	Hydrogen	218.0	54	Xenon	0
2	Helium	0	55	Caesium	76.1
3	Lithium	159.4	56	Barium	180
4	Beryllium	324.3	57	Lanthanum	431.0
5	Boron	562.7	58	Cerium	423
6	Carbon	716.7	59	Praseodymium	355.6
7	Nitrogen	472.7	60	Neodymium	327.6
8	Oxygen	249.2	61	Promethium	n.a.
9	Fluorine	79.0	62	Samarium	206.7
10	Neon	0	63	Europium	175.3
11	Sodium	107.3	64	Gadolinium	397.5
12	Magnesium	147.7	65	Terbium	388.7
13	Aluminium	326.4	66	Dysprosium	290.4
14	Silicon	455.6	67	Holmium	300.8
15	Phosphorus	314.6	68	Erbium	317.1
16	Sulfur	278.8	69	Thulium	232.2
17	Chlorine	121.7	70	Ytterbium	152.3
18	Argon	0	71	Lutetium	427.6
19	Potassium	89.2	72	Hafnium	619.2
20	Calcium	178.2	73	Tantalum	782.0
21	Scandium	377.8	74	Tungsten	849.4
22	Titanium	469.9	75	Rhenium	769.9
23	Vanadium	514.2	76	Osmium	791
24	Chromium	396.6	77	Iridium	665.3
25	Manganese	280.7	78	Platinum	565.3
26	Iron	416.3	79	Gold	366.1
27	Cobalt	424.7	80	Mercury	61.3
28	Nickel	429.7	81	Thallium	182.2
29	Copper	338.3	82	Lead	195.0
30	Zinc	130.7	83	Bismuth	207.1
31	Gallium	277.0	84	Polonium	146
32	Germanium	376.6	85	Astatine	n.a.
33	Arsenic	302.5	86	Radon	0
34	Selenium	227.1	87	Francium	72.8
35	Bromine	111.9	88	Radium	159
36	Krypton	0	89	Actinium	406
37	Rubidium	80.9	90	Thorium	598.3
38	Strontium	164.4	91	Protactinium	607
39	Yttrium	421.3	92	Uranium	535.6
40	Zirconium	608.8	93	Neptunium	n.a.
41	Niobium	725.9	94	Plutonium	n.a.
42	Molybdenum	658.1	95	Americium	n.a.
43	Technetium	678	96	Curium	n.a.
44	Ruthenium	642.7	97	Berkelium	n.a.
45	Rhodium	556.9	98	Californium	n.a.
46	Palladium	378.2	99	Einsteinium	n.a.
47	Silver	284.6	100	Fermium	n.a.
48	Cadmium	112.0	101	Mendelevium	n.a.
49	Indium	243.3	102	Nobelium	n.a.
50	Tin	302.1	103	Lawrencium	n.a.
51	Antimony	262.3	104	Unnilquadium	n.a.
52	Tellurium	196.7	105	Unnilpentium	n.a.
53	Iodine	106.8			

Table 10 Enthalpy of formation of gaseous atoms of the elements $\Delta H_f^{\ominus}$ at 298.15 K and 0.1 MPa in order of $\Delta H_f^{\ominus}/kJ\ mol^{-1}$

74	Tungsten	849.4	8	Oxygen	249.2
76	Osmium	791	49	Indium	243.3
73	Tantalum	782.0	69	Thulium	232.2
75	Rhenium	769.9	34	Selenium	227.1
41	Niobium	725.9	1	Hydrogen	218.0
6	Carbon	716.7	83	Bismuth	207.1
43	Technetium	678	62	Samarium	206.7
77	Iridium	665.3	52	Tellurium	196.7
42	Molybdenum	658.1	82	Lead	195.0
44	Ruthenium	642.7	81	Thallium	182.2
72	Hafnium	619.2	56	Barium	180
40	Zirconium	608.8	20	Calcium	178.2
91	Protactinium	607	63	Europium	175.3
90	Thorium	598.3	38	Strontium	164.4
78	Platinum	565.3	3	Lithium	159.4
5	Boron	562.7	88	Radium	159
45	Rhodium	556.9	70	Ytterbium	152.3
92	Uranium	535.6	12	Magnesium	147.7
23	Vanadium	514.2	84	Polonium	146
7	Nitrogen	472.7	30	Zinc	130.7
22	Titanium	469.9	17	Chlorine	121.7
14	Silicon	455.6	48	Cadmium	112.0
57	Lanthanum	431.0	35	Bromine	111.9
28	Nickel	429.7	11	Sodium	107.3
71	Lutetium	427.6	53	Iodine	106.8
27	Cobalt	424.7	19	Potassium	89.2
58	Cerium	423	37	Rubidium	80.9
39	Yttrium	421.3	9	Fluorine	79.0
26	Iron	416.3	55	Caesium	76.1
89	Actinium	406	87	Francium	72.8
64	Gadolinium	397.5	80	Mercury	61.3
24	Chromium	396.6	2	Helium	0
65	Terbium	388.7	10	Neon	0
46	Palladium	378.2	18	Argon	0
21	Scandium	377.8	36	Krypton	0
32	Germanium	376.6	54	Xenon	0
79	Gold	366.1	86	Radon	0
59	Praseodymium	355.6			
29	Copper	338.3	61	Promethium	n.a.
60	Neodymium	327.6	85	Astatine	n.a.
13	Aluminium	326.4	93	Neptunium	n.a.
4	Beryllium	324.3	94	Plutonium	n.a.
68	Erbium	317.1	95	Americium	n.a.
15	Phosphorus	314.6	96	Curium	n.a.
33	Arsenic	302.5	97	Berkelium	n.a.
50	Tin	302.1	98	Californium	n.a.
67	Holmium	300.8	99	Einsteinium	n.a.
66	Dysprosium	290.4	100	Fermium	n.a.
47	Silver	284.6	101	Mendelevium	n.a.
25	Manganese	280.7	102	Nobelium	n.a.
16	Sulfur	278.8	103	Lawrencium	n.a.
31	Gallium	277.0	104	Unnilquadium	n.a.
51	Antimony	262.3	105	Unnilpentium	n.a.

Table 11 Densities of the solid elements at 298 K, unless otherwise specified/kg m^{-3}

1	Hydrogen [11 K]	76.0	54	Xenon	3540
2	Helium (liq., 4 K)	124.8	55	Caesium	1873
3	Lithium	534	56	Barium	3594
4	Beryllium	1847.7	57	Lanthanum	6145
5	Boron	2340	58	Cerium (α)	8240
6	Carbon (diam.)	3513	59	Praseodymium	6773
7	Nitrogen [21 K]	1026	60	Neodymium	7007
8	Oxygen [55 K]	2000	61	Promethium	7220
9	Fluorine (liq., 85 K)	1516	62	Samarium	7520
10	Neon [24 K]	1444	63	Europium	5243
11	Sodium	971	64	Gadolinium	7900.4
12	Magnesium	1738	65	Terbium	8229
13	Aluminium	2698	66	Dysprosium	8550
14	Silicon	2329	67	Holmium	8795
15	Phosphorus (P_4)	1820	68	Erbium	9066
16	Sulfur (α)	2070	69	Thulium	9321
17	Chlorine [113 K]	2030	70	Ytterbium	6965
18	Argon [40 K]	1656	71	Lutetium	9840
19	Potassium	862	72	Hafnium	13 310
20	Calcium	1550	73	Tantalum	16 654
21	Scandium	2989	74	Tungsten	19 300
22	Titanium	4540	75	Rhenium	21 020
23	Vanadium	6110	76	Osmium	22 590
24	Chromium	7190	77	Iridium	22 420
25	Manganese	7440	78	Platinum	21 450
26	Iron	7874	79	Gold	19 320
27	Cobalt	8900	80	Mercury (liq.)	13 546
28	Nickel	8902	81	Thallium	11 850
29	Copper	8960	82	Lead	11 350
30	Zinc	7133	83	Bismuth	9747
31	Gallium	5907	84	Polonium	9320
32	Germanium	5323	85	Astatine	n.a.
33	Arsenic (α)	5780	86	Radon (liq., 211 K)	4400
34	Selenium	4790	87	Francium	n.a.
35	Bromine [123 K]	4050	88	Radium	*c.* 5000
36	Krypton [117 K]	2823	89	Actinium	10 060
37	Rubidium	1532	90	Thorium	11 720
38	Strontium	2540	91	Protactinium	15 370 (est.)
39	Yttrium	4469	92	Uranium	18 950
40	Zirconium	6506	93	Neptunium	20 250
41	Niobium	8570	94	Plutonium	19 840
42	Molybdenum	10 220	95	Americium	13 670
43	Technetium	11 500	96	Curium	13 300
44	Ruthenium	12 370	97	Berkelium	14 790
45	Rhodium	12 410	98	Californium	n.a.
46	Palladium	12 020	99	Einsteinium	n.a.
47	Silver	10 500	100	Fermium	n.a.
48	Cadmium	8650	101	Mendelevium	n.a.
49	Indium	7310	102	Nobelium	n.a.
50	Tin (β)	7310	103	Lawrencium	n.a.
51	Antimony	6691	104	Unnilquadium	n.a.
52	Tellurium	6240	105	Unnilpentium	n.a.
53	Iodine	4930			

Table 12 Densities of the solid elements at 298 K, unless otherwise specified, in order of density/kg m^{-3}

76	Osmium	22 590	40	Zirconium	6506
77	Iridium	22 420	52	Tellurium	6240
78	Platinum	21 450	57	Lanthanum	6145
75	Rhenium	21 020	23	Vanadium	6110
93	Neptunium	20 250	31	Gallium	5907
94	Plutonium	19 840	33	Arsenic (α)	5780
79	Gold	19 320	32	Germanium	5323
74	Tungsten	19 300	63	Europium	5243
92	Uranium	18 950	88	Radium $\quad c.$	5000
73	Tantalum	16 654	53	Iodine	4930
91	Protactinium	15 370 (est)	34	Selenium	4790
97	Berkelium	14 790	22	Titanium	4540
95	Americium	13 670	39	Yttrium	4469
80	Mercury (liq.)	13 546	86	Radon (liq., 211 K)	4400
72	Hafnium	13 310	35	Bromine [123 K]	4050
96	Curium	13 300	56	Barium	3594
45	Rhodium	12 410	54	Xenon	3540
44	Ruthenium	12 370	6	Carbon (diam.)	3513
46	Palladium	12 020	21	Scandium	2989
81	Thallium	11 850	36	Krypton [117 K]	2823
90	Thorium	11 720	13	Aluminium	2698
43	Technetium	11 500	38	Strontium	2540
82	Lead	11 350	5	Boron	2340
47	Silver	10 500	14	Silicon	2329
42	Molybdenum	10 220	16	Sulfur (α)	2070
89	Actinium	10 060	17	Chlorine [113 K]	2030
71	Lutetium	9840	8	Oxygen [55 K]	2000
83	Bismuth	9747	55	Caesium	1873
69	Thulium	9321	4	Beryllium	1847.7
84	Polonium	9320	15	Phosphorus (P_4)	1820
68	Erbium	9066	12	Magnesium	1738
29	Copper	8960	18	Argon [40 K]	1656
28	Nickel	8902	20	Calcium	1550
27	Cobalt	8900	37	Rubidium	1532
67	Holmium	8795	9	Fluorine (liq., 85 K)	1516
48	Cadmium	8650	10	Neon [24 K]	1444
41	Niobium	8570	7	Nitrogen [21 K]	1026
66	Dysprosium	8550	11	Sodium	971
58	Cerium (α)	8240	19	Potassium	862
65	Terbium	8229	3	Lithium	534
64	Gadolinium	7900.4	2	Helium (liq., 4 K)	124.8
26	Iron	7874	1	Hydrogen [11 K]	76.0
62	Samarium	7520			
25	Manganese	7440	85	Astatine	n.a.
49	Indium	7310	87	Francium	n.a.
50	Tin (β)	7310	98	Californium	n.a.
61	Promethium	7220	99	Einsteinium	n.a.
24	Chromium	7190	100	Fermium	n.a.
30	Zinc	7133	101	Mendelevium	n.a.
60	Neodymium	7007	102	Nobelium	n.a.
70	Ytterbium	6965	103	Lawrencium	n.a.
59	Praseodymium	6773	104	Unnilquadium	n.a.
51	Antimony	6691	105	Unnilpentium	n.a.

Table 13 Electrical resistivities of the elements at 298 K/10^{-8} Ωm

1	Hydrogen	n.a.	54	Xenon	n.a.
2	Helium	n.a.	55	Caesium	20.0
3	Lithium	8.55	56	Barium	50
4	Beryllium	4.0	57	Lanthanum	57
5	Boron	1.8×10^{12}	58	Cerium	73
6	Carbon (graph.)	1.375×10^3	59	Praseodymium	68
7	Nitrogen	n.a.	60	Neodymium	64.0
8	Oxygen	n.a.	61	Promethium	50 (est.)
9	Fluorine	n.a.	62	Samarium	88.0
10	Neon	n.a.	63	Europium	90.0
11	Sodium	4.2	64	Gadolinium	134.0
12	Magnesium	4.45	65	Terbium	114
13	Aluminium	2.6548	66	Dysprosium	57.0
14	Silicon	1×10^5	67	Holmium	87.0
15	Phosphorus (P_4)	1×10^{17}	68	Erbium	87
16	Sulfur	2×10^{23}	69	Thulium	79.0
17	Chlorine	n.a.	70	Ytterbium	29.0
18	Argon	n.a.	71	Lutetium	79.0
19	Potassium	6.15	72	Hafnium	35.1
20	Calcium	3.43	73	Tantalum	12.45
21	Scandium	61.0	74	Tungsten	5.65
22	Titanium	42.0	75	Rhenium	19.3
23	Vanadium	24.8	76	Osmium	8.12
24	Chromium	12.7	77	Iridium	5.3
25	Manganese	185.0	78	Platinum	10.6
26	Iron	9.71	79	Gold	2.35
27	Cobalt	6.24	80	Mercury	94.1
28	Nickel	6.84	81	Thallium	18.0
29	Copper	1.6730	82	Lead	20.648
30	Zinc	5.916	83	Bismuth	106.8
31	Gallium	27	84	Polonium	140
32	Germanium	4.6×10^5	85	Astatine	n.a.
33	Arsenic	26	86	Radon	n.a.
34	Selenium	1×10^6	87	Francium	n.a.
35	Bromine	n.a.	88	Radium	100
36	Krypton	n.a.	89	Actinium	n.a.
37	Rubidium	12.5	90	Thorium	13.0
38	Strontium	23.0	91	Protactinium	17.7
39	Yttrium	57.0	92	Uranium	30.8
40	Zirconium	40.0	93	Neptunium	122
41	Niobium	12.5	94	Plutonium	146
42	Molybdenum	5.2	95	Americium	68
43	Technetium	22.6 (373 K)	96	Curium	n.a.
44	Ruthenium	7.6	97	Berkelium	n.a.
45	Rhodium	4.51	98	Californium	n.a.
46	Palladium	10.8	99	Einsteinium	n.a.
47	Silver	1.59	100	Fermium	n.a.
48	Cadmium	6.83	101	Mendelevium	n.a.
49	Indium	8.37	102	Nobelium	n.a.
50	Tin (α)	11.0	103	Lawrencium	n.a.
51	Antimony	39.0	104	Unnilquadium	n.a.
52	Tellurium	4.36×10^5	105	Unnilpentium	n.a.
53	Iodine	1.3×10^{15}			

Table 14 Electrical resistivities of the elements at 298 K in order of resistivity/10^{-8} Ωm

16	Sulfur	2×10^{23}	41	Niobium	12.5
15	Phosphorus (P_4)	1×10^{17}	73	Tantalum	12.45
53	Iodine	1.3×10^{15}	50	Tin (α)	11.0
5	Boron	1.8×10^{12}	46	Palladium	10.8
34	Selenium	1×10^{6}	78	Platinum	10.6
32	Germanium	4.6×10^{5}	26	Iron	9.71
52	Tellurium	4.36×10^{5}	3	Lithium	8.55
14	Silicon	1×10^{5}	49	Indium	8.37
6	Carbon (graph.)	1375	76	Osmium	8.12
25	Manganese	185.0	44	Ruthenium	7.6
94	Plutonium	146	28	Nickel	6.84
84	Polonium	140	48	Cadmium	6.83
64	Gadolinium	134.0	27	Cobalt	6.24
93	Neptunium	122	19	Potassium	6.15
65	Terbium	114	30	Zinc	5.916
83	Bismuth	106.8	74	Tungsten	5.65
88	Radium	100	77	Iridium	5.3
80	Mercury	94.1	42	Molybdenum	5.2
63	Europium	90.0	45	Rhodium	4.51
62	Samarium	88.0	12	Magnesium	4.45
67	Holmium	87.0	11	Sodium	4.2
68	Erbium	87	4	Beryllium	4.0
69	Thulium	79.0	20	Calcium	3.43
71	Lutetium	79.0	13	Aluminium	2.6548
58	Cerium	73	79	Gold	2.35
59	Praseodymium	68	29	Copper	1.6730
95	Americium	68	47	Silver	1.59
60	Neodymium	64.0			
21	Scandium	61.0	1	Hydrogen	n.a.
66	Dysprosium	57.0	2	Helium	n.a.
39	Yttrium	57.0	7	Nitrogen	n.a.
57	Lanthanum	57	8	Oxygen	n.a.
56	Barium	50	9	Fluorine	n.a.
61	Promethium	50 (est.)	10	Neon	n.a.
22	Titanium	42.0	17	Chlorine	n.a.
40	Zirconium	40.0	18	Argon	n.a.
51	Antimony	39.0	35	Bromine	n.a.
72	Hafnium	35.1	36	Krypton	n.a.
92	Uranium	30.8	54	Xenon	n.a.
70	Ytterbium	29.0	85	Astatine	n.a.
31	Gallium	27	86	Radon	n.a.
33	Arsenic	26	87	Francium	n.a.
23	Vanadium	24.8	89	Actinium	n.a.
38	Strontium	23.0	96	Curium	n.a.
43	Technetium	22.6 (373 K)	97	Berkelium	n.a.
82	Lead	20.648	98	Californium	n.a.
55	Caesium	20.0	99	Einsteinium	n.a.
75	Rhenium	19.3	100	Fermium	n.a.
81	Thallium	18.0	101	Mendelevium	n.a.
91	Protactinium	17.7	102	Nobelium	n.a.
90	Thorium	13.0	103	Lawrencium	n.a.
24	Chromium	12.7	104	Unnilquadium	n.a.
37	Rubidium	12.5	105	Unnilpentium	n.a.

Table 15 NMR frequencies of nuclei* at a field of 2.3488 T (^{1}H = 100 MHz)/MHz

#	Nucleus	Freq	#	Nucleus	Freq
1	Hydrogen	100.000	54	Xenon-129	27.660
2	Helium-3	76.178	55	Caesium-133	13.117
3	Lithium-7	38.863	56	Barium-137	11.113
4	Beryllium-9	14.053	57	Lanthanum-139	14.126
5	Boron-11	32.084	58	Cerium-139	10.862
6	Carbon-13	25.144	59	Praseodymium-141	29.291
7	Nitrogen-15	10.133	60	Neodymium-143	5.437
8	Oxygen-17	13.557	61	Promethium-147	13.51
9	Fluorine-19	94.077	62	Samarium-147	4.128
10	Neon-21	7.894	63	Europium-151	24.801
11	Sodium-23	26.451	64	Gadolinium-155	3.819
12	Magnesium-25	6.120	65	Terbium-159	22.678
13	Aluminium-27	26.057	66	Dysprosium-163	4.583
14	Silicon-29	19.865	67	Holmium-165	20.513
15	Phosphorus-31	40.481	68	Erbium-167	2.890
16	Sulfur-33	7.670	69	Thulium-169	8.271
17	Chlorine-35	9.798	70	Ytterbium-171	17.613
18	Argon-39	6.6	71	Lutetium-175	11.407
19	Potassium-39	4.667	72	Hafnium-177	3.120
20	Calcium-43	6.728	73	Tantalum-181	11.970
21	Scandium-45	24.290	74	Tungsten-183	4.161
22	Titanium-49	5.638	75	Rhenium-187	22.513
23	Vanadium-51	26.289	76	Osmium-187	2.282
24	Chromium-53	5.652	77	Iridium-191	1.718
25	Manganese-55	24.664	78	Platinum-195	21.499
26	Iron-57	3.231	79	Gold-197	1.712
27	Cobalt-59	23.614	80	Mercury-199	17.827
28	Nickel-61	8.936	81	Thallium-205	57.708
29	Copper-63	26.505	82	Lead-207	20.921
30	Zinc-67	6.254	83	Bismuth-209	16.069
31	Gallium-71	30.495	84	Polonium-209	28
32	Germanium-73	3.488	85	Astatine	n.a.
33	Arsenic-75	17.126	86	Radon	n.a.
34	Selenium-77	19.092	87	Francium	n.a.
35	Bromine-81	27.006	88	Radium	n.a.
36	Krypton-83	3.847	89	Actinium-227	13.1
37	Rubidium-87	32.721	90	Thorium-229	1.5
38	Strontium-87	4.333	91	Protactinium-231	12.0
39	Yttrium-89	4.899	92	Uranium-235	1.790
40	Zirconium-91	9.330	93	Neptunium-237	11.25
41	Niobium-93	24.442	94	Plutonium-239	3.63
42	Molybdenum-95	6.514	95	Americium-241	5.76
43	Technetium-99	22.508	96	Curium-247	0.75
44	Ruthenium-101	4.941	97	Berkelium	n.a.
45	Rhodium-103	3.172	98	Californium	n.a.
46	Palladium-105	4.576	99	Einsteinium	n.a.
47	Silver-109	4.652	100	Fermium	n.a.
48	Cadmium-113	22.182	101	Mendelevium	n.a.
49	Indium-115	21.914	102	Nobelium	n.a.
50	Tin-119	37.272	103	Lawrencium	n.a.
51	Antimony-121	23.930	104	Unnilquodium	n.a.
52	Tellurium-125	31.596	105	Unnilpentium	n.a.
53	Iodine-127	20.007			

*Where there are two or more isotopes that can be observed by NMR spectroscopy, only the one that is commonly used is included in this table.

Table 16 NMR frequencies of nuclei* at a field of 2.3488 T
(^{1}H = 100 MHz) in order of frequency/MHz

1	Hydrogen-1	100.000	58	Cerium-139	10.862
9	Fluorine-19	94.077	7	Nitrogen-15	10.133
2	Helium-3	76.178	17	Chlorine-35	9.798
81	Thallium-205	57.708	40	Zirconium-91	9.330
15	Phosphorus-31	40.481	28	Nickel-61	8.936
3	Lithium-7	38.863	69	Thulium-169	8.271
50	Tin-119	37.272	10	Neon-21	7.894
37	Rubidium-87	32.721	16	Sulfur-33	7.670
5	Boron-11	32.084	20	Calcium-43	6.728
52	Tellurium-125	31.596	18	Argon-39	6.6
31	Gallium-71	30.495	42	Molybdenum-95	6.514
59	Praseodymium-141	29.291	30	Zinc-67	6.254
84	Polonium-209	28	12	Magnesium-25	6.120
54	Xenon-129	27.660	24	Chromium-53	5.652
35	Bromine-81	27.006	22	Titanium-49	5.638
29	Copper-63	26.505	60	Neodymium-143	5.437
11	Sodium-23	26.451	44	Ruthenium-101	4.941
23	Vanadium-51	26.289	39	Yttrium-89	4.899
13	Aluminium-27	26.057	19	Potassium-39	4.667
6	Carbon-13	25.144	47	Silver-109	4.652
63	Europium-151	24.801	66	Dysprosium-163	4.583
25	Manganese-55	24.664	46	Palladium-105	4.576
41	Niobium-93	24.442	38	Strontium-87	4.333
21	Scandium-45	24.290	74	Tungsten-183	4.161
51	Antimony-121	23.930	62	Samarium-147	4.128
27	Cobalt-59	23.614	36	Krypton-83	3.847
65	Terbium-159	22.678	64	Gadolinium-155	3.819
75	Rhenium-187	22.513	94	Plutonium-239	3.63
43	Technetium-99	22.508	32	Germanium-73	3.488
48	Cadmium-113	22.182	26	Iron-57	3.231
49	Indium-115	21.914	45	Rhodium-103	3.172
78	Platinum-195	21.499	72	Hafnium-177	3.120
82	Lead-207	20.921	68	Erbium-167	2.890
67	Holmium-165	20.513	76	Osmium-187	2.282
53	Iodine-127	20.007	92	Uranium-235	1.790
14	Silicon-29	19.865	77	Iridium-191	1.718
34	Selenium-77	19.092	79	Gold-197	1.712
80	Mercury-199	17.827	90	Thorium-229	1.5
70	Ytterbium-171	17.613	96	Curium-247	0.75
33	Arsenic-75	17.126	85	Astatine	n.a.
83	Bismuth-209	16.069	86	Radon	n.a.
57	Lanthanum-139	14.126	87	Francium	n.a.
4	Beryllium-9	14.053	88	Radium	n.a.
8	Oxygen-17	13.557	97	Berkelium	n.a.
61	Promethium-147	13.51	98	Californium	n.a.
55	Caesium-133	13.117	99	Einsteinium	n.a.
89	Actinium-227	13.1	100	Fermium	n.a.
91	Protactinium-231	12.0	101	Mendelevium	n.a.
73	Tantalum-181	11.970	102	Nobelium	n.a.
71	Lutetium-175	11.407	103	Lawrencium	n.a.
93	Neptunium-237	11.25	104	Unnilquadium	n.a.
56	Barium-137	11.113	105	Unnilpentium	n.a.

*Where there are two or more isotopes that can be observed by NMR spectroscopy, only the one that is commonly used is included in this table.

Table 17 Ionization energies of neutral atoms
$\Delta E(M \rightarrow M^+)/kJ\ mol^{-1}$

1	Hydrogen	1312.0	54	Xenon	1170.4
2	Helium	2372.3	55	Caesium	375.7
3	Lithium	513.3	56	Barium	502.8
4	Beryllium	899.4	57	Lanthanum	538.1
5	Boron	800.6	58	Cerium	527.4
6	Carbon	1086.2	59	Praseodymium	523.1
7	Nitrogen	1402.3	60	Neodymium	529.6
8	Oxygen	1313.9	61	Promethium	535.9
9	Fluorine	1681	62	Samarium	543.3
10	Neon	2080.6	63	Europium	546.7
11	Sodium	495.8	64	Gadolinium	592.5
12	Magnesium	737.7	65	Terbium	564.6
13	Aluminium	577.4	66	Dysprosium	571.9
14	Silicon	786.5	67	Holmium	580.7
15	Phosphorus	1011.7	68	Erbium	588.7
16	Sulfur	999.6	69	Thulium	596.7
17	Chlorine	1251.1	70	Ytterbium	603.4
18	Argon	1520.4	71	Lutetium	523.5
19	Potassium	418.8	72	Hafnium	642
20	Calcium	589.7	73	Tantalum	761
21	Scandium	631	74	Tungsten	770
22	Titanium	658	75	Rhenium	760
23	Vanadium	650	76	Osmium	840
24	Chromium	652.7	77	Iridium	880
25	Manganese	717.4	78	Platinum	870
26	Iron	759.3	79	Gold	890.1
27	Cobalt	760.0	80	Mercury	1007.0
28	Nickel	736.7	81	Thallium	589.3
29	Copper	745.4	82	Lead	715.5
30	Zinc	906.4	83	Bismuth	703.2
31	Gallium	578.8	84	Polonium	812
32	Germanium	762.1	85	Astatine	930
33	Arsenic	947.0	86	Radon	1037
34	Selenium	940.9	87	Francium	400
35	Bromine	1139.9	88	Radium	509.3
36	Krypton	1350.7	89	Actinium	499
37	Rubidium	403.0	90	Thorium	587
38	Strontium	549.5	91	Protactinium	568
39	Yttrium	616	92	Uranium	584
40	Zirconium	660	93	Neptunium	597
41	Niobium	664	94	Plutonium	585
42	Molybdenum	685.0	95	Americium	578.2
43	Technetium	702	96	Curium	581
44	Ruthenium	711	97	Berkelium	601
45	Rhodium	720	98	Californium	608
46	Palladium	805	99	Einsteinium	619
47	Silver	731.0	100	Fermium	627
48	Cadmium	867.6	101	Mendelevium	635
49	Indium	558.3	102	Nobelium	642
50	Tin	708.6	103	Lawrencium	n.a.
51	Antimony	833.7	104	Unnilquandium	n.a.
52	Tellurium	869.2	105	Unnilpentium	n.a.
53	Iodine	1008.4			

Table 18 Ionization energies of neutral atoms $\Delta E(M \rightarrow M^+)$ in order of energy/kJ mol^{-1}

2	Helium	2372.3	22	Titanium	658
10	Neon	2080.6	24	Chromium	652.7
9	Fluorine	1681	23	Vanadium	650
18	Argon	1520.4	72	Hafnium	642
7	Nitrogen	1402.3	102	Nobelium	642
36	Krypton	1350.7	101	Mendelevium	635
8	Oxygen	1313.9	21	Scandium	631
1	Hydrogen	1312.0	100	Fermium	630
17	Chlorine	1251.1	99	Einsteinium	619
54	Xenon	1170.4	39	Yttrium	616
35	Bromine	1139.9	98	Californium	608
6	Carbon	1086.2	70	Ytterbium	603.4
86	Radon	1037	97	Berkelium	601
15	Phosphorus	1011.7	93	Neptunium	597
53	Iodine	1008.4	69	Thulium	596.7
80	Mercury	1007.0	64	Gadolinium	592.5
16	Sulfur	999.6	20	Calcium	589.7
33	Arsenic	947.0	81	Thallium	589.3
34	Selenium	940.9	68	Erbium	588.7
85	Astatine	930	90	Thorium	587
30	Zinc	906.4	94	Plutonium	585
4	Beryllium	899.4	92	Uranium	584
79	Gold	890.1	96	Curium	581
77	Iridium	880	67	Holmium	580.7
78	Platinum	870	31	Gallium	578.8
52	Tellurium	869.2	95	Americium	578.2
48	Cadmium	867.6	13	Aluminium	577.4
76	Osmium	840	66	Dysprosium	571.9
51	Antimony	833.7	91	Protactinium	568
84	Polonium	812	65	Terbium	564.6
46	Palladium	805	49	Indium	558.3
5	Boron	800.6	38	Strontium	549.5
14	Silicon	786.5	63	Europium	546.7
74	Tungsten	770	62	Samarium	543.3
32	Germanium	762.1	57	Lanthanum	538.1
73	Tantalum	761	61	Promethium	535.9
27	Cobalt	760.0	60	Neodymium	529.6
75	Rhenium	760	58	Cerium	527.4
26	Iron	759.3	71	Lutetium	523.5
29	Copper	745.4	59	Praseodymium	523.1
12	Magnesium	737.7	3	Lithium	513.3
28	Nickel	736.7	88	Radium	509.3
47	Silver	731.0	56	Barium	502.8
45	Rhodium	720	89	Actinium	499
25	Manganese	717.4	11	Sodium	495.8
82	Lead	715.5	19	Potassium	418.8
44	Ruthenium	711	37	Rubidium	403.0
50	Tin	708.6	87	Francium	400
83	Bismuth	703.2	55	Caesium	375.7
43	Technetium	702			
42	Molybdenum	685.0	103	Lawrencium	n.a.
41	Niobium	664	104	Unnilquadium	n.a.
40	Zirconium	660	105	Unnilpentum	n.a.

Table 19 Abundance of elements in the Earth's crust
[p.p.m. = g per tonne (1000 kg)]

1	Hydrogen	1520	54	Xenon	2×10^{-6}
2	Helium	0.008	55	Caesium	3
3	Lithium	20	56	Barium	500
4	Beryllium	2.6	57	Lanthanum	32
5	Boron	10	58	Cerium	68
6	Carbon	480	59	Praseodymium	9.5
7	Nitrogen	25	60	Neodymium	38
8	Oxygen	474 000	61	Promethium	trace
9	Fluorine	950	62	Samarium	7.9
10	Neon	7×10^{-5}	63	Europium	2.1
11	Sodium	23 000	64	Gadolinium	7.7
12	Magnesium	23 000	65	Terbium	1.1
13	Aluminium	82 000	66	Dysprosium	6
14	Silicon	277 000	67	Holmium	1.4
15	Phosphorus	1000	68	Erbium	3.8
16	Sulfur	260	69	Thulium	0.48
17	Chlorine	130	70	Ytterbium	5.3
18	Argon	1.2	71	Lutetium	0.51
19	Potassium	21 000	72	Hafnium	3.3
20	Calcium	41 000	73	Tantalum	2
21	Scandium	16	74	Tungsten	1
22	Titanium	5600	75	Rhenium	4×10^{-4}
23	Vanadium	160	76	Osmium	1×10^{-4}
24	Chromium	100	77	Iridium	3×10^{-6}
25	Manganese	950	78	Platinum	$c.\ 0.001$
26	Iron	41 000	79	Gold	0.0011
27	Cobalt	20	80	Mercury	0.05
28	Nickel	80	81	Thallium	0.6
29	Copper	50	82	Lead	14
30	Zinc	75	83	Bismuth	0.048
31	Gallium	18	84	Polonium	trace
32	Germanium	1.8	85	Astatine	trace
33	Arsenic	1.5	86	Radon	trace
34	Selenium	0.05	87	Francium	nil
35	Bromine	0.37	88	Radium	6×10^{-7}
36	Krypton	1×10^{-5}	89	Actinium	trace
37	Rubidium	90	90	Thorium	12
38	Strontium	370	91	Protactinium	trace
39	Yttrium	30	92	Uranium	2.4
40	Zirconium	190	93	Neptunium	nil
41	Niobium	20	94	Plutonium	trace
42	Molybdenum	1.5	95	Americium	nil
43	Technetium	7×10^{-4}	96	Curium	nil
44	Ruthenium	$c.\ 0.001$	97	Berkelium	nil
45	Rhodium	2×10^{-4}	98	Californium	nil
46	Palladium	6×10^{-4}	99	Einsteinium	nil
47	Silver	0.07	100	Fermium	nil
48	Cadmium	0.11	101	Mendelevium	nil
49	Indium	0.049	102	Nobelium	nil
50	Tin	2.2	103	Lawrencium	nil
51	Antimony	0.2	104	Unnilquadium	nil
52	Tellurium	$c.\ 0.005$	105	Unnilpentium	nil
53	Iodine	0.14			

Table 20 Abundance of elements in the Earth's crust in order of abundance [p.p.m. = g per tonne (1000 kg)]

#	Element	Abundance		#	Element	Abundance
8	Oxygen	474 000		42	Molybdenum	1.5
14	Silicon	277 000		67	Holmium	1.4
13	Aluminium	82 000		18	Argon	1.2
26	Iron	41 000		65	Terbium	1.1
20	Calcium	41 000		74	Tungsten	1
11	Sodium	23 000		81	Thallium	0.6
12	Magnesium	23 000		71	Lutetium	0.51
19	Potassium	21 000		69	Thulium	0.48
22	Titanium	5600		35	Bromine	0.37
1	Hydrogen	1520		51	Antimony	0.2
15	Phosphorus	1000		53	Iodine	0.14
25	Manganese	950		48	Cadmium	0.11
9	Fluorine	950		47	Silver	0.07
56	Barium	500		34	Selenium	0.05
6	Carbon	480		80	Mercury	0.05
38	Strontium	370		49	Indium	0.049
16	Sulfur	260		83	Bismuth	0.048
40	Zirconium	190		2	Helium	0.008
23	Vanadium	160		52	Tellurium	$c.$ 0.005
17	Chlorine	130		79	Gold	0.0011
24	Chromium	100		44	Ruthenium	$c.$ 0.001
37	Rubidium	90		78	Platinum	$c.$ 0.001
28	Nickel	80		43	Technetium	7×10^{-4}
30	Zinc	75		46	Palladium	6×10^{-4}
58	Cerium	68		75	Rhenium	4×10^{-4}
29	Copper	50		45	Rhodium	2×10^{-4}
60	Neodymium	38		76	Osmium	1×10^{-4}
57	Lanthanum	32		10	Neon	7×10^{-5}
39	Yttrium	30		36	Krypton	1×10^{-5}
7	Nitrogen	25		77	Iridium	3×10^{-6}
3	Lithium	20		54	Xenon	2×10^{-6}
27	Cobalt	20		88	Radium	6×10^{-7}
41	Niobium	20		61	Promethium	trace
31	Gallium	18		84	Polonium	trace
21	Scandium	16		85	Astatine	trace
82	Lead	14		86	Radon	trace
90	Thorium	12		89	Actinium	trace
5	Boron	10		91	Protactinium	trace
59	Praseodymium	9.5		94	Plutonium	trace
62	Samarium	7.9		87	Francium	nil
64	Gadolinium	7.7		93	Neptunium	nil
66	Dysprosium	6		95	Americium	nil
70	Ytterbium	5.3		96	Curium	nil
68	Erbium	3.8		97	Berkelium	nil
72	Hafnium	3.3		98	Californium	nil
55	Caesium	3		99	Einsteinium	nil
4	Beryllium	2.6		100	Fermium	nil
92	Uranium	2.4		101	Mendelevium	nil
50	Tin	2.2		102	Nobelium	nil
63	Europium	2.1		103	Lawrencium	nil
73	Tantalum	2		104	Unnilquadium	nil
32	Germanium	1.8		105	Unnilpentium	nil
33	Arsenic	1.5				

Index

The elements are listed alphabetically in the main part of the book. The following properties are given for each element where known. Some properties are listed in separate tables, pp. 223–47, for all the elements.

The elements in alphabetical order with formulae and atomic numbers

Element	Symbol	Number	Element	Symbol	Number
Actinium	Ac	89	Molybdenum	Mo	42
Aluminium	Al	13	Neodymium	Nd	60
Americium	Am	95	Neon	Ne	10
Antimony	Sb	51	Neptunium	Np	93
Argon	Ar	18	Nickel	Ni	28
Arsenic	As	33	Niobium	Nb	41
Astatine	At	85	Nitrogen	N	7
Barium	Ba	56	Nobelium	No	102
Berkelium	Bk	97	Osmium	Os	76
Beryllium	Be	4	Oxygen	O	8
Bismuth	Bi	83	Palladium	Pd	46
Boron	B	5	Phosphorus	P	15
Bromine	Br	35	Platinum	Pt	78
Cadmium	Cd	48	Plutonium	Pu	94
Caesium	Cs	55	Polonium	Po	84
Calcium	Ca	20	Potassium	K	19
Californium	Cf	98	Praseodymium	Pr	59
Carbon	C	6	Promethium	Pm	61
Cerium	Ce	58	Protactinium	Pa	91
Chlorine	Cl	17	Radium	Ra	88
Chromium	Cr	24	Radon	Rn	86
Cobalt	Co	27	Rhenium	Re	75
Copper	Cu	29	Rhodium	Rh	45
Curium	Cm	96	Rubidium	Rb	37
Dysprosium	Dy	66	Ruthenium	Ru	44
Einsteinium	Es	99	Samarium	Sm	62
Erbium	Er	68	Scandium	Sc	21
Europium	Eu	63	Selenium	Se	34
Fermium	Fm	100	Silicon	Si	14
Fluorine	F	9	Silver	Ag	47
Francium	Fr	87	Sodium	Na	11
Gadolinium	Gd	64	Strontium	Sr	38
Gallium	Ga	31	Sulfur	S	16
Germanium	Ge	32	Tantalum	Ta	73
Gold	Au	79	Technetium	Tc	43
Hafnium	Hf	72	Tellurium	Te	52
Helium	He	2	Terbium	Tb	65
Holmium	Ho	67	Thallium	Tl	81
Hydrogen	H	1	Thorium	Th	90
Indium	In	49	Thulium	Tm	69
Iodine	I	53	Tin	Sn	50
Iridium	Ir	77	Titanium	Ti	22
Iron	Fe	26	Tungsten	W	74
Krypton	Kr	36	Unnilpentium	Unp	105
Lanthanum	La	57	Unnilquadium	Unq	104
Lawrencium	Lr	103	Uranium	U	92
Lead	Pb	82	Vanadium	V	23
Lithium	Li	3	Xenon	Xe	54
Lutetium	Lu	71	Ytterbium	Yb	70
Magnesium	Mg	12	Yttrium	Y	39
Manganese	Mn	25	Zinc	Zn	30
Mendelevium	Md	101	Zirconium	Zr	40
Mercury	Hg	80			